Seals of Approval for
"The POWERMIND System"

"People often feel the need for more control in their lives. They talk about things they want to do, but never get around to *doing* them. They talk about the importance of personal growth, but lack the commitment to actually grow. They talk about the importance of balancing their personal and work priorities, but don't have a system for *doing* it.

"This book, The POWERMIND System, introduces a unique self-management program that can help you lead a more meaningful, satisfying life. By using these proven techniques, you will discover what you really value ⸍ how to make decisions consistent with your values. You will learn to live ⸍ ⸍ purpose,' making sure that you get more of what you want out of l⸍

"At last, there is a book that brings it all t⸍ psychological, and the scientific. The POWERMIN⸍

⸍MMUNI-CARE

⸍C.

"You hold in your hands priceless principles that can take a lifetime to learn. Michael Monroe Kiefer captures the essence of success in this modern-day self-help classic. This powerful book will enrich the lives of those who are willing to study and work to apply this proven system.

"The POWERMIND System provides a solid foundation for future achievements."

> **Brian Tracy**
> Author, *Maximum Achievement* and *The Universal Laws of Success and Achievement*

"Intermingled with a scientific background and personal experiences Mr. Kiefer has obviously gleaned a tremendous understanding of mental processes through studies in this field. In his own personal style, he has formulated a very in-depth treatise. One must concentrate on each step in working through this comprehensive array of thought processes. However, by doing so one gains lasting benefits."

> **Jerry Caldwell, Ph.D.**
> President
> ImmGen, Inc.

"Depressed? Lost? Out of control?
"Michael Monroe Kiefer is a man on a mission. A mission to help YOU! Let him take you for a ride on the highways of life's riches and speed you toward your goals. You'll be thrilled when you learn you can easily be in the driver's seat too.

"The signposts up ahead are wealth, power, success, and happiness. Work with the principles and *techniques* in The POWERMIND System. Enjoy the ride!"

Joe Robles
Program Development Officer
Rutgers University

"Mr. Kiefer used an interesting mechanistic and physiological approach, which proved unique and scientific in explaining how autogenic conditioning techniques work. While some books mention similar techniques, most fall short of in-depth explanations of what is happening in the human brain when you perform these mental regimes. This lends tremendous credibility to both lessons 7 and 8, which might otherwise seem silly to a technical professional. This also offers the reader true incentive to confidently practice the techniques for goal attainment.

"On closing the book, I feel it describes a well thought out system of principles and practical methods that are easily understood and applicable to all seekers of success. It is a book well worth reading for getting your life organized and on a positive track. It is a wonderful text for life success, covering a person's entire psychological lexicon. Definitely a work worthy of a trained scientist's seal of approval!"

Sam Galewsky, Ph.D.
Assistant Professor of Biology
University of North Dakota

"It seems that in America today, everyone wants something for nothing, believing they have the right to sit back and expect someone else to take care of them. The POWERMIND System is dead on target in its call to personal responsibility. Michael Monroe Kiefer hones in on the timeless truth that you are ultimately responsible for yourself.

"If you think you are trapped or even if you think you have it all together, The POWERMIND System has something for you. It provides you with practical, down-to-earth methods for evaluating your life and maximizing your potential, showing you the great power you have to really become master of your life.

"I was amazed at what I learned and how motivated I was by the system. If you want to better your life, if you could use help getting direction, if you need motivation to improve yourself *and help others*, The POWERMIND System is for you.

"Michael is also right on the money—quite literally. His urging to 'pay yourself first' puts the simple concept of saving for the future in a whole new light. Overall one of the most powerfully motivating books I have read. If it doesn't light your fire, your wood is wet."

Wanda M.H. Carmichael, M.D.
Texas

"This is **THE SOURCE** for the best, proven, time-honored techniques for improving your life. Useful for people of all walks of life and of all ages—whether an adolescent discovering the world or an adult redefining his/her life or simply wanting to do better. Look no further, because The POWERMIND System is all you need.

"Captivating right from the table of contents! Mr. Kiefer writes with gusto and bravura, giving life to his words and inciting us constantly into action. We never feel distant while reading this book. This is your own personal self-discovery retreat, and Mr. Kiefer is there to guide you through every workshop. The after-lesson visits with the author are particularly good. This book was so useful and fun for me; I was sorry when I finished reading it! Also, The POWERMIND System acknowledges that everyone is different. Mr. Kiefer gives us numerous techniques and encourages us to use the most suitable and comfortable for us. Part IV, High Achievement, is that must-have, tasty icing on the cake!"

Dr. Lynda S. Hagen-Vaissiére
Molecular Virologist
Avignon, France

"WELL WRITTEN, APPLIED, AND TIMELY! The POWERMIND System is an excellent blueprint of how to properly set and accomplish goals in all facets of our lives—personal, financial, occupational, etc. Most people never get where they desire, because they have not clearly defined their goals and objectives. Hence, they end up living their lives with no real goals other than short-term gratification.

"This book provides thorough discussion and procedures for defining and setting goals that are consistent with one's abilities (which, as is pointed out, may be more than one currently believes), desires, and values. Scientific, proven, and easy-to-use techniques are clearly explained. Helpful examples are given. The principles are valid for all.

"If the college students I work with would apply the steps in this book, most would develop a better sense of purpose, develop better lifelong study habits, learn more, get better grades, and have more successful lives. They would be forced to define what 'success' is for them—the first and most important step in achieving it."

Paul J. Hicks, Jr., Ph.D.
Assistant Professor
Penn State

"The POWERMIND System is an inspiring and most useful total life management method. It is the first book I have ever read that is so comprehensive. I was most impressed by the fact that all the lessons, correspondingly, provide the reader with easy-to-follow techniques to implement the POWERMIND system's teachings. No other book gives as many of these valuable hands-on tools to immediately work with.

"The money goals lesson includes a unique set of 'awakening charts' that show everyone how anyone can accumulate a fortune with a consistent savings plan and some self-discipline. How exciting for us all in a day and age when the economy seems to offer so little to the average person.

"Some of my favorite sections included the Reticular Formation, the Dendrite Cabling Process in the brain, Treasure Charting, and of course How to Become a

Self-Made Millionaire. I found that trying the many suggestions offered in the book is a great deal of personal fun, and insures me progress toward achieving my goals.

"My twelve-year-old daughter, Laura, read the Superlearning lesson. She said, 'Michael Monroe Kiefer has a way with words,' and is eager to read the entire book. I think it will serve as both foundation and scaffolding for her to build her own future success. Throughout the entire POWERMIND system Mr. Kiefer conscientiously holds to the highest moral and ethical standards. Gender-neutral examples, religious courtesies, and emphasis on setting non-self-serving goals and helping others lend a truly humanitarian flare to his work.

"I highly recommend The POWERMIND System to you and your entire family."

Maria Ann Nally
Senior Financial Analyst
Intecom Inc.

"Get ready to take off the blinders and see the unlimited potential you possess—and can tap—with the help of this book. I have been fortunate enough not only to read Mr. Kiefer's new book, The POWERMIND System, but also to witness his own amazing transformation effected by the testing and honing of the techniques laid out so masterfully in these pages. His unique melding of science and spirituality has not been seen since the classic self-help writings from the early part of this century.

"Mr. Kiefer's truly scientific approach will gratify any reader disappointed with many current self-help books based strictly on theory and abstract suggestions.

"No mere light reading, The POWERMIND System is a textbook for the serious success student. A careful study of the work will undeniably change the way you view the world and understand the workings of the human mind.

"If nothing else, browse the section on *superconscious thought induction*. You will realize it is not just chance that this book, and your future, now rest in your hands. Do not let the opportunity to own this fascinating self-help classic, unparalleled in its practicality, pass you by."

Douglas Mead
Co-owner Kwik Kopy Printing
Minnesota

"Well researched and thoroughly thought out, The POWERMIND System is brimming with effective examples and useful tools to help success students take each new step forward. Many times I have read an author's impressive philosophy, only to be discouraged at finding myself so far away from my new-found ideal. There seems to be no apparent bridge from my old ideas to the author's worthy ideals. Mr. Kiefer has drawn on years of research in the human achievement field to build this bridge for the reader. In this way his system is ultimately practical. Mr. Kiefer's extensive scientific training has proven an asset in a field otherwise replete with anecdotal theory."

Douglas W. Grissom
Medical Student

THE POWERMIND™ SYSTEM

Twelve Lessons on the
Psychology of Success

MICHAEL MONROE KIEFER

Author: Michael Monroe Kiefer

Copy Editor: Carol A. Kennedy
Title: The POWERMIND™ System
Subtitle: Twelve Lessons on the Psychology of Success
Edition: First Edition
U.S. place of publication: City: Edina State: MN
Published by: Kiefer Enterprizes International Press Division

First Printing: April 1995
Library of Congress Catalog Card Number: 95-94200
ISBN 0-9645934-0-8

Cover Design: "Diamond Mind" by Michael Monroe Kiefer

The word "POWERMIND" is a trademark owned by Michael Monroe Kiefer. The POWERMIND System created and printed in the U.S.A.

Kiefer Enterprizes
Michael Monroe Kiefer (President)
22320 Albatross Circle, Suite #2
Farmington, Minnesota 55024
24-Hour Hotline: 612-460-8205

Dedicated to my daughter: ARIEL MONROE KIEFER

Through the miracle molecule DNA, my molecular history has been transferred to you. My mental history can now be transferred to you through this masterwork. The POWERMIND System represents the distilled knowledge I gathered from over ten years of research and personal experimentation in the area of human achievement. The wisdom contained in these pages is for you!

DNA to DNA
Mastermind to Mastermind
Dreams into Reality
Thoughts into Things

"Be not deceived; God is not mocked (fooled): for whatsoever a man soweth, that shall he also reap."

Galatians 6:7

The Universal Law of Sowing and Reaping Is Immutable!

The Author's Acknowledgment of Assistance Rendered Him for The POWERMIND System Project

The system you are about to read is the result of a unique scientific research project on human achievement.

I have been more than ten years in gathering and classifying information. Personal experimentation and cooperative alliances led to the organization of this life management method. During the course of the project, I have received valuable assistance either in person or by studying the works of the following people.

Jesus Christ
Dr. Alan R. Zimmerman
Brian Tracy
Dr. Denis Waitley
Jim Rohn
Og Mandino
Zig Ziglar
Anthony Robbins
Stephen R. Covey
Melvin Powers
Dr. Gerry Schmidt
Robert McDonald
Douglas Grissom
Don B Carmichael M.D.
Dr. James K. Van Fleet
J. Martin Kohe
Thomas Alva Edison
Ralph Waldo Emerson
Abraham Maslow
Thomas Jefferson
Andrew Carnegie
Alexander Hamilton
Billy Sunday
Edwin C. Barnes
Abraham Lincoln
William James
Orison Swett Marden
Dr. Brenda J. Dunne
Dr. Shad Helmstetter
Connierae Andreas
Ed Foreman
Douglas Mead
Bert Decker
Jerry Caldwell Ph.D.
U.S. Andersen

Napoleon Hill
James W. Newman
Dr. Maxwell Maltz
Earl Nightingale
Dr. Norman Vincent Peale
George S. Clason
Claude M. Bristol
Dr. Joseph Murphy
Edgar Cayce
W. Clement Stone
William H. Danforth
Charles Faulkner
Dr. Kelly Gerling
Steve Andreas
Dr. Elmer Gates
Sam Galewsky Ph.D.
John Hanten
Dr. Alexander Graham Bell
Dr. Russel H. Conwell
Samuel Adams
John Hancock
Benjamin Franklin
Henry Ford
Samuel Smiles
Benjamin Kidd
W.H.M. Stover
James Allan
Dr. J.B. Rhine
Dr. Robert G. Jahn
Dr. Gary Lynch
Eileen McDargh
Tim Hallbom
Suzi Smith
Wanda M.H. Carmichael M.D.
Dr. Frank Channing Haddock

Manuscript Reviewers

Carolyn Sue Kiefer
Gerald Monroe Kiefer
Wanda M.H. Carmichael M.D.
Sam Galewsky Ph.D.
Douglas Mead
Douglas Grissom
John Hanten
Maria Ann Nally

Printing/Production

Milton Adams

Word Processors

Jo Kill Moderie
Kathy Cooper

My Wife

Carolyn Sue Kiefer

My Daughter

Ariel Monroe Kiefer

My Parents

Gerald Monroe Kiefer
Mary Kiefer

TABLE OF CONTENTS

Prelude to the System

Overview

The following prelude contains a congratulatory statement for all readers of the system. This is followed by a section where I reveal to you a glimpse of my own personal struggle on the high roads of human achievement. I think you'll find it quite fascinating! The third section contains my three challenges, since you are about to become one of the travelers on these roads. The last two sections are previews of the guideposts that lie ahead. Enjoy the ride!

Prelude to the System

Congratulations to the "Good Reader"

Congratulations! Reading this book will prove to be one of the best investments of time and money you will ever make. An investment in self-education always pays handsome dividends. By learning the principles and practicing the techniques described in this book you will become knowledgeable, powerful, confident, successful, well respected, and capable of having a strong positive influence on other people's lives. By developing self-awareness, setting worthy goals, understanding mental mechanics, and achieving self-set goals you will build tremendous personal power. You will gain thought clarity, the ability to make quick decisions, and the *power of will* required to take immediate action. You will also have fun as you embark on your exciting self-improvement journey.

As you learn the concepts and techniques in this book, test them out for yourself before making any snap judgments. Keep in mind this is one of the most highly researched self-help books ever created. It's been critically reviewed by respected scientists and doctors and bears their seal of approval.

You have within you right now the potential to bring more health, more wealth, more power, more success, more freedom into your life than you ever dreamed possible. You don't need to *"acquire"* this potential, you already possess it. You just need to learn how to use it, direct it, understand it, so you can apply it in all departments of your life. That's where I can help. As you READ this book you'll gain this specialized knowledge.

My mind reaches out to you, to touch yours through time and space, to have a positive impact on your life. Though we may never meet in person, our minds will be melded as you work through this book. I will be your personal mentor page after page, sharing my knowledge and life experiences with you, making an investment of *life into life*.

This book is the formal publication of The POWERMIND System research project. It contains the greatest discovery of my life. *Join* me as we launch into a date with destiny!

"Tis the good reader that makes the good book; in every book he finds passages which seem to be confidences or asides hidden from all else and unmistakably meant for his ear; the profit of books is according to the sensibility of the reader; the profoundest thought or passion sleeps as in a mine, until it is discovered by an equal mind and heart."

Ralph Waldo Emerson
American success philosopher
Author of numerous essays,
including the famed
"Compensation"

The Author's Amazing Transfiguration

No goals, no future

I believe a snapshot of my own story will aid many readers on their self-improvement journey. Read well, for I myself was nearly caught in the clutches of certain disaster. Here is a glimpse of what happened to me.

When I finished my formal education in college, I vowed I would never read another book again. I was burned out on reading textbooks, writing research papers, taking notes, studying for exams, etc. With two high technology science degrees under my belt, I was glad my days of study were over. What a relief! It was finally time to get a professional-level job and relax for the rest of my life.

Many people adopt this same diseased attitude even sooner than I did; for example, this occurs for some people right after they graduate from high school. They say symptomatic things like "Thank God, school is over, no more reading, no more tests, no more boring homework, and no more people telling me what to do." I found out later to my amazement that this was the wrong attitude, very wrong.

I felt my first professional job after college was quite good, but I often wondered how people became really successful in life. Even with all my formal education, I couldn't seem to figure it out, I didn't even know how to go about figuring it out. So I did what most people around me did. I became a practiced cynic. I went along with the rest of the crowd! I would explain away my own mediocre station in life by parroting how lousy the companies were, the wages, the policies, the taxes, the management, etc. I of course *wasn't responsible* at all for the situation in which I now found myself.

My major goals in life from a very early age were to get my college degrees and then get a good job. After these were achieved I had no other major life goals to pursue, so I drifted for a couple of years. Had it not been for a number of very fortunate events occurring in rapid succession, my life and future would never have undergone the amazing transfiguration. I'll explain these keynote events in more detail in the following passages.

The Wake-Up Call

At the ripe old age of 28, I felt as if dark days were upon me. My health was failing, I had developed a serious negative attitude, I ate junk food, I slept much of the time, and I hadn't touched a book in over two years. I packed fat onto my 5'8" frame, peaking out at a pork-loving, candy-crunching 225 pounds, and my wife became very frustrated with me. The energetic, high-achieving genetic engineer she had married was reduced to an overweight cynical sleepaholic.

One evening while I slept, my wife took a special interest in my snoring habit, probably because it was so loud she couldn't get back to sleep. She noticed during the night I would stop breathing for up to twenty-five seconds at a time, then cough and sputter for breath. This would occur multiple times within a single hour.

As time went on, I developed a dramatic excessive sleeping habit, which was getting increasingly worse as I gained more weight. My doctor said that high blood pressure medicine would soon be necessary for me. My wife continued with her disappointment in me, which led to numerous ongoing arguments. To put it mildly, my life was not going well.

One Christmas we went to visit my wife's family. After gorging myself on Christmas dinner, I fell asleep on the couch as was customary for me after a meal. After my "nap" I awoke to see her sister's husband, an anesthesiologist named Dr. Don B Carmichael, staring at me. He told me I had what is medically termed "sleep apnea."

In my case, the sleep apnea was caused by my tonsils and adenoids being abnormally large (a genetic defect). The weight I had packed on exacerbated the condition by adding neck fat around my throat. Dr. Carmichael explained that shortly after I fell asleep, my throat muscles would relax, allowing my tonsils to collapse into my windpipe, effectively cutting off my breathing. After twenty-five seconds or so my autonomic nervous system caused me to cough, gasping for air. This would occur dozens of times throughout the night. I, however, was completely unaware of these activities. I just felt tired all the time, even after sleeping for twenty-four hours straight!

Dr. Carmichael suggested I have the tonsils and adenoids checked out, so I did. My doctor at home recommended removing them. Before the tonsillectomy, I was given a mild sedative and immediately fell asleep. Because of the sedative, I was unable to unconsciously clear my throat when my tonsils collapsed into my windpipe. I was told later that a nurse passing by me happened to notice I was blue, so they rushed me in for an emergency operation before I died on the gurney.

When I fully recovered from the operation, I was astounded with the newfound energy I gained. With the breath of new life I decided it was time to do something meaningful with my life. I started eating better, exercising regularly, and getting my body into respectable shape. That operation gave me a new lease on life and I was going to make good use of it. It was literally my wake-up call! I will always be grateful to Dr. Carmichael for encouraging me to get my genetically defective tonsils removed.

Turning Point #1 - Dr. Alan Zimmerman

With my body now in shape, I started searching for a subject that intensely interested me. In college I had minored in psychology and was always helping people with their problems. I enjoyed helping them and it gave me a sense of accomplishment and fulfillment. My father (Gerald Monroe Kiefer) suggested that I take some management classes, so I did. I began attending adult education classes, professional development seminars, and workshops.

One of these workshops was conducted by Dr. Alan Zimmerman at The Management Center in Minneapolis, Minnesota. At the beginning of class, Dr. Zimmerman had a volunteer from the audience come up and hold her arms straight out from her sides while he tried to push them down. He was testing for her general level of arm strength. Then he had the person repeat out loud after him a series of negative verbal self-affirmations such as "I am ugly, I am a loser, I am stupid" for about thirty seconds. He then asked the person to hold her arms out again. This time he was able to push the person's arms down effortlessly! Being formally trained as a scientist, I was immediately skeptical of this demonstration. I asked Dr. Zimmerman if he would perform the exercise on me. The exact same results occurred!

I was most impressed by the idea that thinking certain thoughts affects energy levels in the body and that this can be *consciously controlled.* After the demonstration I was intrigued by the material Dr. Zimmerman presented during his workshop. He covered many topics such as self-image psychology, risk taking, memory techniques, deep relaxation methods, and mental programming.

After class I asked him where I could get more information on affirmations. He recommended Dr. Norman Vincent Peale's classic book, *The Power of Positive Thinking.* Dr. Zimmerman also had individual cassette tapes available on other topics. I bought a dozen of them and listened carefully to each one. Dr. Zimmerman had a research-oriented style, presenting only information solidly backed by research study after research study. This greatly appealed to my scientific mind.

After listening to his tapes I made the decision to become a "success scientist." I didn't know exactly how to go about doing this at the time, but I knew that was my next goal in life. I had a burning desire to help people lead more effective, worthwhile lives. Dr. Zimmerman was to become my first living role model.

Turning Point #2 - Earl Nightingale and Brian Tracy

I decided to visit the local library in search of videotapes on the physiology of the human brain, psychology, personal achievement, business management, self-development, and other topics. The local library where I live is a tiny one, so I thought there was only a slim chance that it would have any tapes. But, lo and behold, it had quite a few. However, only two tapes were in stock at the time.

The first one was Earl Nightingale's *The Strangest Secret;* the second one was Brian Tracy's *10 Keys to Personal Power.* Little did I know at the time, but good fortune had dealt me a royal flush in these two videos. Earl Nightingale's tape had an uncanny potent effect on my mind. I would describe it as "almost hypnotic." I watched the tape over and over again. It contained a critical piece to the life puzzle that I had always missed. My mental wheels were spinning incessantly after my exposure to that tape.

When the tape's message was deeply engraved onto my subconscious mind, I knew I could achieve my goal of becoming a success scientist if I kept concentrating on it intensely. (Even though I still had no concrete plan of action, just a burning desire and an unquenchable thirst for more self-development knowledge.)

A few days later, I popped the Brian Tracy tape into the VCR. I watched him for about five minutes, then screamed upstairs to my wife, Carolyn. I said, "Carolyn, come quickly, you've got to see this man!" I was astonished with his unique insight, his vocabulary, and his captivating stagecraft. I told my wife, "That man will serve as another role model for me and I will work to become like him."

I went back to the library, searching for more Brian Tracy tapes. I found one titled *24 Techniques for Closing the Sale*, and another, *Negotiating Strategies*. Instead of watching TV or movie videos on my weekends, I watched Brian Tracy tapes. I watched him over and over again on Friday night, Saturday morning, Saturday night. I remember my wife calling to me at Midnight on a Saturday evening, asking me if I was coming to bed. I told her I was almost finished taking my notes on yet another Tracy tape!

I noticed the phone number for the Nightingale Conant Corp. on the videotape labels, so I called them to get a catalog. What an eye opener that was! I started buying cassette albums and out-of-print self-help books to augment the seminars and workshops I was attending. I studied and learned, studied and learned. I remember my friends at work asking me what I did all weekend, and I said, "I listened to cassette tapes, read old books, watched training videos, and took very good notes." At the time I was also working full time as a DNA fingerprinting research lab manager.

Turning Point #3 - The Project Unfolds

If ever a man was on a mission to find the secrets of great success in life, I was he. Fortunately for me my formal education in science came in handy at this point. I knew how to research information, perform controlled experiments, and use deductive reasoning methods. I also had an excellent understanding of the physiology of the human body.

I started intensively scanning many libraries, scientific journals, new and used bookstores, video and audiotape catalogs, seminar schedules, and other sources. I started running international book searches to find very rare out-of-print books. I started backtracking to find original sources of information. I started enlisting the aid of many scholarly mentors and clever business people.

As my journey into the human achievement archives continued, I met Napoleon Hill, Dr. Maxwell Maltz, Claude M. Bristol, Dr. Frank Channing Haddock, Samuel Smiles, Dr. Joseph Murphy, U.S. Andersen, Ralph Waldo Emerson, William James, Orison Swett Marden, Dr. J.B. Rhine, and a host of other *teachers through time*. All of them labored to put their life philosophies, tools, and techniques into print to serve as guideposts for a select few travelers on the *high roads of human achievement*.

My book collection started to grow into a veritable gold mine. Each author made magnificent deposits in the unfinished room of my basement that came to be called my library! I could now go "mining for gold" every evening and especially on weekends.

Turning Point #4 - Dr. Denis Waitley

One weekend on my quest for more knowledge in a used bookstore, I spied an inconspicuous cassette album by Dr. Denis Waitley titled *The Psychology of Winning*, priced at twenty dollars. I bargained the proprietor down to fifteen dollars, went home, and started listening to it. After hearing the second side of tape one I ran upstairs to play it for my wife. I plugged the recorder in and we listened to Dr. Waitley together.

I couldn't believe how concise he was, how he synthesized so many concepts with precise practical wisdom. The cassette album really took me on an inner journey of self-discovery. On one side of each tape he went over a self-development concept, on the other side he showed exactly how to develop yourself in regards to the concept. I thought that was an excellent way to organize a cassette album. (I found out later thousands of other people thought the same thing!) I now had a third living role model to add to my growing self-help battalion.

Every day driving to and from work I feasted on a rich diet of thoughts and ideas from great people of poise and power. I was up, bright-eyed, every morning, telling my wife, "My Teacher is waiting for me in the truck. I don't want to be late for class!" She was delighted with the changes she saw in me. She encouraged me to keep watching, listening, reading, collaborating, and studying! I was on fire, gathering knowledge. I knew I was approaching something big, really big. I was very near to a major discovery.

Turning Point #5 - Birth of The POWERMIND System Project

I reasoned: From my research and my personal life experiences, I had discovered many secrets of success. I knew these would help millions of people achieve greatly if they were somehow exposed to them. However, someone would first need to systematize the secrets of success, forging them into a practical life guide with universal application, then disseminate it to the people of the world. THAT SOMEONE WOULD BE ME!

The need for a highly effective personal guide to life's riches was recognized and The POWERMIND System project was born! My success scientist goal had automatically come to realization. If I could muster the stamina required to compose a complete life guide, then I could teach people how to lead successful, enjoyable, worthwhile, fulfilling lives. My mission to find the secrets of success was indeed successful. My next mission was to create this guide and to more fully develop my teaching ability.

In order to do this I would need to make great personal sacrifices in terms of time and money. I would need to align myself physically, mentally, and spiritually for the task at hand. I would need to pray for help, guidance, and strength. I would need to enlist the aid of many others—scientists, financial experts, psychologists, doctors, engineers, and of course my family. I would need to dedicate myself to becoming a professional speaker so that I could effectively teach others what I learned. I would need to pour my heart and soul into the project, thereby imbuing the final product with the power to save lives!

Turning Point #6 - Meeting Brian Tracy

During the later phases of the project I learned about the Peak Performers Network (PPN) in Minneapolis, Minnesota, and boom! I was hit like a ton of bricks. I found out Brian Tracy was giving seminars for them. What a very special occasion that would be for me. I was finally going to meet in person one of the men I had spent so many late nights and weekends with. He gave two half-day seminars; of course I attended both!

I went up to meet him and told him I was working on a self-help project. I asked him two very important questions, bought his *Universal Laws of Success and Achievement* album, had my picture taken with him, and was happily on my way. (I knew our paths would cross again in the future.)

I kept attending PPN seminars and learned from all the fine speakers they brought practically to my doorstep. Each one had his or her own story, style, and special message to spread. I had found a class of people that I needed to study very carefully.

Turning Point #7 - Mr. Jim Rohn

One evening at a PPN seminar a speaker came to town by the name of Mr. Jim Rohn. I thought I might miss that talk because I had previously made other plans, but something unusual happened so that I was able to attend.

Blastoff! Five minutes into Mr. Rohn's talk the magic moment of recognition occurred. I knew I was in the presence of a true success. He had a completely unique style. Much of his message was carefully crafted into potent stories. I thought, wow, here is something different. Entertaining, witty stories, each one doubly loaded with a dose of real value on the philosophy of success. Mr. Rohn was able to shed new light on many principles of successful living. His personal struggle hit home with me and served as grist for my mill. He described his own journey on the high roads of human achievement with unparalleled style and charisma.

Mr. Rohn also referenced the Bible in many of his stories. I started carefully reading the Bible after his presentation.

Two of Mr. Rohn's messages came crashing home in my mind after his presentation. The first message was that he started with little, not even a college degree, but through serious self-education was able to achieve financial independence. He said, *"Work harder on yourself than you do on your job."* The second message was the idea that everyone has special *talents or gifts*, and that if you develop these they will take you wherever you want to go. He said, *"If you work on your gifts they will make a room for you."* I was doing what Mr. Rohn recommended all along by simultaneously developing my two main natural talents, which are *research scientist* and *teacher.*

Mr. Rohn said one of his greatest joys in life now is to affect people with his teachings and come back later to collect the stories. He said, *"You can't buy that with money. You have to go out and do the deed."* Mr. Rohn greatly affected me and became my fourth living role model.

The POWERMIND System's Purpose

I had eight years of college, two science degrees, and never once heard anything about what I was researching. I thought,

how awful to go to school for so long and still be totally ignorant of how to really succeed in life. I wanted to combat this
problem for other people.

I was determined that The POWERMIND System would be
designed to *lead the field* in helping the person just starting out.
By "starting out" I mean *starting to study how to be successful
in life*, which isn't taught in school. The system would lay out
the basic blueprint for the beginner. Once finished with The
POWERMIND System, the serious success student would be in
a position to move on to more advanced material. The system
would also serve as scaffolding on which the serious student
could hang any previously learned information, thereby greatly
enhancing his or her overall understanding of life.

The POWERMIND System that you will soon read represents the completion of a long-term multidisciplinary research
project to create an easy-to-understand personal guide to life's
riches. My goal in creating The POWERMIND System is to
help you reach yours. *I trust the book will serve its intended purpose!*

A Personal Word from the Author

And now a personal word for my role models, the big four:
Dr. Alan Zimmerman, Mr. Brian Tracy, Dr. Denis Waitley, and
of course Mr. Jim Rohn. To each of you I wish to formally
express my personal thanks for helping me work my way out of
the darkness and into the light. Without your guidance and inspiration I would be but another silent man among the masses.

And to all my readers, may you, your families, and your
friends benefit from the MASSIVE HUMAN EFFORT AND
CUMULATIVE LIFETIMES OF KNOWLEDGE CON-
TAINED IN THIS BOOK!

*"As water reflects a face, so a person's work reflects their
soul."*

> **Michael Monroe Kiefer**
> **American success scientist**
> **Principal investigator for**
> **The POWERMIND System**
> **Project**

The POWERMIND System Challenges and Basis

The first challenge you face is to **read this entire book!** The second challenge is to **be completely open to what you read.** This second challenge will require you to perform your own personal experimentation. The third challenge is that of **mental maturity.** Will you serve as a teacher for the less fortunate? Will you, once being exposed to the life-saving information contained in these pages, seek to educate others? We'll revisit this last challenge again at the very end of this book.

The POWERMIND System has been carefully designed to systematically teach you the specialized knowledge and practical techniques you will need to attain the riches of life. Some of the techniques can be used directly off the page, others are templates that you will use to build your own tools according to your own individual needs and desires.

The POWERMIND System is based on an all-encompassing human truth: *habitual thinking and mental imagery guides your destiny.* The great self-development pioneer Earl Nightingale searched for many decades to find the so-called secret of success. He found it on New Year's Day 1950. He later revealed his discovery in an album entitled *The Strangest Secret*, which has now sold well over one million copies. The secret was this: *"We become what we think about."* It was stated another way by Ralph Waldo Emerson, the famous American philosopher: *"A man is what he thinks about all day long."* As you work through this book, I will explain this concept in much greater detail.

This book emphasizes success principles popularized from the late 1800s to the present day. It is interesting to note that throughout the history of humankind, success principles seem to be lost and then rediscovered by only a *select few* in every generation. Since the beginning of civilization, relatively few people have ever attained great success in life. This has to do with a person's possession of specialized life management knowledge and subsequent use of it. Some people learn early, becoming wildly successful while still young. Most people of the world, however, have never learned at all. They have led forgotten, mediocre, dismal lives to the bitter, tragic end.

By using The POWERMIND System you can modify the circumstances in your life, taking direct control *over* them. I have scientifically researched the method contained in this book, finding it to be valid through my own personal experiences and the personal experiences of hundreds of others. I now put it in the hands of those who have not studied or experienced what I have. With the information in this book you can trim off years of trial and error experiences, cutting short a potentially painful journey to a successful, rewarding, worthwhile, and fulfilling life.

Use this book in times of trouble, in times of need. It has extraordinary power and is an ever-present sterling servant, standing by your side as a personal guide.

"The POWERMIND System helps all, hurts none!"

Michael Monroe Kiefer
American success scientist
Principal investigator for
The POWERMIND System
Project

The Need for a Life Guide

The POWERMIND system fills the need for a weapon to combat needless personal suffering and misery that is so commonplace in the world today. It was written as a comprehensive life guide.

Can you answer these questions? Why are some people happy and others miserable? Why do some people live their lives in luxurious homes while others eke out a meager existence in a trashy slum? Why are some people astonishing successes and others pitiful failures? Why is one person an outstanding leader and immensely popular while another is a mediocre bum? Why are some people capable of accomplishing genius-level work rapidly while others toil relentlessly for a lifetime without accomplishing anything worthwhile? Why are some people miraculously healed of so-called incurable diseases while others remain sickly and quickly die? Why do some people lacking a high school education became multimillionaires while many Ph.D.s are unemployed? The POWERMIND System answers all of these questions and many more!

What We Do Not See

Few people recognize the fact that if they were to change their current thoughts and actions, redirecting this same energy toward the achievement of worthwhile goals, they would inevitably become successful.

Most people have a tendency to let their minds drift, thereby dissipating this thought energy. They lack meaningful goals, which causes them to wander aimlessly through life. They move from one everyday problem to the next, listening to the crowd, leading lives of terror, bewilderment, frustration, and despair! They also feel overpowered by circumstances, thinking they cannot accomplish anything worthwhile with their lives; thus they kill off the inner drive to try.

A basic life guide is what these people need to revitalize their inner drive. Specialized knowledge and its practical application is one of the few true transfiguring powers in life. It is the power by which consciousness is unfolded and the soul liberated. The quotations below should be considered carefully as you prepare yourself for full exposure to The POWERMIND System!

"What we do not see, what most of us never suspect of existing, is the silent but irresistible power which comes to the rescue of those who fight on in the face of discouragement."

Napoleon Hill
Success philosopher
Author of *Think and Grow Rich, Law of Success, Science of Personal Achievement,* **and** *Mental Dynamite*

"What this power is I cannot say; all I know is that it exists and it becomes available only when a man is in that state of mind in which he knows exactly what he wants and is fully determined not to quit until he finds it."

Dr. Alexander Graham Bell
Vibrational theory scientist
Inventor of the telephone

Part I

Lesson Number 1

1 ▶ Self-Analysis

Overview

I cannot tell you exactly what you should do with your life—*no one can*. This decision requires serious soul searching, which you and you alone must do. I can, however, assist you in the process by presenting you with revealing lines of questioning and self-analysis instruments to help you help yourself to discover what you need to know: your weaknesses, your personal life values, your major definite purpose in life, your natural talents, and a possible career utilizing your natural talents.

Most people in the world will never take the time to sit down, to think long and hard about what is right for them to do with their lives. Consequently, they lead unhappy, unfulfilled, miserable lives of quiet desperation. They wind up old, bitter, broke, and embarrassed, sucking on the icicles of regret.

Use due time and care in working through each of the five self-analysis instruments. It is not necessary to rush or hurry—I recommend that you don't. Your time will be well spent, because each instrument will reveal to you a deeper understanding of yourself. What you find out about yourself here will help you to determine many possibilities for short-term as well as long-term goals.

This lesson consists of a series of five very rigorous, thought-provoking self-analysis instruments. It is the most important part of the book because what you learn here will set the foundation for how you proceed with the rest of the book and possibly the rest of your life.

Many people who buy this book will muse through this section casually, hungry only for the goal-setting and high-achievement techniques. I call on you now to discipline yourself, to work through this lesson very carefully before going on. This book has been painstakingly designed to be worked through systematically. What you learn in each lesson builds your mind, preparing you for the next lesson.

Be fair and honest throughout this self-analysis. You owe it to yourself and those people who are important to you. Good luck!

The POWERMIND System
Part I. Self-Assessment

Self-Analysis

Introduction to Self-Analysis Instrument Design

We will begin some instruments in this lesson with a broad sweep of general questions, then systematically zero in, becoming more and more specific. By the process of looking broadly, then reducing the areas of concern, prioritizing within these areas, and then focusing on what needs to be worked on first, you will be following a systematic reduction procedure. The general process is outlined below.

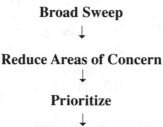

Broad Sweep

↓

Reduce Areas of Concern

↓

Prioritize

↓

Focus on High-Priority Items

You cannot do everything in life—there simply isn't enough time—so you need a systematic method to help you create a foundation on which to build your life. The entire self-analysis lesson taken collectively is designed to help you create this basic life foundation. By the end of this lesson you will have learned:

A. The 37 Key Characteristics for Success
B. The Single Activity that can Completely Prevent Success in Life
C. Your Personal Life Values
D. The 8 Mind-Sets of Personal Power
E. The Principle of Alignment
F. Your Natural Talent(s)
G. How to Align Your Natural Talent(s) with a Career
H. Possible Skills to Develop for Wealth Creation
I. Valuable Insight into Your Major Definite Purpose in Life

In the goal-setting part of this book you will utilize much of this valuable information further.

(1) The Master Test for Success

◆ What key characteristics are necessary for success in life?
◆ Is there one behavior that can completely prevent success?

This is a very simple self-analysis tool. There are only two possible answers for each question: yes or no. Each question addresses a specific personal characteristic. In my research I have found these characteristics to be imperative for true success. You may already have some of these characteristics well developed, others less well developed. They are all necessary for true success. If you are weak in one or more of them, you must work on developing that characteristic.

People tend to waste tremendous amounts of time on unimportant matters because they don't know what is important and what is unimportant. These thirty-seven characteristics are most definitely important and well worth developing.

1. Do I have a **major definite purpose** in life?
2. Do I possess sufficient **self-confidence** to actively pursue my major definite purpose in life?
3. Do I **save at least 10% of my total income** and invest it for retirement?
4. Am I **enthusiastic** in my undertakings?
5. Do I have a good degree of **self-discipline**?
6. Do I usually **do more than is asked of me**?
7. Can I **concentrate single-mindedly** on a task until it is completed?
8. Can I **adapt myself to people whose opinions differ from mine**?
9. Do I have **patience with other people**?
10. Do I **treat other people with respect**?
11. Can I **rally the support of others** to help me achieve my goals?
12. Am I **creative** enough to solve most of my own problems?
13. Am I able to **control my emotions** when they are detrimental to my success?
14. Do I have good **reasoning ability**?

15. Do I **correct my errors and learn from my mistakes**?
16. Do I **teach other people what I know** to help them improve their lives?
17. Do I **manage my time well**?
18. Do I try to **make other people feel good about themselves**?
19. Am I **rarely sick** with colds, flu, allergies?
20. If **my relatives put my ideas down, am I still able to pursue them**?
21. If **my friends put my ideas down, am I still able to pursue them**?
22. Am I a **leader**?
23. Do I have a **set of goals for the future**?
24. Are my **goals clearly written down on paper**?
25. Do I **review my goals daily**?
26. Do I **read books, listen to tapes, or watch videos** to make me more effective?
27. Do I **rarely worry**?
28. Do I **take courses or seminars** to make me more effective?
29. Do I **belong to professional organizations** related to my career?
30. Do I **belong to organizations that help make me a better person**?
31. Do I **control my own destiny**?
32. Are my **decisions congruent with my set of personal life values**?
33. Do I **have at least one person who truly loves me**?
34. Do I **regularly set and achieve increasingly difficult goals** for myself?
35. Do I **understand how my conscious, subconscious, and superconscious minds work**?
36. Do I have a **good relationship with God**?
37. Do I have a **set of personal life values that guide me in all that I do**?
38. When I profit does it **infringe on the personal rights of other people**?

A yes answer to questions 1-37 will largely determine your degree of success. If you answered no to any one of them you now have an idea of what you could work on improving. These are the thirty-seven characteristics necessary for true success.

If you answered yes to question 38 you are currently a failure. A yes answer to that question is particularly devastating. Personal destruction *must come* to the individual engaged in profit at the *expense* of other people. I urge you to cease this activity at once—the consequences are severe, according to the Universal Law of sowing and reaping, from which there can be no escape!

"Whatsoever a man soweth, that shall he also reap."

Galatians 6:7

The Universal Law of sowing and reaping is immutable!

(2) The 8 Mind-Sets of Personal Power

This instrument is designed to allow you by introspection to identify critical areas where you may be weak and also areas of perceived strength. It is uniquely revealing by design, as you will see when you are completely finished with it.

Personal Power categories have been divided into eight mind-sets. They are:

1. Future Expectation
2. Personal Motivation
3. Self-Image
4. Life Direction
5. Life Control
6. Self-Discipline
7. Self-Esteem
8. Image Projection

1. Future Expectation

Circle the number that applies to you. A 1 stands for strongly agree and a 5 for strongly disagree.

strongly agree .... *strongly disagree*

1. Generally speaking, my future is very bright.   1 2 3 4 5
2. My health will get better and better as time goes on.   1 2 3 4 5
3. Problems that come up are really opportunities in disguise.   1 2 3 4 5
4. The future image I hold of myself in one year looks promising.   1 2 3 4 5
5. I look forward to tomorrow.   1 2 3 4 5
6. I look forward to what will happen to me in the next year.   1 2 3 4 5
7. My income will increase dramatically as time goes on.   1 2 3 4 5
8. I am gaining more and more control of my destiny every day.   1 2 3 4 5
9. I will be more successful a year from now than I am today.   1 2 3 4 5
10. I know exactly where I will be in life one year from now.   1 2 3 4 5

2. Personal Motivation

1. There are really only 1 to 3 things that are holding me back. These are:
    1.
    2.
    3.
2. Those things stop me from doing these 1 to 3 things that are really important to me:
    1.
    2.
    3.
3. My main goal in life right now is: _____

4. When I have time to think: (Circle one)
   I am worrying about something going wrong
   I am thinking about how I can achieve my goals
5. My thoughts are usually focused on: (Circle one)
   How to make money
   The many possible ways I could lose money
6. I think more about: (Circle one)
   Health problems
   My good health
7. Generally speaking I am a: (Circle one)
   Follower
   Leader
8. I would rather have someone else take responsibility for my life. Yes or No (Circle one)
9. If I could see a way for me to become successful but it might be difficult at first, I would still jump at the chance. Yes or No (Circle one)
10. There is really no way for me to become successful, so it is useless for me to try. Yes or No (Circle one)

3. Self-Image

1. I think about my mission in life:
   A. daily
   B. monthly
   C. yearly
   D. not at all
   (Circle all that apply)
2. Generally speaking I am a good person.   Yes or No
3. I have a true purpose on earth.   Yes or No
4. I am a goal-striving person.   Yes or No
5. I have no real goals in life.   Yes or No
6. My health is quite good.   Yes or No
   Why?_____
7. My health is poor.   Yes or No
   Why? _____
8. I would like to be good at _____.
   Why aren't you?_____

9. I could be wealthy if I_____.
   Why don't you? _____

10. I could be a leader if I_____.
    Why don't you? _____

11. I would be in control of my life if I _____.
    Why don't you? _____

12. I am most proud of _____ in my life.

4. Life Direction

1. My life long goal is

   _____.

2. Three years from now I will be

   _____.

3. If I continue my current financial practices I will have this
   much money saved in
   1 year _____ (dollar amount)
   3 years _____ (dollar amount)
   5 years _____ (dollar amount)
   I have no idea!

4. I have saved _____ (dollar amount) over the past 5 years.

5. My main goal over the next year is to _____.

6. I have a good deal of control over my health.   Yes or No

7. I know what I have to do to become successful.   Yes or No

8. I know what I have to do to become financially
   independent.   Yes or No

9. I know what I have to do to become a
   self-directing individual.   Yes or No

10. I have researched my plans for the future and
    they are sound.   Yes or No

11. I have a plan for achieving my major definite
    purpose in life.   Yes or No

5. Life Control

1. Luck is the main factor controlling my life.   Yes or No

2. I am a very superstitious person.   Yes or No

3. There is so much *I have to do* I really have
   no choices.   Yes or No

4. Some people may have unlimited choices in
   life but I'm not one of them.   Yes or No
5. Who controls my life?

   _____

6. I could have more control over my life if I

   _____.

7. I would really like to _____ but I don't
   because of _____.
8. I would be under less stress if I

   _____.

9. My life is off track because of

   _____.

10. My life is on track because of

   _____.

6. Self-Discipline

1. I finish what I start.   Yes or No
2. I can't break bad habits no matter how
   hard I try.   Yes or No
3. I think about what I can do but can't seem
   to get motivated to do it.   Yes or No
4. My body is out of shape.   Yes or No
5. I can control my spending.   Yes or No
6. I am a weak person physically.   Yes or No
7. I have strong determination.   Yes or No
8. I keep track of my progress toward my
   goals in writing.   Yes or No
9. I have a set of clearly written goals.   Yes or No
10. I have a set of clearly written personal
    life values.   Yes or No
11. I usually go along with the crowd.   Yes or No
12. I can't study when everyone else is playing.   Yes or No
13. The greatest obstacle I have overcome in
    my life is _____.
    (Did this involve self-discipline?)

7. Self-Esteem

1. I like myself.   Yes or No
2. I am proud of my body.   Yes or No
3. I am proud of my job.   Yes or No
4. I am proud of my profession.   Yes or No
5. If I enjoy myself too much it bothers me.   Yes or No
6. I feel awkward when someone compliments me. Yes or No
7. I see the good in most people I meet.   Yes or No
8. I always take care of myself.   Yes or No
9. I am a shy, reserved person.   Yes or No
10. Other people irritate me often.   Yes or No
11. I am almost never wrong.   Yes or No
12. I would rather be _____ than who I am.

8. Image Projection

1. I try to look my best at all times.   Yes or No
2. I listen 50% of the time and talk 50%
   of the time.   Yes or No
3. I listen to others intensely, trying to
   understand them fully.   Yes or No
4. I ask for feedback when I talk to people
   so I can be sure they understand me.   Yes or No
5. People generally feel comfortable talking
   to me.   Yes or No
6. People confide their problems in me and
   often seek my advice.   Yes or No
7. The opposite sex is readily attracted to me.   Yes or No
8. I have good posture (stand erect, head up,
   shoulders back, sit erect, etc.).   Yes or No
9. I speak clearly and forcefully.   Yes or No
10. I am neat and well groomed.   Yes or No

Now go over each mind-set again, answering the questions just like the first time, but this time imagine you are the perfect person you wished yourself to be. Now how would you answer each of them? There will probably be some important differences in the answers.

Review your two sets of answers and determine the mind-set in which you are most inconsistent. Also look at any inconsistencies in the other mind-sets so you are *aware* of what you need to work on to become the perfect you.

This self-analysis instrument was designed to get you to *think* by revealing your own perceived strengths and weaknesses: strengths to develop further and weaknesses to eliminate. Make a written list of what you really think you need to work on in the eight mind-sets of personal power.

(3) Determination of Your Personal Life Values

◆ What is the single most important value in your life?

◆ What are your core values?

Principle: Self-fulfillment depends on the triple alignment of personal life values, natural talent(s), and goals.

By determining your personal life values and setting goals that are supported by these values, you will automatically become a happier, more effective human being. Many people are unhappy simply because they haven't spent the time to get a clear idea of what is really important to them in life. Everyone has values, but if these are not clearly defined a person can easily wind up working on goals that conflict with their values. You need to know exactly what your life is based on. Without a set of core values to anchor your life, you will drift aimlessly.

Another important reason for determining your personal life values is to serve as a reference check when you determine your goals and consider/reconsider your career. You need to check all your goals against your personal life values list to be sure there is no conflict. If conflict of this kind exists it will create an inner feeling of anxiety, your actions will never "seem right." This feeling must be eliminated; otherwise you can't put your heart and soul into your goals. You must be able to focus your entire being into your goals, and you can't do that if you have core value conflicts. Conflicts of this nature will literally eat you up from the inside out!

Your goals not only must be free from inner conflict with your values but should in fact *support* one or more of your life values. Your deepest personal values will become motivating forces for you if your goals support one or more of them. In this way, when you achieve a goal you'll also gain a sense of true fulfillment.

I stress complete alignment with regard to personal life values, your natural talent(s), and goals (we will discuss natural talents in the next section and then goal setting in Part II of The POWERMIND System). If you use your natural talent(s) in some way to achieve your goals, which in turn support your life values, then the greatest sense of fulfillment accompanies the accomplishment of that goal. Alignment in three areas, personal life values, natural talent(s), and goals, is critical to self-fulfillment.

This self-analysis instrument is uniquely designed to help you uncover your personal life values. I've listed life values in eight separate categories to serve as thought starters. It is well worth your time to go to a quiet place and think very carefully while you perform this self-analysis. You may want to do one category per day or spend an entire weekend to complete the whole instrument. The eight categories are as follows:

1. Family
2. Personal
3. Social
4. Financial
5. Career
6. Health
7. Creativity
8. Spiritual

Circle a number from 1 to 5 with 1 being *extremely* important and 5 being not important. Keep in mind that many items on these lists may be very important to you, but you should be searching for the distinction between *extreme* importance and just importance. Simply marking all the items with a 1 will render the instrument useless!

1. Family

extremely important   *not important*

1. Participating in family holidays (Christmas, New Year's, Thanksgiving, etc.)   1 2 3 4 5
2. Participating in family celebrations (awards, birthdays, graduations, etc.)   1 2 3 4 5
3. Being part of a loving family   1 2 3 4 5
4. Being a positive influence on my family   1 2 3 4 5
5. Being able to handle family problems   1 2 3 4 5
6. Having a happy family   1 2 3 4 5
7. Being affectionate toward my family   1 2 3 4 5
8. Spending time with my family as a group   1 2 3 4 5
9. Getting strength from my family   1 2 3 4 5
10. Leading my family   1 2 3 4 5
11. Maintaining a wonderful marriage   1 2 3 4 5
12. Developing and keeping my sexual relationship with my spouse (physical love)   1 2 3 4 5
13. Developing and keeping my spiritual relationship with my spouse (mental love)   1 2 3 4 5
14. Being supportive of my spouse's goals   1 2 3 4 5
15. Having good relationships with my brothers and sisters   1 2 3 4 5
16. Maintaining healthy relationships with my mother and father   1 2 3 4 5
17. Developing and keeping good relationships with my in-laws   1 2 3 4 5
18. Keeping excellent relationships with my sons and daughters   1 2 3 4 5
19. Spending time with my children individually   1 2 3 4 5
20. Participating in my children's activities (sports, plays, concerts, etc.)   1 2 3 4 5
21. Being supportive of my children's goals   1 2 3 4 5
22. Taking part in my children's education   1 2 3 4 5
23. Instilling my values into my children   1 2 3 4 5
24. Teaching my children how to set and achieve goals in life   1 2 3 4 5

2. Personal

1.	Having time by myself	1 2 3 4 5
2.	Being attractive to the opposite sex	1 2 3 4 5
3.	Feeling that I am still young	1 2 3 4 5
4.	Meeting obligations to my family	1 2 3 4 5
5.	Meeting obligations to my friends	1 2 3 4 5
6.	Meeting obligations to my colleagues	1 2 3 4 5
7.	Living my life according to my own set of core values	1 2 3 4 5
8.	Doing challenging work	1 2 3 4 5
9.	Continuously improving myself	1 2 3 4 5
10.	Being energetic and enthusiastic	1 2 3 4 5
11.	Standing up for my beliefs	1 2 3 4 5
12.	Taking reasonable risks	1 2 3 4 5
13.	Managing my time well	1 2 3 4 5
14.	Being honest	1 2 3 4 5
15.	Increasing my value to other people	1 2 3 4 5
16.	Being in control of my life	1 2 3 4 5
17.	Being neat and well groomed	1 2 3 4 5
18.	Becoming a leader	1 2 3 4 5
19.	Having self-confidence	1 2 3 4 5
20.	Having an inner sense of self-worth	1 2 3 4 5
21.	Being a productive person	1 2 3 4 5
22.	Speaking well and expressing myself clearly	1 2 3 4 5
23.	Completing what I start	1 2 3 4 5
24.	Having worthy goals in life	1 2 3 4 5

3. Social

1.	Being a leader in organizations I belong to	1 2 3 4 5
2.	Being a leader at work	1 2 3 4 5
3.	Following a strong leader	1 2 3 4 5
4.	Belonging to a group or club	1 2 3 4 5
5.	Starting new relationships (personal friends)	1 2 3 4 5
6.	Starting new relationships (business associates)	1 2 3 4 5
7.	Being popular	1 2 3 4 5
8.	Listening to others carefully to understand them	1 2 3 4 5
9.	Being charming and charismatic	1 2 3 4 5

10.	Being the center of attention	1 2 3 4 5
11.	Having a positive influence on other people's lives	1 2 3 4 5
12.	Having a good sense of humor	1 2 3 4 5
13.	Being sensitive to other people's feelings	1 2 3 4 5
14.	Knowing more people next year than I do today	1 2 3 4 5
15.	Being honest with other people	1 2 3 4 5
16.	Doing volunteer work (churches, hospitals, etc.)	1 2 3 4 5
17.	Being active in community organizations	1 2 3 4 5
18.	Being active in politics	1 2 3 4 5
19.	Contributing regularly to the well-being of others	1 2 3 4 5

4. Financial

1.	Having just enough money to live comfortably	1 2 3 4 5
2.	Being financially independent	1 2 3 4 5
3.	Having money for vacations and recreation	1 2 3 4 5
4.	Having a nice home	1 2 3 4 5
5.	Having lots of "toys" (boats, cars, planes, motorcycles, etc.)	1 2 3 4 5
6.	Turning my ideas into cash	1 2 3 4 5
7.	Increasing my net worth in terms of cash value	1 2 3 4 5
8.	Contributing to charities	1 2 3 4 5
9.	Having enough money to support other people's business endeavors	1 2 3 4 5
10.	Continuously increasing my income	1 2 3 4 5
11.	Having financial independence at or before retirement age	1 2 3 4 5
12.	Working harder mentally rather than physically to earn money	1 2 3 4 5
13.	Having a retirement fund	1 2 3 4 5
14.	Having a good life insurance policy	1 2 3 4 5
15.	Having an education fund for my children	1 2 3 4 5
16.	Becoming debt free	1 2 3 4 5
17.	Truly earning all the money I make	1 2 3 4 5
18.	Helping others achieve their financial goals	1 2 3 4 5

5. Career

1. Getting increasingly better jobs within my company   1 2 3 4 5
2. Getting increasingly better jobs with different companies   1 2 3 4 5
3. Using my abilities fully at my job   1 2 3 4 5
4. Having more job responsibilities   1 2 3 4 5
5. Having less job responsibilities   1 2 3 4 5
6. Being recognized for my achievements   1 2 3 4 5
7. Having opportunities for advancement at work 1 2 3 4 5
8. Having good relationships with my coworkers   1 2 3 4 5
9. Contributing at my job to help my company   1 2 3 4 5
10. Taking classes or reading to improve myself in my career   1 2 3 4 5
11. Being neat and well organized   1 2 3 4 5
12. Managing my time wisely   1 2 3 4 5
13. Carefully planning my activities   1 2 3 4 5
14. Having the ability to impress other people with my job   1 2 3 4 5
15. Being competent to do the work I am paid for 1 2 3 4 5
16. Being the best at what I do for a living   1 2 3 4 5
17. Being my own boss   1 2 3 4 5
18. Owning my own business   1 2 3 4 5
19. Being happy with my job   1 2 3 4 5

6. Health

1. Having a strong, muscular body   1 2 3 4 5
2. Having a low level of stress   1 2 3 4 5
3. Controlling my appetite   1 2 3 4 5
4. Controlling my blood pressure   1 2 3 4 5
5. Feeling I am in control of my body   1 2 3 4 5
6. Controlling my temper   1 2 3 4 5
7. Being happy most of the time   1 2 3 4 5
8. Feeling in control of my life   1 2 3 4 5
9. Having an excellent memory   1 2 3 4 5
10. Rarely getting colds or flu   1 2 3 4 5
11. Having a body that I am proud of   1 2 3 4 5

12. Exercising regularly   1 2 3 4 5
13. Eating proper foods   1 2 3 4 5
14. Being good at sports   1 2 3 4 5
15. Being full of energy   1 2 3 4 5
16. Living to a very old age   1 2 3 4 5
17. Being sexually active (able to satisfy and
    be satisfied)   1 2 3 4 5
18. Being more healthy next year than I am today   1 2 3 4 5
19. Being physically attractive to the opposite sex   1 2 3 4 5

7. Creativity

1. Having a wide variety of new ideas to
   implement   1 2 3 4 5
2. Being open to new ideas from other sources
   (people, books, etc.)   1 2 3 4 5
3. Putting other people's creative ideas into action 1 2 3 4 5
4. Putting my own creative ideas into action   1 2 3 4 5
5. Appreciating beauty in the world   1 2 3 4 5
6. Being innovative   1 2 3 4 5
7. Enjoying new and challenging activities   1 2 3 4 5
8. Having an intense interest in my tasks   1 2 3 4 5
9. Using my mind instead of my back to
   achieve results   1 2 3 4 5
10. Being challenged to solve difficult life
    problems   1 2 3 4 5
11. Being engaged in widely differing activities   1 2 3 4 5
12. Exploring new things (places, people, ideas)   1 2 3 4 5
13. Making things with my hands (clothes,
    crafts, machines, etc.)   1 2 3 4 5
14. Exploring new ways to improve myself   1 2 3 4 5
15. Devising new ways to teach others what I know 1 2 3 4 5
16. Using my imagination productively   1 2 3 4 5
17. Working with others to solve problems   1 2 3 4 5
18. Working with others to generate ideas   1 2 3 4 5
19. Being active in the arts (sculpture, painting,
    music, etc.)   1 2 3 4 5

8. Spiritual

1. Having a good relationship with God	1 2 3 4 5
2. Meeting religious obligations	1 2 3 4 5
3. Teaching others my religion	1 2 3 4 5
4. Donating my time to my religious organization	1 2 3 4 5
5. Recruiting for my religious organization	1 2 3 4 5
6. Raising money for my religious organization	1 2 3 4 5
7. Studying my religion	1 2 3 4 5
8. Studying other religions	1 2 3 4 5
9. Searching for life's true meaning	1 2 3 4 5
10. Contemplating God	1 2 3 4 5
11. Devoting time each day to prayer	1 2 3 4 5
12. Asking for God's help in my life	1 2 3 4 5
13. Asking God to help other people	1 2 3 4 5
14. Being thankful for what I now have	1 2 3 4 5
15. Developing myself spiritually	1 2 3 4 5
16. Aligning my actions with God's will	1 2 3 4 5
17. Giving and receiving God's love	1 2 3 4 5
18. Having piece of mind	1 2 3 4 5
19. Deriving security in life through faith in God	1 2 3 4 5

When you have finished with the eight categories, your next step is to get out a clean sheet of paper, write each category title down, and under each one write out all the items after which you circled a 1. If you have other values I did not list that you consider to be in class 1, add them to your list at this time.

Now take a closer look at every number 1 value listed on your sheet. Under each category rank the number 1 values in order of importance to you, numbering them 1-3 or 1-5 or 1-6 or however many you have in order to prioritize the total number of items under that category. Do this for each category. If you didn't mark any number 1s under a category, delete it from your sheet.

Looking over all your prioritized lists under each life values category ask yourself this question: **"What is my single most important value in life?"** Put a star by it.

Take out another sheet of paper and at the top of the page write "These values are the most important in my life and will guide me in all that I do." Then in your best handwriting, write them all out. You now know what is your single most important value in life and what your core values in life are, and have in your possession a prioritized categorical list of them.

◆ ◆ ◆

You have just been through a systematic method of determining personal life values. Review your list carefully, for it tells you what areas are of extreme importance to you. This is the first forward step in managing your life. This list will serve as a guide for the decisions you make and the actions you take in life from this moment onward.

Whatever you do must never conflict in any way with this list of personal life values or your life will be unfulfilled! Creating a personal life values list is also the first step in utilizing the principle of *alignment*.

(4) Uncovering Your Natural Talent(s)

Principle: Everyone in the world has at least one natural talent, even you!

Ask yourself these key questions:
Do I possess latent abilities?
Could my career be based on my natural talent(s)?
Should my career be based on my natural talent(s)?

Most people possess multiple natural talents, any one of which if capitalized on could make them a fortune, give true meaning to their lives, or both. This is a multiple question self-analysis tool specifically designed to help you uncover your natural talent(s).

Here Is a Roadblock to Success to Consider before This Analysis

People tend to become bogged down or weakened by minor everyday problems. They focus on these little cares, making their lives miserable and goal attainment seemingly impossible. They are unhappy and resentful and feel cheated by life. This is both an awful feeling and an unnecessary one, yet millions of people feel this way. They allow tiny obstacles to block their pathway to personal success and happiness rather than developing their God-given talent(s).

They say things like "I deserve more, the world owes me," or "If that's all they pay, I'll work as little as possible." Let me be the first to tell you, "The world owes you nothing." You are the one who owes. You owe it to yourself, your family, and your country to develop your natural talents to the fullest extent.

Everyone feels good when they perform well; in the area of your natural talent(s) is where you have a competitive advantage to perform better than anyone else. Natural talent development is a primary key to success in life. Your special talent(s) or gift(s) if developed fully will benefit you and everyone close to you—guaranteed!

"If you work on your gifts, they will make a room for you."

Jim Rohn
America's foremost business
philosopher; author of *The*
Five Major Pieces to the Life
Puzzle, *Seven Strategies for*
Wealth and Happiness, **and**
The Seasons of Life

Section 1. Determination of Natural Talents

This self-analysis instrument enables you to uncover your natural talent(s). You will pursue a relatively easy line of questioning for this analysis. You may need to think on and off for a couple of days as new ideas spring to mind. When you have finished you will have gained a working knowledge of your natural talent(s). Many people take their talent(s) for granted, not realizing everyone *doesn't* have it.

The self-examination is split into two sections; the second section is more applied than the first. Section 2 forces you to examine your talent(s) with respect to a possible career. This will encourage you to again think about the all-important principle of alignment. In Section 2 you will consider the principle of alignment with regard to both natural talent and career.

◆ ◆ ◆

Take out a sheet of paper and answer the following questions.

The self-unfoldment questions are:

1. Thinking back in your past, what have you done that seemed to be very easy for you to do?
2. What types of things do you learn quickly?
3. What do you seem to have a special "knack" for?
4. What tasks or jobs can you perform exceptionally well?
5. Thinking back in your past, what have other people praised you for that you considered routine?
6. What can you do that is a "cinch" for you?
7. What can you do easily, or better than average, that most other people seem to "struggle" with?
8. Thinking back in your past, have people ever made these types of comments to you?
   A. "You are really good at this," or
   B. "You are a *natural* at this," or
   C. "That's amazing how did you do that?" or
   D. "Wow, I wish I could do that like you" or
   E. "This is so easy for you, but so hard for me."
9. In question 8, identify all the activities you can possibly remember hearing those types of comments for, and list them.
10. After answering questions 1-8, what do you "feel" your natural talent(s) might be? List all of them.

Now ask yourself questions 11-37:

11. Do I possess natural artistic ability to paint, draw, sculpt, etc.?
12. Do I have exceptional physical attractiveness to the opposite sex?

13. Do I have sports skill? If so, what sport? What position?
14. Do I have a particular aptitude for machines? What type (cars, motors, computers, electronics, etc.)?
15. Am I mechanically inclined?
16. Do I have exceptional scientific or analytical ability?
17. Do I have exceptional mathematical ability?
18. Do I have exceptional writing ability? If so, what form (business, poetry, fiction, advertising, etc.)?
19. Do people enjoy listening to me when I speak?
20. Am I particularly entertaining to other people?
21. Am I an extremely good counselor of other people?
22. Do I have an exceptional memory?
23. Is there any particular subject that I learn easily and quickly?
24. Is my body particularly suited to a certain line of work (for example, very small body weight like a racehorse jockey, or very big and strong like a football lineman, or tall like a basketball player, etc.)?
25. Do I have any specialized skills? If so, was it easy for me to acquire them?
26. What have I formally been trained in and why did I choose it?
27. Do I have additional specialized training in the trades (for example, heavy equipment, carpentry, welding, beautician, etc.)? If so why did I choose it?
28. Do I have any college degree(s)? If so, why did I select my major?
29. Do I possess an exceptional ability to complete tasks?
30. Do other people naturally seem to respect me as their leader?
31. Do I possess an exceptional ability to sell things?
32. Do I possess musical talent? With instruments or singing?
33. Do I possess inventive ability?
34. Do I possess a natural ability to craft things?
35. Considering everything in life, what interests me the most?
36. Am I able to organize people to perform a task?
37. Are children readily entertained by me?

Look over your answers carefully. Your natural talent(s) may be a gold mine for you if it can be fully utilized or further developed in your line of work. Section 2 of this self-analysis tool will give you added insight in the area of possible careers based on your natural talent(s).

Section 2. Aligning Natural Talent(s) with a Career

If you kept getting the same answers for some of the questions in Part I, then you probably have a good idea of your natural talent(s). Those questions should have allowed you to identify at least one, and possibly more. If you have identified one or more, list them on a sheet of paper and ask yourself these questions in regard to each of them:

1. Do the talents listed have anything in common?
2. What is the essential skill or skills required to be excellent at them? Another way to ask question 2 is to use a different perspective. Ask this: If someone was very good at this (your talent), what skill or skills would be required of the person?
3. Is there any way I can develop my talent(s) further?
4. Is there any way I can earn money with my talent(s)?
5. Could I make a career out of such talent(s)?
6. Is there a way I can serve other people with my talent(s)?
7. If I were to become the best at my talent(s), would it be worth my time and effort?
8. If I were to make a living using my natural talent(s), would I be happy?
9. What is my greatest achievement so far in life? Why?
10. Did I utilize my natural talent(s) for that achievement?

You should now have a good handle on your natural talent(s). A person who can develop natural abilities to the fullest extent tends to be happy and gains a sense of fulfillment. I'll now state five key questions for you to consider very carefully, with your added insight.

- Do I possess hidden abilities?
- Could my career be based on my natural talent(s)?
- Should my career be based on my natural talent(s)?
- How can I use my natural talent(s) to improve my career?
- Is there some way I can develop my natural talent(s) further at my current job?

(5) Personal Inventory for Wealth Creation

In many cases it is worthwhile for a person to take a personal inventory to determine if he or she has any specialized training that could be useful in earning more money. Another important aspect of this particular inventory is that it addresses the *amount* of training a person has. It is possible that additional training in a certain area could be beneficial in netting more money. This line of questioning is designed to get you to think about what you already have that could be capitalized on or improved on for wealth creation.

1. Do I have a high school diploma? If not, would it be beneficial to get one?
2. Do I have a two-year college degree? If not, would it be beneficial to get one?
3. Do I have a four-year college degree? If not, would it be beneficial to get one?
4. Do I have a master's degree? If not, would it be beneficial to get one?
5. Do I have a Ph.D. degree? If not, would it be beneficial to get one?
6. Do I have any specialized training in a particular trade (for example, electrician, plumber, auto mechanic, refrigeration, etc.)? If not, would it be beneficial to get some?
7. Do I have any advanced training in business management or sales? If not, would it be beneficial to get some?
8. Are there any specialized skills that I have, that I could use to earn money?
9. Do I have any skills that I could use to provide a special service to other people?

10. Can I, right now, think of any training that I could obtain
    that would enable me to earn money or earn more money
    than I currently make?

Questions 11-17 refer to starting/operating a small business of your own.

11. Is there any way I could produce a product or provide a ser-
    vice out of my home or on my own?
12. What equipment would I need to purchase?
13. Who could I get to help me?
14. Where could I raise money for this?
15. How could I market this product or service?
16. What need does my product or service fill?
17. What makes my product or service different/better from
    current vendors?
18. Why would people buy my product or service?
19. Why would people buy from me versus other suppliers?
20. Is there anything I currently have the ability to do that can
    help me earn more money?

An After-the-Lesson Visit with the Author

(1) The Master Test for Success

This self-analysis instrument provided you with thirty-seven
key questions, each addressing personal characteristics necessary for success in life. It also introduced you to the Universal
Law of sowing and reaping. This Universal Law will be emphasized and elaborated on throughout the entire POWERMIND
system, for it is the supreme law governing the universe.

One application of this law is that if you profit from taking
advantage of or abusing other people, this same measure must be
returned to you. The apparently successful person who has
gained power through taking advantage of others has fate
patiently waiting just around the corner with a stuffed club—and
it isn't stuffed with cotton!

(2) The 8 Mind-Sets of Personal Power

Future expectation revealed to you how you expect your future to be. It showed whether your expectations are positive or negative. Your expectation of the future determines to a large degree how your actual future will turn out. This is called the self-fulfilling prophecy.

Personal motivation was to serve as an aid in figuring out what you want to do and give you clues as to what's holding you back. It also addressed your inner drive for achievement.

Self-Image allowed you to determine how you view yourself and stimulated you to think about how to improve on your current self.

Life Direction revealed whether you know where your life is headed, that is to say, whether you have a clear idea or not.

Life Control analyzed your feelings in regards to your perceived control over your life, whether you think you are in charge or "someone else" is in charge.

Self-Discipline addressed whether you have the stamina necessary to achieve long-term goals.

Self-Esteem revealed whether you have a good degree of self-love. Remember you can never love anyone more than you love yourself. When people love themselves they are at ease with others, readily give and accept compliments, are free from jealousy, and take excellent care of themselves. This is not arrogance, it is high self-esteem!

Image Projection allowed you to determine how you impact others.

(3) Determination of Your Personal Life Values

This is one of the most important parts of the entire POWERMIND system because by introspection and reflection you were able to determine what your life is based on. The list of core values you made serves to guide and direct your decisions. Without knowing what your life values are, your decision making becomes erratic because you have no points of reference.

The principle of self-fulfillment was also stated: *Self-fulfillment depends on the triple alignment of personal life values, natural talent(s), and goals.*

You should now have in your possession a neatly handwritten list of your core values. These should be prioritized, with your primary value in life labeled with a star. You will be using this list in the goal-setting section to be sure your goals are not in conflict with any of these core values.

(4) Uncovering Your Natural Talents

Most people have lots of fun with this instrument because when they start it they believe they have no natural talents. After completing it, they see they do!

After completion of Section 1 you should have a good idea of at least one natural talent that you possess. Your mind is then turned in Section 2 to the idea that perhaps your whole career could be based on that one special talent or set of talents. This would indeed be beneficial to you as well as those around you. Should you base your career on your natural talent(s)? I believe so!

(5) Personal Inventory for Wealth Creation

This instrument allowed you to think about what you already have in terms of special skills and training. You then determined whether there were any ways you could increase your current skill levels to increase your earnings.

In the last part you were asked to consider providing a product or service on your own outside of your current employer. This is the beginning of what is called *entrepreneurial thinking*. More than half of the self-made millionaires in the U.S. are entrepreneurs. They made it by starting their own business. That should get your mind cooking!

◆ ◆ ◆

You should now have in your possession:

1. An idea of what personal characteristics are necessary for success in life
2. A working knowledge of the eight mind-sets of personal power
3. A prioritized list of your personal life values

4. Knowledge of your natural talent(s)
5. Knowledge of how to use your natural talent in a career
6. Information on skills or training you might pursue further for increased wealth

I hope you found all five of the self-analysis instruments uniquely revealing and rewarding. These are the first forward steps on your journey of self-discovery and self-mastery. The better you understand yourself, the better off you'll be in life.

The transformation process has already begun; you have now learned many valuable skills, such as entrepreneurial thinking, reflecting, introspection, systematizing, prioritizing, and writing your thoughts on paper. These skills will serve you well throughout the rest of this book and throughout life.

Armed with the personal information gleaned from this lesson, you are now prepared to move into Part II of The POWER-MIND System. Keep up the good work!

GOAL SETTING

Part II

Lesson Numbers 2,3

◆2▶ General Goal Setting

Overview

This lesson is divided into three modules. The first module covers the basics of goal setting theory. The second module consists of a collection of eight specific techniques you can immediately use for goal setting. The third module reviews important points covered in the previous two modules. It also explains the fascinating physiological basis in the human brain that makes these goal setting techniques so effective. Lesson Two of The POWERMIND System ends with a potent call to action. The three modules are outlined for previewing below.

The POWERMIND System
Part II. Goal Setting

General Goal Setting: Module I. Goal Setting Theory

General Goal Setting: Module II. 8 Techniques for Goal Setting

General Goal Setting: Module III. Goal Setting Principles

General Goal Setting: Module I. Goal Setting Theory

Importance of Goal Setting

Principle: No objective always leads to no end.

It is extremely important for you to know exactly what you want to **be, have,** or **do** in life. You can attain your dreams and go where you want to in life only if you have goals clearly "set in mind." The clearer your goals, the better off you are. Your mind cannot focus effectively on a vague objective. Most people don't get anywhere in life simply because they have no idea where they want to go. These people live without purpose, with no clear-cut predetermined objectives in mind. They wander aimlessly through life, with an unfocused *powerless mind,* getting nowhere! Everyone knows *no objectives always leads to no end.*

University studies have shown that only about 3% of the general population ever write out their goals clearly on paper. These studies also have shown that of this small percentage, nearly 100% achieve all their goals. So it is very easy for you to walk away from the 97% crowd who don't set or achieve goals in life!

At Yale University in 1953 a study was begun on the graduating seniors, and only 3% had done all the proper steps in goal setting; another 10% had partially set goals; and 87% had set no goals at all. In 1973, twenty years later, it was found that the 3% who properly set goals had accomplished more than the 97% who did not. The study also showed that the elite 3% were worth more financially than the other 97% combined!

"Give me a stock clerk with a goal and I'll give you a man who will make history, but give me a man without a goal and I'll give you a stock clerk."

> **J.C. Penney**
> **Founder of the J.C. Penney**
> **stores**

Goals are not limited to individuals. Entire nations can be motivated to remarkable action by a common goal. In 1960 the country of Japan set the goal of becoming the leading steel-producing country in the world. Even though Japan had no natural iron ore and no coal to produce steel, they achieved their *seemingly impossible* goal. In 1970 they set the goal of being the number one nation in the world in automobile production. U.S. automakers scoffed at this, saying it couldn't be done—to their dismay it happened!

Why is it the majority of people do not have clearly written goals? I can think of four possible answers.

1. They simply don't know what they want out of life.
2. They don't realize the power of goal setting.
3. They don't know *how to* properly set goals.
4. They don't have the self-discipline it takes to think their goals out in detail ahead of time and write them down. (Can you imagine a person having the self-discipline to achieve a major life goal if they don't even have the self-discipline to write out what the goal is on a sheet of paper?)

This entire lesson is designed to help you overcome all four of these life-destroying dilemmas.

"I have observed that setting a goal makes no appeal to the mediocre. But to those fired with an ambition to really greatly achieve, setting a goal becomes a program that stirs the inner soul to action."

> **William H. Danforth**
> **Chairman of the board,**
> **Ralston Purina Co., 1940**
> **Author of more than twelve**
> **books, including *I Dare You!*,**
> ***Power*, and *Four Golden Keys***

People without Purpose

Many scientific studies have shown most people are unfocused, wandering through life with no clue as to what they want to **be**, **have**, or **do**. Hence they become apathetic and cynical, and do nothing. There is a lot of talk on the problems of time management as an excuse for not achieving anything, but the fact of the matter is this: people don't lack time, *they lack direction*. Time management is pointless unless you have a set of life goals you are working towards. **There is no need at all to manage your time if you have no goals!**

So many people are shortsighted, going from day to day in utter delusion, thinking somehow everything in life will work out fine for them. They never think about who will care for them when they are old or what their purpose on this earth is. They have no patience and seek instant gratification of all their whimsical wants. They go through life casually drifting from one self-created disaster into another.

All too often their "wake-up" call is life shattering. The pink slip at the job notifying them they've been laid off, the chained doors at the plant with a note reading "shut down, moved to Mexico," the unforeseen heart attack, colon cancer, nervous breakdown, severe arthritis, or family breakup. They are like corks floating aimlessly in the vast ocean of life, eventually getting waterlogged and sinking to a deep watery grave.

Without purpose, life is meaningless. A person who has absolutely no goals in life, no short-term goals, no long-term goals, none at all, will literally shrivel up and die. I will back this statement up with two common examples that you have probably witnessed.

First example: What happens to many extremely productive career-driven people when they retire? If their job was their life, when the job ends, in less than two years many of their lives do as well (unless they have set new life goals for themselves!).

Second example: If a husband and wife team have been very close for many, many years, when one dies the other follows suit shortly thereafter. One spouse was the other's "whole life." When one is gone, the other is not far behind. The survivor decides that he or she has "nothing more to live for."

However, a surviving spouse who develops new interests or new goals, or finds a new partner, may live on for a long, long time, but tragically this doesn't happen to everyone.

So many people get scripted into believing their lot in life is predetermined. They think they can't do anything about it, they see themselves as the victims of fate. Usually in childhood these people were taught to **FOLLOW** everyone else, to be like the rest of the low-performing 97% crowd. They were told things like "Children should be seen and not heard," "Color between the lines," "Don't touch that," "Follow the rules," "You can't do that," "Who do you think you are." The *creative leadership* drive was literally bred out of them.

Early on, the incessant bombardment of self-limiting beliefs was blasted into them, stifling their inner drive to succeed as well as their creativity. Children aren't usually taught to question authority or to think for themselves, judge for themselves, or determine who exactly set the rules they are to live by.

Relatively few people in the world have really big goals or great desires. Most shuffle through life shiftlessly, accepting whatever fate befalls them, adapting to circumstances rather than controlling them. Accepting their particular lot in life as "fixed" or "unchangeable," they make little mental or physical effort to break out of their mental prison, to better themselves, or to strive for more than shear personal poverty or at best mere mediocrity. They engage in self-destructive fantasizing, such as endless watching of the lives of the rich and famous people on TV or at the movie theater. They vicariously live the great dreams of others, never raising their own sights high enough to realize that they too could be one of them. Instead of working toward clearly defined goals of their own, they remain spectators on the sidelines of the great game of life—and they even have to *pay* to get in! By fantasizing their *time* away on nonproductive activities, they pay the heavy price of living a very small, pitiful, unfulfilled life of regret!

F.E.A.R. and Reality

People without a fixed goal in mind are working toward nothing and working for nothing! How can anyone achieve a goal when they have no idea where it is or what it looks like? People without goals are like ships without rudders, floundering around in the ocean of life *hoping* to someday land on treasure island.

Early in life they are taught to believe in F.E.A.R. (False Evidence Appearing Real), and this *becomes reality* to them. They become *socially conditioned* to adopt and believe the negative self-limiting attitudes and misperceptions of other people they associate with. Usually these people are family and friends. (Most people are highly susceptible to the influence of others with whom they associate.)

The flea trainer story illustrates this conditioning concept. Fleas won't jump out of a jar with no lid after they have been placed in one with a lid for a short period of time. They become conditioned to stop jumping higher than the lid even after the lid has been completely removed!

This same type of conditioning occurs in people with regards to big life goals. They get bluffed into believing that they can't get what they truly want out of life, so they stop trying.

They never learn what they are really capable of doing. They never explore their full potential because they never pursue really big goals. Their minds are filled with thoughts of lack and limitation, and they believe in F.E.A.R. They never achieve personal excellence because their minds are limited by their incorrect thinking patterns.

The *average* person goes to their grave never even knowing what they were capable of doing. This phrase sums it up nicely: "Here lies John Doe, he gave up on his goals at age 20, but we didn't bury him until age 73!"

"What you do today and in the immediate days that follow is the thing that will prove whether or not you possess the spirit of the priceless few who DARE."

> **William H. Danforth**
> **Chairman of the board,**
> **Ralston Purina Co., 1940**
> **Author of more than twelve**
> **books, including *I Dare You!*,**
> ***Power,* and *Four Golden Keys***

Negative Default Goals

**Principle: The subconscious mind will accept dominant
conscious thoughts as commands and
immediately act on them.**

Many times a person unconsciously sets a "default goal."
That is, whatever thoughts they allow to occupy their conscious
minds on a continuing basis will serve as goals for them. They
will automatically begin to move toward whatever they think
about on a continuing basis.

You will begin to bring into your life whatever you think
about, dwell on, imagine, or are emotional about. This happens
whether you consciously decided on the thoughts as "goals" or
simply allowed something to become the center of your attention. If your thinking is not rigorously controlled and focused on
positive goals, you will think negatively, and these thoughts
become negative default goals.

Many people *unconsciously* set negative default goals for
themselves—they actually set goals to fail! They didn't write
these down on a sheet of paper and say "failure is my chief goal
in life," but because they have unconsciously decided to focus
their thoughts on their worries and problems, continuously
thinking about all the reasons why they *can't* do what they want
to do, they set up impossibility, inactivity, cynicism, and failure
as a negative default goal.

They worry constantly about failing, imagining in vivid
detail with high emotion all the terrible consequences if they
fail. They visualize a negative foreboding future for themselves,
combining feelings of fear, apathy, depression, and failure with
these ominous visions, thereby emotionalizing them. They drive
these thoughts and images right into the root of their subconscious mind, and indeed their subconscious mind acts on that
powerful command with all its tremendous power. They do, in
fact, achieve their negative self-set default goals. They become
failures in life just like they thought! They have done the *exact
opposite* of **POSITIVE GOAL SETTING.**

"Present thoughts determine your future. Sure Enough."

James W. Newman
Creator of the PACE seminar
Author of *Release Your*
Brakes

The Self-Image

To further your understanding of how your dominant thoughts affect your circumstances in life, it will help if we look at what is called a person's self-image. Your self-image involves what type of person you think you are and in what type of environment you feel comfortable. Your goals in life will always be directly related to your self-image. Your self-image determines who you are, where you feel comfortable, how you dress, what friends you have, what job you do, what type of home you own, what car your drive, which social activities you engage in, what recreational events you attend, etc. A person's surroundings tend to reflect the person's own self-image.

A common illustration of this is student dorm rooms in college. Every student's room is different one week into the semester. In the beginning of the semester all the rooms are the same, but within one week, they are transformed; each room reflects the self-image of its occupant. Posters and flags are hung, furniture is replaced, decorations of all kinds abound. Whatever is in the mind of the occupant is *expressed in the external environment*. Their likes, hobbies, desires are all graphically displayed in the room.

A tragic illustration of self-image in action was the government-funded slum cleanup projects. The slums were destroyed, the old buildings were leveled, and new ones were erected in their place. The previous inhabitants were moved back in and quickly converted the new buildings into a slum again. The people weren't bad people. They were just behaving in a perfectly normal (to them) and predictable fashion based on their self-image.

Reverse the slum situation above and you'll see this point more clearly. Let's move **you** into the insect-infested filth of a slum apartment. What would you do first? Probably start cleaning up a bit, right? *Changing the environment to reflect your internal self-image* in your mind. You will begin by making things a bit more comfortable (to you). You'll start to make your surroundings more like the way things are "supposed" to be (according to you).

Everyone does this. My point in these illustrations is this: Your outer world, both environment and circumstance, reflects what's in your inner mind (self-image) because you actively set about to make it that way! Whatever is set in your mind motivates you to actively reflect it in your external environment.

So what does all this have to do with goal setting? As you continuously think about your goals in your mind, you change your self-image. When this happens your actions start to automatically change, tending to move you toward goal-achievement. You begin noticing goal-related opportunities and start taking advantage of them.

Goals, once driven into the subconscious section of the mind, alter your self-image. Once the mental self-image is altered, a conflict is set up between what is in your mind and your external surroundings. This then activates the subconscious mind to begin working on conflict resolution. Creativity, expansion of awareness, sensory enhancement, mental energy, and both conscious and unconscious actions all begin to operate in harmony to change your environment so it coincides with the new self-image.

Goal Setting: The Quintessential Skill for a Successful Life

Principle: Goal setting allows for the management of change in a direction most profitable for the individual.

Why are goals essential? There is one guarantee in life: It will change. No matter how hard you or anyone else tries to resist, change will inevitably occur. Time stands still for no one. With the passage of time change occurs.

If you have a set of goals you are progressively working toward, you can effectively manage this change in the direction you want change to occur. If you allow change to "happen to you," the consequences may be good or bad, but are usually bad. Instead of allowing change to happen to you as most people do, you can set goals giving you the power to take control of your future. If you set goals you are taking a conscious, active role in controlling change. By controlling change, you inevitably control your destiny.

Properly set goals also make your future look appealing, motivating you to take action. If the future appears frightening, bleak, dismal, lugubrious, how motivated are you? The key to self-motivation is to be proactive rather than reactive, and by setting your own goals you are being proactive.

Goal Setting Reduces Stress by Creating an Enticing Future

Principle: To the degree that you believe you can control your future, your level of negative stress will be reduced.

Many people have tremendous amounts of negative stress in their lives because they don't have their future well designed. They are filled with fear of the future. They rely on other people to set their goals for them both at work and in their personal lives. By not setting any goals of their own they are putting their lives in the hands of someone else. "Someone else" may not have what **they** really want in life planned for them. Here is what someone else may have planned for you: NOT MUCH!

Goal setting allows you to have an imagined future, thereby giving you a certain degree of control over it. In essence by setting goals you create a framework in your mind of what your own future has in store for you. This reduces negative stress! *To the degree that you believe you can control your future, your level of negative stress will be reduced.*

The side benefit of this belief is that your creative ability and natural potential are also allowed to flow more freely, giving you a better chance of actually achieving the goals you have set. The very act of setting a goal has the direct effect of relaxing you, which immediately improves your ability to achieve that goal! As negative stress is reduced your positive emotions increase and your true potential can pour out into your effort, speeding you toward the goal. The mental stages of this effect are outlined below.

Eight Stages of Goal Achievement

I. Goal is conceived

↓

II. Goal is set in writing

↓

III. Goal is reviewed daily

↓

IV. Goal achievement is believed

↓

V. Negative stress is reduced

↓

VI. Positive emotional flow increases

↓

VII. Achievement potential increases

↓

VIII. Goal is more rapidly achieved

By its very nature, goal setting helps you to combat depression. In fact, a major cause of depression is that a person feels they have no direct control over their life, and no sense of purpose. Without goals this is quite true. When I had no short-term or long-term goals in my life, I can assure you I was severely depressed, unhealthy, and cynical.

Constantly moving toward a worthy goal has a multitude of beneficial psychological and physical effects. Setting goals has an uncanny power to create enthusiasm inside you. You begin to look forward to your future. Your journey to the goal is exciting and challenging. Your actions change, your emotions change, you become more active, more alive, more healthy. Each day becomes meaningful. Goal setting is what makes all this possible.

Happiness and Winning Goals

Principle: All mental states can be cultivated.

Happiness is entirely a mental state—sought by many, found by few. The external environment doesn't really affect your happiness. Most of what happens to you happens to everyone else too. It's your interpretation, perception, and reaction to what happens that has the real effect.

All mental states can be cultivated, so you have the power to control happiness by controlling your thinking. Most people are unhappy because they have no clearly defined worthy goals toward which to work. If you have no goals in life, let me ask you this simple question: What are you doing here? Are you doing anything at all worthwhile, or are you simply existing here, waiting for your body to wear out and die? If you don't have any worthy goal you are working toward, I'll be bold and suggest you are in big trouble. Notice I use the word "worthy." This is key, because goals must be meaningful and inspirational, at least to you and hopefully to others as well.

When you push yourself, using all the power within you to achieve, maximizing your inner resources, your creative energies, pouring your heart and soul into winning a goal, then you are cultivating happiness. As you see yourself making progress in winning your goals you become happier.

Certainly you are happy once you have achieved the goal, but this happiness is usually only fleeting happiness. You are soon discontented, looking for a new goal, pursuing a new desire, pushing yourself, growing as an individual, seeing what all you can do with yourself and your life. That's when the happiness returns. Happiness is a by-product of laboring to win worthy goals. People who wonder if they are happy or not are indeed happy, because if they were unhappy they would certainly know it!

Mind-Set of the Goal Setter

Principle: Chance favors the prepared mind.

Imagine two line workers in a factory. Call them Lee and Chris. In Lee's mind is the goal of getting promoted in the next

five years. In Chris's mind is no career goal at all except showing up for work every day and collecting a weekly paycheck.

Lee begins taking definite actions to move toward that five-
year goal of a promotion by searching for information, taking
classes, planning, reading books, talking to others, working on
ways to prepare for the next higher job. Chris wastes time
watching TV, drinking beer, attending sporting events, and gam-
bling. Don't you think at the end of five years Lee will have
moved into a more favorable position, well ahead of Chris? It's
not likely Chris will have advanced much intellectually in the
same time period, but it is highly likely Lee will have advanced
quite far.

Now Lee is not guaranteed a promotion, but if Lee's actions
are consistent in moving him in that direction, Lee will be
assured progress well beyond Chris, who was engaged in no
self-development at all. Lee, being well prepared for promotion,
may seek it out at a new company if his current employer does-
n't offer him a promotion.

Do you see how having a definite career goal helps in aligning both your thoughts and actions? Since more than 90% of the
people in the U.S. have no clearly written goals at all, do you see
how **easy** it is for you to move ahead of the pack? Goal setting
has many advantages not obvious upon casual observation.

Goal setting orients your subconscious mind so it can actively work on what you want to achieve. With no objective to work
toward, it doesn't know what to do for you. In the example
above, Lee, who prepares for promotion ahead of time, increases
his chances of getting it.

If by some strange method Chris was promoted instead of
Lee, Chris wouldn't be able to do the job because Chris never
prepared for the job. So in fact *Chris can't do the job even if it is
offered,* because Chris didn't prepare for it. If you were a super-
visor, which person would you choose to promote? A person
unprepared, lacking motivation, and unable to do the job or one
who studied, worked hard, was competent, eager, and motivated
to do the job? If the opportunity comes for a higher position, the
prepared person obviously stands a better chance of receiving it.
You see now a simple illustration of the principle that: *Chance
favors the prepared mind.*

What is Lee to do if he is not selected for the promotion? Lee still has a number of profitable options available. Being confident in the five years of preparation, Lee could seek a higher position at another company, could use his inborn creativity to figure out ways to work independently, perhaps part-time at first, or could seek out business alliances with others who have similar skills or diverse skills and form a type of cooperative enterprise. People who prepare for opportunities never waste the time, because in actuality they invest in themselves. What they learn can never be taken away from them, and if they *apply their mind* they will find ways and means to reap a harvest from their efforts.

Using the Power of Imagination to Break the Time Barrier

Principle: Goal setting allows you to design your future ahead of time.

Why is a powerful imagination so important? Answer: So you can design your future in vivid detail in your mind ahead of time. Examine my answer carefully. Read it three times, let it soak in. You must design your own future in vivid detail ahead of time. Why? Simple answer: If you don't someone else will. Do you want to design your own future or do you want to leave it to someone else? What if you don't like the future "someone else" has in store for you? What if it's a future that will make you sad, unhealthy, miserable, and broke?

Here's another question. Who is designing your future for you right now? I hope you can see the value of designing your own future. It's your life; you should take on the *personal responsibility* to design it.

Let's examine the second part of my initial answer to the first question—"ahead of time." Isn't that an interesting statement, "ahead of time"? Your imagination can allow you to see your future before time has caught up with it. You can project yourself into the future by using your power of imagination. What a remarkable, uniquely human ability that is. No other creature on this planet can "project itself into its future in its own mind." Humans can easily do this; not only that, but they can imagine multiple futures for themselves based on different plans of action they could follow. This is one aspect of reasoning ability.

With the power of imagination time is no longer a barrier. You don't need to actually wait five years to see what you could do in the time between the present and five years from now. Combine the essence of the two parts of the answer I gave to the question: an ability to (1) design your future in vivid detail in your mind, (2) ahead of time. We call this two-part process GOAL SETTING! Why not take advantage of your latent powers of imagination. It's a natural ability that all humans possess. I recommend using it!

Goal setting puts a structure onto your future, a sort of mental scaffolding for you to work from. When the mind has a framework and a vision it will *expect* to realize it. You then bring what's known as the Universal Law of expectation into play. This Universal Law is stated as follows: **What you expect to happen usually does.** Why? Because your mind will work toward bringing any *goal you vividly imagine with strong emotion to realization.*

7 Helpful Hints to Keep in Mind *Before* Setting Personal Goals

These seven helpful hints will serve as a powerful aid to help you in determining your goals.

1. Balance. Select goals in multiple departments of your life. Choose from major categories such as health, financial, career, education, family, spirituality, etc. Select one or more in these various categories so your whole life isn't totally focused on improvement in only one area. You are capable of working more than one goal simultaneously, but don't try to work twenty or thirty major goals simultaneously, that's way too many. I personally prefer less than five. However, you can have ten or fifteen lined up for the future.

When you identify what you want to achieve in each of these areas, **write it down!** Get used to the idea of writing. *The skill of thinking on paper is of utmost importance.*

2. Comfort. When you write your goals out on paper, be sure they are exactly what you really want. *Think ahead of time* to make sure you will be comfortable with your goals if you actually achieve them. Think about the future impact they will have on your life, your family, and the lives of those close to you. Be sure you can handle the changes in your lifestyle and the additional responsibility that goes along with attaining your goals.

3. Realism. You must have at least a 50/50 belief that you are actually capable of achieving the goal at the time the goal is set. This is the 50/50 rule of goal setting. You must feel you have about a 50/50 chance of achieving the goal you describe. A goal should both excite and challenge you. It should be outside your current ability, forcing you to grow as a person. When you think about your goals, they should fill you with feelings of eager anticipation and enthusiasm rather than feelings of inadequacy or foolishness.

If you set your goal too high, you may not be able to imagine yourself as already possessing it. This is dangerous because you need to be able to project yourself into the future in your imagination as if you already have the goal. If the goal is too easy it doesn't inspire; if it's too difficult to imagine as a possibility for you it also doesn't inspire.

Only you can decide what you feel you have a 50% chance of achieving. Don't play it too safe; push yourself, otherwise you won't grow. Remember you have great potential inside waiting to be released. You aren't in competition with anyone else, you are always after a "personal best." Don't get caught up competing with others or getting sidetracked working on someone else's goals because they are popular goals. Work on self-set goals, goals that have true meaning to you.

4. Precision. Describe the goals on paper in explicit detail. Systematically analyze each goal. Think about each one individually. As you think and write you will be creating a crystal-clear vision in your *mind's eye*. This is **exactly** what you want to do. This crystal-clear vision is then charged with positive emotion (happiness, enthusiasm, pleasure, expectancy) to bring it to life. You need to have clarity and feel good about your self-set goals.

The more vivid and exact you can be using your imagination, the more likely you are to get exactly what you want. In other words, the more precise you can be about your goals, the better your chances of achieving them.

For example, a vague goal might be, I want to save some money. A more precise goal would be, I want to have five thousand dollars in a savings account at XYZ Bank by January 15 of next year. Your subconscious mind doesn't have a good idea of what you want in the first case, and I might add, neither do you!

5. Confidentiality. Goal setting is a very serious personal business. Only tell your most *trusted inner circle*. If you don't want to tell anyone at all then DON'T. It's okay if it's just between you and God. The reason for this is that others may try to put you down or tell you your goals are silly or foolish. This can ruin your desire. Only if you trust that the other person(s) will honestly support you, may they be told. Anyone that can't be trusted 100% should be told nothing!

Bragging about your goals and your progress is also to be avoided. Many people are so insecure, feel so out of control in their own life that they don't think anyone else can improve or gain control in their life. These insecure people can quickly destroy the weak-minded individual or beginning success student, keeping them suppressed at the point where they give up before getting started. You don't ever want to invite any negative feedback or destructive criticism from others, so be careful!

6. Closeness to Nature. Natural settings have a potent effect on the human mind. I believe this can be very powerful in clearing one's thoughts. Getting away from the hustle and bustle of everyday life is helpful in enabling you to set your goals or reevaluate your life. Annoying phone ringing, city traffic, hordes of people, children, pressing responsibilities, and so on, all interfere with the mind's thinking process.

In setting your goals, if possible I suggest the nature retreat or back to nature approach. You need not travel to exotic places, although that would certainly be nice; for many the neighborhood park will suffice. The key element in the naturalistic approach is to get away from other people, isolating yourself in a natural setting.

It is important for you to be alone when doing this; at this point others can't assist you anyway. You need time for internal reflection; just you, nature, and God. Notice your surroundings, become *in tune* with nature. Take some time to write out what you *must be, have,* and *do* in your life from this point forward. This is a very personal experience, which most people *never* do!

This you must do alone in the workshop of your own mind. Your own personal opinion is all that counts here; other people's advice is all right to consider, but only you can decide what is important, correct, and inspirational for you. Solitude, nature, inner reflection, and closeness to God are four keys to great success in life.

7. Aim High. Psychiatrists treat people all the time who have mentally crippled themselves by setting up preprogrammed boundaries or limitations in their mind. These people can be identified by what they say. They say things like "I could never do that" or "I'm not talented enough." I agree with them—as long as that self-limiting mental program is played in their mind, they never will accomplish much!

They focus their thoughts on their limitations, so they never even think of really high goals. They also tend to get caught up early on in the planning and strategy phases of goal setting, centering on problems and obstacles, giving up the goal even before making any real attempt.

Aiming high is the ability to disregard the strategy of how to achieve a goal while determining the goal. For example, an auto mechanic cannot think creatively about completely restoring a classic car if he is bogged down with thinking about fixing a flat tire, repairing a muffler, replacing a cracked windshield, fixing brakes, sanding small rust spots, etc. The little jobs become overwhelming and get in the way of his thinking. He can't see the beautifully painted and waxed masterpiece if he fixes his gaze on all the little jobs at once.

You need to do only one thing to aim high: determine your goals first, without worrying about the strategy of how to achieve them. This is the art of aiming high!

"All who have accomplished great things have had a great aim, have fixed their gaze on a goal which was high, one which sometimes seemed impossible. . . ."

> **Orison Swett Marden**
> **Author of *Pushing to the Front***

General Goal Setting: Module II. 8 Techniques for Goal Setting

Introduction to Goal Setting Techniques

Now that you understand the extreme need to set goals, this module will provide you with eight different goal setting techniques. Each one is described in step-by-step detail. After reading through all of the techniques, go back and pick the one that seems to be the most fun, interesting, and inspirational to you. Feel free to try some of the other techniques for additional goals. One or more techniques may ideally suit your personal needs. Use those first, but be open to trying the others in the future.

(1) The 15-Step Systematic Goal Setting Method

Principle: **Power is organized effort. Without organization there is no power.**

This is an easy fifteen-step method with universal application that can be used for setting any goal. It can fit anything you want to **be, have,** or **do** and will serve you well. I have included eleven thought-starter categories for possible goals and a few general examples for each, but always keep in mind that **you must determine what your goals in life should be!** I only offer suggestions. This fifteen-step method has enjoyed widespread application.

The 11 Thought-Starter Categories

1. **Physical Objects** — cars, boats, trucks, jewelry, clothes, real estate, planes, etc.

2. **Health** — exercise programs, eating habits, ideal body weight, personal grooming, sex life, personal hygiene, posture.

3. **Family** — being a patient listener, forgiving mistakes, being a good role model, being supportive, being respectful and loving, spending time together, doing activities together.

4. **Financial** — annual salary, living within a specific budget, amount of life insurance, health insurance, elimination of debt, investments such as savings accounts, stocks, bonds, real estate.

5. **Social** — sense of humor, listening ability, manners, empathy, etiquette, speaking skill, helping others.

6. **Spiritual** — peace of mind, major definite purpose in life, closeness to God, religious study, prayer habit, involvement in a religious organization.

7. **Mental** — creativity, culture of positive mental attitude, taking courses, acquiring a personal library, obtaining specialized knowledge, keeping a personal journal, reading skills, writing skills, diplomas, degrees, certifications, licenses.

8. **Career** — job satisfaction, job knowledge, personal effectiveness, excellence in job performance, time management, contributions to company, obtaining the ideal job.

9. **Relational** — increasing friends, business associates, love life, family, supporting those close to you.

10. **Travel and Vacations** — places to see, how to get there, who to go with.

11. **Personality** — leadership skills, patience, elimination of fear, emotional control, culture of courage, developing poise, self-confidence, self-esteem, elimination of negative traits. Since personality goals are a little more difficult for most people to comprehend, I'll cite an example.

Personality Modification Example

If you want to change a trait such as shyness, you might start with a small attainable goal. Chat a little with any new people you might meet, then gradually try to achieve longer and longer conversations. For example, try talking to everyone at a party a little, even if it is just to say hello, how are you? What do you do for a living? Or single out one person you don't know and talk to him or her for a while. There are many strategies you could use, but the idea is to do something you wouldn't normally do now. The behavior has to be out of character for you, because you want to change your current character. The new trait, such as boldness, is to replace the old one, such as shyness.

All personality goals should be approached using a gradual systematic process like the example above illustrates. Start with small incremental changes that are the least intimidating for you, then continue working your way up until you finally achieve the ultimate goal or your personality trait rises to the desired level.

◆ ◆ ◆

Review yourself now and determine which of the eleven categories you might need to set goals in. When you are finished with your rough goal set, put it away and forget about it for one day. Then look at it and add anything new you can think of to it. You are now ready to begin the fifteen-step systematic goal setting method.

The 15 Steps

1. Examine each rough goal closely and write out **why** you want it. If you can't think of a single good reason why you want a goal on the list, cross it off, because you don't really want it. Put the list away for a day. Pull it back out and see if you can think of any additional reasons why you want the remaining goals on the list.

2. Review the goal set and rank the items in order of importance to you. Ask the question "How important is it for me to achieve this goal?" Rank the goals in order of importance from 1-X (X being the total number of goals on your list).

3. Examine the top three in each category you selected carefully. Determine if deep down you feel you deserve or should have this. Drop any out you don't feel worthy of. Ask the question, "Is the goal morally correct by my standards?" Select a total of only one to ten top goals for the rest of the steps.

4. Clarify in your mind exactly what is desired; be very specific.

5. Write it out on a piece of paper.

6. Generate rough potential plans that *could* work to enable you to achieve each goal.

7. Set the date by which you *expect* to attain each goal by estimating how much total time you think it would take for achievement. A good way to do this is by working the goal backwards from the estimated deadline. Determine what would need to be done between now and the estimated deadline date. Subdivide these tasks into shorter time increments—yearly, quarterly, and monthly milestones. Think about what you would need to do in the next month to move you to your first month's milestone for each major goal. Then break the first monthly milestone into four weekly milestones if possible. This is the process of working backward from a future goal deadline to the present day.

8. Determine whom you will need to enlist to help you. You usually need to get other people involved in helping and supporting you in your major goals. People you trust can significantly contribute to building you emotionally by providing support and inspiration. Even two people, when they work together in the spirit of perfect harmony, can accomplish uncommon goals.

9. Do your own research and determine if your tentative plan for each major goal is a feasible one.

10. Polish the plan by checking it with people **you trust** who have more expertise and experience than you do. Ask them to find flaws in your plans and offer improvement; learn from their experience and insight. Make any necessary modifications.

11. Set sub-deadlines for any major milestones or mini-goals. Break the newly polished plan into pieces, working backward from your revised goal deadline. Determine what mini-goals must be met along the way and by what dates they must be accomplished. Make a written chart of your plan, with dates on all mini-goals so you know exactly what must be done by what date in order for you to achieve the major goal by the final deadline.

12. Start working your plan; monitor your progress every day in a journal or keep track on a progress chart for each major goal.
13. Periodically reevaluate your whole plan to be sure you are on track, and modify your plan and dates as necessary whenever you gain new information. Don't be afraid to modify your plans. The major goals are what is important, not precisely how you get there. No plan works perfectly from start to finish; modifications will be necessary, so be flexible.
14. As you begin working a goal plan, make special note of what goes well and what is difficult. Your best learning comes from the working of a plan IF YOU KEEP TRACK AS YOU GO. There's nothing worse than NOT learning from your own experiences!
15. Persist! Keep working the plan. If you reach an impasse, keep trying until you figure a way around, over, under, or through it. Keep working the plan, don't stop until you've achieved the goal. Keep working the plan! Modify the plan but never lose sight of the main goal. Keep working the plan!

If you hit a major obstacle, remember the great magician/escape artist Harry Houdini, who tried to get out of a world-famous jail cell in an exhibition event. He tried and tried to get out; finally after two hours of effort he collapsed in exhaustion and fell against the cell door, and the door miraculously opened! The jailers forgot to lock it! It was never locked in the first place except in Houdini's own mind. Many people can stop you temporarily but no one can stop you permanently. **NEVER LOSE SIGHT OF THE GOAL!**

◆ ◆ ◆

Everyone faces difficult periods in life, but having a set of clearly defined goals supported by solid plans of action helps you to weather the storms of life. Without short-range and long-range goals, the problems of everyday life can push you off course. If a ship gets blown off course the captain makes corrections to keep it heading towards its destination. He follows compass readings, maps, and daily progress charts to plot the course right through or around rough storms and strong currents. Eventually the ship arrives at its destination; the storms that are weathered mean experience gained for both captain and crew. Don't ever abandon a goal at the first signs of difficulty.

Don't be afraid to modify your original plan of action, especially if you figure out a short cut as you go. And never stop if you hit an unexpected roadblock—just change your plan, but keep heading straight for the goal.

Time marches on. Be persistent, discipline yourself to stay with it! Keep working and moving toward your goals every day. Remember you haven't lost until **you** stop trying. As long as you persist it's not over. The goal is not lost. Running into a roadblock gives you the opportunity to be creative; when you solve a problem write down how you solved it for future reference.

"A problem solved is a difficulty mastered."

**Michael Monroe Kiefer
American success scientist
Principal investigator for
The POWERMIND System
Project**

When you achieve a goal, replace it with a new one. If a goal is no longer important to you due to a change in circumstances beyond your control, scratch it off the list. Systematically work through your goal list throughout your life, adding new ones, deleting obsolete ones, keeping a running tally of the ones that you accomplish in your personal journal.

You may want to compile and keep a yearly master list in your journal too. Add your journals to your personal library. Personal journals document your life and will be extremely useful to you in years to come as you review them and reflect on your past achievements.

Life is tough for everyone, but if you push yourself life seems to be much easier. Life can be fun, happy, and fulfilling if managed right. Becoming goal oriented, focusing your energy on meaningful goals, and working on them daily will always make your future look bright and your life truly worth living. Your life is what YOU make of it!

Summary of the 15-Step Systematic Goal Setting Method

1. Write out your goals and the reasons why you want to achieve them.
2. Rank your goals in order of importance.
3. Determine if you are worthy of your goals and if they are morally correct; narrow the list to a total of 1-10 major goals.
4. Clarify the major goals in your mind.
5. Clarify the major goals on paper in writing.
6. Generate a potential plan of action for each major goal.
7. Set an expected deadline to achieve each major goal.
8. Determine whose help you will need to win each goal.
9. Examine the potential plan for feasibility by doing your own research.
10. Have others you trust who have experience greater than your own examine the putative plan for flaws.
11. Set mini-goals or milestones with deadlines along the highway to your major goal.
12. Implement your plan of action and monitor your progress in a personal journal.
13. Periodically reevaluate your plan and modify it as necessary.
14. Learn from your experience what works well and also what doesn't work well.
15. **Persist! Never, never give up!!!**

(2) Wish Crafting

"The reason most people face the future with apprehension instead of anticipation is because they don't have it well designed."

> **Jim Rohn**
> **America's foremost business philosopher; author of** *The Five Major Pieces of the Life Puzzle, Seven Strategies for Wealth and Happiness,* **and** *The Seasons of Life*

This is another powerful technique you can use, which employs a number of important principles that are simultaneously integrated into one method. In wish crafting, you are asked to compile three separate goal lists or wish lists: one containing everything you want to **have**, one containing everything you want to **do**, and one containing what you want to **be**. I'll explain the steps for creating the first wish list, then explain the principles behind this unique method.

Constructing the Want-to-Have Wish List

Here is how to construct your first wish list. This wish list will contain all the material objects in this world you would like to **HAVE**. It may have hundreds of items on it or just a few. Don't limit yourself. Include all kinds of material objects, such as boats, cars, trucks, snowmobiles, summer houses, cabins, land, jewelry, stocks, clothing, money, etc.

Step 1. Write out all your physical desires. Take a sheet paper and completely exhaust your mind; then set this list aside for one day and come back to it the second day. Read the list over and write out any new items that come to mind on the second day. Set the list aside for two days, then come back to it once again. Look it over and add any new items that come to mind. Use careful thought to completely drain your mind of all your physical *desires.*

Step 2. Prioritize your wish list. Put a 1 next to all the items you have a burning desire for. Put a 2 next to those items you would like to have, and a 3 next to the items that would be nice to have but you could really do without them.

Step 3. Further prioritize the wish list. Transfer all items you put a 1 next to onto another sheet of paper. Look at this list carefully. If you could only have one item on the entire list, what would it be? Put an A next to it. From the remaining items on the list, ask the same question, "If I could have only one item from this reduced list, what would it be?" Put a B next to this item. Repeat this process until you run out of letters or items on the list, whichever comes first.

Step 4. Clarify the main goals on paper. Take the top item on the list, the one that is marked A, and put this on a separate piece of paper. Examine it and make it as specific as you can. For example, if you said you want a new car but you really meant a 1999 Lamborgini countach S, it should be rewritten as: a 1999 red Lamborgini countach S with red leather interior, Hoosier tires, six-speed transmission, black pinstripes, tinted windows, a USA #1 license plate, etc. Take the item marked B and the item marked C and do the same thing. You should now have the top three goals clearly written out.

The idea is to clearly write out the object in as much detail as you possibly can. Describe it on paper as if you were ordering the object from the manufacturer and they had no idea at all what you wanted.

◆ ◆ ◆

The basic wish crafting technique incorporates many fundamentals of high-performance thought, enabling you to lead a multipointed mental attack on the all-important question, **"What do I want to have?"** The five thought methods employed are:

- ◆ Free Thinking
- ◆ Delayed Thought Expansion
- ◆ Systematic Prioritization
- ◆ Zero-Based Thinking
- ◆ Written Thought Clarification

◆   **Free thinking** is the ability to use your imagination to the fullest extent without self-imposed restrictions. Most people limit their imaginations with "imaginary" boundaries. Whenever the desire for an expensive material object enters their mind, they quickly delete it as a possibility for them to ever possess.

The reason for this is extensive early *childhood conditioning* that causes them to think of all the reasons why owning such an object is "impossible" or "bad" for them. They tend to focus their thoughts on all the reasons why they could or should **not** have the object rather than how to actually get it.

With this negative mind-set they can't think of a single way to practically, honestly obtain the object. They say things like "I'm being realistic," which simply means "I've quit before I've tried," or "Only crooks have these things." As you apply free thinking you eliminate these self-imposed mental blocks and simply allow yourself to dream big dreams.

◆   **Delayed thought expansion** enables your mind to digest the question you've posed to it. By concentrating on a question intensively for a short time, you form a command to your subconscious mind. Your subconscious mind will continue to work on the command, stimulating new thoughts to "pop" into your head. You may have missed some important items in your first concentration session. By waiting, then concentrating some more, you will be able to capture all your true desires on paper.

◆   **Systematic prioritization** continues to distill your desires in an organized manner. By setting priorities you can separate the simple wish from the *burning desire*. The items that float to the top of the prioritized list take on a new meaning when compared side by side as the rest sink to the bottom.

◆   **Zero-based thinking** is related to systematic prioritization but gives added emotional depth to the process. Instead of making a cursory comparison, you are asked to analyze more deeply each item on your wish list. Each item is taken individually and compared side by side to every other item on the list with the key question, "If I could have only one item on this whole list, what would it be?" This causes you to further determine which items you back with real emotion (*burning desire*).

It is a powerful stand-alone method, which can be applied to any dream list, or even a things-to-do list, to figure out priorities.

◆   **Written thought clarification** is the last technique that we come to, which we will continue to use time and time again throughout The POWERMIND System. It is the hallmark tool of all highly successful people. Putting your thoughts in the form of words onto paper imparts a sort of *magical quality* to them because:

WHEN THOUGHTS ARE PLACED ON PAPER IT IS THE FIRST TIME THAT THEY HAVE BEEN TAKEN OUT OF THE MENTAL REALM AND TRANSFERRED INTO THE PHYSICAL BY HUMAN HAND. It also causes you to clarify the thoughts in your own mind by forcing you to define them in your own language. Your whole mind is activated, drawing upon your subconscious memory banks and imagination to formulate a word picture of the thoughts.

Did you ever notice great thinkers are usually great writers? The two go hand in hand. Development of one complements the other. If you write well you think well, and if you think well you write well. The two are inseparable.

This idea of clarifying your thoughts into mental pictures and words is extremely important for subconscious programming, which will be discussed in much more detail in the High Achievement part of this book. You are now ready to make your second wish list.

Constructing the Want-to-Do Wish List

Now that you are familiar with the basic wish crafting technique, I ask you to apply it to the second wish list. This is a list of all the things you want to **DO** in the next year. You can make other lists for three years, five years and ten years, but let's focus for now on the upcoming year. Take the same time, about one week, to create this list. The examples again are limitless. Here are just a few thought starters.

1. Travel to Europe
2. Write a book
3. Climb a mountain
4. Visit a foreign country

5. Go skydiving
6. Travel cross-country
7. Build a race car
8. Meet the President of the U.S.
9. Build a church
10. Restore an antique
11. Be a missionary for a year
12. Start/finish a college degree
13. Have dinner with a movie star
14. Sail around the world
15. Run a marathon
16. Become a millionaire
17. Start your own company
18. Get promoted
19. Start a new career
20. Take a vacation with your family

The next steps to take are only summarized below, because they are exactly the same as for your first wish list.

◆ Prioritize these items just like you did with the items you would like to *have*. Select the top items you would most like to do by putting a 1 next to all the things you would really like to do, a 2 next to the things you would enjoy doing, and a 3 next to the items that would be sort of fun but not necessary.
◆ Transfer all the items with a 1 after them onto a new page and prioritize them using zero-based thinking, comparing each item against the rest.
◆ Finally, use written thought clarification and detail the three major to-do items out. Make them as specific as you can, then put these with the items from your first wish list.
◆ Refer to the previous pages for more detailed instruction.

Constructing the Want-to-Be Wish List

The last wish list will be made in a slightly different fashion: assemble a list of all the possible careers you might enjoy, in other words, what you would like to **BE**.

Stage 1. Career Selection

Step 1. If you could do any job or have any career in the world, what would it be? Take one single hour and press yourself to come up with twenty-one possible careers options on paper. Time yourself with a timer. By allowing yourself only one hour, your strongest career desires will readily surface. These are the only ones you want to list.

Step 2. When you are done, wait a day, then come back and review the list, add to it, wait a day, etc. Repeat this process for a week.

Step 3. Prioritize your list, by using the zero-based thinking method, which goes like this: "If you could do any job in the world except your very first choice, what would it be?" Pursue this question until all the possible careers on your list are prioritized. You now have a list of up to twenty-one possible careers ranked in order of priority.

Step 4. Now look at the careers you numbered one through five. Do they have anything in common? Write out what they have in common, to give you insight into what career you would most like.

Step 5. Now select out the top three. What do these three in *particular* have in common?

Step 6. Take the one you have selected as choice 1 and ask yourself this heart pounding question: ***Why don't I have this job right now?***

Stage 2. Barrier/Benefit Analysis

Step 1. With your number-one career selected, write it out on the top of a sheet of paper. Draw a line down the middle of the page.

Step 2. List all the barriers stopping you from doing that job on the left side of the page, and on the right side of the page list all the benefits to you if you had that job.

Step 3. With the barriers all listed, put a 1 by the most difficult barrier for you to overcome, a 2 next to the second biggest, and so on.

◆ ◆ ◆

You now have a summary of what job/career you want in life, what is stopping you from having it, and what the benefits to you would be if you had that job.

In the earlier self-assessment part you determined your natural talent(s). Always try to maximize the use of your natural talents in the job or career you select.

You also made a set of personal life values. Check each of your goals against this list to be sure you aren't in conflict with any of these. You never want to be working at cross-purposes with yourself! Keep yourself in triple alignment: **life values** in line with **life goals**, achieved by direct or indirect utilization of **natural talent(s)**.

Also ask yourself these final questions in regard to your life goals: Are these worthy goals for me? Should I have these? Do I feel comfortable asking God to help me in achieving these goals? If you don't answer yes to all three questions, then reconsider your goals, because you are *out of alignment!*

◆ ◆ ◆

It is now time for you to do a systematic breakdown of your one-year wish list goals. From each of your three wish lists take the number-one item and determine what would need to be accomplished each month over the next twelve months in order for you to achieve the goal at the end of the twelfth month. Basically you are working backwards from the main goal deadline. You are setting twelve individual mini-goals or milestones that correspond to each month in the year. If you can't figure out all twelve at once, do as many as you can.

In this one-year plan you should identify what problems you currently see standing in your way and what you will need to do to overcome them. Decide who you may need to help you—people, groups, organizations—and write them down too.

Once this is complete, take your first milestone and break it into four smaller milestones, corresponding to the four weeks in a month. Your last step is to break the first week milestone into seven parts, corresponding to the seven days in a week.

As you complete one week's worth of projected progress, plan out the next week. By breaking a year-long goal into smaller pieces, you make it much more manageable and it doesn't seem so overwhelming. (Remember you can use this same procedure for three-year, five-year, even ten-year goals.)

You may have trouble defining the six- to twelve-month milestones, but make your best guess; as you begin working your plan, the later pieces will fall into place. You will also gain new information along the way as you start progressing toward the goal, which may alter your original plan of action. This is okay as long as you keep the main goal at the forefront of your consciousness at all times. So what if you figure out a shortcut to a one-year goal in three months and achieve what you thought would take twelve months in three! Just set another goal for yourself and begin work on that one!

(3) Pyramiding

Here is another goal setting technique, called pyramiding. The first step is to take out a sheet of paper and write your goal at the top of a pyramid. Then divide the pyramid into horizontal layers. Each layer of the pyramid represents a milestone that must be passed along the goal path before you can ascend to the major goal at the top of the pyramid. A deadline is always listed for each of the milestones, so you have a definite time frame in which you must work to advance to the next higher level. You must determine both the number of layers and the reasonable deadline dates for each milestone.

Each pyramid graphically represents a single summarized goal plan. Pyramids can represent long-range (three years or more) or short-range (one year or less) goals. As you ascend the pyramid, completing milestones, you color in each of the layers. The summarized descriptions of the milestones are listed to the side of the layers. A goal pyramid is a brief pictorial representation so you can easily visualize the entire scope of a major goal and keep track of your progress in one single place. The following are a few examples.

Goal: Driving my new red Corvette in 2 years, January 1999.

- ◆ Make down payment, pick up new red Corvette January, 1999 (Goal Achieved!)
- ◆ Have $17,707.96 invested by January 1, 1999
- ◆ Sell current car for $5,000 in December, 1998, add this to investment, now have $13,442.54
- ◆ Sell snowmobile for $3,000 by June 1, 1998, and add this to investment, now have $6,866.70
- ◆ Have $2,734.06 invested by January 1, 1998
- ◆ Save $200.00 per month starting January 1, 1997; put this in an investment that yields a 10% return

Goal: Having a job as a college professor in 13 years by June 1999

- ◆ Be a college professor by June 1999 (Goal Achieved!)
- ◆ Apply for assistant professor jobs early in 1999
- ◆ 2 more years of work as a post - doc, finish in 1998
- ◆ 4 more years of college, graduate with Ph.D. in 1996
- ◆ 2 more years of college, graduate with M.S. degree in 1992
- ◆ Go to college 4 years, graduate with B.S. degree in 1990
- ◆ Graduate from high school 1986

Goal: Travel to Europe in January 1999 for a total cost $6,638

- ◆ Touchdown on the tarmac in London, England! (Goal Achieved!)
- ◆ Have $6,638.10 invested by January 1, 1999 (ready to fly!)
- ◆ Sell motorcycle for $1,000; add to investment, have $4,871.44 by the end of January 1998
- ◆ Have $3,871.44 in the investment by January 1, 1998
- ◆ Have $2,486.75 by January 1997 in investment
- ◆ Add $1,000 Christmas bonus to investment
- ◆ Have $1,367.03 in investment by the end of December 1996
- ◆ Save $100 per month, put this in an investment that yields a 10% return, start January 1, 1996

The main points of pyramiding are to set reasonable achievable deadlines underneath the "big" goal. Stick to the milestone deadlines as well as you can. Discipline yourself to work consistently, moving up from layer to layer on schedule. Only then can the big goal be achieved on time. Achievement of the big goal is totally dependent on the achievement of the milestones on the pyramidal layers under it. Don't forget to chart your progress by coloring in layers of the pyramid as you ascend to the top!

This technique allows you to plan either long-range or short-range goals easily. It organizes your thoughts and actions, focusing your mind and body in one direction. Power is organized thought combined with organized physical effort. Without organization there is no power.

The fundamentals of this goal setting technique are very similar to the others: writing the goal down in detail, setting a deadline for attainment, figuring out what needs to be done by *working backward* from the date you set as the main deadline and then setting milestones back to the present time.

You should keep the goal pyramids where you can see them every day to serve as a constant reminder of where your life is headed. On the ceiling above your bed or on the bathroom mirror are two possible locations. Every morning you will wake up and see that your life is moving up the layers of the goal pyramids!

(4) Treasure Charting

This goal setting technique is only a few thousand years old, but I think it is worth mentioning. Egyptian tombs were often decorated with what are called treasure charts. Whenever a royal child was born, the Egyptians would start a tomb for them. The walls of these tombs were ornately decorated with pictures of the child's entire "prophesied" life up to their death.

The pictures were all painted during the child's first few years of life. The best things in life were depicted. Frescocs would depict the child being educated, marrying, inheriting the kingdom, winning wars, having an abundance of food, helping the people, and so on. A whole set of lifelong goals would be "treasure charted" on the walls of their tomb.

The high priest would then imbue the paintings during *highly emotional* religious ceremonies with chants, incense, and music to give the paintings special "magical powers." The ceremonies lended heavy *emotional charging* to the images that were being *imprinted on the child's subconscious mind at a very young age.* These images were being programmed directly into the child's subconscious mind, where they took root. It was an early form of *childhood conditioning* or mind shaping. Since the child's earliest memories would be of these paintings depicting a successful life, the child would have a good chance of growing up to have an extremely high sense of importance, self-confidence, self-esteem, and future expectation.

A treasure chart was in fact a life goals map. The royal child's whole set of life goals would be mapped out on the walls of his tomb. So the question now becomes, how can you create a type of treasure chart for yourself?

Building a Personal Treasure Chart

1. Get a large poster board and collect pictures that represent what you want from life. A quick review of some goal categories for you to consider are physical health, career, family, relationships, material goods, spirituality, education, serving others. Magazines, brochures, advertisements, etc., are a great source for colorful pictures to use on your personal treasure chart. Remember to pick photos representing multiple goals you wish to achieve in various goal categories.

2. Paste or tape the pictures representing your number-one goal in life as a collage at the center of the board. Paste the other life goals pictures in a cluster around it. Each of the other goals has its own mini collage area surrounding the central goal. You can have many photos for each goal collage.

3. When you've finished roughing out the treasure chart, go back to it every day for about a week, adding any additional pictures to the individual goal collages as you see fit. You of course can add pictures that seem fitting at any time, but spend a week diligently searching for photos to represent your goals.

4. The fourth step is to put biting, emotionally charged words or phrases from magazines or newspapers under each of the goal collages. If you can't find "power words" that fit, write your own around each goal collage with a marker.

5. Once you've depicted each goal with both power words and colorful pictures, write out a one-page description of what each goal means to you. Paste these on the back of the treasure chart.

6. You should now place the date by which you think you can achieve each goal above its collage. Place the treasure chart where you can see it at least twice, preferably more times, a day. On waking in the morning and just before dropping off to sleep at night are ideal times. On the ceiling above your bed is an excellent location. The bathroom is another good location. Refrigerator doors are also good. Places that you look often are key.

7. Once one goal on the treasure chart is achieved, remove the collage signifying that goal and replace it with a new goal collage. Your personal treasure chart should only be seen or known about by you and the most trusted people in your life. Your personal treasure chart is not a public poster for all to see! It's private, important, and yours!

◆ ◆ ◆

The main point of treasure charting is to get both a verbal and pictorial representation of your goals posted on a board where you can see it every day.

Treasure charts are not only ideal for the individual but are also useful for families, sports teams, and corporations. The team or corporation treasure charts should, however, be in places where everyone can see them often. For example in the locker room, coffee room, or cafeteria.

Why Are Treasure Charts Effective?

Each side of the cerebral cortex of the human brain has different functions. Speech, language, and calculation are centered in the left hemisphere, while artistic concepts and special perception are centered in the right hemisphere (Sperry, 1987). Right brain/left brain laterlization has most extensively been studied by the Nobel Prize winner Roger Sperry, who studied "split brain" patients to determine brain hemispherical function. Sperry's work has shown specific functional localization. So what exactly is happening in the brain when you use the treasure charting technique?

◆ First and foremost, the treasure chart as a whole stimulates your subconscious mind each time you look at it.
◆ Second, the pictures stimulate the right hemisphere of your cerebral cortex, or "right brain" for short. This is the location of your brain's visual, spacial, and creativity centers.
◆ Third, the words stimulate the left hemisphere of your cerebral cortex, or "left brain," where speech and language centers are located. By combining the words with the pictures you stimulate the corpus callosum (neural connections

between the right and left brain), improving right brain/left brain intercommunication. This allows you to more efficiently utilize your whole brain's creative powers of thought. As each hemisphere of the brain is stimulated along with the communication center between them, you automatically move toward your goals faster in terms of both thought and action.

◆ Fourth, treasure charts help maintain goal focus. People's minds tend to "drift" with time, forgetting about what's really important. Seeing the treasure chart two or more times per day keeps your whole mind on track and on course, focused constantly on your own goals, thereby eliminating this natural drift effect. Simply looking at the treasure chart daily tends to focus your thinking on goal achievement.

◆ Fifth, when you look at the treasure chart it helps to motivate and energize you to take action. Your desire then spurs you on to enthusiastic activity.

◆ Sixth, treasure charts reduce negative stress, because if you know what you want in life and are actively engaged in getting it, negative stress automatically goes down.

◆ Why do a treasure chart? So you wind up with treasures in life instead of trinkets!

Roger Sperry's pioneering brain research was cited from <u>Biology</u>, *Neil A. Cambell, copyright 1987, The Benjamin/Cummings Publishing Company.*

(5) The Self-Artistry Technique

This particular technique utilizes the power of your right brain and is very effective as a goal setting technique. The right hemisphere of the cerebral cortex in the human brain is the source of creativity, visual imagery, spacial perception, and artistic talent, as Roger Sperry demonstrated in the late 1980s. Since this technique is designed to stimulate your right brain, colors and graphic representations are very important, just like in treasure charting. You will need poster board and colored pens/pencils/chalk or paints.

The first step is to draw or paint yourself, as you feel inside right now, on a piece of poster board. What I mean is to exaggerate the features of your "self-portrait" in relation to how you currently feel about yourself and your life. For example, if you feel you have great intelligence, draw your head overly large. If you feel you are physically very strong, exaggerate your muscles. If you feel old, draw a wrinkled face and a gray-haired head. However you feel about yourself, try to depict that graphically in your drawing. Artistic skill is unimportant, the picture need make sense only to you. You are just trying to make a graphic representation accenting how you feel about yourself, whether your feelings are positive or negative. Be as honest as possible.

When you are done with this part, draw out what things are important to you in your life. If you have a family, you might put family members around you. Make their closeness to you and detail represent importance. For example, if you have a turbulent relationship with a spouse, make him or her gray, shaded, and distant from you. If you have a pet you love, paint it in full vibrant color right next to you. Place what is important to you close to you, in color, and in detail. Whatever is not as important to you should be in dark shades, in less detail, and far away. If it's not important at all leave it out.

Here are some other examples. A tyrannical, abusive spouse may be depicted as towering over you in black, holding a chain around your ankles, representing control. If my wife were doing this exercise she would paint our daughter in her arms in a beautiful pink dress with a smile on her face.

You may also want to put your place of employment in the background, large or small depending on its importance to you. Remember, put important things close, large, and in detail and less important things further way, smaller, and in less detail.

Use colors to represent your feelings: red could signify love, black could signify death or hatred, purple - royalty, white - purity or holiness, yellow - happiness, and so on. After you've finished set it aside for a day or up to a week, modifying it as you see fit.

Now get another board or canvas and draw out the "perfect" you. Imagine yourself standing in front of a mirror. Imagine this "other you" one year to five years from now. How would you feel? What would you look like? What would you have accomplished? What skills would you have learned? What friends would you have? Where would you live? What would your hobbies be? What job would you have? You must decide for yourself what the perfect you would be like!

This new you is basically a graphic representation of the way you *want to be*. Accentuate the features that you would **ideally** like to have. If you are overweight now and would like to be trim, draw a slimmer you. If you feel you are too emotional and not logical you may want to draw a tiny heart representing less emotion. If you want to be a happier person, you might draw a big smile on your face.

Now, in the area surrounding the perfect you draw in what you *want to have* in your life. Perhaps a new car, house, boat, maybe even a baby. If you are single you might draw in a spouse holding your hand, smiling at you, signifying friendship or love. A new getting-in-shape program could be signified by jogging shoes or weights, a tennis racquet or swimming suit, near you.

Now, place the two drawings up next to each other where you can see them every day. Put an X on the feature in the original self-artistry portrait you want to change, and circle the new features on the "ideal you" portrait you want to gain. Focus your thoughts each day on eliminating the X features and gaining the circled features.

The Self-Artistry Technique Review

You now hold in your possession in the two self-artistry drawings your current station in life as you see it and your desired station in life. The difference between the first drawing and the second one represents some of your personal goals.

This is a dramatically revealing technique, which has helped many people uncover their strongest desires in life. Whenever you feel motivation lacking, look at your self-artistry drawings to inspire you.

Those of you who are parents may want to teach this simple goal setting technique to your children. They will have fun and you will be teaching them one of the most important skills in life, that of setting goals. Incidentally, you'll also be stimulating their creative abilities, which are underdeveloped in greater than 90% of children in the U.S. Give your kids a head start in life, teach them well. Proper early education always alleviates later struggle in life!

You could also have the whole family contribute by making a whole family "present day self-artistry portrait" and a family "ideal future self-artistry portrait". This helps build family ties because everyone contributes something and gives the family a set of group goals to work on, instilling a sense of **unity** and belonging. Children really get into this, they love crayons, colored pencils, pens and paints, etc. (Most adults do too, but won't admit it!)

(6) The Focused Visualization Technique

Focused visualization is yet another potent method that can be used for setting goals in the mind. It is important not only to visualize your goals but visualize them as already achieved. Visualizing goals as if you have already achieved them is the primary difference between wishing, hoping, and daydreaming and the scientific skill of focused visualization. Why? The **emotional charge** is missing from wishing, hoping, and daydreaming. It's pleasant enough for you to ponder these thoughts, but without strong emotional charging the beneficial effects of focused visualization on your brain are drastically decreased. The brain chemicals and other body hormones don't stimulate rapid reengineering of the brain's physical structure in hoping and wishing. Strong positive emotional charging is the key to this type of stimulation.

In focused visualization you think intensively about the goal *as if it has already been attained*. You vividly imagine the reality of it, you see it in color, feel and hear the congratulatory remarks of other people. You think of how you'll actually feel at the moment you've finally won the goal!

If it's a trophy signifying winning a competition, you should feel the coolness of it in your hands. If it's a slimmer figure, you should feel your hands running over your shapely stomach, buttocks, and thighs. In focused visualization the goal is *already yours.* You don't think about getting it because you have it (in your mind). You ponder your own reaction and the reactions of others when the goal is won.

This is the contrast between **hoping** for something and **having** something. You tingle with enthusiasm and excitement when you have it. In focused visualization you are also free from any self-doubt that often accompanies hoping and wishing.

Here is an experiment that you can try that illustrates strong **positive emotional charging**. Select something you would like to have. Let's say a new home. Close your eyes and hope or wish for a new home. How do you feel? Now use focused visualization, see yourself walking around in your home, feel the white marble fireplace. Invite your friends over, see their smiling faces admiring you and your new home. Show them around, take them into every room, explain the features to them. Relax in your living room, look around your new home and say, "Wow, it's all mine, all paid for, what a beauty!"

I hope you can see the difference between the two states of mind now. How the "hoping for something" doesn't emotionally charge you up nearly as much as "focused visualization" does. That **positive wonderful feeling** is what I call positive emotional charging. In hoping for something that positive emotional charge is missing; the imagined experience is not realistic. However, in focused visualization your imagined experience is very, very realistic **and that's the key!**

Detailed imagery of the goal combined with strong positive emotional charging is essential. Wishful thinking leaves you feeling drained, empty, and frustrated. Focused visualization leaves you feeling inspired, motivated, and full of energy. That internal self-generated energy can then be channeled into activity that is expended to actually achieve your goal. One method, wishing and hoping, *drains* energy (that's the one most people use). The other, focused visualization, *generates* energy (that's the one only a few use). This short technique can be used every day and in conjunction with any other goal setting technique previously discussed. It will speed you toward your goals and motivate you to action!

(7) The Inner Game of Life: A Goal Setting Self-Discovery Exercise

This goal setting exercise contains a series of reflective questions designed to make you look at life's larger picture. In answering them you will gain a greater understanding of yourself and your life. Write out your answer to the following questions on a sheet of paper.

1. What do I really enjoy doing?
2. What do I really enjoy reading about?
3. In general, what interests me immensely?
4. What do I think I would enjoy doing but haven't researched enough to "know" the answer?
5. What do I spend hours doing because I just love doing it?
6. What would I do if I didn't have to go to work everyday?
7. If I had a million dollars what exactly would I do with it?
8. If I had all the money I would ever need, would I work at my current job? If not what would I do with my time? Why?
9. What specific types of activities am I greatly interested in?
10. What can I easily pay attention to for hours on end?
11. What can I become absorbed in learning more about?
12. If I knew failure was impossible, what would be my biggest dream?
13. If I rubbed an Aladdin's lamp and a genie popped out saying, "I will grant you three wishes," what would they be?
14. If I knew that I had five years to live and that I would die on the exact day ending the fifth year, what would I do between now and then?
15. What if the time frame in question 14 was changed to three years to live, what then? One year to live?
16. You don't need to respond to this question, it's only meant to make you think: What makes you think you will live another five years, one year, six months, one month, one week, one day, one minute?
17. When you are dead, what would you like to have left behind for your family, your friends, the people of the world?
18. If you look back at your past five years, what was the most important thing you did? Why?
19. If you look back at your past one year, what was the most important thing you did? Why?

Review

Now review what you have written. As you contemplate the answers to these questions they may hold the golden keys to some future goals. This line of questioning is extremely potent and revealing, cutting to the very core of your *persona*.

You should be doing what interests you in life and what you enjoy for self-fulfillment. Questions 1-11 will give you insights in this area. Questions 12-19 probe into what some of your deepest goals might be.

This exercise is used to help you determine some big life goals for yourself, rooting out what's meaningful from what's nice. The purpose of the exercise is to get you to think more deeply about your life rather than just thinking about simple material goods, such as a new car or a new watch. It also gets you thinking about long-range goals. Material goods can limit so many people's visions of life that they never stop and think of what life is really all about. Think carefully as you ponder some possible future goals.

(8) The 3-Year Dream

This is the very last technique I will cover for helping you determine some life goals for yourself. It's very short and sweet. Here it is: Imagine what you would most want your life to be like in three years if you were guaranteed success in all areas. What type of person would you be? What education would you have? What relationships would you have? How much wealth? What material possessions? What would be the physical condition of your body? What personal powers? Where would you live? What would you have accomplished? What job would you have? Let your mind run free.

1. Write out your answers on a piece of paper. Take up to a week if necessary.
2. At the end of that time ask this question, "What are the most important items for me to accomplish in this description?"
3. Prioritize the list.
4. Take the top three and see what they have in common.

5. Write out what you would need to do to accomplish the top three in three years. This short exercise gives you insight into some long-range (three-year) goals.

Aligning Goals with God

"Finally, my brethren, be strong in the Lord, and in the power of his might."

Ephesians 6:10

Once you have decided on any goal, be sure it is a worthy one by asking yourself these check questions: "Can I dedicate myself to the goal emotionally?" "Can I actually see myself achieving the goal?" "Is it really a possibility for me?" **"Do I think *I can do it?"*** You must be able to *align* yourself in these important areas first; then the big questions come in: "Is it a morally correct goal?" "Can I dedicate myself spiritually?" "Does this goal feel right to me?" If you feel the goal sounds "good" on the outside, but it feels wrong on the inside, it's not a morally correct goal for you. The starlight question to ask when aligning goals with God is this: **If I were standing before God, would I be comfortable asking for divine assistance in achieving this goal?** If you feel uneasy asking for God's aid in winning your goal, it is probably not ethically, morally, or spiritually correct.

For example, getting a promotion so you can have power **over** others to get revenge or to dominate, control, and mistreat them is wrong. On the outside the goal sounds good, "to be promoted," but on the inside it's morally wrong because the reasons are unethical. Most people would like a promotion, but if you want it to control people or influence them in a negative way, I suggest you reevaluate this goal and yourself. Ask yourself, "Should I want this goal?" and "What are my reasons for wanting it?" If you can honestly feel good about your answers, then be very frank and in your prayers each day ask for God's help very specifically. If you are willing to work for a goal and believe you should have it, be bold and ask for God's help!

"Ask and it will be given to you; seek and you will find; knock and the door will be opened to you. For everyone who asks receives; he who seeks finds; and to him who knocks, the door will be opened."

Matthew 7:7-8

If you have no belief in God, you can never obtain true fulfillment in life. You may have many material successes, but true life success will elude you. True success has a strong spiritual element to it.

The Power of a Things-to-Do List

"Never begin the day until it is finished on paper."

Jim Rohn
America's foremost business philosopher; author of *The Five Major Pieces to the Life Puzzle, Seven Strategies for Wealth and Happiness,* **and** *The Seasons of Life*

The concept of a daily things-to-do list serves as an excellent simple formula, capturing the essence of the entire goal setting process. Let's break it down into its four component parts and examine each one individually.

1. Think of what **needs** to be done and write it down.
2. Prioritize the items on the list in order of importance.
3. Work down the list sequentially.
4. If you hit something that cannot be completed that day for some reason, move it to tomorrow's list.

These are the four basic steps to writing out your daily things-to-do list. This enables you to organize your thinking as well as forcing you into efficient time management. Here is a question for you to consider: If you are not currently working each day using a prioritized written list of objectives, what are you using as a guide so you know what to do? Possible answers: Someone else tells me exactly what to do each day (author's comment: not a good answer!). I just wait and see what comes up (author's comment: not a good answer!). I don't have time to make a well thought out prioritized list, I'm busy keeping all the crises in my life under control (author's comment: not a good answer!). I do a little of this or that but I'm going to get really busy tomorrow (author's comment: not a good answer!).

The necessity for having a things-to-do list as a guide should be obvious. Without a written list to work from, your thinking is unclear, your actions are disorganized, your priorities are unknown, and your energies are dissipated. You work in a highly inefficient manner, wasting the whole day away. Structuring the day on paper first is essential for it to be productive and well spent, and I do mean spent, since time cannot be packaged up and saved for later use. *Never begin the day until it is finished on paper.* I'll detail out the four steps for you.

In Step 1. Sit down, relax, and think for a few minutes, *thinking ahead in time in your imagination,* picturing the day as you wish it to be. This develops two essential mental powers: (1) projecting your behaviors into the future (thinking things out ahead of time), and (2) flashing brief mental images of yourself doing the tasks, seeing them through to completion with positive emotion (positive emotional charging).

Writing a brief summary of what you need to do focuses your thoughts into a brief concise memory prompt. Just a few words represents an entire task you need to accomplish. The brief phrase or sentences triggers a host of related thoughts. This develops thought clarity as well as exercising your memory.

In Step 2. By prioritizing the list you develop organizational skills. When prioritizing a set of daily duties, you are exercising a major skill of time management. You go over in your head what needs to be done first, second, third, etc. If you work on unimportant tasks first, the important tasks might never get done; you may in fact run out of time! This happens to so many people because they didn't prioritize their list. Hence they wind up spending major time on minor tasks.

In Step 3. You develop self-discipline. You must discipline yourself to work on high-priority tasks first as you work down the list sequentially. Sticking to a well thought out plan until it is completed requires self-discipline; your daily things-to-do list is a mini plan of action. If you don't discipline yourself in daily activities, how could you ever hope to discipline yourself to sticking to a six-month, one-year, or three-year plan of action? Without daily self-discipline, all long-term planning is an exercise in futility!

In Step 4. You develop mental flexibility. If a task simply cannot be finished that day for an unforeseen reason, make a decision to scrap the task or move it to another day. No plan is perfect, so changing it may be inevitable. Flexibility is an excellent leadership characteristic to develop.

Now then, with a completed daily things-to-do list as a base, let's review the basic goal setting process one final time. If you have a goal in mind that cannot be accomplished in one day, sit down with pen and paper and determine logically and honestly how long you think it will take for you to accomplish it. Write it out in vivid detail so you know exactly what must be done by when. Then you schedule the work backwards.

For example, let's say you have determined it will take one year to achieve a particular goal. A year is twelve months. The goal can then be broken down into twelve monthly milestones. Figure out what twelve milestones would need to be met in order for the main goal to be achieved.

Now prioritize these in a sequence, numbering them 1 to 12. You now know the twelve milestones and the order in which they need to be achieved. Move now to milestone number 1, break it into four parts, each representing four mini-milestones. Prioritize these 1 to 4, break number 1 into seven parts for each day of the first week, prioritize it 1 to 7. Then each day prepare your daily things-to-do list.

You now have in your hands a rough one-year plan and a highly detailed plan for the first month. If you can break any of the twelve milestones into four parts, go ahead. If you feel you can plan out two months, do it.

The reason for not planning out each of 365 days all at once is because the plan will change after you have been working on it for a couple of months. These adjustments can be made in the following months. As you gain more information, more changes will be necessary. By not detailing out each day of the whole year and structuring your detailed plan too far in advance, you build flexibility into your overall plan. You still have a good overall plan, because you know the twelve milestones needed for goal accomplishment, and these probably will not change drastically, so that planning effort is not wasted on your part.

It should now be more apparent that a daily things-to-do list is absolutely essential to achieve any long-term goals. A two-year, three-year, five-year, or ten-year goal is set up in a similar fashion. The closer the time perspective, day or month, the more highly detailed the plan should be. The further out, such as the eleventh and twelfth month for a one-year goal, the more sketchy the plan. As you move from month-to-month closing on the goal each upcoming month's tasks become clearer and clearer. However, the major goal must always be absolutely clear from the very start. Stephen R. Covey, author of the best-selling book *The Seven Habits of Highly Effective People,* says, "Begin with the end in mind."

With a five-year goal, the first-year activities will probably be much more clearly defined than the fifth-year activities. But you should still have a good general idea of what needs to be done in the fifth year.

This process of working backwards from the end goal is independent of the goal itself whether it's saving money for a new car, starting a business, becoming an Olympic champion, or building a personal fortune. This goal setting process has universal application! Long-range goal setting involves a goal, a daily things-to-do list, careful thought, imagination, organized planning, self-discipline, mental flexibility, and YOU!

General Goal Setting: Module III. Goal Setting Principles

6 Basic Goal Setting Concepts to Remember

(1) Obstacles Can Always Be Overcome
(2) The Goal Setting Process
(3) Concentration
(4) Small Goals Win Big Goals
(5) Goal Setting Strategy: Options and Flexibility
(6) Qualities of Big Goals

(1) Obstacles Can Always Be Overcome

If a particular goal's importance is greater than anything else in your life, it can be achieved. Everything in the world achieved by people started in the mind of a single person as their goal (dream). From landing on the moon, to starting businesses, to building skyscrapers, to creating computers, they all hatched as an idea in a single person's mind before they became a reality. Many obstacles blocked the way in bringing the goals to fruition, but they were all overcome.

"What the mind of man can conceive and believe, it can achieve."

Napoleon Hill
Success philosopher
Author of *Think and Grow Rich, Law of Success, Science of Personal Achievement,* and *Mental Dynamite*

"Success" is defined as "the progressive realization of a worthy ideal" by self-development pioneer Earl Nightingale. Therefore any person regularly engaged in achieving a goal that he or she considers important is by definition successful. Any person not so engaged is a failure. Everyone in the world could be successful by Earl Nightingale's definition, but studies have shown that only 3 to 5% of the population is successful by that definition, that is, only three to five out of every one hundred people are working toward clearly defined worthy goals. I might add that working toward a goal includes overcoming obstacles. *Are you successful? Are you working toward a clearly defined goal?*

(2) The Goal Setting Process

Ask people what they want in life and many will say health, wealth, happiness, power, success. These are not goals at all because they are too general. What exactly do *you* want to be, to have, to do? *A successful fulfilling life is created by the systematic process of setting and achieving progressively more difficult, interesting, and rewarding goals.* You will accomplish more in five years than most people do in a lifetime if you follow proper goal setting procedures. Goal setting is an art. Goals give you something meaningful to live for and a true sense of fulfillment once they are achieved. They give direction and purpose to your earthly struggle. If you don't know what you want out of life, what are you doing?

Many people are unsuccessful because they do not prioritize and focus; they haphazardly try to achieve too many goals at once. You usually make the fastest progress on a small set of goals at a time.

Each long-term goal should be broken down into smaller components, called mini-goals or milestones. When you do this, the long-term goal appears easier to achieve and you will achieve the milestones quickly, giving you momentum. This helps keep you motivated and on track toward the long-term goal.

(3) Concentration

Think about your goals as often as you can, be very specific, set deadlines, and get a clear mental picture of the goal.

"We become what we think about."

> **Earl Nightingale**
> **Self-development pioneer**
> **Author of** *The Strangest*
> *Secret, Lead the Field,* **and**
> **Cofounder of the Nightingale**
> **Conant Corp.**

See yourself in your *mind's eye* as having already attained the goal. After sixteen years of searching for the so-called secret of success, from 1933 to 1950, Earl Nightingale found it on New Year's Day 1950: You are the sum total of your thoughts.

Concentrated thinking automatically moves you toward your goals. A person with a goal is one with a dream, a purpose, and a mission. As soon as you set a goal in your mind, then on paper, it will seem almost magical how you will come up with strategies to achieve that goal. You will "happen" to come by information you need, when you need it. You'll also be far more creative than ever before and you will succeed!

The goal must also be interesting to you; if you aren't interested you won't be receptive to acquiring the necessary knowledge to achieve it. It's hard to work on uninteresting goals. You need to be able to concentrate, and you can't concentrate on a goal if it isn't very interesting. Concentrated thought enables you to become unified and focused; without concentrated persistent thinking on the goal you are doomed to low performance.

What you gain when you achieve a goal is not nearly as important as the person that you become. You'll gain greater mental and physical strength, increased knowledge, skills, success habits, personal power, and a *heightened level of awareness.* Goal Setting allows you to **be**, **do**, and **have** more of everything. You'll use more of your potential, expand your mind, your body, your soul. Goals give your life purpose, power, speed, and direction. You'll gain greater self-esteem, feel fulfilled in life, be more motivated, and *accomplish the seemingly impossible.* Concentrating single-mindedly on a goal, keeping that goal at the forefront of your consciousness, is key!

(4) Small Goals Win Big Goals

**Principle: The achievement of small goals trains and pre-
pares you to achieve big goals.**

As you get into the habit pattern of setting goals and achieving them, you start to build self-confidence. Part of the reason
for breaking a big long-term goal into smaller milestones is to
help you build increasing self-confidence by winning the smaller
ones. This keeps you motivated because you see yourself making consistent progress on a regular basis toward the big goal.
You build skill, competence, courage, and foresight as you go.

*The achievement of small goals trains and prepares you to
achieve big goals.* This is a basic principle of high-achievement
living. You start small, then steadily improve in ever-increasing
increments. It's not important where you start as long as you
consistently improve over time. Remember, a successful life,
which may consist of seventy-five years or more, is built one
successful day at a time!

(5) Goal Setting Strategy: Options and Flexibility

I've stressed over and over in this lesson the idea of subdi-
viding big goals into smaller and smaller ones, then working on
achieving these mini-goals or milestones one at a time. This
allows you to set up a rough time scale as to when each milestone can be met. If you don't have enough information on how
to achieve a goal or to accurately gauge the time required, here
are two easy methods to help you.

First, talk with other people who would be able to give you
more accurate information; second, do your own research by
reading up on how other people accomplished similar tasks. You
can tap *other people's* knowledge to possibly give you a strategy
and time frame to achieve *your* goals. Don't be afraid to directly
use someone else's strategy or modify a strategy you learn
about.

Your modification will probably be necessary because your
particular strengths and weaknesses will differ from everyone
else's. There is always more than one way to achieve the same
goal, but having multiple strategies in mind helps you to develop

the perfect one for you. This is the beauty of using your own creative mind and natural talents. Try to develop multiple strategies to achieve your goals, and then evaluate which one you think will work best for you. Leave all options open when first developing strategies, and be flexible!

One last word. Don't ever be afraid to abandon a goal if something in your life changes drastically and makes the goal unimportant or obsolete for you. Just set a new goal to replace it.

(6) Qualities of Big Goals

All goals must be precise, tangible, measurable, and exciting, not vague, lifeless, or boring. You must narrow your life focus to a set of clearly defined goals; otherwise you will become confused and your energies dissipated. The power and time you have on this earth is limited, so focusing on just a few goals at a time is key. Goals need to be very specific in order for you to focus your attention and energy on them.

Goals must also be believable. If you think a goal is an outrageous one, impossible for you to ever achieve, you'll never achieve it. In goal setting the 50/50 rule reigns supreme! I mentioned this rule earlier but it's worth repeating. The rule goes like this: In order to know if a goal is gauged properly for you, you must feel you have a 50/50 chance at achieving it when you start. If you feel you have a 90% chance of not achieving a goal, you will not be motivated because it seems too difficult at the start. If you feel you have a 90% or greater chance of achieving it, then it won't motivate you because it's too easy.

You should also have a main goal in life. This main goal should also be larger than your own life. What I mean by this is that it should transcend you, having the capability to impact other people's lives in a beneficial way. Napoleon Hill refers to this as a "major definite purpose." A selfish goal inspires no one. In order to achieve a big long-term goal you will need to enlist the help of other people. Other people won't be motivated to come to your aid if you work on a totally self-serving goal.

"I will induce others to help me by my willingness to help others."

> Napoleon Hill
> Success philosopher
> Author of *Think and Grow
> Rich, Law of Success, Science
> of Personal Achievement,* and
> *Mental Dynamite*

Goals that can be achieved in a few days or weeks are small ones, although small goals are always part of a long-term goal. Goals that take many months or years are long-term goals.

As you start to base your life on a solid foundation of personal life values, worthy goals aligned with God, utilizing your natural talents in some way to achieve these goals, you will feel very good about yourself. Using your natural talents makes you feel good, and knowing that you are laboring towards God-supported worthy goals makes you feel even better. This is why figuring out personal life values and natural talents and goal setting are so vital to your life's success.

Your life is then focused, because you are serving a specific meaningful purpose, which in turn makes your life fulfilling. In this way your life *gains total alignment*, takes on new meaning, becomes worthwhile and important. As you look on your past after a hard-fought goal is finally won, you will then be able to say that the battle, discipline, and labor were worth it. You will be able to safely say, it was all in all a small price to pay for the success you earned. Really big goals expand your consciousness, benefit others, and make life worth living!

"The ultimate reason for setting goals is to entice you to become the person it takes to achieve them."

> Jim Rohn
> America's foremost business
> philosopher; author of *The
> Five Major Pieces to the Life
> Puzzle, Seven Strategies for
> Wealth and Happiness,* and
> *The Seasons of Life*

The Physiological Basis for Heightened Awareness: The Power of the Reticular Formation

This is one of the most important sections in the entire POWERMIND system. The physiological basis behind most mental conditioning techniques is explained right here!

Principle: **People are alert and aware of what is present in their environment to the degree that it has pre-assigned significance or importance to them.**

In many sections of this lesson I've alluded to the fact that proper goal setting procedure causes you to have an expanded awareness and sensory enhancement. What is the physiological basis that allows for this heightened level of awareness? Neurologists call it the **reticular formation**, or **RF** for short. It is a small finger like area located in the middle of the human brain. Most college biology textbooks with a chapter on the human brain discuss the RF.

The reticular formation serves as a vital link in determining states of awareness. Almost all neural fibers (connections) reaching the cerebral cortex (center of consciousness) from the five sense organs must pass through the RF. Thus the RF is essentially a filter that selects which sensory information reaches the cerebral cortex (conscious awareness). (See General Goal Setting, Diagram RF.)

The RF has two other very important functions as well. First, it continuously sends signals out to all skeletal muscles, maintaining a certain degree of tension in the human body known as muscle tone; second, the RF serves to keep you alert and awake. The most important function of the RF for our current discussion, however, is its role as a **sensory filter.**

All incoming information (sensory stimulation) coming in from your five senses (sight, hearing, touch, taste, smell) is filtered to some degree by the RF before it reaches the cerebral cortex (center for consciousness) of your brain. All information still comes into your subconscious mind, but you aren't consciously aware of it. Only a tiny fraction of what your senses detect is consciously perceived. The RF is the biological organ in the brain that allows only *"significant"* or *"important"* information from the environment to pass into conscious awareness from the five senses. Here are three simple examples that illustrate RF function.

First example. Did you ever want to purchase a particular kind of car? You started thinking about it, *concentrating on it, visualizing it* with *strong emotional desire*. Later you started "seeing" these types of cars everywhere on the roads. They now somehow seem to be popping up everywhere; you can easily spot them a mile away. You are very **alert** to and **aware** of them in your surroundings.

Second example. You read an unfamiliar word in a book, you look it up in the dictionary, read its definition, you concentrate on it for a while. Now in the next few days you'll see the word again and again; it starts to "appear" everywhere.

Third example. Hunters become very **alert** and **aware** of the type of game they are hunting. They develop a keen eye and can spot the particular game at long distances. They read hunting magazines, study the game's habits, seasonal appearances, likely locations, etc. They concentrate on their particular specialty game. They thus develop an uncanny skill of being able to see the game when untrained people cannot. Unskilled hunters are often amazed at the experienced hunter's *"spotting"* skill.

This is all possible because of the RF in your brain, which can be effectively utilized to help you achieve *all your goals* with seemingly uncanny skill. You'll be able to spot opportunities all around you. There are no magical or occult forces operating here, it's just simple brain physiology. As you focus on a goal, thinking about it often, concentrating on it, visualizing and charging it with the emotion of desire, you activate your RF to allow all incoming sensory information in regard to that goal to pass through to conscious awareness. Now, when the subconscious mind takes in sensory information through the five senses from the environment that may be related to a **PREPRO-GRAMMED** goal, it "flashes" that to the conscious mind by way of the RF and you become instantly **aware** of it.

General Goal Setting Diagram RF

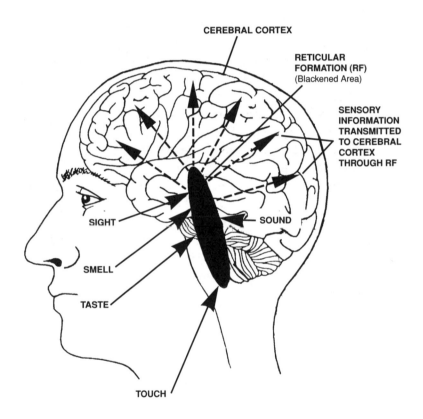

Impulses from sensory organs must pass through the reticular formation before reaching the cerebral cortex (center of conscious awareness).

People are alert and aware of what is present in their environment to the degree that it has preassigned significance or importance to them. Here are a few more examples of RF function. Can a mother hear her screaming child in a crowded grocery store? Can you hear your child's voice among a crowd of other children playing at a picnic? Can you pick out the voices of people you know at a party? Do you see how you can "tune in," so to speak? You have adjusted your RF to these specific sensory inputs. The goal setting techniques in this lesson were specifically designed to help you adjust your RF!

As you moved through this goal setting lesson I've stressed:

◆ Thought clarity, getting a clear picture in your *mind's eye* of your goals.

◆ Feeling as if your goals are already won so you are highly emotional about them, thereby assigning them a high degree of importance in your mind. (Emotionalizing a thought assigns importance to it.)

◆ Writing out your goals, which forces intensive *concentration,* again reinforcing thought clarity.

◆ Visualizing the goals, which preprograms your greatest sense, your sense of sight.

◆ Thinking every day about your goals, morning, noon, and night.

◆ Telling individuals *you trust* about your goals, thereby reinforcing them in your own mind and programming their minds to help you.

I wasn't using these methods for the fun of it! All of these serve to adjust the RF in your brain. By using daily affirmations, concentration, visualization, positive emotional charging, and verbal repetition of your goals, you alter your RF. You program yourself to become instantly aware of anything in your environment that may help you achieve your goals. By having absolute clarity and using daily affirmations, concentration, and visualization techniques to adjust the RF, you make your mind become like a highly sensitive, sophisticated goal-seeking machine. You will learn more about the RF in the High Achievement part of this book, for it is the basis of the two most scientific forms of **autogenic conditioning, verbal self-affirmations** and **imagineering.**

Most people alter their RF but aren't even aware of it. Have you ever tuned out your spouse or children? You have the ability to do this because of the RF in your brain. Have you ever been driving and suddenly realized you are lost? Now every road sign glares out at you. You are instantly very alert and focused on figuring out where you are and how to get back on track.

By properly setting goals into the subconscious section of the mind, you adjust your RF, which then alerts you to opportunities present in your environment that will make it possible for you to achieve your goals with astonishing speed! You will be shocked at what you notice, and so will everyone you know. You'll most certainly be stunned into action after reading the upcoming autogenic conditioning part of this book, if for no other reason than to prove to yourself that you possess this amazing power!

Remember, the subconscious mind's primary function is to achieve goals. It is like a powerful goal-seeking machine. Your conscious mind sets (programs) the goal into the subconscious machine. Most people set no goals at all; thus they are unaware of this latent power. They are wandering, forever lost on the highways of life, seeking no goals and finding no opportunities! They are taking a careless drive through life with no destination in mind, winding up inevitably at the *crossroads of doom!*

Activating Other People's Reticular Formation

In the previous section I told you about the RF. You can adjust other people's RF as well. You do this by telling people **you trust** about your goals in great detail. In so doing you will be programming their subconscious minds to help you, enlisting their mindpower by adjusting their RF for **your** goals. This greatly expands your own potential for gain because their five senses now begin operating on your goals! Since most people have no clearly defined goals of their own, you can enlist them to work on yours. They will now notice information in their environment related to your goals, because they are keyed in or tuned in to **your** goals. You could help other goal seekers by having them tell you about their goals as well. This can work both ways for mutual benefit.

Talk enthusiastically to other people **you trust** about your goals. Use words to create vivid images in their minds, talk to them often about *your* goals to keep them keyed in on your goals. They will then stay programmed! They will keep thinking about *your* goals, and start to see things in their environment related to *your* goals and, you hope, bring that information back to you!

For example, I told one of my close friends one time about a project I was working on. He went home and told his wife about it because he was thinking about it all afternoon. She told him she had read a book that might be of interest to me. The next day he brought the book to me, and indeed it was very useful for my project.

You can set this sort of chain reaction in motion, and then hours, days, weeks, even years later others may bring you materials and information. Give this a try and watch what happens!

The Time Is Now

Principle: Laboring toward worthy goals brings new life.

Daily life offers limitless opportunity for constant fulfillment, physically, mentally, socially, and spiritually, by working on worthy goals. Remember how you felt when you were 6, waiting to grow up? At 16 life is endless, at 30 life is getting shorter, at 40 comes mid-life crisis, the emotional brick wall. Mid-life crisis for some is the achievement of all early life goals, or it could be the bitter realization of not achieving any worthwhile goals at all. Some people find themselves locked into lifeless relationships with a spouse or has-been lover, others are completely frustrated with lack of career development, and so on. At 50 life is so very short, and at 60 life is pointless for many. They say, "Why live any longer?" The feeling of life's accumulated failure has caught up with them because they didn't set goals!

Time management is extremely important, and the proper setting of goals allows you to manage your time (your life) well.

If you want to lose weight, become energetic, gain enthusiasm, increase your income, remove bad habits, improve your love life, relationships, career, education, personal power, **THEN DO IT!**

"If you want to change the future you must change what you are doing in the present."

> **Brian Tracy**
> **Human achievement expert**
> **Author of** *Maximum Achievement, The Psychology of Achievement,* **and** *Universal Laws of Success and Achievement*

Set your goals, write them down, set deadlines for their achievement, and get busy working a plan. Let your daily watchword be action, **action, ACTION!** In this way unstoppable momentum can be yours! The evils of procrastination and an unfulfilled life of regret can be totally eliminated with worthy goals. *Laboring toward worthy goals brings new life.* The time is now!

"All must labor either with hand or head."

> **Samuel Smiles**
> **Author of the classic self-help series** *Self Help, Thrift,* **and** *Character*

An After-the-Lesson Visit with the Author

You have just been through one of the most comprehensive lessons on goal setting ever created. If you feel a little mind-weary, that's good, you should. I worked you systematically through basic goal setting theory, explaining the secret powers of goal setting as well as the absolute necessity of worthy goals for living a successful fulfilling life. Goal setting is a master skill of success because it allows you to get exactly what you want in life while others mill about aimlessly.

A big problem people have once they are convinced of the benefits and importance of goal setting is they really don't know what they want to **be, have,** or **do.** The series of eight goal setting techniques in Module II were meant to aid you in getting a very good handle on these big three goal setting questions. Not only were the techniques designed to systematically answer all three of these questions, but they also taught you step by step how to properly set goals. You were also introduced to the reticular formation (RF) in your brain, which allows you to become "sensitized" to information and opportunities in your environment.

Your last obstacle to overcome is that of self-discipline. Time is forever ticking away, and your clock is running out just like everyone else's. The time to get started is NOW! If you try something and it doesn't work, just try again, but don't ever lose sight of your goals. Persistence is self-discipline in action. Many times the difference between success and failure boils down to a person having just a little more self-discipline. The man or woman who sticks it out just a little bit longer when the chips are down usually ends up the winner!

As with the whole POWERMIND system, you must choose to use what makes sense to you. Even if you just picked up a few pieces of information in this lesson, use them, put them into action in your life right now! Remember it's usually the person with just a slight edge who ends up winning. This lesson provided you with far more than a slight edge over more than 90% of the general population. So think, set your goals carefully, make great plans, and capitalize on every opportunity that comes your way, speeding you on to high achievement. *Always remember, it only takes one good idea to transform your whole life!*

"There is one quality which one must possess to win, and that is definitiveness of purpose, the knowledge of what one wants, and a burning desire to possess it."

Napoleon Hill
Success philosopher
Author of *Think and Grow Rich, Law of Success, Science of Personal Achievement,* **and** *Mental Dynamite*

3 Money Goals

Overview

This lesson is divided into three modules concerning basic wealth creation. The first module deals with proper career selection. The second module goes over the proper attitudes for wealth creation, and the third module is an in-depth study of exactly how to build a personal fortune. The three modules are outlined below.

"The finest thing you can give others is the knowledge of the law of prosperous thinking, and they will never want for any good thing in life."

> **Dr. Joseph Murphy**
> **Author of** *The Power of Your Subconscious Mind, Your Infinite Power to be Rich,* **and** *The Amazing Laws of Cosmic Mind Power*

Money Goals: Module I. Proper Career Selection

The Grasshopper and the Bee (a fable)

A grasshopper, half starved with cold and hunger, came to a well-stored beehive at the approach of winter, and humbly begged the bees to relieve his wants with a few drops of honey.

One of the bees asked him how he had spent his time all the summer, and why he had not laid up a store of food like them.

"Truly," said he, "I spent my time very merrily, in drinking, dancing, and singing, and never once thought of winter."

"Our plan is very different," said the bee. "We work hard in the summer to lay by a store of food against the season when we foresee we shall want it; but those who do nothing but drink, and dance, and sing in the summer, must *expect to starve* in the winter."

"You must get good at one of two things: sowing in the spring or begging in the fall."

Jim Rohn
America's foremost business
philosopher; author of *The*
Five Major Pieces to the Life
Puzzle, Seven Strategies for
***Wealth and Happiness*, and**
The Seasons of Life

What's in Store for You?

The United States Department of Health and Human Services conducted a study in 1990 (SSA, 1990). They found these shocking results: For every one hundred people starting a career in the U.S., they all fell into one of the following four categories at age 65:

- ◆ 25 WERE DEAD
- ◆ 20 HAD ANNUAL INCOMES OF LESS THAN $6,000
- ◆ 51 HAD ANNUAL INCOMES BETWEEN $6,000 AND $35,000 (WITH A MEDIAN ANNUAL INCOME OF $12,000 PER YEAR)
- ◆ 4 HAD ANNUAL INCOMES OF $35,000 OR MORE

The United States is clearly the richest nation in the entire world, yet millions are poverty stricken even after forty or more years of hard labor. These people did not plan for their future. They left their financial destiny in the hands of **someone else**. They *thought* somehow everything would miraculously work out okay for them. They *thought* someone would take care of them.

They did not take action, they did not study money, they did not set money goals for themselves, they simply **followed the crowd**. They did what most people did: THE WRONG THING!!! They wound up broke, embarrassed, bitter, and old. Instead of paying the small price of daily disciplined saving, they paid the high price of regret and disgrace.

What is your plan for wealth creation? Do you have any money goals? How much do you have stored by for the winter? How far in debt are you? Remember, with no plan for wealth creation you are planning for poverty. Don't get caught in this trap; set money goals and work diligently on a sound financial plan for yourself. Save a portion of all you earn and store it by for the winters of life!

Statistical source. U.S. Department of Health and Human Services, *SSA Publication #13-11871-6190, 1990.*

Examination of Current Job: A 42-Question Self-Test

Principle: It's hard to build a fortune or enjoy life when you hate your job.

Wealth creation begins with having the job for which you are best suited. In this self-test, you will be asked to answer a series of questions about your current job and line of work. These questions are specifically intended to give you insight as to whether you have chosen the right career or not. If you haven't (and most people haven't), you will gain valuable information about yourself so that you can more accurately determine what would be the proper career for you. *It's hard to build a fortune or enjoy life when you hate your job!*

1. What is the most enjoyable part of your job?
2. Why did you select the job you now have?
3. Why did you select the particular line of work you do?
4. What are the aspects of your job that you find particularly rewarding?
5. Do you like working for the company that employs you? Why? Why not?
6. Do you like working for your boss? Why? Why not?
7. If someone else offered you a 10% salary increase for a similar job with similar benefits, would you leave your current job?
8. What is the least enjoyable part of your job?
9. What are all the aspects of your job you find particularly displeasing?
10. If you were to receive a 10% pay cut, would you stay at your current job? If not, what would you do?
11. If you could have any job *within* *your* *company* what would it be? What additional skills/training would you need to get that job?
12. If you could have any job *in the world* what would it be? What additional skills/training would you need to get that job?
13. What are all the factors that you consider to be stopping you from getting the ideal job *within* *your* *company?*
14. Is your ideal job *in the world* the same as the ideal job *at* *your company?*
15. If your ideal job in the world does not exist at the company you are currently working for, why are you there?
16. Do you know where to get information to find out what skills/training are required for your "ideal job in the world?"
17. Does your current job utilize your *natural talents?*
18. Do you feel you are growing or stagnating in your current job?
19. Does your current job make use of your "brains" or "brawn"?
20. If you used your "brains" more, could you use your "brawn" less?

21. Do you know anyone who currently has the job that you consider to be "ideal"? If you do, do you know how that person got the job?
22. Is there anyone who has the job you consider to be ideal who will honestly tell you how they got it and what skills/training are necessary to get it?
23. If you do not know anyone personally who has what you consider to be the ideal job, are there books available in the library or bookstore about someone that has/had what you consider to be the ideal job? Would it be beneficial for you to read those books?
24. Are there any individuals **you can trust** who will help you get the ideal job within or outside your company?
25. If your ideal job lies outside your company, do you know anyone in that company that can help you to "get in"?
26. Overall, do you like your current job?
27. Would you be a happier person if you had a different job?
28. Would you be a happier person if you were in a different line of work?
29. Overall, do you like the line of work you are in?
30. List all the lines of work you think you would like better than your current line of work.
31. Overall, do you think you are in the job for which you are best suited?
32. Overall, do you think you are in the line of work for which you are best suited?
33. Are you interested in your current job?
34. Are you interested in your line of work?
35. What are all the lines of work that you are intensely interested in?
36. Do you feel it would benefit you personally and the people you care about to have a job for which you are best suited?
37. Do you feel it is worth whatever time and energy is necessary for you to obtain the ideal job?
38. Looking back over the past year, would you say your job was very enjoyable to you?
39. If you answered no to question 38, do you realize it is physically unhealthy to engage for extended periods of time in activities that you do not enjoy?

40. If you had a long-term (three or more years) plan of action that could get you your ideal job would you follow through with it?
41. Do you feel you should work for what you receive in life, or do you think it should be given to you for free?
42. If you were to stay in your current job for the next ten years, would you be happy? Five years? Two years?

Review

Now go over your answers carefully, reflecting on them. The goal in this self-analysis is to uncover aspects of your job and line of work that you haven't considered before, thereby giving you greater insight as to what your proper career might be. Most people will never go through this sort of rigorous career analysis. They will work mindlessly at a job or series of jobs all their lives, never taking the few hours or days to really consider if they are in the job or line of work for which they are best suited.

It is possible that you are now employed in the perfect job. If you are, I salute you, for you are among a select few individuals in the entire world. If this is the case, my hope is that after completing this self-test you have far greater confidence in yourself to continue pursuing your current career goals. If you are not in this elite category, I ask that you now consider the specialized design of this self-analysis instrument.

This instrument was designed to cause you to **think** about:

◆ What you like and dislike in your current job
◆ Whether your line of work is correct for you
◆ Whether your company is best suited to *your* needs
◆ Whether you should consider different jobs or different lines of work
◆ Whether your skills and abilities are utilized at your current job
◆ Whether you need additional skills/training to get your ideal job
◆ Whether you could be tapping into other people for information
◆ Whether you should start reading books about people who have had your ideal job
◆ The vital question of *interest:* If you aren't interested in your job, you can never excel in it

The following is a brief explanation of what each of the questions is designed to uncover.

Questions 1, 2, and 3 make you think about what you like and dislike about your job and what the reasoning behind your job selection was. Many people chose their job or line of work on a whim or on the advice of others, never considering their individual fit with the job.

Questions 4 and 5 look at what is rewarding and displeasing in your job; this is a subtle variation on likes and dislikes.

Question 6 addresses the question of liking your boss. It is hard to be happy and productive working for a boss you dislike or don't respect.

Question 7 delves into your drive for money. All things being equal, would you leave where you are for a 10% raise. If you answered yes, you are mainly money driven, and your employer means little to you.

Questions 8 and 9 ask you to consider the most displeasing aspects of your current job so you know what to avoid when seeking a new job.

Question 10 is the reverse of Question 7. Basically put, would a 10% pay cut be enough to motivate you to seek a different job? Is money or your love of the line of work a bigger motivation for you? Most people say money is their sole motivation because they are in the wrong line of work.

Question 11, in two parts, allows you to figure out where a possible career goal might be *within* your company and what you would need to do to prepare for it.

Question 12, also in two parts, asks you to broaden your imagination scope to include the whole world, then asks what training you might need to obtain the ideal job. The answer to Question 12 may put you on the path to a new and very rewarding career.

Question 13 asks you to identify what stands in your way, preventing you from getting the best job available to you at your company. Answers to this question could be used as career goals for you to work on. Eliminating them would make the attainment of that job a more realistic possibility for you. The two areas to consider are, What skills/training are needed? and What barriers do I need to eliminate? Therein lie some of the most crucial items for you to consider working on.

Question 14 asks you to consider whether your ideal job in the world exists at your current company.

Question 15 is meant to stimulate your thinking so that you expand it to outside your company, if your ideal job is not even there. Is the company right for you? Or should you move on?

Question 16 asks whether you know where to get information on obtaining the ideal job.

Question 17 addresses your *natural talents*. Are your natural talents being utilized at your current job? If they aren't, it is most likely you consider the job dissatisfying.

Question 18 is designed to see whether you are developing in your job.

Questions 19 and 20 seeks to find out whether you are using your head or your back and whether you realize that *higher income always comes from using your head, not physical labor.*

Questions 21 and 22 ask whether there is any role model that you can study for tips or pointers to help you. Gaining experience from a mentor is extremely useful and saves tremendous amounts of time.

Questions 23 and 24 ask whether you know what it took or what methods other people used to secure the type of job you want. Also, whether you know and trust someone who can teach you. These questions also suggest the idea of reading books to help you. This opens your mind to the idea that you don't need to know anyone personally if there are books written about the role models you need to study. It presses you to *study* and allows you no excuse for not learning how to get the best job for yourself.

Question 25 (one of my favorites) asks if you can form a network of helpers who can be of value to you in securing a better job outside your current company. People in other companies often have connections there and, if they are *trustworthy*, may help you to get in.

Questions 26-32 analyze your feelings about your work and ask you to generate possible alternatives based on your *natural career fit.*

Questions 33-35 ask if you are interested in your work. It is impossible to be the best at anything you are not intensely interested in . The more interested you are in a subject, the more you will learn about it. Interest enables you to be more receptive to new information and be more creative.

Question 36 asks you to consider the negative impact on your family or the people close to you if you are unhappy with your work. A common story goes like this. The guy yells at his wife and kids each night. He apologizes later to his wife, saying, "Just another FIFTEEN YEARS till I retire, honey, then everything will be okay".

Question 37 asks whether you have the stamina to pursue your ideal job.

Question 38 asks whether historically (past year) you enjoyed your job.

Question 39 asks whether you realize the poor health implications that come from being in the wrong job. Are you sickly, do you hate your job, is there correlation? Are you taking into account the long-term health effects of working in a job you don't find enjoyable?

Questions 40 and 41 determine whether you have the self-discipline and proper mind-set to follow though on a plan of action. Question 41 gets at the proper mind-set more specifically, because there is no such thing as something for nothing. Anyone who professes "something for nothing" as a truth is wrong. This question basically addresses your work ethic. Many people have the wrong one, figuring somehow the world owes them. Again, there is no such reality as something for nothing. *The Universal Law of sowing and reaping is immutable! As ye sow, so shall ye reap. Sow good, reap good, sow evil, reap evil, sow nothing, reap nothing!*

Question 42 addresses your long-term time perspective at your job, getting you to think again. Is your career future bright or dismal? ***It won't change if you don't change it.***

❖ ❖ ❖

Now go back over your answers one more time with the added dimension of the test's design and *THINK AGAIN!*

If you have made a thorough effort in the analysis, congratulations are in order. You should now have a much greater understanding of the operation of your mind in regard to your career. Some of you will be delighted! If you are not in that category, you may feel discouraged and depressed. Take heart; this book is designed to save you from a life of regret.

Remember, millions of people work in mindless, mind-rotting jobs all their lives, never taking the time to really consider if they are in the right job or line of work. Many don't know what questions to ask. It is the rare exception to find a person in the job that is perfect for them.

In completing this self-test you should now be happy. Why? Because you now know if you are doing the right thing or the wrong thing, and knowing now is always better than knowing later. If indeed you are in the wrong job or line of work, be glad you are reading this book. As you move on you will learn more specific techniques for getting your ideal job, if that's your goal. Already a few of the keys have been revealed to you in this self-test. They are listed below but will be elaborated on more throughout this book.

14 Keys to a Successful Career

1. Think about *why* you want to be in a certain line of work and think carefully about changing from your current line of work.
2. Most people are not solely money driven in their careers; usually other factors drive them. By identifying these other factors, you can enrich your career.
3. Identify needed training/skills that would help you get your *ideal job.*
4. Strive for an *ideal job*, not one that is just a notch better.
5. Identify what is keeping you from obtaining your ideal job.
6. A major part of job happiness comes from utilizing natural talents in your job.

7. Use of brains, not manual labor, always nets more cash in a career.
8. Study role models (living or dead) to help you obtain the ideal job.
9. Read! Read! Read! A wealth of knowledge and highly skilled teachers through time are at your beck and call in the local library!
10. Network and enlist the help of others.
11. Interest in your job is of utmost importance.
12. *Learn* from your past mistakes. Don't regret your past, treat your past as a school.
13. Develop a long-term perspective; look into your future a few years or more with the power of your imagination.
14. Education, self-discipline, and labor are the three roads leading to the ideal job.

3 Pieces to the Career Puzzle

Principle: Your career must involve your personal interests in order for you to be a true success.

Principle: The wisest use of your time is time spent on self-education.

Principle: The more people you serve, the more money you can make.

There are only three pieces in this basic system of career selection:

1. Intense Interest
2. Specialized Knowledge
3. Service to Others

1. Intense Interest. Your first piece in the ideal career selection puzzle is to find whatever has intense interest to you. I stressed the issue of interest in the self-assessment part of this book as well. This is usually something that you enjoy doing very much, that you are good at, and that involves use of your *natural talents.*

In order to become one of the best at your job, you must be intensely interested in it, love doing it, and be naturally suited to it. Many people are bored with their jobs eventually, ending up hating them. This attitude does not lead to quality work, excellence, happiness, good health, or personal success—please don't be overwhelmed with my bold statement of truth!

If you have a job you are unhappy with, you will communicate this to people around you, consciously by griping and complaining and unconsciously in multiple subtle ways. If you resent your boss or employer, feeling you deserve more than you are paid or that you should receive more recognition, you are immediately separating yourself from the organization. You then are no longer a productive part of the company. You act as a worn-out or broken gear in the company machine. You don't give 100%, because you have in fact "fired" yourself. Later, if you are laid off or fired because of a "personality conflict" (which is always the number-one reason for firing), it is partly your fault. Your heart was not in your work and you lacked skill in finding the ideal job for yourself. If it's hard for you to have a good attitude toward your job, begin your search immediately for one you *can* have a good attitude toward.

Interest is key here for this very reason. It's hard to have an eager positive attitude toward something you hate doing or are bored with. When you are intensely interested in anything, you are hungry for more information. Your mind is receptive, absorbing new knowledge like a dry sponge absorbs water.

This leads to mastery in that area of expertise, which in turn increases your personal value tremendously. After all, a local, state, national, or world authority on any subject can make more money than someone who is not an expert. If you can't wait to leave your job at the end of the day or you don't look forward to going in on Monday morning with eager anticipation, you aren't that interested in your job. *Your career must involve your personal interests in order for you to be a true success.*

2. Specialized Knowledge is the second piece. You must also continue to keep up with your chosen field, staying current in your area of expertise. We all know how hard it is to study a subject we are not *interested* in. That's why intense interest comes first: it enables you to gain specialized knowledge.

Through my window of personal experience, I saw many people who felt once they graduated from college they were finished learning. (I was one of them!) This is a **SERIOUS MIS-TAKE!** Continuous learning is the only way to increase your personal value. Interest is the driving force necessary to motivate you toward lifelong learning.

Now you are probably thinking, "I know what I like to do, what I am interested in, and what I can gain specialized knowledge about, but how can I make a living at it?" This is mainly up to your own creative ability; however, in the High Achievement part of this book I outline specific methods you can use to release your creative problem-solving abilities. The answer is always within your reach. You just need a way to grab hold of it, and that's where I can definitely help. The answers will be different for everyone because of each person's unique combination of natural talents.

I won't keep you in total suspense, however, so here is one method you can use right now. Direction will come if you persist in thinking this thought: "How can I earn money at _____?" or "How can I provide a product or service to others with _____?" Fill in the blank with your special interests or what you know how to do well or your natural talents. As you begin gathering specialized knowledge in your area of interest, creative ideas will begin to flow through your mind like a river; it will spin incessantly with creativity. If you set your mind to figuring out a way to make a living at what you are interested in, you'll certainly find a way to do it. Devote time each day and concentrate for about fifteen minutes, repeating silently or out loud, "How can I make money with _____?" Do this over and over, then write down any ideas that come to mind. If you really latch onto the right answer you'll hardly be able to sleep at night; you'll know deep down inside it's right!

When you aren't interested in your job, you tend either to **not** think about it much or to think about it in a negative light, suppressing all your creativity. When you don't use your natural talents you tend to be unhappy. You'll also not be very good at your job, whatever it is, because you aren't naturally suited to it.

I'll explain the value of specialization. You need to learn more about your job than anyone else. If your job is a broad-based one, then specialize in a certain aspect of it. Create an area of expertise where *you* are the expert. For example, if you are interested in and love fishing, you might become a professional fisherman such as those seen on TV. You could then specialize in freshwater fishing or saltwater fishing. Once the waters are selected, choose the type of fish, such as rainbow trout, large-mouth bass, catfish, or perch, or in saltwater blue marlin, grouper, barracuda, haddock, etc. You could specialize even further to a region of the country, a certain state, a certain county, certain lakes, etc. Do you see the pattern? We keep becoming more and more specialized, defining the area of expertise further and further.

Going fishing is not traditionally thought of as a multimillion-dollar career—that's why I picked it as an example. It could indeed become a multimillion-dollar career if you are interested enough to obtain the *specialized knowledge* necessary to become a world-class expert! Many professional bass fisherman, experts in certain lakes, make substantial livings as fishing guides, doing TV spots, writing books, producing videos, and endorsing products. These people know the lakes, the lures, the techniques, the equipment, the fish, the seasons, the weather conditions, and all the other details. They are world-class experts in their area of expertise, and people will always pay big money for the best!

There are thousands of careers, any one of which can make you rich if you are dedicated to being the best. The attitude of striving to be the best is an entirely different attitude than making a mediocre living at a going-nowhere job to pay some lousy bills! Having a mundane job to pay the lousy bills and support the family isn't success at all, *it is existing without living.*

Push yourself to be the best in your job by gaining specialized knowledge. The happiest people are those who do the best that is within them. These people have mastered an area of expertise. Keep improving yourself in some way every day in your chosen field. Take each day as a learning experience. Learn as much as you can; self-education will net you all the riches and happiness you could possibly want. Don't ever stop learning. Always strive to learn and grow as a human being. Time is short, use it wisely. *The wisest use of your time is time spent on self-education.*

"Formal education will make you a living; self-education will make you a fortune."

> **Jim Rohn**
> America's foremost business
> philosopher; author of *The
> Five Major Pieces of the Life
> Puzzle, Seven Strategies for
> Wealth and Happiness*, and
> *The Seasons of Life*

3. Service to others. This third piece of the career puzzle states that you must *serve other people* in some way in order to reap the greatest rewards in life. A self-serving career is a self-defeating one. Being interested and an expert won't earn you any money unless you can serve others. Your career must be a noble one, serving others as well as yourself. A selfish career or goal will always end in defeat.

You must try to serve mankind or benefit humanity in some way with your special expertise and *natural talents*. Highly successful people love their work; they use their natural talents to perform a service to others. They base their line of work on high ideals that help humankind in some way.

The more people you serve, the more money you can make. By the Universal Law of sowing and reaping, if you serve others, rewards will be poured on you in abundance. It can be no other way. Serving other people must return benefit to you.

The three pieces to successful career selection are now stated for your careful consideration:
1. Intense Interest
2. Specialized Knowledge
3. Service to Others

I will now briefly review and tie together these three pieces in the next section.

Putting the Career Puzzle Together

**Principle: Interest allows you to gather specialized
        knowledge.**

This short section will put the whole career puzzle together
for you. There are five basic instructions:

1. Determine what your intense interests are.
2. Obtain a wealth of knowledge in one or more of these areas.
3. Figure out a way to make money at what you love doing.
4. Figure out ways to improve the quality of your product or
   service to others.
5. Determine ways to provide your product or service to more
   people.

Again, I will briefly discuss the all-important principle of
alignment. If you select a career dealing with a subject that interests you, you will be receptive to obtaining more information
about it. This allows you to gain specialized knowledge, which
increases your personal value IF you can figure out a way to
make money with the information.

*Special note: As discussed in the self-assessment section,
            natural talents are usually directly involved
            with your intense interests.*

Interest allows you to gather specialized knowledge. The
trick then is to determine **how to** use this specialized knowledge
to increase the quality of a product/service or to provide such to
more people or to provide such at lower cost than what is currently available. This will enable you to earn money. If you can
align all five of the above instructions, your career will skyrock-
et!

Here is exactly how to do it!

1. Determine interests. Make a list of:
   a. Your intense interests
   b. What you enjoy doing
   c. What you can spend much of your time on without
      becoming fatigued

2. **Obtain a wealth of knowledge in one or more of the items listed above.** Get books at the library, buy books at the bookstore, take classes, listen to cassette tapes, watch instructional videos about one or more of them. Learn all you can. Become a specialized-knowledge-gathering machine!

3. **Figure out how to make money at what you love doing.** Ask yourself each day, "How can I make money at (put your interests here)?" Make a list of possible ways and add to it daily until you find the one that you think will work. Ask other people whom **you trust** this question: "If all you knew how to do was (put your interest here), how would you go about making money?" Keep a list of your ideas as well as the ideas gathered from other people.

4. **Figuring out ways to improve quality.** Ask yourself, "How can I improve the quality of (product or service) that interests me?" Ask others the same question. Keep a list of ideas.

5. **Determining new and bigger markets.** Ask yourself, "How can (product or service) be provided to more people?" Ask others the same question. Keep a list of ideas.

Whichever one of these five is giving you trouble, keep working on that one. Ask other people whom you trust for help, take notes on answers that come to you and what others tell you. Review the list of answers periodically; eventually the right answer will come if you **persist**. You could also ask God for divine guidance in your prayers.

"If any of you lack wisdom, let him ask of God, that giveth to all men liberally, and upbraideth not; and it shall be given him."

James 1:15

Money Goals: Module II. Winning Attitudes for Wealth Creation

Attitudes That Block Wealth Creation

Greed, bitterness, envy, and jealousy are attitudes that always block personal wealth. Have you ever said to yourself or heard others say, "Those rich people, they are all crooks" or "I knew them when they were poor, and they are rich now. They must be thieves or swindlers." See if you can determine why these people are reacting that way. Perhaps they are having financial difficulty in their own lives, causing them to be jealous, envious, or bitter? Did their friends become rich and successful while they remained poor? Condemning others who have achieved financial freedom causes a person to block their own financial success.

Having a goal of being rich when deep down you really despise rich people is self-defeating. Do you want to despise yourself? If you think being rich is "bad," your attitude must change in order for you to fire up your creative abilities and release your potential to gain wealth.

2 Major Reasons for Having Wealth-Blocking Attitudes

1. Childhood Conditioning
2. Misquoting the Bible

Why don't many people feel they should be rich? Some people were raised in superstitious families that **wrongly** believed there was virtue in poverty. This belief was instilled during childhood and has been carried over into adulthood. Poverty is ignorance, sickness, devastation, self-destruction, sadness, and embarrassment. There is no virtue at all in it.

The second major cause on the religious side comes from parents or teachers who misinterpret the scriptures. They cite the often-heard misquote "Money is the root of all evil." A more accurate transcription is "For the *love of* money is a root of all kinds of evil" (1 Timothy 6:10). Don't blame the Bible for personal poverty.

I'll explain both of these causes for malconditioned attitudes towards wealth creation more thoroughly in the following sections, because I feel they are keeping many people from their rightful monetary riches.

Dangers of Condemning the Wealthy

Many people who are struggling because they don't have enough money condemn those who are rich. They feel that a wealthy individual must be engaged in illegal operations or be somehow ruthless. Part of the reason why these people are unsuccessful at wealth creation is because they are condemning the very thing they need. They are jealous, envious, covetous, and in many cases quite ignorant!

Ask them how many self-made millionaires they know on a personal basis. I'll bet not many. They learn about the wealthy from the twisted tabloid papers and the news media. They know nothing first hand. They also have a crooked view that money is somehow evil or bad, that you have to be a bad person to have lots of money.

When people are jealous of others they set up a negative mind-set. This suppresses their own ability to attain wealth. Instead of *studying the process* of wealth creation or focusing on how to get wealthy themselves, they simply say things like "The rich must be crooks," or "I don't want to be a crook," or "I'm an honest good person (so I'll remain poor)," as if there are no honest rich people. Do you see the faulty logic in this line of reasoning? The faulty thinking is this: crooks = the wealthy.

They say "I'm not a crook, so I am not wealthy." They justify their poverty by attaching honor to it, which is also called twisted logic or plain ignorance. The basic flaw is the presupposition that in order to be wealthy you must be a crook. In reality most crooks are very poor, and many very honest people are very wealthy. Wouldn't you like to set the record straight and become a very honest and very wealthy person?

Money: Evil or Good?

Principle: Money isn't evil or good, people are evil or good.

If you were to discover gold or oil in your backyard, would you think your backyard was a source of evil? This "evil" idea comes from people's misunderstandings or false interpretation of money. Money in our society consists of paper, ink, lead, gold, nickel, copper, silver, etc. Are these materials inherently evil? Who of intelligence regards paper and ink as evil objects? The Bible is made out of paper and ink just like money. Wedding rings are made of gold. Are they evil? Certainly what comes into question is the *use* of money.

Let's not confuse the article itself with its use. I will not argue the point that money can be **used** for evil. A surgeon's scalpel can be used to save a life or end one. The possessor determines its **use**. An ambulance can be used to save a life by rushing a person to the hospital or to end a life by running someone over. The **driver** determines its **use**. Nuclear power can be used to heat homes for families and babies or to destroy cities with bombs. The use is the main point here. Who determines how money is used? People do!

More specifically, if it is your money, who determines how it is used? Answer: YOU DO! Now we can quickly tidy up this line of reasoning. *Money isn't evil or good, **people** are evil or good.* Money is simply a tool that people use to do their bidding, whether it is building churches, educating the ignorant, buying illegal drugs, or building bombs.

Poverty as a Disease of Mind

Principle: If you want to be wealthy, study wealth.

Most people don't think of poverty as a mental disease, yet it is. Being poor is not virtuous, it is crippling. People with a physical illness go to a hospital when they are sick. There are no financial hospitals, but there is self-education, which can provide the cure for poverty.

Self-education, in the case of treating poverty as a disease of mind, provides specific treatments for cure. Treatments include increasing your knowledge of money management and reading books on wealth creation. The public libraries have excellent books on wealth creation. Your first *book of cures* for poverty should be *Think and Grow Rich* by Napoleon Hill, your second, *The Richest Man in Babylon* by George S. Clason. Both of these books are readily available in bookstores today, yet they were both written over fifty years ago. *Why do you suppose that is?*

There are thousands of ways to become rich. One is reserved especially for you, but you need to search for it! This is one of my particular areas of specialization. The techniques in this book have universal application and are readily applied to wealth creation if you set a money goal for yourself. If you are not now financially independent or making good progress toward that end, there is something wrong with your plan—not you, but certainly your plan. If you are saying, "Plan? What plan?" there is your answer to why you aren't wealthy! With no plan for wealth creation there can be no wealth. *If you want to be wealthy, study wealth.*

People aren't meant to live in poverty, dress in rags, and starve to death. The natural state of a human being is prosperous, seeking growth and fulfillment in all areas of life, especially in the finance department. It is important to rid yourself of any diseased attitudes toward money. You shouldn't criticize it or think of it as evil. If you do, you will repel money, not attract it. Your attitude should be one of liking (not loving) money.

You should **love** *using money wisely and constructively as a tool,* which is precisely what it is. This should make you feel great about making more money. You should strive to get all you can, to use it for your benefit and the benefit of others.

When money flows in and out of your life continuously and easily, a proper state of equilibrium is reached. This is the real meaning of the phrase "plenty of money." Plenty of money to do what you want, when you want, and to have what you want. Money alone won't make you happy, but it's certainly easier to become happy when you are rich, and virtually impossible when you are poor. The fact is most rich people are much happier than most poor people. Money has made more people happy than poverty ever has, and you can take that to the bank!!!

The Poverty or Prosperity Mind-Set

People with the poverty mind-set feel helpless, victims of circumstance; they have no money goals in life, are usually depressed and quite cynical. They always live in poverty conditions. They don't have many ideas on how to get rich. They don't read self-help books. They feel there isn't enough; the feeling of lack fills their minds. They are *irresponsible* because their blame list is forever at the forefront of their consciousness, blinding them. They're poor because they see only taxes, their employers, the government, the town, their job, their genetics, their parents, their education, their lack of connections as the causes of their poverty. If they were only to remove the *planks from their eyes* and take a look on the inside, a look at themselves, they would see why they are so poor.

People with the prosperity mind-set are quite different; they see plenty of money for all. They have many creative ideas and their opportunities abound—so many, in fact, they don't have time to pursue them all. They are ardent readers. They are filled with energy and enthusiasm, they are alive and happy. If they don't have much money right now, they are actively engaged in pursuing a practical plan to get it. They look to their own creative ability to get what they want. They don't feel helpless or hopeless. They are in control; they are personally *responsible* for their finances.

It was never intended in the Master's plan for humankind to live in poverty. You should have all the wealth you need for you and your family to live a happy, productive life. Why be satisfied with poverty or mere financial mediocrity? Money should be your friend. You can do a lot of good with it.

All things being equal, can a person with only ten dollars help the needy more than a person with ten million? If each desires to use their money to help the needy, the person with ten million can help more needy people than the person with only ten dollars.

Which mind-set do you have? Are you rich or are you poor? Are you happy or are you sad? Are you *personally responsible* for your finances or is it someone else's fault that you may be poor? Is there a connection?

Money Goals: Module III. Building a Personal Fortune

Learning and Earning: 5 Steps to Wealth

Principle: All the raw materials necessary for you to become wealthy are within your reach.

Principle: To earn more you must learn more.

Principle: A portion of all you earn is by Universal Rights yours to keep.

You must become skilled in the basics of wealth creation. Money obeys certain laws; these laws are universal and unchanging. The laws of money have not changed since its early use in ancient *Babylon* six thousand years ago. Early preparation is key in building a personal fortune. The sooner you learn the laws of money the better off you will be. Your actions can be no wiser than your thinking, and your thinking can be no wiser than your understanding; learning results in earning.

Money is plentiful in the U.S. It's just that only a few people ever **learn** the laws of its acquisition. The U.S. has dazzling wealth and extreme poverty all crowded together with no real system of isolation. You can find penniless beggars in some of the wealthiest parts of the country. *All the raw materials necessary for you to become wealthy are within your reach* here in the U.S.

Step 1. Read! If you are reading this sentence you have a substantial advantage—you can read. You have a brain and you learned how to read. If you can read, you can learn; if you can learn, you can get rich. How? Read! I encourage you to go to a public library, a big one; you will be absolutely astounded at the amount of information on wealth creation available.

To get more wealth you must become a student of wealth. That is you must *study wealth creation*. Get books and read, read, read! Waiting around for someone else to give you money puts you on the fast track to poverty and pennilessness. Some people think two or three manual labor jobs are the keys to wealth. Physical laboring is **NOT** the way to get rich; there is no fortune or future in manual labor jobs. Mental laboring always has been and still is the only way to fortune. Many people work,

work, work and are still poor, getting nowhere. Priceless knowledge is waiting for you in the public library, and the cost of a library card is still nothing. It doesn't get any easier than free. You don't have to clean toilets fourteen hours a day, you only need to read!

You could also visit a bookstore. Wealth creation just happens to be quite popular there. Very good practical books, understandable by even those with limited formal education, await your arrival. In fact some of the finest books on wealth and business were written by people who only have a high school education or less! I am not against a college education. However, it isn't required in order to become a self-made millionaire or billionaire. The truth of this statement is self-evident—study the life histories or teachings of self-made millionaires and you will see that this is true.

Step 2. Study those who are successful with money to see what they did. Find out how others became rich and do similar things to what they did. The principles of wealth creation are always the same. The exact methods always vary. Seek out those who know and who are successful in wealth creation. Take them out to lunch or dinner and ask them for help and guidance. (Be sure you pick up the tab!) The amount of information and ideas you could gather from one on one conversation like that is incredible. Ask them to tell you their story of how they made it. Don't ask them for money, ask them for **information**; in the end it will be worth much more to you.

Do you know anyone who started out with you but now has outstripped you financially? They "made it" so to speak, and you didn't? What did they do? In two words: WHAT HAPPENED? Wouldn't you like to know? *To earn more you must learn more.*

Step 3. Set a specific dollar amount as a personal money goal to be obtained by a specified date. Most people have little money because they never really set any money goals. They don't study wealth creation. They don't ask people who are wealthy how they did it. In other words, they never really try to get rich!

Many people when they look back on their lives find they did succeed at getting most of the things they truly desired, but few actually set any money goals. They may have said they wanted to be rich or have plenty of money, but that wasn't a goal, it was only a whim. Money goals must be turned into concrete plans of action with milestones, deadlines, definite numbers, and timeframes. Time and study are the requirements. Everyone has time. It's equal for all; everyone gets twenty-four hours in a day. How you *spend* it is the *trick!* Set your money goals, write them down, and make it your burning desire to amass a personal fortune!

Step 4. The habit of purposeful systematic saving. *A portion of all you earn is by Universal Rights yours to keep.* How much of your earnings do you keep for yourself? What percentage of your income? Do you spend it all? Surely you don't spend it all and keep none for yourself! Are you like the foolish knave who spends **more** than they earn? I certainly hope not!

Those who keep none of their earnings for themselves may give some to the grocer, the restaurateur, the carmaker, the landlord, the clothes maker, and spend the rest or more on trinkets they do not *need*. What a pity—they forgot to pay themselves! After forty years or more of hard labor they may have saved nothing; worse yet, they may *owe* money! That's worse than working for nothing! What if you get into this habit of spending all you make for five years, ten years, forty years? AT THE END OF A LIFETIME OF LABOR YOU WILL HAVE NOTHING! Sadly enough that's **REALITY** in the U.S., as the government statistics at the beginning of this lesson illustrate. That's the trap that catches practically everyone in the U.S. What a colossal financial prison!

Slaves used to work for a master in the U.S. before the Civil War. The master provided them only with food, clothing, and shelter. They had no money or chance to become wealthy. They were not free; they had no freedom to accumulate riches on their own. Are you a slave? Do you lead the lifestyle of a free person, or are you following the lifestyle of a slave? Be sure to pay yourself first. How much should I save, you ask? At least 10% of your income. Protect your financial freedom; save at least 10% of all you earn, right off the top. Pay yourself first and live free. Financial independence can be yours! Laboring for others is okay, but labor for yourself too. *A portion of all you earn is by Universal Rights yours to keep.*

Step 5. Invest the interest from your savings. How much would you save if you saved 10% of your income for ten years at 10% interest? Even the slow-witted will be quick to respond, roughly one year's salary. However, you may get raises during that ten years, increasing your base salary. So you would have *more* than your first year's annual salary.

The next step to follow is to *invest the interest your savings earns as well.* Don't be foolish and steal from your own fortune by spending the interest that your 10% savings is providing. That's the second mistake most people make. They don't reinvest the interest gained from their savings. The wealth tree grows from a tiny seed; the sooner you plant, the sooner it grows. Fertilize and water it with consistent interest and deposits. In this way it will bear fruit for you much sooner.

10 Basic Rules of Wealth Creation

Principle: Reality is a harsh taskmaster; ignorance of the rules is no excuse.

1. Discipline yourself to live on less than you earn. Save 10% or more of your income.

Your "necessary" expenses will always grow to match or exceed your income unless you employ self-discipline. Don't confuse your "wants" with necessary expenses. You may want a new shiny red sports car, but your rusty brown station wagon works just fine. You generate the proper appreciation for money if you truly earn what you buy instead of buying on credit, running yourself into debt by immediately satisfying one capricious want after another.

If you think rich people have the ability to gratify *all* their wants, you are in error. Human wants are endless; therefore you must pick and choose only what you strongly desire.

As you discipline yourself to live on less than you earn, saving the rest, you'll quickly find it just as easy or hard as before. However, something new will begin to happen: temptation will enter your life as your money hoard grows. You'll be tempted to spend it all. You must refrain from this activity!

This little story may inspire you. A father is talking to his ragged-clothed daughter sitting on his knee. She asks, "Papa, why are we so poor?" He answers, "I don't really know." But in his mind he does know. He thinks to himself, "Because I didn't realize I was spending our family's fortune when I gambled, bought alcohol and unnecessary trinkets. I spent it foolishly, honey, little by little, day by day. I saved nothing for our future. I worked hard, I was honest, but I never learned about money. I never studied wealth. Now we have nothing and I can provide but little for your future. I labored very hard with my hands and my back all my life, but I never worked with my head. I never really learned the rules of wealth creation. I had plenty of time to learn but I didn't study, I never set any money goals. My squandering of our family's potential fortune and my irresponsibility forces us to now live in utter squalor. I did not read, I did not study. Now you must pay for my ignorance! Please forgive me, honey. I just didn't KNOW!" *Reality is a harsh taskmaster; ignorance of the rules is no excuse.* The rest of the rules of wealth creation are now stated so you WILL know!

2. Make a monthly budget and follow it religiously. As you allocate quantities of money each month for specific purposes, don't dip into other pools and spend foolishly. For example, spend food money on food not clothing. Never spend the 10% you are saving for retirement. Allow that to be your greatest desire, which is being fulfilled. Your monthly budget is the wall of defense protecting your fortune from the razor-sharp bite of the poverty vultures.

3. Reinvest the interest from the 10% you are saving for retirement and save that as well. In this way, the money will all be compounding, working in harmony, in a concerted focused effort to be fruitful and multiply. The money itself will gain definiteness of purpose, its purpose being that of growth! Your money will then be *magnetized*, causing it in turn to attract more money, and so on and so forth. The money turns active and dynamic, taking on a personality of its own. As it grows it becomes alive, for it will be your life saver when you retire.

4. Don't kill your fortune. Guard your living treasure from others who want to snatch it from you. People will try to get you into shady investments when they learn of your winter storehouse. Reject what sounds too good to be true, because it is. Keep your fortune safe where you can reclaim it if an emergency arises. The twin powers of **greed** and **temptation** will try to kill your fortune. Shield it from them with the iron will of self-discipline.

5. Seek out those who know how to handle money. Family members and friends are not necessarily the best people to ask. Ask professional financial planners *with successful track records!* Would you ask a race car driver how to lay brick or how to race cars? Would you ask a jeweler about carpentry or jewelry? Would you ask a welder about genetic engineering or welding? Ask successful professional financial planners about planning finances! But be sure to thoroughly check them out. Some of them will take your money in return for *poor* advice!

6. Become competent in handling money yourself. Obtain basic money knowledge and become at least competent on wealth creation. As your savings grows you'll have a newfound sense of pride and independence, knowing you have made sound plans for your future. A sense of joy will fill your heart, a sense of confidence in your own competence and self-discipline. This will help you in more ways than just wealth creation. It will aid you as a person, building your mind, body, and spirit, knowing you are on the only safe fast track to fortune. You'll gain a greater sense of self-worth as well. No one should condemn a person for being wealthy, because they learned how to handle money.

7. Keep your savings safe. Don't take large risks with your savings. A small return on investment is more desirable than losing it all. Gamblers aren't known to be very wealthy. Get-rich-quick schemes seldom if ever work! Don't become a miser either, saving 90% and living on 10%—that's out of balance and it's not healthy or wise.

8. Own your own home. Get a house to live in and pay for it as quickly as possible. Paying rent to the landlord simultaneously builds his fortune and decreases yours! Real estate has always been a safe investment. A good degree of personal pride and satisfaction goes with owning your own dwelling. No matter how plain it may be, at least it is yours—a private place where you and your family can enjoy **unity**.

9. Prepare for misfortune with insurance: life, health, auto, home, disability. Plan for future income in case of emergency. Insure yourself, your children, and your family so you can handle unforeseen dangers in life. Without insurance a fortune can be reduced to pennies in a very short period of time.

Pivotal Rule

10. Cultivate your personal powers. Continue increasing your ability to earn more money with *skills and knowledge.* Network with those who know about money, and exchange information with them. Become wiser and more skillful in wealth creation. There is plenty of money for everyone. Abundance is all around you, so GO GET YOURS!

5 Golden Laws of Money

1. *Money comes easily and in variously increasing amounts to those with the self-discipline to save at least 10% of all they earn and reinvest the interest. The purpose of the saving is to create an estate for their future and their family's future.*
2. *Money works hard to make more money for the wise investor.*
3. *Money stays with cautious owners who invests it under the direction and care of those skilled in its handling. Wise investments multiply surprisingly fast!*
4. *Money runs from those unskilled in its handling. Those who invest it in areas that they are not familiar with or that are not approved of by successful financial planners will soon be without money.*
5. *Money runs from those who invest it in their romantic desires or in the advice of tricksters and schemers (get-rich-quick plans).*

There is no magic in wealth creation. It grows gradually, starting at zero and then steadily building from knowledge, self-discipline, and definiteness of purpose. Year in and year out, by bearing the small burden of consistent, purposeful *systematic saving*, you can achieve your final money goal.

If you are determined to create a personal fortune, you will achieve it, because it awaits all who have determination and definiteness of purpose. Your burning desire has a power that will take on a force of its own; guide this power with knowledge, and all the riches you want will be yours. The golden laws of money as well as the rules of wealth creation have a rich reward *in store* for those who know and abide by them. Poverty patiently awaits the heavy spendthrift, just around the corner *at the approach of winter.*

A Quick Formula to Get Out of Debt

This is a very simple formula you can use to dig your way out of debt. Live on 70% of your income, pay creditors 20%, and save 10%. Always save that 10%. You may live on less than 70% to pay your debts off sooner, but still save the 10%.

Make a list of all your debts and pay the highest-interest debts first. For example, if you have three debts at 18%, 12%, and 8% interest, pay the 18% interest debt first. Stick to this formula and you'll be saving (wealth creation), paying debts, and living on the same old paycheck. Try to dump raises and bonuses or any extra cash you generate into paying off debt or increasing investments.

Set a lifetime money goal of a certain dollar amount of annual income totally from your investments. That number will be your financial independence amount. Calculate how long it would take and how much you would need in order to be able to live solely from the income of your personal fortune. Work toward that end, year in and year out! The 10-20-70% formula is key: Save 10%, pay debts with 20%, and live on 70%. Force yourself to it, use your self-discipline to keep to this formula. You'll start to find money-saving opportunities everywhere, but only if you set a money goal!

Here is one money-saving method you can implement immediately. Negotiate on all your purchases and search for deals. If I told you could save six thousand dollars in twenty minutes, most people would be very interested. It is quite realistic to get six thousand dollars off the price of a twenty-five thousand dollar car in twenty minutes of negotiating. My wife and I personally got four thousand dollars off a used truck in twenty minutes, and we probably could have gotten much more! Ego is all that stands in the way of most people saving by negotiation. Is the nobler person the one who throws money away or the one who saves money?

A Surefire Method to Become a Self-Made Millionaire

Principle: If you don't save any money, you'll never have any money.

If you examine the *"Awakening Charts"* on the following pages, you will see some eye-opening figures. Each chart contains examples of annual incomes, quarterly compounded rates of return, savings as a percent of income, and yearly salary increases. The charts are calculated based on a thirty-year working lifetime, deleting inflation and tax rate effects, since these will vary over time.

Look at Awakening Chart #1 in the annual income of $20,000 per year column (which a bright high school graduate could garner with some business savvy and interviewing skills). Let's say the person invested 10% of their income in an investment yielding a 10% rate of return (10% yield is the standard textbook figure based on decades of stock market averaging). If the individual didn't get a single raise to boost their annual income, in thirty years time they could retire having an annual income of $35,367, (10% return on $353,678), or nearly twice what they were earning for the past thirty years.

If they made $25,000 per year they would have close to half a million dollars stored *away for winter*. Remember, this chart assumes no increase in annual input of savings for the thirty-year time period; you save only 10% per year, or $2,500, and you only earn 10% on your investment. Most people would get raises in thirty years, hopefully making more than they started at after thirty years time! If you and your helpmate had a combined income of $50,000 per year, by following this plan you could retire almost millionaires at $884,194 (see column at $50,000 annual income).

In Awakening Chart #2 our *worker bee* is getting a little smarter. They are now saving 15% of their annual income, but still never got a raise or increased their annual input of savings. At a starting and finishing salary of only $20,000 per year, they retire with well over half a million dollars and an annual income of $53,051 (10% of $530,516) per year—almost two and a half times what they made for the past thirty years!

The person with $30,000 per year income is almost a millionaire at $795,775 from saving 15%. The person with $40,000 per year income strikes pay dirt, becoming a bona fide millionaire! Imagine that, a millionaire from a 15% payroll deduction for thirty years at a $40,000 annual income. You wouldn't even feel it and you could retire a millionaire after thirty years. At all incomes equal to or above $40,000 per year, saving 15% at a 10% rate of return would make you a **MILLIONAIRE** in thirty years.

The squeeze is on in Awakening Chart #3. Our savvy investor saves 20% per year, still too ignorant to ever get even a small raise. However, after thirty years of hard labor on only a $20,000 annual salary, they would have $707,355 packed way, retiring on an annual income of $70,735—almost four times what they made for the past thirty years. The $25,000 annual income person is almost a millionaire at $884,194. Everyone over $30,000 annual income retires a millionaire. The $50,000 per year person or couple are almost **MULTIMILLIONAIRES**. How about that!

Now, we'll be a little more realistic in Awakening Chart #4. We'll assume our would-be investor can manage at least a 5% raise each year at a starting salary of $20,000 per year, consistently saving 10% of their income annually. After thirty years they've got over half a million in the kitty. The $30,000 per year starter is almost a millionaire, and the $40,000 per year starter gets inducted into the millionaire's club for sure!

Look at Awakening Chart #5. The numbers start to jump up even quicker here. With a starting salary of $20,000 per year, with annual salary increases of 5%, saving 15% at a 10% rate of return produces over half a million after only twenty-six years, and after thirty they are almost a millionaire. Everyone starting at $25,000 annually or more cashes out millionaires! The $50,000 per year and above starters cash out multimillionaires.

The heat is on in Awakening Chart #6. Saving 20% of annual salary, starting at $20,000 with salary increases of 5% per year, at a 10% rate of return, after working thirty years our savvy saver cashes out at over one million dollars! We finally got the $20,000 per year starter in the big money club, and look how our $35,000 per year starter wound up, almost into the **big money** double millionaire club, along with everyone else at $35,000 per year and above. Look what the $50,000 per year person did, a millionaire almost three times over! How about them apples!

In Awakening Chart #7 we increase our interest rate of return to 12%, which is possible in a good investment—our $20,000 per year starter reads up on investing a little, saves 20%, but still can't get a raise in thirty years (personality problems of course!). But look, they still cash in their working chips at well over a million. They retire on an annual income of $107,437 (assuming only a 10% rate of return), over six times their ending salary, representing a 165% raise (the raise was worth the wait after all!). Our $40,000 per year person is a multimillionaire, and the $50,000 per year person has over two and a half million.

In our last chart, Awakening Chart #8, our worker bee burns out early after only twenty-five years. They earned a 12% rate of return, saved a strong 20%, did well with raises of 5% per year starting at $20,000. They are almost a millionaire with $838,698 in savings. (Not bad since they may not have started saving a dime until age 40 and can retire comfortably at age 65.) The $25,000 annual income starter retires a millionaire, as well as everyone else with only twenty-five years of work.

Now I urge you to study these awakening charts very carefully. There is nothing magical about them. I'm deliberately trying to show you that **it's not necessary to wind up broke and embarrassed at age 65!** If you look at the charts you can get some idea of the financial *possibilities* without much effort at all. Some people say, "Well, I can't afford to save anything." My answer: "Well, you'll never have anything." *If you don't save any money, you won't ever have any money, and that's a very safe bet!*

AWAKENING CHART #1
HOW MUCH MONEY YOU WILL HAVE

	$20,000		$25,000		$30,000		$35,000		$40,000		$45,000		$50,000	
ANNUAL INCOME	10%		10%		10%		10%		10%		10%		10%	
RATE OF RETURN	10%		10%		10%		10%		10%		10%		10%	
SAVINGS AS A % OF INCOME	0%		0%		0%		0%		0%		0%		0%	
YEARLY SALARY INCREASE														
YEAR	ADDITION	BALANCE	ADDITION	BALANCE	ADDITION	BALANCE	ADDITION	BALANCE	ADDITION	BALANCE	ADDITION	BALANCE	ADDITION	BALANCE
1	$2,000	$2,000	$2,500	$2,500	$3,000	$3,000	$3,500	$3,500	$4,000	$4,000	$4,500	$4,500	$5,000	$5,000
2	2,000	4,208	2,500	5,260	3,000	6,311	3,500	7,363	4,000	8,415	4,500	9,467	5,000	10,519
3	2,000	6,644	2,500	8,306	3,000	9,967	3,500	11,628	4,000	13,289	4,500	14,950	5,000	16,611
4	2,000	9,334	2,500	11,668	3,000	14,001	3,500	16,335	4,000	18,668	4,500	21,002	5,000	23,336
5	2,000	12,303	2,500	15,379	3,000	18,455	3,500	21,531	4,000	24,606	4,500	27,682	5,000	30,758
6	2,000	15,580	2,500	19,476	3,000	23,371	3,500	27,266	4,000	31,161	4,500	35,056	5,000	38,951
7	2,000	19,198	2,500	23,997	3,000	28,797	3,500	33,596	4,000	38,396	4,500	43,195	5,000	47,995
8	2,000	23,191	2,500	28,989	3,000	34,786	3,500	40,584	4,000	46,382	4,500	52,180	5,000	57,977
9	2,000	27,598	2,500	34,498	3,000	41,398	3,500	48,297	4,000	55,197	4,500	62,096	5,000	68,996
10	2,000	32,463	2,500	40,579	3,000	48,695	3,500	56,811	4,000	64,927	4,500	73,043	5,000	81,159
11	2,000	37,834	2,500	47,292	3,000	56,750	3,500	66,209	4,000	75,667	4,500	85,126	5,000	94,584
12	2,000	43,761	2,500	54,702	3,000	65,642	3,500	76,582	4,000	87,522	4,500	98,463	5,000	109,403
13	2,000	50,304	2,500	62,880	3,000	75,456	3,500	88,032	4,000	100,608	4,500	113,184	5,000	125,761
14	2,000	57,526	2,500	71,908	3,000	86,290	3,500	100,671	4,000	115,053	4,500	129,434	5,000	143,816
15	2,000	65,498	2,500	81,873	3,000	98,248	3,500	114,622	4,000	130,997	4,500	147,371	5,000	163,746
16	2,000	74,298	2,500	92,872	3,000	111,447	3,500	130,021	4,000	148,596	4,500	167,170	5,000	185,745
17	2,000	84,011	2,500	105,014	3,000	126,017	3,500	147,019	4,000	168,022	4,500	189,025	5,000	210,028
18	2,000	94,733	2,500	118,416	3,000	142,099	3,500	165,782	4,000	189,465	4,500	213,148	5,000	236,831
19	2,000	106,567	2,500	133,209	3,000	159,850	3,500	186,492	4,000	213,134	4,500	239,776	5,000	266,417
20	2,000	119,630	2,500	149,537	3,000	179,445	3,500	209,352	4,000	239,260	4,500	269,167	5,000	299,075
21	2,000	134,049	2,500	167,561	3,000	201,074	3,500	234,586	4,000	268,098	4,500	301,611	5,000	335,123
22	2,000	149,965	2,500	187,456	3,000	224,948	3,500	262,439	4,000	299,930	4,500	337,422	5,000	374,913
23	2,000	167,533	2,500	209,417	3,000	251,300	3,500	293,184	4,000	335,067	4,500	376,950	5,000	418,834
24	2,000	186,926	2,500	233,657	3,000	280,388	3,500	327,120	4,000	373,851	4,500	420,583	5,000	467,314
25	2,000	208,331	2,500	260,414	3,000	312,496	3,500	364,579	4,000	416,662	4,500	468,745	5,000	520,827
26	2,000	231,958	2,500	289,948	3,000	347,937	3,500	405,927	4,000	463,917	4,500	521,906	5,000	579,896
27	2,000	258,039	2,500	322,548	3,000	387,058	3,500	451,568	4,000	516,077	4,500	580,587	5,000	645,096
28	2,000	286,826	2,500	358,533	3,000	430,239	3,500	501,946	4,000	573,653	4,500	645,359	5,000	717,066
29	2,000	318,603	2,500	398,253	3,000	477,904	3,500	557,555	4,000	637,205	4,500	716,856	5,000	796,506
30	2,000	353,678	2,500	442,097	3,000	530,516	3,500	618,936	4,000	707,355	4,500	795,775	5,000	884,194

AWAKENING CHART #2
HOW MUCH MONEY YOU WILL HAVE

ANNUAL INCOME	$20,000		$25,000		$30,000		$35,000		$40,000		$45,000		$50,000	
RATE OF RETURN	10%		10%		10%		10%		10%		10%		10%	
SAVINGS AS A % OF INCOME	15%		15%		15%		15%		15%		15%		15%	
YEARLY SALARY INCREASE	0%		0%		0%		0%		0%		0%		0%	
YEAR	ADDITION	BALANCE	ADDITION	BALANCE	ADDITION	BALANCE	ADDITION	BALANCE	ADDITION	BALANCE	ADDITION	BALANCE	ADDITION	BALANCE
1	$3,000	$3,000	$3,750	$3,750	$4,500	$4,500	$5,250	$5,250	$6,000	$6,000	$6,750	$6,750	$7,500	$7,500
2	3,000	6,311	3,750	7,889	4,500	9,467	5,250	11,045	6,000	12,623	6,750	14,201	7,500	15,779
3	3,000	9,967	3,750	12,458	4,500	14,950	5,250	17,442	6,000	19,933	6,750	22,425	7,500	24,917
4	3,000	14,001	3,750	17,502	4,500	21,002	5,250	24,502	6,000	28,003	6,750	31,503	7,500	35,003
5	3,000	18,455	3,750	23,069	4,500	27,682	5,250	32,296	6,000	36,910	6,750	41,523	7,500	46,137
6	3,000	23,371	3,750	29,213	4,500	35,056	5,250	40,899	6,000	46,741	6,750	52,584	7,500	58,427
7	3,000	28,797	3,750	35,996	4,500	43,195	5,250	50,395	6,000	57,594	6,750	64,793	7,500	71,992
8	3,000	34,786	3,750	43,483	4,500	52,180	5,250	60,876	6,000	69,573	6,750	78,269	7,500	86,966
9	3,000	41,398	3,750	51,747	4,500	62,096	5,250	72,446	6,000	82,795	6,750	93,145	7,500	103,494
10	3,000	48,695	3,750	60,869	4,500	73,043	5,250	85,217	6,000	97,390	6,750	109,564	7,500	121,738
11	3,000	56,750	3,750	70,938	4,500	85,126	5,250	99,313	6,000	113,501	6,750	127,688	7,500	141,876
12	3,000	65,642	3,750	82,052	4,500	98,463	5,250	114,873	6,000	131,284	6,750	147,694	7,500	164,105
13	3,000	75,456	3,750	94,320	4,500	113,184	5,250	132,049	6,000	150,913	6,750	169,777	7,500	188,641
14	3,000	86,290	3,750	107,862	4,500	129,434	5,250	151,007	6,000	172,579	6,750	194,152	7,500	215,724
15	3,000	98,248	3,750	122,810	4,500	147,371	5,250	171,933	6,000	196,495	6,750	221,057	7,500	245,619
16	3,000	111,447	3,750	139,309	4,500	167,170	5,250	195,032	6,000	222,894	6,750	250,756	7,500	278,617
17	3,000	126,017	3,750	157,521	4,500	189,025	5,250	220,529	6,000	252,033	6,750	283,537	7,500	315,042
18	3,000	142,099	3,750	177,623	4,500	213,148	5,250	248,673	6,000	284,198	6,750	319,722	7,500	355,247
19	3,000	159,850	3,750	199,813	4,500	239,776	5,250	279,738	6,000	319,701	6,750	359,664	7,500	399,626
20	3,000	179,445	3,750	224,306	4,500	269,167	5,250	314,029	6,000	358,890	6,750	403,751	7,500	448,612
21	3,000	201,074	3,750	251,342	4,500	301,611	5,250	351,879	6,000	402,147	6,750	452,416	7,500	502,684
22	3,000	224,948	3,750	281,185	4,500	337,422	5,250	393,659	6,000	449,895	6,750	506,132	7,500	562,369
23	3,000	251,300	3,750	314,125	4,500	376,950	5,250	439,775	6,000	502,600	6,750	565,425	7,500	628,251
24	3,000	280,388	3,750	350,486	4,500	420,583	5,250	490,680	6,000	560,777	6,750	630,874	7,500	700,971
25	3,000	312,496	3,750	390,620	4,500	468,745	5,250	546,869	6,000	624,993	6,750	703,117	7,500	781,241
26	3,000	347,937	3,750	434,922	4,500	521,906	5,250	608,891	6,000	695,875	6,750	782,859	7,500	869,844
27	3,000	387,058	3,750	483,822	4,500	580,587	5,250	677,351	6,000	774,116	6,750	870,880	7,500	967,645
28	3,000	430,239	3,750	537,799	4,500	645,359	5,250	752,919	6,000	860,479	6,750	968,039	7,500	1,075,599
29	3,000	477,904	3,750	597,380	4,500	716,856	5,250	836,332	6,000	955,808	6,750	1,075,284	7,500	1,194,760
30	3,000	530,516	3,750	663,146	4,500	795,775	5,250	928,404	6,000	1,061,033	6,750	1,193,662	7,500	1,326,291

AWAKENING CHART #3
HOW MUCH MONEY YOU WILL HAVE

ANNUAL INCOME	$20,000		$25,000		$30,000		$35,000		$40,000		$45,000		$50,000	
RATE OF RETURN	10%		10%		10%		10%		10%		10%		10%	
SAVINGS AS A % OF INCOME	20%		20%		20%		20%		20%		20%		20%	
YEARLY SALARY INCREASE	0%		0%		0%		0%		0%		0%		0%	
YEAR	ADDITION	BALANCE	ADDITION	BALANCE	ADDITION	BALANCE	ADDITION	BALANCE	ADDITION	BALANCE	ADDITION	BALANCE	ADDITION	BALANCE
1	$4,000	$4,000	$5,000	$5,000	$6,000	$6,000	$7,000	$7,000	$8,000	$8,000	$9,000	$9,000	$10,000	$10,000
2	4,000	8,415	5,000	10,519	6,000	12,623	7,000	14,727	8,000	16,831	9,000	18,934	10,000	21,038
3	4,000	13,289	5,000	16,611	6,000	19,933	7,000	23,256	8,000	26,578	9,000	29,900	10,000	33,222
4	4,000	18,668	5,000	23,336	6,000	28,003	7,000	32,670	8,000	37,337	9,000	42,004	10,000	46,671
5	4,000	24,606	5,000	30,758	6,000	36,910	7,000	43,061	8,000	49,213	9,000	55,364	10,000	61,516
6	4,000	31,161	5,000	38,951	6,000	46,741	7,000	54,532	8,000	62,322	9,000	70,112	10,000	77,902
7	4,000	38,396	5,000	47,995	6,000	57,594	7,000	67,193	8,000	76,792	9,000	86,391	10,000	95,990
8	4,000	46,382	5,000	57,977	6,000	69,573	7,000	81,168	8,000	92,764	9,000	104,359	10,000	115,954
9	4,000	55,197	5,000	68,996	6,000	82,795	7,000	96,594	8,000	110,394	9,000	124,193	10,000	137,992
10	4,000	64,927	5,000	81,159	6,000	97,390	7,000	113,622	8,000	129,854	9,000	146,086	10,000	162,317
11	4,000	75,667	5,000	94,584	6,000	113,501	7,000	132,418	8,000	151,334	9,000	170,251	10,000	189,168
12	4,000	87,522	5,000	109,403	6,000	131,284	7,000	153,164	8,000	175,045	9,000	196,926	10,000	218,806
13	4,000	100,608	5,000	125,761	6,000	150,913	7,000	176,065	8,000	201,217	9,000	226,369	10,000	251,521
14	4,000	115,053	5,000	143,816	6,000	172,579	7,000	201,342	8,000	230,106	9,000	258,869	10,000	287,632
15	4,000	130,997	5,000	163,746	6,000	196,495	7,000	229,244	8,000	261,994	9,000	294,743	10,000	327,492
16	4,000	148,596	5,000	185,745	6,000	222,894	7,000	260,043	8,000	297,192	9,000	334,341	10,000	371,490
17	4,000	168,022	5,000	210,028	6,000	252,033	7,000	294,039	8,000	336,044	9,000	378,050	10,000	420,055
18	4,000	189,465	5,000	236,831	6,000	284,198	7,000	331,564	8,000	378,930	9,000	426,296	10,000	473,663
19	4,000	213,134	5,000	266,417	6,000	319,701	7,000	372,984	8,000	426,268	9,000	479,551	10,000	532,835
20	4,000	239,260	5,000	299,075	6,000	358,890	7,000	418,705	8,000	478,520	9,000	538,335	10,000	598,150
21	4,000	268,098	5,000	335,123	6,000	402,147	7,000	469,172	8,000	536,197	9,000	603,221	10,000	670,246
22	4,000	299,930	5,000	374,913	6,000	449,895	7,000	524,878	8,000	599,861	9,000	674,843	10,000	749,826
23	4,000	335,067	5,000	418,834	6,000	502,600	7,000	586,367	8,000	670,134	9,000	753,901	10,000	837,667
24	4,000	373,851	5,000	467,314	6,000	560,777	7,000	654,240	8,000	747,702	9,000	841,165	10,000	934,628
25	4,000	416,662	5,000	520,827	6,000	624,993	7,000	729,158	8,000	833,324	9,000	937,489	10,000	1,041,654
26	4,000	463,917	5,000	579,896	6,000	695,875	7,000	811,854	8,000	927,833	9,000	1,043,812	10,000	1,159,792
27	4,000	516,077	5,000	645,096	6,000	774,116	7,000	903,135	8,000	1,032,154	9,000	1,161,174	10,000	1,290,193
28	4,000	573,653	5,000	717,066	6,000	860,479	7,000	1,003,892	8,000	1,147,305	9,000	1,290,718	10,000	1,434,132
29	4,000	637,205	5,000	796,506	6,000	955,808	7,000	1,115,109	8,000	1,274,410	9,000	1,433,712	10,000	1,593,013
30	4,000	707,355	5,000	884,194	6,000	1,061,033	7,000	1,237,872	8,000	1,414,711	9,000	1,591,549	10,000	1,768,388

AWAKENING CHART #4
HOW MUCH MONEY YOU WILL HAVE

ANNUAL INCOME	$20,000		$25,000		$30,000		$35,000		$40,000		$45,000		$50,000	
RATE OF RETURN	10%		10%		10%		10%		10%		10%		10%	
SAVINGS AS A % OF INCOME	10%		10%		10%		10%		10%		10%		10%	
YEARLY SALARY INCREASE	5%		5%		5%		5%		5%		5%		5%	
YEAR	ADDITION	BALANCE	ADDITION	BALANCE	ADDITION	BALANCE	ADDITION	BALANCE	ADDITION	BALANCE	ADDITION	BALANCE	ADDITION	BALANCE
1	$2,000	$2,000	$2,500	$2,500	$3,000	$3,000	$3,500	$3,500	$4,000	$4,000	$4,500	$4,500	$5,000	$5,000
2	2,100	4,308	2,625	5,385	3,150	6,461	3,675	7,538	4,200	8,615	4,725	9,692	5,250	10,769
3	2,205	6,960	2,756	8,700	3,308	10,440	3,859	12,180	4,410	13,920	4,961	15,660	5,513	17,400
4	2,315	9,998	2,894	12,497	3,473	14,996	4,052	17,496	4,631	19,995	5,209	22,495	5,788	24,994
5	2,431	13,466	3,039	16,833	3,647	20,200	4,254	23,566	4,862	26,933	5,470	30,300	6,078	33,666
6	2,553	17,417	3,191	21,771	3,829	26,126	4,467	30,480	5,105	34,834	5,743	39,188	6,381	43,543
7	2,680	21,905	3,350	27,382	4,020	32,858	4,690	38,334	5,360	43,811	6,030	49,287	6,700	54,763
8	2,814	26,994	3,518	33,742	4,221	40,490	4,925	47,239	5,628	53,987	6,332	60,736	7,036	67,484
9	2,955	32,751	3,694	40,938	4,432	49,126	5,171	57,314	5,910	65,502	6,649	73,689	7,387	81,877
10	3,103	39,253	3,878	49,067	4,654	58,880	5,430	68,693	6,205	78,507	6,981	88,320	7,757	98,133
11	3,258	46,586	4,072	58,233	4,887	69,879	5,701	81,526	6,516	93,172	7,330	104,819	8,144	116,465
12	3,421	54,843	4,276	68,554	5,131	82,265	5,986	95,975	6,841	109,686	7,697	123,397	8,552	137,108
13	3,592	64,128	4,490	80,160	5,388	96,192	6,285	112,224	7,183	128,256	8,081	144,289	8,979	160,321
14	3,771	74,557	4,714	93,196	5,657	111,835	6,600	130,475	7,543	149,114	8,485	167,753	9,428	186,392
15	3,960	86,257	4,950	107,821	5,940	129,385	6,930	150,949	7,920	172,513	8,910	194,078	9,900	215,642
16	4,158	99,369	5,197	124,211	6,237	149,054	7,276	173,896	8,316	198,738	9,355	223,581	10,395	248,423
17	4,366	114,051	5,457	142,563	6,549	171,076	7,640	199,589	8,731	228,101	9,823	256,614	10,914	285,127
18	4,584	130,475	5,730	163,093	6,876	195,712	8,022	228,331	9,168	260,949	10,314	293,568	11,460	326,187
19	4,813	148,833	6,017	186,041	7,220	223,249	8,423	260,457	9,626	297,666	10,830	334,874	12,033	372,082
20	5,054	169,337	6,317	211,672	7,581	254,006	8,844	296,341	10,108	338,675	11,371	381,009	12,635	423,344
21	5,307	192,224	6,633	240,279	7,960	288,335	9,287	336,391	10,613	384,447	11,940	432,503	13,266	480,559
22	5,572	217,751	6,965	272,188	8,358	326,626	9,751	381,064	11,144	435,501	12,537	489,939	13,930	544,377
23	5,851	246,207	7,313	307,758	8,776	369,310	10,238	430,861	11,701	492,413	13,164	553,965	14,626	615,516
24	6,143	277,909	7,679	347,386	9,215	416,864	10,750	486,341	12,286	555,818	13,822	625,295	15,358	694,773
25	6,450	313,210	8,063	391,512	9,675	469,815	11,288	548,117	12,900	626,420	14,513	704,722	16,125	783,024
26	6,773	352,498	8,466	440,622	10,159	528,747	11,852	616,871	13,545	704,995	15,239	793,120	16,932	881,244
27	7,111	396,203	8,889	495,254	10,667	594,304	12,445	693,355	14,223	792,406	16,001	891,456	17,778	990,507
28	7,467	444,801	9,334	556,001	11,200	667,201	13,067	778,401	14,934	889,601	16,801	1,000,802	18,667	1,112,002
29	7,840	498,817	9,800	623,521	11,760	748,226	13,720	872,930	15,681	997,634	17,641	1,122,338	19,601	1,247,043
30	8,232	558,833	10,290	698,541	12,348	838,249	14,406	977,958	16,465	1,117,666	18,523	1,257,374	20,581	1,397,082

AWAKENING CHART #5
HOW MUCH MONEY YOU WILL HAVE

ANNUAL INCOME	$20,000		$25,000		$30,000		$35,000		$40,000		$45,000		$50,000	
RATE OF RETURN	10%		10%		10%		10%		10%		10%		10%	
SAVINGS AS A % OF INCOME	15%		15%		15%		15%		15%		15%		15%	
YEARLY SALARY INCREASE	5%		5%		5%		5%		5%		5%		5%	
YEAR	ADDITION	BALANCE	ADDITION	BALANCE	ADDITION	BALANCE	ADDITION	BALANCE	ADDITION	BALANCE	ADDITION	BALANCE	ADDITION	BALANCE
1	$3,000	$3,000	$3,750	$3,750	$4,500	$4,500	$5,250	$5,250	$6,000	$6,000	$6,750	$6,750	$7,500	$7,500
2	3,150	6,461	3,938	8,077	4,725	9,692	5,513	11,308	6,300	12,923	7,088	14,538	7,875	16,154
3	3,307	10,440	4,134	13,050	4,961	15,660	5,788	18,270	6,615	20,879	7,442	23,489	8,269	26,099
4	3,473	14,996	4,341	18,745	5,209	22,495	6,078	26,244	6,946	29,993	7,814	33,742	8,682	37,491
5	3,647	20,200	4,558	25,250	5,470	30,300	6,381	35,349	7,293	40,399	8,205	45,449	9,116	50,499
6	3,829	26,126	4,786	32,657	5,743	39,188	6,700	45,720	7,658	52,251	8,615	58,782	9,572	65,314
7	4,020	32,858	5,025	41,072	6,030	49,287	7,036	57,501	8,041	65,716	9,046	73,930	10,051	82,145
8	4,221	40,490	5,277	50,613	6,332	60,736	7,387	70,858	8,443	80,981	9,498	91,103	10,553	101,226
9	4,432	49,126	5,540	61,408	6,649	73,689	7,757	85,971	8,865	98,252	9,973	110,534	11,081	122,815
10	4,654	58,880	5,817	73,600	6,981	88,320	8,144	103,040	9,308	117,760	10,471	132,480	11,635	147,200
11	4,887	69,879	6,108	87,349	7,330	104,819	8,552	122,289	9,773	139,759	10,995	157,228	12,217	174,698
12	5,131	82,265	6,414	102,831	7,697	123,397	8,979	143,963	10,262	164,529	11,545	185,096	12,828	205,662
13	5,388	96,192	6,734	120,240	8,081	144,289	9,428	168,337	10,775	192,385	12,122	216,433	13,469	240,481
14	5,657	111,835	7,071	139,794	8,485	167,753	9,900	195,712	11,314	223,671	12,728	251,629	14,142	279,588
15	5,940	129,385	7,425	161,731	8,910	194,078	10,395	226,424	11,880	258,770	13,365	291,116	14,849	323,463
16	6,237	149,054	7,796	186,317	9,355	223,581	10,914	260,844	12,474	298,107	14,033	335,371	15,592	372,634
17	6,549	171,076	8,186	213,845	9,823	256,614	11,460	299,383	13,097	342,152	14,734	384,921	16,372	427,690
18	6,876	195,712	8,595	244,640	10,314	293,568	12,033	342,496	13,752	391,424	15,471	440,352	17,190	489,280
19	7,220	223,249	9,025	279,062	10,830	334,874	12,635	390,686	14,440	446,498	16,245	502,311	18,050	558,123
20	7,581	254,006	9,476	317,508	11,371	381,009	13,266	444,511	15,162	508,012	17,057	571,514	18,952	635,016
21	7,960	288,335	9,950	360,419	11,940	432,503	13,930	504,587	15,920	576,671	17,910	648,754	19,900	720,838
22	8,358	326,626	10,447	408,283	12,537	489,939	14,626	571,596	16,716	653,252	18,805	734,909	20,895	816,565
23	8,776	369,310	10,970	461,637	13,164	553,965	15,358	646,292	17,552	738,620	19,746	830,947	21,939	923,275
24	9,215	416,864	11,518	521,079	13,822	625,295	16,125	729,511	18,429	833,727	20,733	937,943	23,036	1,042,159
25	9,675	469,815	12,094	587,268	14,513	704,722	16,932	822,176	19,351	939,629	21,769	1,057,083	24,188	1,174,537
26	10,159	528,747	12,699	660,933	15,239	793,120	17,778	925,306	20,318	1,057,493	22,858	1,189,680	25,398	1,321,866
27	10,667	594,304	13,334	742,880	16,001	891,456	18,667	1,040,032	21,334	1,188,609	24,001	1,337,185	26,668	1,485,761
28	11,200	667,201	14,000	834,001	16,801	1,000,802	19,601	1,167,602	22,401	1,334,402	25,201	1,501,202	28,001	1,668,003
29	11,760	748,226	14,700	935,282	17,641	1,122,338	20,581	1,309,395	23,521	1,496,451	26,461	1,683,507	29,401	1,870,564
30	12,348	838,249	15,436	1,047,812	18,523	1,257,374	21,610	1,466,936	24,697	1,676,499	27,784	1,886,061	30,871	2,095,623

AWAKENING CHART #6
HOW MUCH MONEY YOU WILL HAVE

ANNUAL INCOME	$20,000		$25,000		$30,000		$35,000		$40,000		$45,000		$50,000	
RATE OF RETURN	10%		10%		10%		10%		10%		10%		10%	
SAVINGS AS A % OF INCOME	20%		20%		20%		20%		20%		20%		20%	
YEARLY SALARY INCREASE	5%		5%		5%		5%		5%		5%		5%	
YEAR	ADDITION	BALANCE	ADDITION	BALANCE	ADDITION	BALANCE	ADDITION	BALANCE	ADDITION	BALANCE	ADDITION	BALANCE	ADDITION	BALANCE
1	$4,000	$4,000	$5,000	$5,000	$6,000	$6,000	$7,000	$7,000	$8,000	$8,000	$9,000	$9,000	$10,000	$10,000
2	4,200	8,615	5,250	10,769	6,300	12,923	7,350	15,077	8,400	17,231	9,450	19,384	10,500	21,538
3	4,410	13,920	5,513	17,400	6,615	20,879	7,718	24,359	8,820	27,839	9,923	31,319	11,025	34,799
4	4,631	19,995	5,788	24,994	6,946	29,993	8,103	34,992	9,261	39,990	10,419	44,989	11,576	49,988
5	4,862	26,933	6,078	33,666	7,293	40,399	8,509	47,133	9,724	53,866	10,940	60,599	12,155	67,332
6	5,105	34,834	6,381	43,543	7,658	52,251	8,934	60,960	10,210	69,668	11,487	78,377	12,763	87,085
7	5,360	43,811	6,700	54,763	8,041	65,716	9,381	76,669	10,721	87,621	12,061	98,574	13,401	109,527
8	5,628	53,987	7,036	67,484	8,443	80,981	9,850	94,478	11,257	107,974	12,664	121,471	14,071	134,968
9	5,910	65,502	7,387	81,877	8,865	98,252	10,342	114,628	11,820	131,003	13,297	147,379	14,775	163,754
10	6,205	78,507	7,757	98,133	9,308	117,760	10,859	137,387	12,411	157,014	13,962	176,640	15,513	196,267
11	6,516	93,172	8,144	116,465	9,773	139,759	11,402	163,052	13,031	186,345	14,660	209,638	16,289	232,931
12	6,841	109,686	8,552	137,108	10,262	164,529	11,972	191,951	13,683	219,372	15,393	246,794	17,103	274,216
13	7,183	128,256	8,979	160,321	10,775	192,385	12,571	224,449	14,367	256,513	16,163	288,577	17,959	320,641
14	7,543	149,114	9,428	186,392	11,314	223,671	13,200	260,949	15,085	298,228	16,971	335,506	18,856	372,784
15	7,920	172,513	9,900	215,642	11,880	258,770	13,860	301,899	15,839	345,027	17,819	388,155	19,799	431,284
16	8,316	198,738	10,395	248,423	12,474	298,107	14,552	347,792	16,631	397,477	18,710	447,161	20,789	496,846
17	8,731	228,101	10,914	285,127	13,097	342,152	15,280	399,177	17,463	456,203	19,646	513,228	21,829	570,253
18	9,168	260,949	11,460	326,187	13,752	391,424	16,044	456,661	18,336	521,899	20,628	587,136	22,920	652,373
19	9,626	297,666	12,033	372,082	14,440	446,498	16,846	520,915	19,253	595,331	21,660	669,748	24,066	744,164
20	10,108	338,675	12,635	423,344	15,162	508,012	17,689	592,681	20,216	677,350	22,743	762,019	25,270	846,687
21	10,613	384,447	13,266	480,559	15,920	576,671	18,573	672,782	21,226	768,894	23,880	865,006	26,533	961,118
22	11,144	435,501	13,930	544,377	16,716	653,252	19,502	762,127	22,288	871,003	25,074	979,878	27,860	1,088,754
23	11,701	492,413	14,626	615,516	17,552	738,620	20,477	861,723	23,402	984,826	26,327	1,107,930	29,253	1,231,033
24	12,286	555,818	15,358	694,773	18,429	833,727	21,501	972,682	24,572	1,111,636	27,644	1,250,591	30,715	1,389,545
25	12,900	626,420	16,125	783,024	19,351	939,629	22,576	1,096,234	25,801	1,252,839	29,026	1,409,444	32,251	1,566,049
26	13,545	704,995	16,932	881,244	20,318	1,057,493	23,704	1,233,742	27,091	1,409,991	30,477	1,586,240	33,864	1,762,488
27	14,223	792,406	17,778	990,507	21,334	1,188,609	24,890	1,386,710	28,445	1,584,811	32,001	1,782,913	35,557	1,981,014
28	14,934	889,601	18,667	1,112,002	22,401	1,334,402	26,134	1,556,802	29,868	1,779,203	33,601	2,001,603	37,335	2,224,004
29	15,681	997,634	19,601	1,247,043	23,521	1,496,451	27,441	1,745,860	31,361	1,995,268	35,281	2,244,677	39,201	2,494,085
30	16,465	1,117,666	20,581	1,397,082	24,697	1,676,499	28,813	1,955,915	32,929	2,235,332	37,045	2,514,748	41,161	2,794,165

AWAKENING CHART #7
HOW MUCH MONEY YOU WILL HAVE

	$20,000		$25,000		$30,000		$35,000		$40,000		$45,000		$50,000	
ANNUAL INCOME	12%		12%		12%		12%		12%		12%		12%	
RATE OF RETURN	20%		20%		20%		20%		20%		20%		20%	
SAVINGS AS A % OF INCOME	0%		0%		0%		0%		0%		0%		0%	
YEARLY SALARY INCREASE														
YEAR	ADDITION	BALANCE	ADDITION	BALANCE	ADDITION	BALANCE	ADDITION	BALANCE	ADDITION	BALANCE	ADDITION	BALANCE	ADDITION	BALANCE
1	$4,000	$4,000	$5,000	$5,000	$6,000	$6,000	$7,000	$7,000	$8,000	$8,000	$9,000	$9,000	$10,000	$10,000
2	4,000	8,502	5,000	10,628	6,000	12,753	7,000	14,879	8,000	17,004	9,000	19,130	10,000	21,255
3	4,000	13,569	5,000	16,961	6,000	20,354	7,000	23,746	8,000	27,138	9,000	30,531	10,000	33,923
4	4,000	19,272	5,000	24,090	6,000	28,908	7,000	33,726	8,000	38,544	9,000	43,362	10,000	48,180
5	4,000	25,691	5,000	32,114	6,000	38,536	7,000	44,959	8,000	51,382	9,000	57,805	10,000	64,227
6	4,000	32,915	5,000	41,144	6,000	49,373	7,000	57,602	8,000	65,831	9,000	74,060	10,000	82,289
7	4,000	41,047	5,000	51,308	6,000	61,570	7,000	71,832	8,000	82,093	9,000	92,355	10,000	102,617
8	4,000	50,198	5,000	62,748	6,000	75,297	7,000	87,847	8,000	100,397	9,000	112,946	10,000	125,496
9	4,000	60,499	5,000	75,623	6,000	90,743	7,000	105,873	8,000	120,997	9,000	136,122	10,000	151,247
10	4,000	72,092	5,000	90,115	6,000	108,138	7,000	126,161	8,000	144,184	9,000	162,206	10,000	180,229
11	4,000	85,140	5,000	106,425	6,000	127,710	7,000	148,995	8,000	170,280	9,000	191,565	10,000	212,850
12	4,000	99,826	5,000	124,782	6,000	149,739	7,000	174,695	8,000	199,651	9,000	224,608	10,000	249,564
13	4,000	116,355	5,000	145,443	6,000	174,532	7,000	203,621	8,000	232,709	9,000	261,798	10,000	290,887
14	4,000	134,958	5,000	168,698	6,000	202,437	7,000	236,177	8,000	269,917	9,000	303,656	10,000	337,396
15	4,000	155,897	5,000	194,871	6,000	233,845	7,000	272,819	8,000	311,793	9,000	350,768	10,000	389,742
16	4,000	179,463	5,000	224,329	6,000	269,195	7,000	314,060	8,000	358,926	9,000	403,792	10,000	448,658
17	4,000	205,987	5,000	257,484	6,000	308,961	7,000	360,478	8,000	411,975	9,000	463,472	10,000	514,968
18	4,000	235,841	5,000	294,801	6,000	353,761	7,000	412,721	8,000	471,681	9,000	530,641	10,000	589,601
19	4,000	269,441	5,000	336,801	6,000	404,161	7,000	471,521	8,000	538,881	9,000	606,241	10,000	673,602
20	4,000	307,258	5,000	384,072	6,000	460,887	7,000	537,701	8,000	614,516	9,000	691,330	10,000	768,145
21	4,000	349,821	5,000	437,277	6,000	524,732	7,000	612,187	8,000	699,643	9,000	787,098	10,000	874,553
22	4,000	397,727	5,000	497,159	6,000	596,591	7,000	696,022	8,000	795,454	9,000	894,886	10,000	994,318
23	4,000	451,645	5,000	564,557	6,000	677,468	7,000	790,379	8,000	903,291	9,000	1,016,202	10,000	1,129,113
24	4,000	512,331	5,000	640,413	6,000	768,496	7,000	896,579	8,000	1,024,661	9,000	1,152,744	10,000	1,280,827
25	4,000	580,633	5,000	725,791	6,000	870,949	7,000	1,016,107	8,000	1,161,266	9,000	1,306,424	10,000	1,451,582
26	4,000	657,507	5,000	821,884	6,000	986,261	7,000	1,150,638	8,000	1,315,015	9,000	1,479,391	10,000	1,643,768
27	4,000	744,030	5,000	930,038	6,000	1,116,045	7,000	1,302,053	8,000	1,488,061	9,000	1,674,068	10,000	1,860,076
28	4,000	841,413	5,000	1,051,766	6,000	1,262,119	7,000	1,472,472	8,000	1,682,825	9,000	1,893,178	10,000	2,103,532
29	4,000	951,017	5,000	1,188,772	6,000	1,426,526	7,000	1,664,280	8,000	1,902,035	9,000	2,139,789	10,000	2,377,543
30	4,000	1,074,378	5,000	1,342,973	6,000	1,611,568	7,000	1,880,162	8,000	2,148,757	9,000	2,417,351	10,000	2,685,946

Copyright 1994, Michael Monroe Kiefer

AWAKENING CHART #8
HOW MUCH MONEY YOU WILL HAVE

ANNUAL INCOME	$20,000		$25,000		$30,000		$35,000		$40,000		$45,000		$50,000	
RATE OF RETURN	12%		12%		12%		12%		12%		12%		12%	
SAVINGS AS A % OF INCOME	20%		20%		20%		20%		20%		20%		20%	
YEARLY SALARY INCREASE	5%		5%		5%		5%		5%		5%		5%	
YEAR	ADDITION	BALANCE	ADDITION	BALANCE	ADDITION	BALANCE	ADDITION	BALANCE	ADDITION	BALANCE	ADDITION	BALANCE	ADDITION	BALANCE
1	$4,000	$4,000	$5,000	$5,000	$6,000	$6,000	$7,000	$7,000	$8,000	$8,000	$9,000	$9,000	$10,000	$10,000
2	4,200	8,702	5,250	10,878	6,300	13,053	7,350	15,229	8,400	17,404	9,450	19,580	10,500	21,755
3	4,410	14,204	5,513	17,755	6,615	21,306	7,718	24,857	8,820	28,408	9,923	31,959	11,025	35,511
4	4,631	20,617	5,788	25,772	6,946	30,926	8,103	36,081	9,261	41,235	10,419	46,389	11,576	51,544
5	4,862	28,067	6,078	35,084	7,293	42,101	8,509	49,118	9,724	56,134	10,940	63,151	12,155	70,168
6	5,105	36,695	6,381	45,869	7,658	55,042	8,934	64,216	10,210	73,390	11,487	82,564	12,763	91,737
7	5,360	46,661	6,700	58,326	8,041	69,991	9,381	81,657	10,721	93,322	12,061	104,987	13,401	116,652
8	5,628	58,146	7,036	72,682	8,443	87,218	9,850	101,755	11,257	116,291	12,664	130,828	14,071	145,364
9	5,910	71,353	7,387	89,192	8,865	107,030	10,342	124,868	11,820	142,707	13,297	160,545	14,775	178,383
10	6,205	86,514	7,757	108,143	9,308	129,771	10,859	151,400	12,411	173,028	13,962	194,657	15,513	216,285
11	6,516	103,888	8,144	129,860	9,773	155,832	11,402	181,804	13,031	207,776	14,660	233,748	16,289	259,720
12	6,841	123,768	8,552	154,710	10,262	185,652	11,972	216,594	13,683	247,536	15,393	278,478	17,103	309,420
13	7,183	146,486	8,979	183,107	10,775	219,728	12,571	256,350	14,367	292,971	16,163	329,592	17,959	366,214
14	7,543	172,413	9,428	215,517	11,314	258,620	13,200	301,723	15,085	344,827	16,971	387,930	18,856	431,033
15	7,920	201,972	9,900	252,466	11,880	302,959	13,860	353,452	15,839	403,945	17,819	454,438	19,799	504,931
16	8,316	235,637	10,395	294,547	12,474	353,456	14,552	412,366	16,631	471,275	18,710	530,184	20,789	589,094
17	8,731	273,944	10,914	342,429	13,097	410,915	15,280	479,401	17,463	547,887	19,646	616,373	21,829	684,859
18	9,168	317,494	11,460	396,867	13,752	476,241	16,044	555,614	18,336	634,988	20,628	714,361	22,920	793,735
19	9,626	366,969	12,033	458,711	14,440	550,453	16,846	642,195	19,253	733,937	21,660	825,680	24,066	917,422
20	10,108	423,134	12,635	528,918	15,162	634,702	17,689	740,485	20,216	846,269	22,743	952,052	25,270	1,057,836
21	10,613	486,855	13,266	608,568	15,920	730,282	18,573	851,996	21,226	973,709	23,880	1,095,423	26,533	1,217,137
22	11,144	559,103	13,930	698,879	16,716	838,655	19,502	978,430	22,288	1,118,206	25,074	1,257,982	27,860	1,397,758
23	11,701	640,976	14,626	801,221	17,552	961,465	20,477	1,121,709	23,402	1,281,953	26,327	1,442,197	29,253	1,602,441
24	12,286	733,711	15,358	917,138	18,429	1,100,566	21,501	1,283,994	24,572	1,467,421	27,644	1,650,849	30,715	1,834,277
25	12,900	838,698	16,125	1,048,373	19,351	1,258,047	22,576	1,467,722	25,801	1,677,397	29,026	1,887,071	32,251	2,096,746
26	13,545	957,508	16,932	1,196,885	20,318	1,436,262	23,704	1,675,638	27,091	1,915,015	30,477	2,154,392	33,864	2,393,769
27	14,223	1,091,906	17,778	1,364,883	21,334	1,637,859	24,890	1,910,836	28,445	2,183,812	32,001	2,456,789	35,557	2,729,765
28	14,934	1,243,884	18,667	1,554,855	22,401	1,865,826	26,134	2,176,796	29,868	2,487,767	33,601	2,798,738	37,335	3,109,709
29	15,681	1,415,683	19,601	1,769,603	23,521	2,123,524	27,441	2,477,445	31,361	2,831,365	35,281	3,185,286	39,201	3,539,206
30	16,465	1,609,828	20,581	2,012,285	24,697	2,414,742	28,813	2,817,199	32,929	3,219,656	37,045	3,622,112	41,161	4,024,569

The Evil of Plastic Money

Principle: When your wheel of fortune spins in reverse, someone else's spins forward.

When I graduated from college, I was heavily in debt. Then along came the glorious "free" riches provided to me by my two plastic friends, Mr. V. and Ms. M. I used to visit them often in my special wallet pouch. I'd show them to all the cashiers often. With the influence of my powerful new friends I could buy what I couldn't buy before, eat where I couldn't eat before, go places I couldn't go before. I liked them so much I never left home without them!

Then the mean old mailman came with good news and bad news. The good news was I only needed to pay twenty dollars a month; the bad news was I owed five thousand dollars. My wheel of fortune was spinning in reverse, like it does for so many people caught in the whirlwind of the plastic money pit!

I'm not totally against credit cards. They are convenient in emergency instances or when ordering merchandise by phone. However, watch your hand carefully as you deal with those shimmering cards of silver and gold. *When your wheel of fortune spins in reverse, someone else's spins forward.*

If you are already trapped by debt refer back to the quick get out of debt formula I mentioned earlier. **Save 10%** of your income, pay debts off with **20%**, and live on the **70%** that's left. I've found most people spend all that they make or more than they make to impress other people or satisfy their greed.

They do this for two main reasons: First, they have low self-esteem; second, they lack self-discipline. A person also feels deep internal self-worth usually isn't bent on impressing others with money or expensive items. In the second case, a lack of self-discipline results in the childish attempt to instantly gratify all whimsical wants without restraint.

Marketing Yourself and Personal Packaging

Principle: God looks on the inside, people look on the outside.

Personal packaging is of prime importance on the job, on an interview, when meeting new people, and when making connections. Any marketing expert will tell you that if two products are exactly equal in quality and price, the one in the pretty package will outsell the other.

When you go to a grocery store's fruit and vegetable section, would you buy the muddy carrots with dried brown leaves or the clean, neatly trimmed, bright green and orange ones? How about tomatoes—would you buy the ones laying in a dirty bushel basket on the floor or the clean, shrink-wrapped ones in the fancy green carton? What about canned goods—poor sales on the faded label, dented cans, right? Who buys dented canned goods when a good can is available? The brightly colored eye-catching label sells the product; even though the quality inside may be poorer than that in the poorly labeled can, most people will never know!

So what does this have to do with you and wealth? People judge you by how you look. Many opportunities can come solely from a person's appearance because *God looks on the inside, people look on the outside.* This principle is stated in the Bible: "The Lord does not look at the things man looks at. Man looks at the outward appearance, but the Lord looks at the Heart" (1 Samuel 16:7). Since people are going to be judging you by your outward appearance, here are a few basics of personal packaging:

- ◆ *Be extremely clean. Be sure your personal hygiene is top notch. You must have absolutely no dirt anywhere. Especially keep ears, hair, hands, nails, and feet squeaky clean.*
- ◆ *Always smell nice, with a light fragrance, or have no odors at all.*
- ◆ *Wear clean, pressed, well-fitting clothes. Be sure there are no stains or tears, and wear colors that look good on you.*

- ◆ *Dress for the occasion* at parties, dinner events, or other special events. Dress a step or two up so you stand out in the crowd. You want people to notice you! Always overdress, never underdress.
- ◆ *Hair styles* should be neat and up-to-date (never shaggy, especially for men).
- ◆ *Wear "eye candy"* such as jewelry and makeup. This goes for men too—watches, bracelets, rings are good. Doesn't a Christmas tree look better, with its glittering ornaments and lights, than a plain old pine tree?
- ◆ *Read books* on fashion and wear what your role models wear.
- ◆ *Notice what you get compliments on*. Be very observant to what looks good on you.

Do you have eye appeal? Do your clothes accent your good features? Do you know what colors work well on you? Do you wear clothes that set you apart or make you blend into the crowd unnoticed?

Don't ever make the mistake of thinking how you look doesn't matter. IT DOES! When you look good, you feel good. When you look and feel good your chances of running into opportunities for wealth creation are greatly enhanced. How you look matters, everything matters! Most people won't have any respect for a slipshod dresser who doesn't have any eye appeal.

Money Hunger

Principle: If you start saving 10% of all you earn, you'll start to build a personal fortune.

If you fill a bucket with ten gallons of water and pour out nine each day, what will eventually happen? Answer: In time the bucket will become overflowing. Why? Because every day you left in one more gallon than you took out. That one gallon left in each day builds up until the bucket capacity is reached and it overflows.

If you put in your wallet ten dollars each day and take out nine, eventually your wallet will be stuffed to overflowing. *If you start saving 10% of all you earn, you'll start to build a personal fortune.* This sounds simple, but often the most complex problems yield to very simple solutions.

When you are deprived of food your nose becomes acutely aware of the aromas of good food such as roasting meat, stir-fried vegetables, fresh bread, coffee, apple pie, etc. Your mouth automatically salivates just from the scent. You become hunger driven. If you are deprived of water your thirst grows, you visualize a glass of ice water with the cubes clinking away. Your senses become acutely tuned to sources that may quench your thirst.

As you become hungry for wealth and your hunger burns inside you, your senses become keener. Your thirst for knowledge increases. Your mind clears, it becomes more alert, more alive, more receptive. New opportunities will seem to **miraculously** present themselves.

As your wealth accumulates and your appetite starts to be satisfied, a new sense of strength and freedom will grow within you. So many rags to riches stories tell of people who were deprived of money as youths or grew up in poverty. Their money hunger is what drove them. Their appreciation of wealth was great because they knew the full spectrum, they lived it from near starvation at the bottom of the socioeconomic scale to the top. They became stronger because of their *struggle.* They craved what they could not afford.

So many people who spend all they make don't realize they are sowing their seeds of fortune in the winds of immediate gratification, unaware that the reaping will be a tornado of trouble and suffering in the fall. *Their stores for the winter will be empty and they must expect to starve!*

People who are living beyond their means have poverty awaiting them in old age. The dust of regret will be beneath their poor, wrinkled feet. This can all be avoided with a few simple disciplines and a little extra learning.

Many will read this lesson on money goals and it will have no effect on them; others are already following the rules and obeying the laws of wealth creation. Some will think it too simple, and a choice few will now be inspired by my words. I wrote this for those choice few. Continue your learning and earning. If one person did it, you can learn how to do it too! Work your way out of the darkness of slavery and poverty into the light of fortune and freedom.

This will be a turning point in the lives of many a reader with regard to money handling. You must develop money hunger and set money goals. Only then is it possible to build a personal fortune.

An After-the-Lesson Visit with the Author

"If a man empties his purse into his head, no man can take it from him. An investment in knowledge always pays the best interest."

Benjamin Franklin
America's first self-made
millionaire

I included this lesson on money goals for the simple reason that I've seen more destruction come to individuals, families, and even countries caused by money, its improper handling and use. Lack of basic money management knowledge is one of the major causes of marital breakdown in the U.S. Think about that if you are married. Can you credit money problems as the cause of any of your arguments? You and your spouse must be working in harmony by setting money goals together. One can't save while the other spends!

The government statistics at the beginning of this lesson shocked me when I first saw them, but when I thought back and reflected on my own past I could see clearly how true they were. When I graduated from college I was offered many credit cards. I got almost all of them. I then proceeded to buy many items I had wanted for a long time.

When I got my first job after college I bought more "toys"— a new car, motorcycle, etc. I never once thought of saving a penny! You see, in my mind retirement was something "old people" did and I wasn't old. Thinking ten or twenty years down the road was inconceivable to me. I couldn't even conceive of living for twenty more years. My interests were in buying whatever I wanted, whatever my friends were getting, whatever struck my fancy on a TV commercial or magazine ad. I was heading like a speeding bullet for the lowest category in the government statistics even though I was making a very good salary.

Then my sister and my wife had a powerful effect on me in a conversation. I started to think ahead and realized that if I continued my financial practices I myself would end up broke and embarrassed at age 65, wondering what happened! I realized I needed to make major changes in my thinking and I did.

My father told me one time that he had achieved almost all the goals he had set for himself in life, but he said that he never set any money goals. He said to me, "Don't make that mistake. I've lived that one and it isn't any fun."

I used fairly severe language and illustrations in this lesson on purpose, because I don't want you to end up broke after a lifetime of labor. I encourage you to set money goals just like you would any other major goals in life. Put the dollar amount you want to end up with in writing, with a deadline for achievement, and devise a workable plan to attain it. I've presented you with the simplest, safest plan, which is that of saving 10-20% of your annual income and investing it wisely. Study those Awakening Charts! If you haven't saved anything in the past five or ten years and you aren't planning on saving any money for your future, then you don't need an Awakening Chart to figure out how much money you will end up with. The ultimate taskmasters called **reality** and **inflation** will certainly wake you up at age 65. . . . with a sledgehammer!

"Shortly after I met my mentor he asked me, 'Mr. Rohn, how much money have you saved and invested over the last six years?' And I said, 'None.' He then asked, 'who sold you on that plan?' "

Jim Rohn
America's foremost business philosopher; author of *The Five Major Pieces to the Life Puzzle, Seven Strategies for Wealth and Happiness,* **and** *The Seasons of Life*

MENTAL MECHANICS

Part III

Lesson Numbers
4,5,6

4 ▶ The Triune Mind

Overview

It's time for you take a short break. Put your pen and paper away. Take your life values list and goals list and set them aside for now. You are ready to learn about the fundamental components and operation of your mind. There are no written exercises in this part, just a wealth of practical information. This knowledge will benefit you in two very important ways. First, it will allow you to understand your own mind; second, it will allow you to understand other people's minds.

The POWERMIND System Part III. Mental Mechanics

The Triune Mind: Module I. Three Minds in One

The Triune Mind: Module II. Mental Interactions

The Triune Mind: Module I. Three Minds in One

The Author's Special Preface to Mental Mechanics

Mental Mechanics was included in The POWERMIND System because a fundamental understanding of the human mind is crucial for success in life. Many of the mental techniques you will learn in the High Achievement part of this book would make little or no sense at all to the beginning success student, or anyone else for that matter, who doesn't have the basic knowledge of how their mind operates. A shocking portion of the population don't even know they have a subconscious or superconscious mind, let alone how to effectively make use of them. Many others who are highly successful have been using their subconscious and superconscious minds extensively without realizing it or understanding what they were doing. They gained success by the trial and error method, which may have consumed the greater portion of their life, instead of using a more systematic approach.

The three lessons contained in Mental Mechanics will require an open mind and some serious thought on your part. You should proceed slowly, and backtrack to reread paragraphs or whole sections that don't make any sense to you the first time through. Your rewards in terms of understanding will be immeasurable if you do this. I often reread sections of books a few times to lock in what the author is teaching, especially if I am unfamiliar with the concepts.

You will probably have a number of what are called "ah-ha" experiences as you read through this lesson because you will realize why many previously unexplainable occurrences in your life happened. You will also develop a deeper understanding of why people behave the way they do.

There is a lot of false, trendy, occult literature on the market today that is shrouded in unjustifiable mysticism dealing with "supernatural phenomena," and it is unfortunate that the words "subconscious" and "superconscious" have been attached to some of it. I will dispatch here and now with this sort of approach since it is unscientific and serves to create needless fear and confusion in people's minds. Most of this so called "occult knowledge" literature is useless junk written by starving authors trying to make a fast buck!

However, since this part of The POWERMIND System is sure to cross religious boundaries for many readers, it is necessary for me to state at the outset of this lesson that my approach throughout Mental Mechanics will be straightforward, scientific, and of course highly systematic. It is my intent to teach you practical valuable information that will help you, your family, and those close to you. The best way to teach this sort of information to the beginner is with basic definitions, simple working models, and practical everyday examples anyone can relate to. Mental Mechanics is a real eye opener for many people. **Conceptually this is the most difficult part of The POWER-MIND System to understand**. Open your mind, use due care, and proceed slowly, thinking, rereading, and pausing to reflect as you go!

An Ancient Hindu Legend

There was a time on earth long, long ago when all men were gods. But men sinned and abused the divine so much that Brahma, the god of all gods, decided that the *godhead* should be taken away from men and hidden in a special place where they could never find it and abuse it.

"We will bury it deep in the earth," said the other gods.

"No," said Brahma, "because man will dig down in the earth and find it."

"Then we will sink it in the deepest ocean," they said.

"No," said Brahma, "because man will learn to dive and find it there, too."

"We will hide it on the highest mountain," they said.

"No," said Brahma, "because man will some day climb every mountain on earth and again capture the godhead."

"Then we do not know where to hide it where he cannot find it," said the lesser gods.

*"I will tell you," said Brahma. "Hide it down in man himself. He will never **THINK** to look there."*

Developing a Working Knowledge of the Triune Mind

Principle: The human mind has three components: Two are physical, the conscious and subconscious; one is spiritual, the superconscious.

Principle: The response of your subconscious and superconscious minds is directly related to the most firmly held beliefs in your conscious mind.

Significant progress in any field is impossible without a basic working knowledge of terms, principles, and theory. This section will provide you with these in regard to your mind so you will have some background knowledge to build on. This will enable you to become skilled in operating your conscious, subconscious, and superconscious minds. **The three minds collectively are defined as the triune mind because they function as a single unit.** Most people don't even know they have *three minds in one*, and certainly most people don't have any idea how they operate. Since your mind is your most powerful, most important, most valuable, easily controllable asset in life, you should learn the basics of its operation.

The conscious, subconscious, and superconscious are not really three separate minds, they are really the three parts or subsystems of a single mind. Each one, however, is endowed with separate unique functions. Just like you have a single body with a circulatory system, a nervous system, and a digestive system (three subsystems, one body), your mind has three parts.

As you move through this lesson and the rest of the book these concepts of conscious, subconscious, and superconscious will become clearer and clearer to you. This information will no doubt seem strange at first to many who have no knowledge of the human mind at all, but I will continue to illustrate the fundamentals of mind over and over. By the end of this lesson you should have a good basic understanding of the human mind. Read this section carefully, because the answer to why many "unexplainable phenomena" occur in people's lives is contained right here!

The human mind has three components: Two are physical, the conscious and subconscious; one is spiritual, the superconscious. The conscious mind is also called the logical, rational, thinking, or "program**ming**" mind; the subconscious mind is the instinctive, intuitive, memory storing, or "program**mable**" mind; and the superconscious mind is the spiritual, Universal Force mind, which can be called into operation when the other two minds are working in perfect harmony.

The superconscious mind, since it is the spiritual component of a human being, can also be viewed as your soul. It is this spiritual component of mind that has the power to create according to the nature of your conscious thinking mind. The superconscious mind is responsible for unique inventive insight— "strange" and "miraculous" occurrences that happen in our lives, which most people who lack *specialized knowledge* in this area attribute to chance or luck. It is what enables people to have powers of telepathy, telekinesis, and clairvoyance as well as all other forms of extrasensory perception. "ESP," by the way, simply means not of the five common senses (sight, hearing, smell, taste, and touch), **NOT** black magic or witchcraft.

Briefly, the relationship of the three minds to each other is as follows. As you think certain thoughts in your conscious thinking mind, these habitual thinking patterns are imprinted onto your subconscious mind, affecting your attitudes and behavior. In regard to goals, the subconscious mind can induce the superconscious mind if necessary. An important point to remember is that the subconscious mind carries out commands given it by the conscious mind. It carries out these commands either alone or in conjunction with the superconscious mind, according to the nature of the conscious mind's command. For example, if you are trying to solve a difficult problem or achieve a major goal, then the subconscious mind will call the superconscious mind to its aid. This happens according to the firmness of your conscious mind's *belief* that you can accomplish the task. The stronger and longer the belief is held within the conscious mind, the more intensely the superconscious is induced to action. The subconscious mind induces the superconscious mind to come to its aid in bringing a consciously believed idea or *burningly desired* goal into reality.

This conscious, subconscious, superconscious interaction functions according to the Universal Law of belief. This is an immutable law of nature, just like the law of sowing and reaping. The great Napoleon Hill stated this law in his teachings. He said, "What the mind of man can conceive and believe, it can achieve."

Humans were given free will to choose their beliefs, so this law of belief is neutral and works in a positive or negative way. In the case of negative beliefs, such as certain failure, poverty, self-doubt, and unhappiness, according to the Universal Law of belief all the circumstances necessary to achieve these self-chosen "negative goals" are brought to you. If you have chosen these as goals for yourself by holding these thoughts in your conscious thinking mind on a continuing basis, they will then be attracted to you by your actions as well as superconscious activity.

However, when you hold appropriate specific goals and think more positive thoughts in your conscious thinking mind on a continuing basis, such as perfect health, wealth, power, and success, these are also brought into your life according to the Universal Law of belief. With one caveat: You must have the courage to act by following your intuition, which will lead you to these goals. Positive thoughts without physical action achieve nothing. This idea of faith without physical action traps many people. They concentrate very hard and then wonder why nothing is happening. The quotation below is self-explanatory and addresses this exact issue.

"In the same way, faith by itself, if it is not accompanied by action, is dead."

James 2:17

I bring this point up for an important reason. Many people who study the mind learned from people who were charlatans, not scientists. These people taught that if you sit in a room meditating on success, wealth, happiness, and wisdom it will miraculously be yours. This is not true! Living life requires **right action** along with **right thought**. Sitting under a cactus in the desert, rubbing crystals, chanting, dancing, hoping, praying, wishing for success isn't going to speed you toward your earthly goals at all unless your goal is a bad case of sunburn! You must TAKE ACTION yourself!

The take-home message is this: If your conscious belief in your ability to achieve a goal is made strong enough, you will develop the courage required to take the necessary actions leading to that goal. Your actions will become *automatic* because your belief is so strong. These automatic actions come under subconscious control, which is exactly what you want! As you take action toward your goals, you will also experience unexpected events occurring, seemingly moving your goals toward you. This is caused by induction of your superconscious mind. *The response of your subconscious and superconscious minds is directly related to the most firmly held beliefs in your conscious mind.*

All of these concepts will be explained further as you proceed with this lesson. It would be a good idea to reread this section again if you are totally lost!

The Conscious Mind

Most people are very familiar with the conscious mind; in fact, this is all they think of when dealing with the concept of "mind." I will not go into great length on the conscious mind because the heart of human power lies in the subconscious and superconscious minds. However, a brief description is necessary for the sake of making this lesson comprehensive.

As stated previously, the conscious thinking mind has the capacity to reason. It can make decisions, it is the seat of your free will to choose. Your conscious decisions are made with this reasoning mind.

Many mental activities, such as your ability to make decisions, lend themselves much better to conscious awareness than others. Conscious processes are those processes that can be actively controlled or guided to a high *degree. Degree* is the operative word here, since certain mental processes are much more controllable than others. All thought is really an interplay between all three minds. *Mental activities only seem* to be either conscious, subconscious, or superconscious because of the *degree* to which you seem to have conscious control. In explaining mental mechanics, however, it is easiest to view them as separate at first.

Goal setting is another example of a conscious activity. When you carefully set goals you use the information you have at hand to determine a specific desire. This is done with your conscious reasoning mind. You set goals when you are awake (conscious), not while asleep (unconscious), obviously. You also actively set about to gather the necessary information to develop *reasonable* plans of action to achieve these goals. You must consciously decide from research what information is important for you to gather and what is unimportant. You weigh information on a set of "mental scales."

The conscious mind is also often referred to as the "programmer" because it has the ability to "program" the subconscious mind. This means that when an objective is consciously decided on, such as a goal to achieve or a problem to solve, it immediately becomes an instruction or command for the subconscious mind. The subconscious mind cannot set up its own programs or instructions, it must be instructed by the conscious mind.

It is important for you to note that conscious mind function is inhibited by high stress. When this occurs the subconscious mind takes over and the person functions on instinct, without regard to rational thought. The person behaves illogically because the conscious mind's reasoning ability is impaired. This is easily demonstrated when a person loses their temper—they revert to "animal instincts," not logical clearheaded thinking.

The Conscious Mind — Characteristics and Functions

◆ *Makes Decisions Using the Power of Reason*
◆ *Is the Seat of Free Will to Choose*
◆ *Sets Goals*
◆ *Determines the Importance of Information Using "Mental Scales"*
◆ *Programs the Subconscious Mind*
◆ *Its Function Is Inhibited by High Stress*

The Subconscious Mind

Entire books have been written on the subconscious mind; however, it has just a few fundamental characteristics and functions. I will outline these briefly for you.

The subconscious mind operates most of your *automatic* bodily processes like growth and repair, your heart beat, your digestive system, and so on. These all fall under subconscious control. For the most part the conscious mind doesn't play much of a role in these activities. I am well aware of biofeedback technology, whereby "automatic" (subconscious) bodily processes can be brought under the conscious mind's direct control. However, in ordinary circumstances you don't tell your heart to beat or your throat to sequentially contract when you swallow a piece of food.

The subconscious mind is also the seat of emotion, controlling your body's limbic system (hormone levels). It controls your "fight or flight" survival response. When you sense danger the subconscious mind *automatically* releases the hormone adrenaline into your bloodstream, increasing heartbeat, blood pressure, breathing, etc., to prepare your body for responding to danger by fighting or running. You don't consciously think to do all these things, they happen automatically (instinctively).

There are also two separate types of *learned* behaviors that later become subconsciously controlled as we grow up. The first type of learned behaviors are physical actions such as walking or riding a bicycle. When you first learned how to walk, it was difficult; you had to consciously think about every move. Now, however, that learned behavior has become automatic for you. The second type of learned behaviors are mental actions. These are our attitudes, which are also learned at early ages by how we habitually think. Some people have negative attitudes and react pessimistically to everything automatically. They view life in a negative light; this is a learned or socially conditioned behavior. This is easily proved by asking the question, how many newborn babies have negative attitudes? Negative attitudes must be learned, and then they become subconsciously driven or automatic.

The subconscious mind also houses your memory (memory banks). All the information you have taken in through life experiences, whether they are real or imagined, is recorded and stored in your memory. Everything you ever sensed with your five senses was and is being recorded. Any book you've read, any place you've visited, anything you've tasted, everything you've learned, anything you've ever imagined is in there. These vast subconscious memory banks contain every thought you've ever had, from about four months after you were conceived up until now. All this information is available to your subconscious mind for its use. The subconscious mind operates by **automatic association** of new information with information already stored in its memory banks. (We'll discuss this particular concept further in later sections.)

The subconscious mind can also be thought of as a goal-seeking machine, that is, it will seek to attain specific goals and obey commands given to it by the conscious mind. It is in fact a "programmable" biological machine.

The subconscious mind is programmed by your conscious mind's thoughts and beliefs. It has no power of rejection; it cannot reason out information to see if it is true or not, or if the thought commands given to it are beneficial to the person or not. It can't argue with the conscious mind's belief. The subconscious mind cannot engage in "editing"; it cannot determine whether the conscious thoughts you plant are good or bad, true or false—that's the job of the conscious reasoning mind. If you believe something to be true even though it's really false, your subconscious mind will accept it as true and proceed to operate as if that information were a fact.

The subconscious mind is like the soil, it accepts seeds thrust upon it. Soil will accept flower seeds just as readily as weed seeds. The subconscious mind will accept negative destructive beliefs, thoughts, attitudes, or goals, and in time it will produce in your outer experience the exact reflection of these. By the same token, fortunately for us, it will produce success in our life if beneficial beliefs, thoughts, attitudes, or goals are planted in it. This is what is meant by the Universal Law of sowing and reaping stated in the Bible, *"Whatsoever a man soweth, that shall he also reap"* (Galatians 6:7) or *"As ye sow (into your subconscious mind) so shall ye reap (in your life)."* Our outer experiences and circumstances mirror what has been planted in our subconscious mind.

The subconscious mind also has very powerful conflict resolution and creative problem-solving functions, by setting up a mental conflict between your self and your environment (goal setting). The subconscious mind will automatically cross-reference information in its memory banks and send practical insight, intuition, plans, and answers on how to resolve the conflict to the conscious mind.

Perhaps the most powerful function in regard to conflict resolution and creative problem solving is the subconscious mind's ability to induce the superconscious mind when its standard conflict resolution operations fail. This enables it to tap outside forces and outside sources ("outside" meaning outside the physical body) for information, assistance, guidance, and power.

The Subconscious Mind — Characteristics and Functions

- *Controls Automatic Body Functions (Heartbeat, Digestion, Growth and Repair, etc.)*
- *Is the Seat of Emotion — Controls the Body's Limbic System (Hormones)*
- *Expresses the Survival Instinct — The "Fight or Flight" Bodily Response*
- *Controls Two Types of Automated Behaviors That Have Been Learned: 1. Physical Actions (for example, Walking or Riding a Bike) and 2. Mental Actions (Attitudes)*
- *Houses the Memory Banks (Holds All Real and Imagined Life Experiences)*
- *Is Like a Biological Machine (Goal Seeking by Nature)*
- *Is Programmable and Is Programmed by the Conscious Mind*
- *Lacks "Editing" Capability (Cannot Edit Incoming Information as Real or Imaginary, True or False)*
- *Cannot Determine whether Conscious Thoughts are Helpful or Harmful to the Person*
- *Has Creative Problem-Solving Capabilities*

◆ *Can Resolve Conflict between Self and Physical World*
◆ *Can Instantly Assimilate and Cross-Reference Incoming Information with Stored Information in Memory Banks Automatically*
◆ *Can Induce the Superconscious Mind When Its Standard Methods Fail*

Since the information you just read on the subconscious mind is quite intensive and important, you are now asked to reread this entire section again. Think carefully, because all these concepts will come into play in various ways for the rest of the lessons in this book.

"There is no artist, man of science, or writer of any distinction, however little disposed to self-analysis, who is not aware by personal experience of the unequaled importance of the subconscious."

Gustave Geley
Distinguished French psychologist; author of *From the Unconscious to the Conscious*

The Superconscious Mind

"It is impossible that an outsider should enter into a clear understanding of the mystical spiritual natural world around him and it follows that the teachings and tenets of that spiritual nature world must be more or less a closed book to such a one — a book moreover which he seldom cares or dares to try and open. For this reason the sages concealed much of their profound knowledge from the multitudes because they rightly recognized the limitations of narrow minds and prejudiced opinions. . . . What the fool cannot learn he laughs at, thinking that by his laughter he shows superiority instead of latent idiocy."

Marie Corellie
Author of *The Life Everlasting*

I will use the term "superconscious mind" to refer to the spiritual component of mind. This spiritual component of mind is defined by some as the human spirit or soul. This is perhaps a difficult concept for many to comprehend, especially those who have been subjected to extensive *childhood conditioning* resulting in a narrow-minded view of human nature. Some people believe humans are just advanced animals without any spirit at all. This is unfortunate. It is important to realize that all major religions of the world recognize that humans have a spiritual component.

Beginning in the late 1800s a special breed of scientists and electrical engineers became increasingly interested in this spiritual aspect of the human mind. One such electrical engineer was Charles P. Steinmetz.

"The most important advance in the next fifty years will be in the realm of the spiritual — dealing with the spirit-thought."

Charles P. Steinmetz
World-famous electrical
engineer

Only since the turn of the century have conclusive scientific experiments been performed to prove human beings are capable of what is now loosely termed extrasensory perception. (I might add, not only perception but psychic powers.) Most notable, historically speaking, was the work of the late Dr. J. B. Rhine of Duke University.

His group conducted the first scientific ESP experiments in the 1930s and 1940s. He tested "telepathy," defined as the ability of a person to send or receive thoughts from one person to another; "clairvoyance," defined as the ability to sense objects not visible to the eyes; and also "telekinesis," defined as the ability of a person to influence physical objects. His experiments were sponsored by the British psychologist William McDougall, Fellow of the Royal Society and at the time department head of psychology at Duke University. Rhine's laboratory was called the Parapsychology Laboratory and was the first research laboratory of its kind anywhere.

Rhine's experiments were also the first *systematic* experiments done on the spiritual component of mind. His lab developed standardized tests so the experiments he did could be repeated at other universities. Rhine was very rigorous and applied strict statistical analysis to measure chance versus significant events. He showed that some people do indeed possess striking telepathic, clairvoyant, and/or telekinetic abilities. He also wanted to determine if ESP operated under the known physical laws or if it was subject to physical laws *not yet discovered*.

Rhine's work centering on psychokinesis resulted in the development of his famous "roll of the dice" experiments, which showed certain people could clearly influence the chances of a specific combination appearing when dice were thrown repeatedly *by a machine*. The experimental subject was instructed to concentrate on a specific outcome for the dice roll. Rhine's results showed beyond a shadow of a doubt that some people could indeed influence the dice with concentrated conscious thought. The mechanism of the force of influence was at that time unknown.

"There is no better explanation than the subjects influenced the fall of the dice without any recognized physical contacts with them."

Dr. J. B. Rhine
Founder of Duke University's
Parapsychology Research
Laboratory

Rhine also performed experiments in which individuals would be asked to predict what shapes were on a series of cards that were placed out of sight of the person. He tested whether space (distance) had any effect on a person trying to identify cards by clairvoyance. For telepathy, distance experiments were also performed at both short distances (yards) and long distances (hundreds of miles) away. He found no significant distance effects on clairvoyance or telepathy. Results of a few yards versus hundreds of miles proved equal. Also, walls made of various materials had no inhibitory effects on a person's ESP capability.

Later tests were done to see if ESP was governed by time laws. Space was already shown to have no effect. He found certain people could predict the order of cards equally well in a deck two days or ten days ahead of the time when they would be randomly shuffled *by a machine*. Time had no effect on prophetic powers. His conclusion from these studies was that the human mind had an aspect that was not governed by the known physical laws of time and space, which scientifically proved the human mind has a spiritual component. These experiments sent shock waves throughout academia, as other labs raced to confirm them.

They were confirmed in that other research labs at leading universities determined that the human mind has properties that are not governed by currently known physical laws. Rhine reasoned that since the human mind had properties not governed by known physical laws, it must have an extra physical or spiritual component. He concluded in 1946 that this was proof that man had a soul (Rhine, 1946).

Later on, to quiet the public hysteria that ensued, he said that his evidence was *only highly supportive* and not absolute proof that humans have souls. He said his experiments proved only that *the completely physical nature of man, as commonly believed in intellectual circles, was an incorrect picture.*

Dr. G. R. Schmeidler of the Harvard Psychological Clinic conducted an interesting series of scientific experiments showing telepathy not only was real but was dramatically affected by a person's **belief** in his or her own telepathic ability. He performed what are called "reverse" experiments, which proved telepathic power exists in everyone.

He showed in the 1940s that subjects who did *not* believe in telepathy at all showed scores in telepathy tests far *below* chance. This aided in proving telepathy with *contrary evidence*. If these nonbelieving, below-chance-scoring people had showed only chance scores it would not support telepathic ability. However, since they actually were suppressing telepathic ability with negative belief, they showed telepathic power can be consciously controlled. The subjects who had strong belief in telepathy scored well above chance in telepathy tests; people of average or indifferent belief scored the same as chance. But the negative belief people showed **below chance scores!**

Holding all parameters even, these experiments showed a person's conscious belief can directly affect their telepathy scores by raising or lowering them. Dr. Schmeidler's results fit those of a perfect experiment. He couldn't have asked for better results. If only the strong believer's group had high scores he would be missing the negative control group. If the nonbelievers group scored the same as chance it wouldn't be supportive of the idea that conscious belief can **lower** telepathic ability, but since nonbelievers scored well *below chance* it showed their conscious belief was decreasing their telepathic powers. In effect they were consciously suppressing their natural ability to be telepathic!

More recent research in the 1980s and 1990s has been conducted by Dr. Robert G. Jahn and Dr. Brenda J. Dunne of the Princeton Engineering Anomalies Research Laboratory. Their elegant experimentation deals primarily with two forms of ESP: low level psychokinesis and precognitive remote perception. Their work clearly demonstrates some human beings possess telekinetic power as well as various forms of telepathy. Their work showed these are both time and distance independent (Jahn, 1987, 1988, 1992) just as the early work of Dr. J. B. Rhine demonstrated.

Dr. Jahn also proposes one possible mechanism of influence for thought force, dealing with quantum mechanics similar to what was described by physicist Ernst Schroedinger, who theorized matter has a *dual wave* particle nature. In short, the mechanism deals with thought force as *vibrational energy*. This same type of mechanism for thought force was suspected by vibrational theory scientist Dr. Alexander Graham Bell, success philosopher Napoleon Hill (Hill, 1929) and physicist Niels Bohr (Bohr, 1961), among others. Jahn and Dunne's well-researched book, entitled *Margins of Reality — The Role of Consciousness in the Physical World,* will make the most ardent skeptic think twice! Dr. Robert G. Jahn is a professor of aerospace science and dean emeritus of the School of Engineering and Applied Science at Princeton University (1994). Brenda J. Dunne is the manager of the Princeton Engineering Anomalies Research Laboratory [P.E.A.R.] (1994).

The trail-blazing research of Rhine and the excellent current research of Jahn and Dunne continues to close the gap between man's physical nature and his spiritual nature. These researchers and many others used rigid scientific procedures and highly controlled experiments to study what I call the superconscious faculty of mind. They look to science for answers to difficult controversial questions and try to scientifically characterize the spiritual component of mind. As with the subconscious mind, it is tragic that the mass media and quacks take advantage of people's fears and ignorance for personal profits rather than seeking truth and understanding in science.

"We are at the threshold of our knowledge of the latent psychic powers of man."

> **Dr. Robert Gault**
> **Former professor of**
> **psychology Northwestern**
> **University**

A careful literature search from the late 1800s to today will quickly uncover the undeniable fact that there is a component of mind that generally resides within the human body but can also *exist outside it.* This superconscious component is not bounded by the physical laws of time and space as we currently understand them. Since this is the case, the superconscious mind shares characteristics on an individualized basis with what most people would call God or some people call Infinite Intelligence. I'll use both terms interchangeably.

Albert Einstein showed that our entire universe is made up of only two components: energy and matter. We as human beings are composed of both existing simultaneously. We as human beings emanate various forms of energy since we are composed on a molecular level of vibrating atoms and energy. We emanate heat, magnetic fields, and of course vibrational thought energy from this physical body.

In 1944 Dr. H. S. Burr of Yale University, after performing twelve years of research, concluded that a self-made aura, electrical in nature, surrounds all living things, and all life is connected electrically. This is in fact true but only partially explains the superconscious mind. There is more to the force field phenomenon than can be explained by electricity.

Is it possible that any person can communicate with and invoke the forces of God through efficient use of their superconscious mind? Can this superconscious component of mind be consciously controlled? Based on my research, I believe so. This now opens up a full range of human potentialities that staggers the mind, but only a few of these are pertinent to this book.

"I believe that the mind has the power to affect groups of atoms and even tamper with the odds of atomic behavior, and that even the course of the world is not predetermined by physical laws, but may be altered by the uncaused volition of human beings."

Sir Arthur Stanley Eddington
English mathematician and
astrophysicist

It is important for you to be aware of the fact that the great electrical scientists Thomas A. Edison, inventor of the electric light bulb, Charles P. Steinmetz, electrical engineer, Nikola Tesla, inventor of the air core electrical transformer, Dr. Alexander Graham Bell, inventor of the telephone, and Guglielmo Marconi, inventor of wireless telegraphy, were all intensely interested in telepathy. These men were not considered religious fanatics or easily swayed by magic tricks. They were great creative scientists and inventors who performed rigorous experiments resulting in the formation of the bedrock technologies for our current society. After all, where would we be without electric lights and telephones?

I brought the point up earlier in the subconscious mind section of this lesson that it has the ability to induce the superconscious mind to help it achieve preprogrammed goals, resolve conflicts, and solve problems when its normal modes of action fail. I'll explore this concept a little further now. We know from all religious teachings that God is an all-knowing, all-powerful, ever-present spirit being, so it follows from the scientific research that our superconscious mind is made of the same "stuff," although not nearly as magnificent or powerful. Thus there should be a way for us to induce this superconscious spiritual component of mind to action, and indeed there is. The door is now flung wide open for each of us as human beings possessing a spiritual superconscious mind to obtain all necessary knowledge and activate outside forces to help us achieve our goals by tapping into, utilizing, or drawing upon this superconscious power!

The next obvious question in your mind is, how exactly can I draw upon this latent power to help me? The answer is simple. You probably already know it. It was stressed by the Master Teacher Jesus Christ throughout his entire life.

The Universal Law is now stated: The superconscious mind is induced to action by deep conscious belief, called FAITH!

These Biblical quotations and many more support this Universal Law.

"Everything is possible for him who believes."
Mark 9:23

"According to your faith will it be done to you."
Matthew 9:29

"Come near to God and He will come near to you."
James 4:8

These quotations are not enough, however, for the average person to begin systematically utilizing their superconscious mind in everyday affairs in a practical way. Therefore, as you proceed through the rest of Mental Mechanics I will explain how all three components of mind, conscious, subconscious, and superconscious, interact so you can begin using them effectively.

Armed with this *specialized knowledge* and what is in the rest of this book, you will achieve your goals much more easily. At the conclusion of this book you will have all the theory, understanding, and practical tools necessary to craft a wondrous life for yourself here on earth and perhaps beyond as well!

"There is dormant in each human being a faculty, whether it is developed or not which will enable that particular individual to succeed if the desire for success is present in his conscious mind."

> **Erna Ferrell Grabe and**
> **Paul C. Ferrell; authors of**
> ***The Subconscious Speaks***

Author's Note: I believe that there is a "good" force and an "evil" force, and we can control our superconscious mind's alignment with either by conscious free will. In other words, it is your choice, so choose wisely!

The Superconscious Mind — Characteristics and Functions

- *The Spiritual Component of Mind*
- *Defined by Some as the Human Spirit or Soul*
- *Is the Seat of Psychic Powers (ESP, Telepathy, Telekinesis, Clairvoyance, etc.)*
- *Can Exist Within or Outside the Physical Body*
- *Is Not Bounded by Physical Laws of Time and Space as We Currently Understand Them*
- *Can Communicate with God (Infinite Intelligence)*
- *Serves as a Resource for the Subconscious Mind to Draw on for Conflict Resolution, Problem Solving, and Goal Achievement*
- *Can Obtain All Necessary Knowledge to Achieve Your Goals*
- *Is Induced to Action by Deep Conscious Belief, Called FAITH*
- *Seeks Alignment with Good or Evil*

"The Supernatural is the natural not yet understood."

> **Elbert Hubbard**
> **Success philosopher**
> **Author of *The Message to Garcia***

Scientific References for The Superconscious Mind Section

1. "Scientific Evidence Man has a Soul," Dr. J. B. Rhine, *American Weekly Magazine*, August 25, 1946.

2. "Experiments in Remote Human/Machine Interaction," Brenda J. Dunne and Robert G. Jahn, *Journal of Scientific Exploration* 6, no. 4 (1992): 311-32.

3. "Operator-Related Anomalies in a Random Mechanical Cascade," Brenda J. Dunne, Roger D. Nelson and Robert G. Jahn, *Journal of Scientific Exploration* 2 (1988): 155-79.

4. "Engineering Anomalies Research," Robert G. Jahn, Brenda J. Dunne and Roger D. Nelson, *Journal of Scientific Exploration* 1, no. 1 (1987): 21-50.

5. *Law of Success*, Napoleon Hill (Evanston, IL: Success Unlimited, 1992).

6. *Atomic Theory and the Description of Nature*, Niels Bohr (Cambridge: The University Press, 1961).

The Triune Mind: Module II. Mental Interactions

Conscious/Subconscious Interaction: A 4-Subprocess Working Model

Principle: The degree of conscious awareness you have about anything in your environment is in direct proportion to the degree of importance you have preprogrammed or assigned to it. The degree of importance assigned to sensory input is based on prior experience and/or MENTAL CONDITIONING.

Principle: Environmental stimuli, external or internal, only have meaning to you if you have some information already stored in your subconscious memory banks (mental core) that you can relate them to or associate them with.

Principle: Everything you perceive has been associated with already existing information and emotions stored in your subconscious mental core.

In the previous sections you were introduced to the three components of mind: conscious, subconscious, and superconscious. It's not quite as cut and dried as that since each part interacts heavily with the other parts to form one "Triune Mind." This section will focus primarily on the interplay between the conscious and subconscious minds. Conscious and subconscious interaction can be broken down into a four-subprocess working model. The four subprocesses in this highly simplified model are *association, perception, evaluation, and decision*. This model will serve as a very good basic foundation for later lessons.

The first conscious/subconscious process is called *association*. Your five senses take in information from the environment. The subconscious mind then automatically records and associates this information with existing information in its memory banks. (Remember, earlier I told you one of the characteristics of the subconscious mind was the storehouse of memory.) I will call all of your memory bank data the **mental core**. You are basically unaware of this recording and association process; it is occurring subconsciously or below the level of conscious awareness. (Refer to Mental Mechanics Diagram #1)

The second conscious/subconscious subprocess is called **perception**. It is simply what is happening around you that you are aware of. It is that small portion of information you are conscious of that comes in from your five senses. Your eyes take in what you see, your ears what you hear, your nose what you smell, your tongue what you taste, and your skin what you feel, but all of this stimulation would quickly overload the conscious mind's capacity without some sort of *filtering device*.

Inside your subconscious mind you also monitor information inside your body such as your body position in relation to gravity, body temperature, hormone levels, digestive processes, etc. Neurologists estimate two million or more signals come into your brain every second. You do not actually consciously perceive all this information individually, otherwise you couldn't function. Inside the brain is a "sensory filter" that alerts you to what is important in the environment, and this filter filters out all the unimportant sensory stimulation. The reticular formation (RF), discussed briefly in the general goal setting lesson, is the physical structure inside your brain that allows for this.

Mental Mechanics Diagram #1

<u>ASSOCIATION</u>

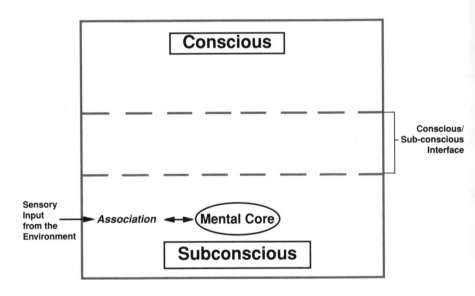

Sensory input is subconsciously recorded and *associated* with existing information housed within the mental core (memory banks).

Here is a simple example to illustrate RF function. When you ride a bike you receive constant input about your position in the environment as well as millions of bits of information on your body movements. This input from your eyes, ears, muscles, skin, etc., is constantly fed into your brain, but you aren't consciously thinking about each bit of information individually. You are able to ride the bike **automatically** (subconsciously) without conscious thought. Your RF (sensory filter) only alerts you to important sensory input, such as your foot slipping off a pedal or the handlebars shaking if you get a flat tire. As long as nothing out of the ordinary happens you are basically unconscious of all the activities required to ride the bike. **Observe!**

The degree of conscious awareness you have about anything in your environment is in direct proportion to the degree of importance you have preprogrammed or assigned to it. The degree of importance assigned to sensory input is based on prior experience and/or MENTAL CONDITIONING.

In other words, you selectively perceive the information signals from your surroundings that you need to be aware of, first, for survival and second, *to achieve **preprogrammed goals**.* I will continue to illustrate this concept because it is a central principle of The POWERMIND System.

You can *sense* much more from your surroundings than you actually consciously *perceive.* You read the words on this page right now, but are you also aware of any sounds, smells, tastes, or bodily functions? Do you hear any background noises? Are you hungry or thirsty? Do you have to go to the bathroom? These may all be registering in your conscious mind but only in a very minor way.

As you read the previous sentences, did you notice yourself instantly **"tuning in"** to those functions for a brief moment? Can you "tune out" people's voices when you concentrate hard on something? Have you ever tuned out your spouse, kids, teachers, or the TV? I'll bet you would instantly become aware of the smell of something burning, the smell of natural gas, or the smell of gasoline if they were present in your environment. You would instantly become aware of these because they represent physical danger, which was *conditioned in* to most people as "dangerous" when they were children. The smell of smoke is subconsciously *associated* with physical danger, so no matter what you were doing, if you smelled smoke you would probably become alerted to it immediately. The RF structure in your brain allows information from your five senses to pass into conscious awareness or blocks its entry into consciousness, recording it into the mental core only. (Refer to Mental Mechanics Diagram #2)

As you *sense* people, events, and all other environmental stimuli in your surroundings every day, all this information is processed and recorded subconsciously. All your life the years of accumulated knowledge have been filed into your subconscious mental core. This mental core of information is constantly growing each moment of your life. Environmental information is instantaneously compared to accumulated information stored in the mental core to determine if you have sensed anything like this before. The mental core also houses your emotional patterns, called *attitudes*, as well as all environmental information you've been exposed to.

The **Association** process occurs largely in the subconscious mind. Here are a few more examples of association. If you hear a sound the subconscious mind asks, "Have I ever heard that sound before?" For a new smell, "Have I ever smelled that smell before?" If you have a pain in your chest it asks, "Have I ever felt that pain before?" In the case of chest pain it may also go further and ask, "What have I learned about chest pain?" "Do I know what the chest pains for a heart attack are like?" **"Is this like that?"** "What have I read about chest pain?" It asks, "What do I **associate** this chest pain with, based on the stored information is my memory banks?"

This memory bank search is the *association* process, whereby new inputs are simultaneously added and compared with existing information within the mental core. The mental core houses all life experiences (real or imagined) plus attitudes or emotions connected with those experiences. **Observe!**

Environmental stimuli, external or internal, only have meaning to you if you have some information already stored in your subconscious memory banks (mental core) that you can relate them to or associate them with.

Mental Mechanics Diagram #2

PERCEPTION

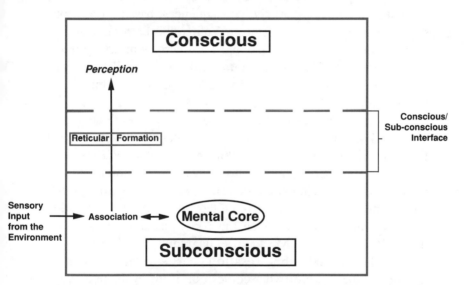

A constant memory file search of the mental core is conducted as information from the environment is sensed. When an environmental stimulus triggers an "important" association based on the comparison of the stimulus with existing information, that associa-tion is flashed to consciousness through the reticular formation filter and the association is consciously *perceived*. The person then becomes instantly aware of it.

If you have a lot of **related** information, experiences, or knowledge already stored in your mental core regarding an environmental stimulus, your perception of it will be very meaningful. **Observe!**

Everything you perceive has been associated with already existing information and emotions stored in your subconscious mental core.

Evaluation is the third mental subprocess used to determine if an environmental stimulus that has been *associated* and *perceived* has any *further significance*. The significance after it is consciously perceived is determined by gauging probabilities, estimating validity, value, and consequences, based on previous experiences with similar stimuli. Your mind both consciously *and* subconsciously asks, "Is what I am perceiving true, important, valuable?" "What is the future of this stimulus?" "The consequences?" "Is this stimulus true/false, good/evil, helpful/hurtful, useful/useless?"

Important sensory input that is perceived is evaluated both consciously, using objective logic, and subconsciously, subjectively based on attitudes held within the mental core. These attitudes or feelings are connected to related information and experiences stored in the mental core. These attitudes regarding related information are consciously called up during the evaluation process, which cycles between the conscious and subconscious mind. (Refer to Mental Mechanics Diagram #3)

The last mental subprocess to occur is called decision. A decision is the result of what comes out of the evaluation cycle. A conscious decision to do something or nothing regarding an environmental stimulus is made. In other words you make a conscious decision to act. In some cases you may also decide to take no action at all. (Refer to Mental Mechanics diagram #4, which completes our four-subprocess model.)

Mental Mechanics Diagram #3

EVALUATION

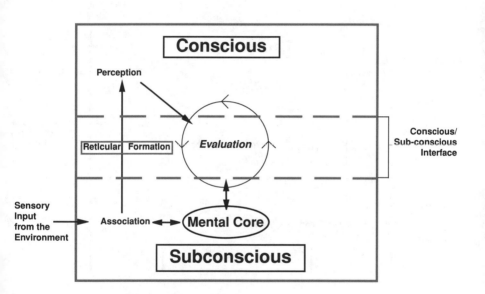

Perceived information is fed into the *evaluation* process cycle, which utilizes both the conscious and subconscious minds simultaneously to determine further significance of an environmental stimulus.

Mental Mechanics Diagram #4

<u>DECISION</u>

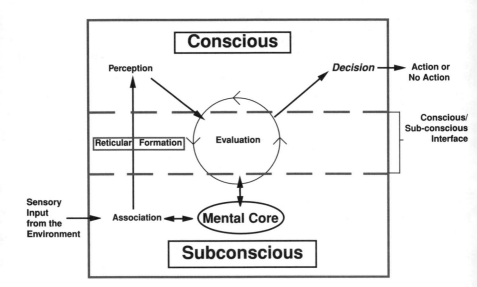

A conscious *decision* to take action or not results from the evaluation process cycle. This is the completed four-subprocess model.
NOTE: This four-subprocess model does not explain all human behavior and mental action. It has its limitations. However, for the beginning success student it serves as a very good basic framework to build on, as you will see in the next section.

Applying the 4-Subprocess Model

Principle: **Human behavior is largely determined by an individual's information AND attitudes held within their subconscious mental core. Also of importance: An individual's mental core is never perfectly accurate and is always changing.**

Let's see how the model works for a simple everyday case. You are driving along the road in your car and the car ahead of you puts on its brakes. Your subconscious mind senses and associates the fact that the car's red brake lights just went on. The RF filter allows the information to flash to conscious awareness because "red brake lights" have significance. You now have **perception** of an important environmental stimulus. You then evaluate it by consciously and subconsciously checking your memory files (mental core) housed in the subconscious mind for past experiences related to this type of information and also for feelings (attitudes) about this information. Based on further associations you evaluate the stimulus with your own unique set of past experiences related to this type of situation. You continue the evaluation cycle to determine what is *probably* going to happen next. The car will probably slow down. So the next mental process is for you to make a conscious **decision**. Your **decision** will determine what you will do next—your decision determines your action, which will probably be to put your foot on the brake pedal to slow down.

The key point of this simple example is to illustrate the basic mental mechanics and also show you that most of your decisions are mainly due to what has already happened to you in life (your own unique *conditioning*). In other words, what is stored in your mental core: the information plus emotion. The information and emotions (attitudes) that you have accumulated and developed in your subconscious mind through the years of living and learning, which I call your mental core, form your reference system or belief system and largely determines your decisions and subsequent actions. Your mental core is the sum total of all the information, feelings, and sensations you have learned about yourself and the world around you. *It is the database, reference system, memory banks, or belief system that represents the total programming of your mind!*

Unlike a computer datbase, however, your mental core includes emotional components or attitudes, that is, how you feel about every bit of information stored in the mental core. You have emotions an electronic computer does not. Your mental core includes emotions along with each piece of raw data. Your mental core serves as your database for you to *associate* and *evaluate* all that you *sense* and *perceive*. Your decisions and subsequent actions, in essence all your behavioral output, will tend to be consistent with your own personal and unique mental core. **Observe!** One of the most important principles of mental mechanics for you to understand is now stated.

Human behavior is largely determined by an individual's information AND attitudes held within their subconscious mental core. Also of importance: An individual's mental core is never perfectly accurate and is always changing.

What is in your mental core differs from what is actually going on. Why? Because your mind perceives everything in a different way than anyone else's in the world. Your perception may be imperceptibly different (essentially the same) or totally different from someone else's. For example: Someone puts you down in a foreign language but says it smiling softly, waving in a friendly manner, on first meeting you. Your perception of a friendly greeting is totally inaccurate. Another person with you who understands the language will be very offended. The same actual event occurred; two totally different perceptions and subsequent actions resulted for you and your friend regarding the same insulting stranger (environmental stimulus). Both of you are acting in a perfectly consistent manner, based on the information stored in each of your mental cores. If your friend had not known the language either, both of you might have had similar misperceptions that the stranger was greeting you kindly.

Did you ever have trouble communicating with someone who speaks your own language? Say to yourself, "Boy, that person sure is strange"? He seems strange to you because his mental core is set up very differently than yours. His accumulation of knowledge and life experiences is different. You can't figure him out because he is operating with a very different mental core or database than you are. His actions seem strange to you because he has different information stored in his mental core.

I'll illustrate this point further. If I hand a ten-month-old baby a thousand-dollar bill, she may play with it, taste it, tear it to pieces, or ignore it. She has no information in her mental core concerning the value of money. Her mental core can't associate it with much except that it's colored paper. You on the other hand would instantly know what it was, understand its value, and probably keep it if it were offered. Your mental core knows the value of money based on **prior experiences** with it.

Let's look at what is going on right now as you perceive my words on this page. You associate them with meanings that are already existing in your mental core. Then you evaluate the validity and usefulness of the information as you *perceive* it and you *decide* what action to take if any. These four basic mental subprocesses (perception, association, evaluation, decision) go on in everyone's mind all the time, and the mental core accounts for the differences in your actions as opposed to the actions of any other person who reads these same words on this same page.

Any two individuals can stand side by side and watch the same event occur, but if their *associations* differ they could make very different decisions and take different subsequent actions.

Your mental core is like a road map that you use to drive on the *highways of life*, but "the map is not the territory." A highly detailed map is not exactly the same as the territory it represents. A map helps out a lot—you can get from Canada to Mexico by car with one—but you know some of the map will turn out inaccurate or incomplete. You know you can't drive your car on the black lines on a piece of paper. You wouldn't be surprised to find some roads changed, some detours, some new roads, some signs changed. You will not expect the map to be perfect. Your mental core is like a road map—a *map in your mind* that you rely on constantly to navigate through life!

You can, however, accomplish more and get to your goals faster with a good map than you could without one. Your map will help you get where you want to go more quickly to the *degree* that it is accurate and complete. Your mental core is your personal representation of the world and you! This is why you must continuously learn as a person, to build and make your mental core (database) as large and as accurate as possible.

In examining the four subprocesses again I'll use another illustration. Suppose you are sitting in your living room, the door nudges open, and a rattlesnake slithers in. What happens?

First you subconsciously sense a change has occurred in your environment, perhaps with your eyes, or possibly your ears. You will then associate the snake with information stored in your mental core. This will likely cause you to be alerted to or perceive the environmental stimulus. Next you enter the evaluation cycle: You evaluate what you know about snakes, your information **and** feelings about them that have been programmed into your mental core from earlier experiences. You continue the evaluation cycle by estimating probabilities. What is the likelihood this is a real rattlesnake or a trick someone is playing on you? Is it dangerous? What will it do if you sit quietly, or run, or pull on its tail? Then you make a decision on what action to take.

The prediction is impossible to make here because everyone will react in their own way depending on how their mental core is set up (programmed). Some will run; some will scream; some will do nothing; some will break out in a cold sweat; some may laugh, thinking it is a joke. A two-year-old may go over and play with it because a two-year-old probably has nothing in their mental core concerning snakes. An older child who has never seen one may find it cute, new, and interesting, moving toward it thinking it would make a fascinating pet.

As each person evaluates the snake, their evaluations and subsequent decisions to take action will be different based on their mental core. Each decision and action will seem rational and logical to each person because each will act in a manner consistent with the information stored within their mental cores.

Here are a few more examples illustrating the potent effect your mental core has on your behavior. When you were a child you "knew" that Santa Claus and the tooth fairy really existed. Later you found out what *you knew to be true was in fact actual-*

ly false! When you see people from foreign countries with differing behaviors such as "odd" religious customs, food prefer-
ences, lifestyles, and so on, remember their behavior is perfectly
normal to them. And *yours is quite odd!* Yet both of you are
behaving logically according to your mental cores. Your past
experiences and earlier programming are what is very different.

Children are extremely susceptible to programming or ***conditioning*** of their mental core because they have very few life
experiences with which to *associate* and *evaluate* what is happening in the world around them. Their past experiences and
information are limited. Their mental core is somewhat empty.
Here are two examples illustrating *childhood conditioning.* If a
child is scratched and bitten (physical pain) by a cat, later in life
this person will probably not like cats. My wife, Carolyn, is
afraid of dogs because as a child she was viciously bitten on her
ankle by a dog. She screamed and screamed but no one was
around to help her. To this day dogs make her very edgy. She
associates and evaluates all dogs based on past experiences and
attitudes stored in her subconscious mental core.

This section on Mental Mechanics was designed to give you
some basic insights into the interaction of the conscious and subconscious mind, using a four-subprocess model. It is very important that you understand the fundamental interaction of these
two minds. Many of the techniques in the High Achievement
part are based on these fundamentals. Without this section laying
the groundwork for you to build understanding, some of the
techniques in that part would not make any sense at all to you.
You wouldn't have any information in your mental core with
which to associate and evaluate the achievement techniques.
That's why this model was included in Mental Mechanics.
Continue your studies; more information follows to build a more
powerful accurate mental core for yourself!

Importance of the Reticular Formation (RF)

Principle: **When you sense something in your environment related to your preprogrammed goals, the subconscious mind will immediately search its memory banks (association) and flash it to conscious awareness (perception).**

In the four-subprocess mental mechanics model I touched on one of the reticular formation functions as being a sensory perception filter. This point is vitally important for you to understand because it bears specifically on the necessity of setting and preprogramming goals into your subconscious mind. I will provide you with more examples specifically illustrating RF function and then briefly explain its importance in regard to the specific purpose of this book.

Are you aware of how your clothes feel on your skin? What's going on inside your body right now? Are you relaxed? How about your heart, is it beating? Is blood pulsating through your body? Is your liver monitoring blood glucose levels and detoxifying poisons? You probably aren't aware of any of these functions because they are largely monitored by your subconscious mind.

You can become aware of some of these functions with the aid of biofeedback machines, but most people are totally unaware of these processes most of the time. They are filtered from conscious awareness by the RF. If something goes wrong, however, you become instantly alerted to the problem, usually with a pain signal.

The RF can be consciously set or "tuned." You can tune out background noises when you read or become acutely tuned in to your child's scream at a large outdoor picnic party. The RF filter sensitivity is turned down when you block sensory input out and turned way up when you require specific important sensory input. In the case of the smell of smoke I mentioned earlier, the RF sensitivity is turned way up. The RF sensory filter is a screen for what sensory input is allowed to pass into conscious awareness. It can be consciously set at any time but once it is set it operates largely under subconscious or automatic control.

You may be thinking, what does all this mental mechanics stuff have to do with me achieving my goals? Here is the answer. You can consciously set your RF so that you are made instantly aware of useful information in your environment regarding your goals. I'll explain.

We know all the resources you need to achieve your goals are all around you in your environment right now: the people, the information, the events, etc. As Dr. Russell H. Conwell said, "You are standing in your own acres of diamonds." But many people don't realize it. They aren't "tuned in" to their environment because they have not set clearly defined goals in their subconscious mind for proper tuning of their RF. They aren't aware of any opportunity even though they are surrounded with opportunity. Their RF filter is not set properly, so it screens out opportunities and information. You can get tuned in using *autogenic conditioning* techniques and a host of the others that I'll go over in great detail in the High Achievement part of this book. But briefly, here is how to tune your RF.

The physiology of the human brain, specifically the RF, requires that you must first have a goal clearly defined in mind and then consciously drive that goal down into the subconscious mind. In doing this you change the setting of your brain's natural sensory filter (RF). Without first having a clearly defined goal in mind, you cannot even begin setting your RF. **Observe!**

When you sense something in your environment related to your preprogrammed goals, the subconscious mind will immediately search its memory banks (association) and flash it to conscious awareness (perception).

Subconscious programming or autogenic conditioning and visualization techniques are key in setting the RF filter. You learned earlier that the subconscious mind contains your past knowledge, emotions, and experiences in its mental core (both imagined and real). **When an important association is made, it will send that information up to the conscious mind so you will become instantly aware of it and perceive it! If the RF is tuned into a specific set of goals it will allow goal-related information to pass into conscious awareness and allow you to perceive what you are sensing.**

The RF has nothing to do with ESP or the superconscious mind at all; it's just a part of your brain. It has nothing to do with religion or metaphysics. It's a real structure in your brain that has an information-filtering function. Just like your kidneys filter your blood, the RF filters environmental information coming in from your five sense organs. As you have come to recognize the smell of smoke as danger, based on childhood conditioning, you will come to recognize people, events, circumstances, and opportunities in your surroundings enabling you to achieve your **preprogrammed** or conditioned goals.

This is why proper goal setting is the single major skill for high achievement in life. With no preprogrammed goals your subconscious mind doesn't know what to make you aware of! The RF allows little to pass into conscious awareness. You achieve nothing because you search for nothing, when in reality everything is all around you. You are now standing in your own acres of diamonds!

This book is organized with self-assessment, goal setting, mental mechanics, and high achievement, *in that order*. That sequence is critical to successful living because that sequence has a strong physiological as well as psychological basis.

If you can grasp the concept of RF function you will be many miles ahead of the average person. I'm going to teach you with extreme precision how to capitalize on this in Lessons 7 and 8 on *autogenic conditioning*.

The Subconscious Mind Revisited

Principle: **To the degree that you experience an event or occurrence vividly in your imagination, it will be logged into your mental core as something that actually happened. This is the basis for autogenic conditioning or mental rehearsal techniques practiced by professional and Olympic athletes, astronauts, actors, and all high achievers.**

Principle: **Emotionalized thoughts have a potent effect on the mental core.**

You learned earlier in this lesson about the subconscious mind. In order to complete your understanding of the subconscious mind, it is necessary to expand on what you learned and go into a little more detail. By properly utilizing your subconscious mind you put tremendous power immediately at your command.

Three unthinking, automatic, robotlike processes go on within the subconscious mind. It is possible to stimulate or condition some of them deliberately through conscious control. If you do not consciously control them they will function automatically, possibly to your detriment, and that's what we want to avoid.

The first subconscious process is **body function**. Certain *automatic* body functions, such as reflexes, were "genetically programmed" into your nervous system at birth. When a doctor hits your knee, it jerks upward. You don't go through the four mental subprocesses of association, perception, evaluation, and decision described in our earlier model. The reflex loop that involves mainly your spinal cord and leg muscles bypasses the model circuit. When the reflex response is over, your conscious mind is notified of what has happened and *then* you perceive it.

All automatic bodily functions such as reflexes, digestion, circulation, respiration are subconscious activities. Breathing is an interesting activity because it is genetically "wired"; however, breathing can immediately be consciously controlled to a high degree at any time you choose. Breathing can be conscious (deliberate; you are aware of control) or subconscious (automatic; you are unaware of control). It's a matter again of degree. Food digestion, blood circulation, hormone balance, and heart beat are also largely under subconscious control (you are unaware).

The human brain also has the unique capability of rewiring its own cellular circuitry, in the body but especially in the brain (Lynch, 1986, 1987, 1988—*Dr. Gary Lynch is at the Center for the Neurobiology of Learning and Memory Bonney Center, University of California, Irvine. He is recognized as a world authority on learning and memory*). This plasticity allows us to consciously rewire the body's cellular circuitry to automate physical activities. Many non-genetically-wired circuits can in fact become "hardwired" through conscious control, and others that were genetically hardwired can be lessened. In other words, you can override the original genetic blueprint or consciously create a new cellular blueprint for many activities. You can in effect *rewrite much of the brain's blueprints*. For example, speaking, reading, walking, playing the piano, eating with silver-ware, riding a bicycle were not genetically programmed in; you learned them years ago. You can *become* consciously aware of these activities, but your performance will probably drop as you try to think about each step. You are most often better off to let the activity **FLOW** naturally, *automatically* (subconsciously).

A professional bowler further illustrates this point. Pros don't think about how many steps to take on the approach or how to release the bowling ball. It has been consciously hard-wired. Their approach and release are performed in a free-flow-ing manner. It is *automatic* (subconsciously controlled). The entire approach is automatic, hardwired from repetition of the task hundreds of times. When they think consciously about their approach they become awkward, and their scores most certainly go down. The great professional bowler Earl Anthony rolled hundreds of games with no pins simply to hardwire his approach. He said the pins *"annoyed him"* as he was trying to develop the *"perfect approach"* during each practice session.

Like physical activities, there are also automated mental activities. For example, 2+2=?, 4+4=?, 10-0=? These simple equations don't require much thought for you now. But they did at one time require a great deal of *conscious effort*. For example 5+5=? The number 10 "pops" into your conscious mind from the subconscious mental core instantaneously! How about 5436.2 + 284.33, come on, quick! This one requires a little more con-scious effort for you to figure out because you were never drilled on this. Most of the behaviors and skills that you now perform extremely well are ones you have *automated*.

When a skill or activity is *automated* your *conscious mind is free* to think of other things. For example, while driving your car do you focus your thoughts on how firmly to hold the steering wheel? Do you concentrate on how to operate the brake pedal and accelerator pedal? Of course not, that doesn't take any conscious effort at all.

Secretaries don't think of where to put their fingers on the keyboard to type, they don't "hunt and peck" for letters. It's all *automatic* for them. Much of your behavior, in fact most of your behavior, is automatically controlled by either genetic hardwiring or your own conscious hardwiring through the process of repetition and practice.

It is very difficult for a pro bowler to get rid of a flaw once it has crept into their style. They need to **recondition** themselves by *consciously* eliminating the flawed aspect and retaining the rest.

The second subconscious process, the information plus emotion storage system discussed earlier, is called the **mental core.** All thoughts and feelings that occur in your conscious mind are and have been stored and recorded in the subconscious mental core. Many of your mental activities, such as your attitudes and idle thoughts, are also functioning *automatically,* possibly to your *detriment* instead of benefit, but you may not now be aware of it. Thank your lucky stars you are reading this, becoming **aware** of this. It is imperative that you understand this concept. Whatever you "experienced" at a conscious level, whether it was real or vividly imagined, is recorded in your subconscious memory banks that make up your mental core. You always record your own somewhat distorted version of any event you perceive. This makes your mental core real to you, and this is quite useful, but remember, *your reality* is always somewhat inaccurate, incomplete, and different from anyone else's. **Observe!**

To the degree that you experience an event or occurrence vividly in your imagination, it will be logged into your mental core as something that actually happened. This is the basis for autogenic conditioning or mental rehearsal techniques practiced by professional and Olympic athletes, astronauts, actors, and all high achievers.

Vividly imagined experiences become a part of your "experience files" (memory banks), serving as a reference to guide and direct subsequent behavior. This is part of the reason why *autogenic conditioning, imagineering,* and *visualization* techniques work. Emotion + vivid imagination = reality. "Vivid" is defined as the full stimulation of your five senses (usually); however, the focus is on sight and sound.

If you experience events emotionally and vividly in your imagination, they are accepted and recorded subconsciously in your mental core as events that actually happened. This may seem like a genetic design flaw of the human mind; however, it can be utilized to help you. *This peculiar quality of the human mind allows us to take deliberate conscious control of reshaping our subconscious mental core and in so doing altering our automatic behaviors.*

Humans have the unique dimension that emotion causes information, whether true or false, to have a much more profound effect on their behavior because the information gets "locked" into the mental core with the strong emotion. **Observe!** *Emotionalized thoughts have a potent effect on the mental core.*

By mixing high emotion with an imagined (synthetic) experience, that experience alters the mental core in such a way as to influence the association and evaluation subprocesses discussed earlier.

The third subconscious mental process is **conflict resolution**, which can be physiological (memory searches) or spiritual (the subconscious induces the superconscious mind). If there is a conflict between what you want (a goal) and your current situation, creative energy can be unleashed to *resolve the conflict.* Your subconscious mind works automatically, based on information housed in the mental core, to help you resolve a conflict or solve a problem. This is a physiological function. However, if this physiological method fails the subconscious mind can use a spiritual mode, involving the power of the superconscious mind to come to its aid in resolving the conflict or solving a problem. The superconscious mind has the ability to make alterations in the world around you. This is discussed in more detail in the next section.

Scientific References for The Subconscious Mind Revisited Section

1. "Neuroanatomical Plasticity: Its Role in Organizing and Reorganizing the Central Nervous System." Christine Gall, Gwen Ivy, Gary Lynch, *Human Growth*, vol. 2 (Plenum Publishing Corp., 1986), ch. 15.

2. *Synapses, Circuits and the Beginnings of Memory*, G. Lynch (Cambridge: MIT Press, 1987).

3. "Structure — Function Relationships in the Organization of Memory," G. Lynch and M. Baudry, in *Perspectives in Memory Research*, ed. M. S. Gazzaniga (Cambridge: MIT Press, 1988).

Superconscious Thought Induction

"Everyone who is seriously involved in the pursuit of science becomes convinced that a Spirit is manifest in the Laws of the Universe."

Albert Einstein
The World's Most Famous
Scientist

Its now time to detail out your ultimate mind force, your superconscious mind. Many readers will now be skeptical as I lock the third section of the mind into its proper place. Some people do not believe that human beings have a spiritual component. (That's too bad.) This section will be almost useless to them. I haven't included it to try to convince them that they have a superconscious mind. My intent is to teach the *serious success student* how it operates!

The serious student will be richly rewarded with interesting answers to perplexing events that occur in people's lives. Since what I will now teach crosses religious boundary lines, I encourage you to be open-minded as you read. The conclusions are drawn from my own personal experiences as well as solid research by world-class scientists who specialize in the study of this particular topic.

When I started my research for this lesson I wanted hard answers to the awesome capabilities of the human mind. I did not find all the answers, but I found some. They add up to good sense in my mind, as well as to many others who are experts in this specific area. I hope you find the information practical and useful, if not absolutely fascinating!

When you set a goal and consciously program it into your subconscious mental core, you are setting up a conflict inside the mental core between you and your environment. By programming I mean thinking about the goal daily, affirming it, visualizing it, etc. This can induce the creative forces of your superconscious mind, and I do mean "creative" in a literal sense. When you do this, it is like a nuclear reactor being activated.

A real nuclear reactor (a breeder-style reactor) consists of a core of radioactive material brought together in one place. The way you "turn on" a nuclear reactor is to remove control rods made of boron, which absorb flying atoms. As you remove the energy-absorbing boron rods that are embedded in the heart of the nuclear core, atoms and subatomic particles begin to fly out at an enormously fast rate of speed, colliding with each other, generating heat. The human mind works in an analogous fashion.

When you program in a goal, you'll be astonished at your creative ability that is unleashed. This creative energy is always there, but it lies dormant in most people. By setting up a conflict in your mental core between the way things are right now and the way you would desire things to be, you induce subconscious creativity. The subconscious mind can then call the superconscious mind to its aid if necessary. The superconscious mind then radiates the necessary thought energy outside your body to resolve the conflict (achieve the desired goal). This is the ***principle of superconscious thought induction.***

Through the unification or focusing of the conscious and subconscious minds on a specific goal, or clearly defined set of goals, the superconscious mind can be induced to action. The superconscious mind can bring about changes in you and your environment so the conflict is resolved. This then brings you once again into harmony with your world.

Your superconscious mind can tap into "outside" sources and draw upon outer forces for information, power, or inspiration, generating a type of force field around you. This force field is much like a magnet, serving to attract people and events into your life and you into theirs in order to speed you toward your goals. This "superconscious effect," as I call it, is responsible for all the "strange chance happenings" that occur when a person focuses single-mindedly on a burningly desired goal or small set of goals.

Carl Jung, the great psychoanalytical theoretician, believed in a human ability to tap an outside source for information. He called this outside source the "collective unconscious." Napoleon Hill, the greatest success philosopher ever produced by the U.S., called it "Infinite Intelligence." Most people simply call it God.

Focusing on one goal or a small set is best, because as you focus on more than one goal you dilute the superconscious effect. Your personal energy and powers are not unlimited. Conscious concentrated *focus is critical* to inducing the superconscious mind to action. By its very nature you cannot induce the superconscious to action unless you have first programmed the goal into the subconscious mental core. That is to say, the conscious and subconscious must be working in complete harmony before the superconscious mind will be activated. You must burningly desire to achieve a goal with all your heart. Being wishy-washy will not induce the superconscious mind; you must truly desire, hope, pray, **and** have faith in its power. All your energies must be devoted to the single-minded achievement of your ultimate purpose.

A simple example of a superconscious effect is that a stranger is drawn into your life. This stranger then provides you with exactly what you need to achieve your goal or solve a particular problem on your goal path. When you desire a specific goal it's like setting the exact frequency of thoughts radiating from your subconscious mental core. The goal determines your thought frequency, so to speak. You tune in to your goal just as you do when you tune in your car radio to a particular station. If you want rock music, you tune into a rock station; for classical music you tune into a classical station. The radio waves for all the stations are in the air all the time; you just tuned into them with your car radio so you can hear what you want to hear. The human brain can also tune into thoughts that are in the air. *This goes far beyond what could be explained by the reticular formation alone.* Your superconscious mind is like your mental radio, and your conscious mind is like the tuner. It's just a matter of tuning into what you need to achieve your goal. The materials, answers, and opportunities are all around you right NOW. (Refer to Mental Mechanics Diagram S)

But you need to learn some specific techniques to tune in; focused concentration and solemn prayer are two such techniques.

Powerbonding Defined

"Powerbonding" is the synchronization and harmonious operation of your conscious, subconscious, and superconscious minds. These automatically become synchronized when you direct all your conscious thoughts toward a specific purpose, single goal, or set of goals. In doing *autogenic conditioning* techniques (you will learn these in the High Achievement part), you facilitate the powerbonding process. Powerbonding is also termed *scientific self-direction* (SSD).

In powerbonding you consciously focus on a certain idea, such as solving a problem, developing a plan of action, or achieving a goal you want. You convey this to the subconscious mind by adding the component of *positive emotional charging*—feeling the reality of the event, the happiness, the joy, and sense of achievement that goes with the successful outcome of the idea you are focusing on. As time goes on and you continuously practice this procedure daily, holding these success-oriented thoughts as often as possible in your conscious mind, they will be brought into reality, as long as you continue to act in accordance with your natural movements or hunches from that point onward.

A powerbonded individual is at a heightened state of mental **alertness** in regard to his or her goal. The subconscious mind is now continuously scanning, processing, and analyzing all new environmental information coming in through the five senses **as it relates to the programmed goal.**

Mental Mechanics Diagram S

THE SUPERCONSCIOUS EFFECT

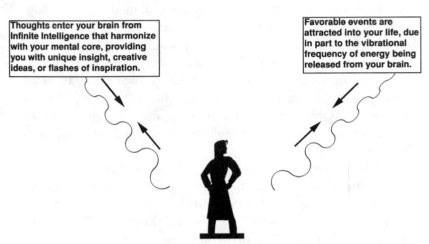

Thoughts enter your brain from Infinite Intelligence that harmonize with your mental core, providing you with unique insight, creative ideas, or flashes of inspiration.

Favorable events are attracted into your life, due in part to the vibrational frequency of energy being released from your brain.

Your brain radiates thought waves according to what's in your subconscious mental core.

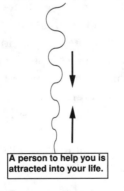

A person to help you is attracted into your life.

The "superconscious effect" is defined broadly as your goals being attracted toward you and you toward them without any physically trace-able actions on your part.

This bonding of the conscious, subconscious, and superconscious minds generates a mental force field like a magnet (superconscious power) around the individual. Here is an analogy to help illustrate this force field concept. The difference between a plain bar of iron and a magnet is the *alignment* of the atoms contained within it. In a plain iron bar the polarity of the molecular domains are pointed in different directions randomly. In a magnet, however, the polarity of all molecular domains are lined up, pointed in the same direction. It is this ***internal alignment*** of the polarities of individual atoms that allows the magnetized bar of iron to have a magnetic field around it. Once magnetized, the bar has a force field surrounding it that is not present in an unaligned ordinary bar of iron. All iron has the potential to become magnetized. And the number of internal molecular polarities that are aligned determines the strength of a magnet's magnetic field.

It is similar with the human mind—the better *aligned* your conscious, subconscious, and superconscious minds are, the stronger the mental (superconscious) force field surrounding you. By setting and focusing your thinking vividly on your goals, you align the three minds, inducing superconscious activity. The superconscious activity is the mental force field or aura that surrounds and can transcend the physical human body, affecting other people and external events.

When your whole triune mind is in complete harmony you are powerbonded. If you are completely powerbonded negatively you will be very unhappy, have low self-esteem and no self-confidence, consider yourself a failure in life, be depressed, repressed, and lethargic, hate the world, and have poor circumstances in your life. When positively powerbonded you will feel good about yourself, be enthusiastic, have self-confidence, have high self-esteem, be altruistic, and have favorable circumstances in your life.

Positive powerbonding requires one additional element: You must be focused on achieving **worthy** goals. When powerbonded on worthy goal achievement, you will feel very good about yourself and like the world. Only a few people, less than 5% of the general population, are positively powerbonded (completely focused on worthy goals).

What you are now learning is based on the physiology of the human body, Universal Law, and the fundamentals of human nature.

The Wheels of Mind Model: Conscious, Subconscious, Superconscious Interaction

"There are no unnatural or supernatural phenomena, only very large gaps in our knowledge of what is natural. . . . We should strive to fill those gaps of ignorance."

Edgar Mitchell
Apollo 14 Astronaut
Founder, Institute of Noetic Sciences

It's time now to bring the three components of mind together into a unified interactive model. The Wheels of Mind Model on the following page is a conceptual diagram to help illustrate the interplay between all three minds.

The three minds, conscious, subconscious, and superconscious, each are endowed with separate and distinct attributes and powers, as you learned earlier. No one questions the fact that the conscious mind is located in the brain. The subconscious is also in the brain, but the superconscious mind can be either in or out and is capable of extending far from the physical body. The superconscious mind can affect the external world, affecting other people and events, moving you toward them and them toward you.

The lines or belts in the Wheels of Mind Model (Refer to Mental Mechanics Diagram W) represent *thought energy pathways;* the wheels represent the three units of mind. You see clearly now why alignment (powerbonding) of the three minds is important. All minds must be turning in the same direction. By this I mean focused on the same goal. With no alignment of thought (powerbonding), the conscious mind and subconscious mind wheels do not turn in the same direction.

Mental Mechanics Diagram W

THE WHEELS OF THE MIND MODEL

(Conscious, Subconscious, Superconscious Interactions)

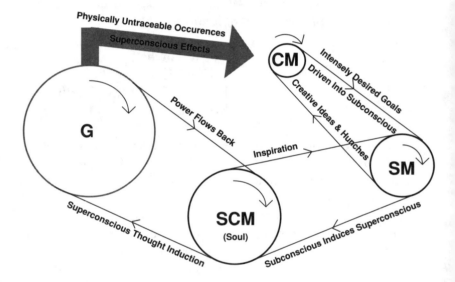

CM = Conscious Mind
SM = Subconscious Mind
SCM = Superconscious Mind (Soul)
G = God (Infinite Intelligence)

The diagram above is a conceptual model to help illustrate the interplay between the three minds and their interconnection with God. The lines connecting the circles represent power belts to help illustrate the direction of thought energy flow.

Look carefully at the diagram of the model and observe. If the conscious mind wheel turns clockwise as illustrated, it will in turn spin the subconscious mind wheel. However, if the conscious mind wheel spins clockwise and the subconscious mind wheel spins counterclockwise (out of alignment) the flow of thought energy along the pathway (belt) does not occur. I discussed earlier the idea of driving your goal into the subconscious mental core. That's what causes the subconscious mind wheel to turn. If your goal is not made into burning desire, you won't generate enough conscious mind power to spin the larger subconscious mind wheel. A hope, whim, or wish does not have the necessary conscious mind power to drive the subconscious mind wheel.

Once a burningly desired goal has activated the subconscious mind wheel, it in turn begins to spin in harmony with the conscious mind wheel. The goal "conceptually" has moved down the right-hand side belt from conscious to subconscious. But notice the left side of the belt also returns to the conscious mind wheel from the subconscious wheel. What returns from the subconscious mind is creative thoughts, ideas, **answers to questions,** plans to achieve goals, unique insights, hunches, intuition, etc. These types of thoughts flow up to conscious awareness from the subconscious mind along the left thought energy pathway.

Notice now that the subconscious mind wheel is also connected to a much larger superconscious mind wheel. As the subconscious mind wheel turns it also drives the superconscious mind wheel. If normal subconscious activity is not enough to do the job asked of it by the conscious mind, it will call upon the superconscious mind along the bottom belt pathway. As you see, the belt is a continuous loop, so the superconscious mind must also return thoughts, ideas, inspiration, and so on, to the subconscious mind, which will then be able to shuttle them to the conscious mind.

Let's take a closer look at this superconscious mind wheel because it is also connected by a belt to what most people call God. I've stated earlier that the superconscious mind is our spiritual component, which can communicate with or invoke a higher power. When this happens our thought pathway belts may or may not be used at all. This is where external events occur in your life without any "conventional" or physically traceable explanation. It seems like chance or luck. Also any ESP-type abilities will stem from this source by way of the superconscious mind.

So with our model completed, let's see how it works when you are working in complete harmony (powerbonded). When I talk about the harmonious operation of the whole triune mind I mean all three mind wheels spinning in the same direction.

The first step is that the conscious mind decides on a specific goal that is worthy, meaning it will benefit others in some way. This immediately gives the goal the potential to invoke God. (Remember, I stressed earlier not to focus on completely self-serving goals. When you start playing with this type of power you want to be sure you are aligned with the correct source.)

The worthy goal is then concentrated on, focused on, visualized, burningly desired, prayed for, etc. This activates the subconscious mind wheel. When this occurs your actions become **automatic** and you develop courage to take action on your creative ideas, hunches, and inspiration received from the subconscious mind. Also the RF filter is set so your physical body operates at a heightened level of awareness; your senses are acutely tuned in to all information in your environment as it relates to your goals, allowing you to **perceive** what you could not perceive before.

As the subconscious mind wheel turns, the superconscious wheel is moved to action, invoking God to come to your aid in achieving your worthy goal (superconscious thought induction). Seemingly chance occurrences start happening in your life that "miraculously" help you to overcome obstacles along the highway of success to your goals—such as an event occurring to shortcut the time you originally thought necessary to achieve your goal. Any number of outside, strange, or weird **beneficial** phenomena may occur, speeding you to the goal.

Your whole mind operates like a magnificent machine, in harmony with itself and the world around it, benefiting everyone with whom it comes into contact.

A few final points to remember: The whole mind machine is controlled by the thoughts held in your conscious mind. **The conscious mind commands the entire operation. You and everyone else has the ability to consciously command this mind power.**

Conscious control of the superconscious effect is the most powerful and highest state of mental development a human can achieve. This has sometimes been referred to as the development of an **"iron will."** No single individual can stand in the way of a positively powerbonded iron-willed person. In most cases a positively powerbonded person can negate the negative effects of thousands, if not millions, of others.

Wise Men on the Subconscious

William James, former Harvard professor and the father of American psychology, said, *"The power to move the world is in your subconscious mind."* It is widely recognized by those who have researched the subject of mind that whatever is pressed into the subconscious mind will be experienced in your outer existence. This will be manifested in circumstances, conditions, people, and events. Whatever is on the inside will be experienced on the outside. Thoughts turn into reality. One of the main reasons for personal misery in the world is that so many people are totally ignorant of the interaction of their conscious, subconscious, and superconscious minds.

The much heralded **Tomb of Hermes** was opened with great anticipation because people thought the secret of the ages was contained within it. The tomb contained this message: *"As within, so without, as above, so below."* (The people's suspicions were right!) To put it in modern terms: *As within* your mind, *so without* outside your mind. *As above,* as the conscious mind believes, *so below* the subconscious mind brings forth. This law was also stated by other wise men, such as Jesus, Moses, Isaiah, Buddha, Zoroaster, Laotze, and all the wisest of the wise in every generation throughout human history.

The internal images consistently held in your conscious mind cause the reaction, which is what you become and the external circumstances of your life. Your external world conforms to and reflects back to you what is in your internal world. The image you impress on your subconscious mind is always mirrored in your external world. External action *follows* internal action. Most people will live all their lives and never understand what you just read!

"As water reflects a face, so a man's heart reflects the man."

Proverbs 27:19

The Universal Law of life, stated as the physical law of rest and motion, action and reaction, sowing and reaping, cannot be broken. Impressions made on the subconscious mind are mirrored by expression in your body and environment. They will eventually be in harmony. Change the impressions on the subconscious mind and the expression in body and environment must **follow**. This is Universal Law!

Thinking negative destructive thoughts generates negative forces inside you, which must be born out externally. Afflictions in the body such as ulcers, heart disease, hypertension, arthritis, many skin diseases, digestive problems, headaches, cancer, and other serious illness can result. I'm not saying your mental state is the sole contributor in all cases of illness; however, the medical journals will back up the statement that a person's mental state is usually a major factor in most diseases. How you feel about yourself deep down inside is the impression you've made on your subconscious mind. This is what is then expressed in all phases of your life. It simply cannot be otherwise!

Millions of people do physical injury to themselves with the negative ideas they entertain in their conscious minds. Worry, bitterness, anger, hatred, jealousy, vengefulness, and fear are the mental needles of emotional poison delivering their toxic dose to the subconscious mind. A baby isn't born negative; no one says, "Oh, what a poor baby, it's so negative, filled with hatred, fear, bitterness, jealousy, anger, worry, etc."

Negativity is learned, it's conditioned or programmed. As you start to change your conscious thoughts by thinking more positively, more optimistically, setting worthy goals for yourself, you slowly reshape your mental core. In so doing you automatically change the direction of your life and your future.

Review of the Triune Mind: The Parody of Nonbelievers

Those who do not accept the teachings in this lesson but are well schooled in their respective fields and highly successful sometimes condemn thought power. They make no effort to learn the mental mechanics operating behind their success. Yet if they are truly successful they have unknowingly made use of what is in this lesson. They may also flatly deny any principles that are not in line with their scripted belief systems, summarily rejecting anything to the contrary. Another quote from Marie Corellie, the great English novelist, sums it up nicely.

"The very idea that any one creature (human) should be fortunate enough to secure some particular advantage which others, through their own indolence or indifference, have missed is sufficient to excite the envy of the weak or the anger of the ignorant."

Marie Corellie
Author of *The Life Everlasting*

As stated earlier in the beginning of this lesson, there are three unique entities of the human mind: conscious, subconscious, and superconscious. Characteristic functions and processes occur within each. The first was the conscious mind, with which most people are highly familiar. This part of the mind directly expresses only a tiny fraction of our true mental potential. It is the thinking mind, which uses logic and reason. Unfortunately, much of the general population is unskilled in using even this faculty of mind. The conscious mind is characterized by being the control or command center for the subconscious mind. It has the power of free will, as well as reasoning ability. Whatever it has faith in is imprinted upon the subconscious mind. The conscious mind has the job of editing information and protecting the subconscious mind from false or harmful information by using its reasoning ability.

How do the conscious mind and the subconscious interact? The conscious mind functions as the programmer for the subconscious mind. What the conscious mind thinks and believes, the subconscious absorbs into the mental core and accepts as operating instructions to act on.

The real power to solve problems and achieve goals lies in utilizing the subconscious mind. If you continuously concentrate or focus on certain thoughts, goals, or solutions to problems, the subconscious internalizes them as operating instructions. The subconscious mind can draw on all the information you have ever taken into your brain from the day you were born to today (memory banks). This vast subconscious storehouse contains all your knowledge; it is the keeper of your mental core. The subconscious and conscious working together in harmony have the ability to multiply knowledge, imagine or create new thoughts, making use of past experiences. The subconscious mind can also invoke the superconscious mind.

The superconscious mind is that part of the mind that is induced to action based on the conscious and subconscious minds working in harmony. When the conscious mind continuously thinks certain thoughts, such as dwelling on a goal, this gets driven into the subconscious mind, aligning the two. When this occurs, the subconscious mind can induce the superconscious mind to come to its aid. This is called superconscious thought induction and results in superconscious effects.

Superconscious effects are the strange occurrences we commonly attribute to luck or chance. The superconscious mind is characterized by the ability to tap into or communicate with Infinite Intelligence or God for information. It is the source for everyone's natural ability to develop ESP. The superconscious mind is that spiritual component of the human mind that exists inside **OR** outside the physical body. In this definition, the superconscious mind is likened to the human spirit or soul.

Since humans have a component of mind that is totally spiritual, this spiritual component can by its very nature communicate with the All Knowing (God). Conscious control of your soul is the sixth and one of the most difficult highways of power to travel, *the highway of the sovereign soul*. I don't expect everyone to accept all the concepts of mind covered in this lesson immediately; therefore I have included a recommended reading list.

*"As to the learning that any person gains from school educa-
tion, it serves only like a small capital, to put him in the way of
beginning learning for himself afterwards. Every person of
learning is finally his own teacher."*

Thomas Paine
American Revolutionary
Coauthor of the United States
Declaration of Independence

Michael Monroe Kiefer's Powerbook Library

(Recommended Reading for the Very Serious Student!)

1. *The New Testament*
2. *The Seasons of Life*, Jim Rohn
3. *The Power of Your Subconscious Mind*, Dr. Joseph Murphy
4. *Law of Success*, Napoleon Hill
5. *The Power of Positive Thinking*, Dr. Norman Vincent Peale
6. *Power of Will, Power for Success*, and *The Personal Atmosphere*, all three by Dr. Frank Channing Haddock
7. *The Unconscious*, Morton Prince, M.D.
8. *See You at the Top*, Zig Ziglar
9. *Margins of Reality—The Role of Consciousness in the Physical World*, Dr. Robert G. Jahn and Dr. Brenda J. Dunne
10. *Psycho-cybernetics*, Dr. Maxwell Maltz
11. *Cosmic Consciousness*, Richard Maurice Bucke, M.D.
12. *Mental Radio*, Upton Sinclair
13. *Higher Cortical Functions in Man*, A.R. Luria
14. *The Life Everlasting*, Marie Corellie
15. *Law of Psychic Phenomena*, Thomas J. Hudson
16. *The Subconscious Speaks*, Erna Ferrell Grabe and Paul C. Ferrell
17. *The Magic of Believing* and *TNT The Power Within You*, both by Claude M. Bristol
18. *Your Greatest Power*, J. Martin Kohe

19. *The Science of Power,* Benjamin Kidd
20. *Three Magic Words* and *The Greatest Power in the Universe,* both by U.S. Andersen
21. *Empires of the Mind,* Dr. Denis Waitley
22. *The Magic of Thinking Big,* Dr. David J. Schwartz
23. *The Higher Powers of Mind and Spirit,* Ralph Waldo Trine
24. *Mental Power Through Sleep Suggestion,* Melvin Powers
25. *Maximum Achievement* and the classic six-cassette-tape album entitled *The Psychology of Achievement,* both by Brian Tracy

That should keep you busy for a while!

Faith and a Resolute Will

"The greatest discovery of the nineteenth century was not in the realm of physical science, but the power of the subconscious touched by faith. Every individual can tap into an eternal reservoir of power that will enable them to overcome any problem that may arise. All weaknesses can be overcome, bodily healing, financial independence, spiritual awakening, prosperity beyond your wildest dreams. This is the superstructure of happiness."

William James
Harvard Psychologist
The Father of American Psychology

It will be quite astonishing to most people, the power they possess and the things that will happen to them once they are positively powerbonded. Productive thoughts will "pop" into their heads and they will begin to see opportunities everywhere in their environment. These opportunities were always there but they just weren't *perceiving* them. It isn't a miracle, it is just the laws of nature and a human being's mental mechanics at work. Being powerbonded can get you very far in life, allowing you to progress rapidly toward your goals. As you continue being powerbonded, your goals will be moving towards you as well!

This is the beauty of superconscious activity. Your goals moving toward you will mean people coming into your life, helping you, enemies becoming allies, seemingly chance occurrences and events happening on a regular, almost predictable basis, giving you unexpected boosts toward your goals. These will trim time and effort off your preplanned journey on your own individual highway of success.

Superconscious effects could result in a known obstacle on your goal path being removed through no direct physical action on your part. For example: A boss who stands in your way to promotion (if promotion is your goal) is removed through no direct effort on your part, be it through firing or voluntarily leaving. An event like this would seem to be "coincidental." It may not be fully due to your own superconscious mind; but as you begin to notice "superconscious effects" playing a more and more significant role in your life, you cannot help but come to the conclusion that this is a unique power of the human mind. It's as if through powerbonding your mind has tapped into some universal energy source, or "eternal reservoir of power" as William James put it.

Your superconscious mind sends out a vibrational beacon or a type of magnetic message, calling out and attracting people and events into your life that you had no direct physical involvement with. Conscious control of superconscious mind is the ultimate phase in the development of a POWERMIND. Conscious control of the superconscious effect is called the **"power of illumination."**

Ignorance of the mechanical function of the human brain and the universal power of the human mind prevents most people from ever reaching this state. A person who is powerbonded functions at their highest capacity; they express their true potential totally in the given area of goal achievement. Powerbonding is the high art of supreme success.

In Dr. Frank Channing Haddock's masterwork book *Power of Will* (in this book the word "will" actually meant soul, not willpower), published in the early 1900s, he refers to powerbonding as an ironclad will. The height of human achievement, the pinnacle of the pyramid of life, the high plains, are for the powerbonded only. When the three minds function as one and that one joins with the Universal for energy, a sense of elation is know to occur. A person becomes aware, enlightened, or in a superconscious state. This is indeed self-mastery! The complete unfoldment of the human soul! (**The highway of the sovereign soul.**)

Effective use of your whole mind is a major skill that you will require in order to live a successful life. The conscious, subconscious, and superconscious minds working in unison have the capacity to bring your dreams into reality. As you learned before, the subconscious mind largely governs our behaviors. It is also your link to the superconscious, which is in turn your link to Infinite Intelligence.

"Ideas come from space. This may seem astonishing and impossible to believe, but it is true. Ideas come from out of space."

Thomas Alva Edison
Scientist/inventor who possessed one of the most creative minds ever to exist

I believe what Edison meant was the idea of tapping into this Infinite Intelligence or Eternal Reservoir.

The Power of an Iron Will

A human possessing an iron will (powerbonded) becomes unconquerable. A completely powerbonded person **must** achieve their goals or die trying. Most people don't think for themselves and become victims of social conditioning, feeding their mind heterosuggestion (suggestions from others) from the mass media.

A single new thought or idea can change the whole direction of your life. How many people do you know throughout history who turned their whole life around when they caught fire with a new idea. By caught fire I mean made it their mission in life. They rallied support, overcame obstacles, and were driven by a strong *internal sense of purpose.* They may have explored new worlds, motivated millions, built businesses, built nations, conquered lands, liberated slaves. These people had no monopoly on mind power. They just knew a few Universal Laws, and in many cases only a handful of mental techniques, which was enough for them to make history.

You have the same potential they had. You have a brain, the biomachine of the mind, and a soul. You only need to use them. You can change your body, beauty, happiness, wealth, power, health, success, etc.

Your thinking however, must be strictly disciplined. What is in your conscious mind is reflected in your outside world. Thoughts are causes, your outer world is the reflected effect — *"As ye sow, so shall ye reap."* The Universal Law of sowing and reaping, cause and effect is inviolate!

Plan your life carefully; if you don't, you are planning to fail. There is no middle ground. Read and reread this book. It is based on Universal Law. Use as many of the techniques as you can; become a master of masters. The superpower combination of the information in this book along with your natural talents is more than enough for you to live a life far better than your wildest dreams. You'll get results, be alert, be alive, live better than ever before. Back your goals with unquestionable faith, an iron will to achieve greatly, and you will become an unstoppable beneficial force to all who come into contact with you!

An After-the-Lesson Visit With the Author

Very few people of the world have been exposed to the concepts you just learned in this lesson. What a mind-expanding journey this must have been for you. I can recall when I first started my research for this lesson. I found that many of the most influential, creative, successful, wealthy people throughout history were studying this same subject. I thought, "They never taught me any of this stuff in college." I went to college for eight years and obtained two high tech science degrees, yet I saw people with no college education running businesses, being healthier than I was, more powerful, wealthier, helping more people in need. I thought, "What are they studying?" Certainly not what I had studied! So I needed to find out. That search led me to many unique discoveries, down some very interesting alleys, and into some very old dust-covered books with brittle yellowed pages.

I was very curious about the conscious, subconscious, and superconscious minds. As my work in this area progressed I found many common threads running through the scientific, philosophical, and religious literature. Many scientists had been discovering the mechanisms operating behind mental principles. My goal in this lesson was then to expose you to the very basic elements in regards to the operation of the human mind. Some of the material contained in this lesson is highly controversial; that's why I relied mainly on solid scientific data rather than entertaining you with an interesting religious or philosophical discourse.

I had to dig into both old and new scientific research to filter out science from science fiction for you, using a skeptical eye. What I have written should not be confused with unproven theories. Mindscience is an exact science. All my formal training has been in science, and I don't believe in claims unsubstantiated by rigorous controlled testing. Most of the principles in this lesson you can test out for yourself to determine their validity. If you had difficulty with this lesson, persistence and continuous study will breed better understanding. The books I recommended in the reading list will help further your understanding.

As you look at the world around you, realize that everything made by humans hatched as a creative thought in one person's mind before it came into materialization. Telephones, televisions, cars, houses, airplanes, sewing machines, spaceships, even money sprang from the human mind.

The secret of success lies in the workings of each person's own unique mind. Thought precedes all actions. Eating, dressing, going to work, walking, and reading are all preceded by a thought. How you walk, talk, dress, all reflect your thinking. What you exhibit outwardly you are inwardly. In terms of self-image psychology, you are what you *believe* yourself to be.

The very idea that thinking and believing can develop a fortune, change your health, increase your personal power, improve your ability to learn, is nothing short of profound!

What you think about in a focused manner and act toward achieving you can usually achieve. Your mind radiates a type of vibrational energy that can directly influence people and events in the world. Thought power is as powerful as anything in this world. So few people understand this concept that they scoff at it without any real knowledge, without doing any research of their own.

Most people block their own success. They do not understand the interplay of their conscious, subconscious, and superconscious minds. With the knowledge of how these interact, you gain a large degree of self-confidence.

Thoughts create after their kind, meaning they attract to you the people, objects, and events that *correlate* with them. Your inner dominant thoughts will control to a great degree your outer circumstances. It is similar to magnetism. You are like a living magnet, attracting to you that which you continuously think about (goals). Thoughts of fear and disaster are just as magnetic as the thoughts of success, but they attract poor health or troubles to us.

Always remember, your subconscious mind is impressionable to all your conscious thoughts; it acts on ideas immediately according to the degree of belief you have; it is totally obedient. It uses all the information stored in its memory banks since before you were born and can induce the superconscious mind's activity. Used destructively it brings failure, sickness, sadness, poverty, etc. Used constructively it brings freedom, success, health, riches, happiness, etc.

To become successful you must fill your conscious mind with constructive, worthy goals. These goals must be accepted as being real, achievable, and already existing in perfect detail in your mind. The subconscious will then have the exact instructions it needs to carry out this command effectively and aid you in achievement.

Thoughts charged with the positive emotion of faith in God and in yourself have power unparalleled. All this power is at your fingertips, you need only use it!

With this new understanding, as you think and look back over your past you will recognize how many seemingly strange events of your life fit neatly together. The random events are all really logically linked, leading you to where you currently are. Even the fact that you are reading this book is not by chance. You were supposed to have it, finish reading it, use it yourself, and help others use it too!

As I close this marvelous mind-expanding lesson, the following quotations are worth pondering.

"A miracle is nothing more or less than this. Anyone who has come into a knowledge of his true identity, of his oneness with the all-pervading wisdom and power, thus makes it possible for laws higher than the ordinary mind knows of to be revealed to him."

> **Ralph Waldo Trine**
> **Author of The LIFE Books,**
> **including *In Tune with The**
> **Infinite, The Alignment of**
> **Life*, and *The Higher Powers**
> **of Mind and Spirit***

"You are searching for the magic key that will unlock the door to the source of power; and yet you have the key in your own hands, and you make use of it the moment you learn to control your thoughts."

"When your desires are strong enough you will appear to possess super human powers to achieve."

> **Napoleon Hill**
> **American success philosopher**
> **Author of *Think and Grow**
> **Rich, Law of Success, Science**
> **of Personal Achievement*, and**
> ***Mental Dynamite***

"You know from past experiences that whenever you have been driven to the wall, or thought you were, you have extricated yourself in a way which you never would have dreamed possible had you not been put to the test. The trouble is that in your everyday life you don't go deep enough to tap the divine mind within you."

Orison Swett Marden
Author of *Pushing to the Front*

Lesson

5 ▸ The Mental Core

Overview

In Lesson 4 you learned from the four-subprocess working model that the mental core is used in both the association and evaluation subprocesses. These two subprocesses guide and direct what you perceive in the environment as well as how you make decisions about what is perceived. The mental core warrants further study, because your attitudes and much of your behavior also stem from what is in your mental core. This lesson is dedicated to expanding your awareness in regard to this unique powerhouse held within the subconscious mind. What you learn here will serve as solid background information, enabling you to have complete comprehension of the High Achievement techniques discussed in Part IV of The POWER-MIND System.

The Mental Core

The 4 Modes of Thought

**Principle: In conscious thought humans use four modes that
contribute to the ongoing development of their
mental core: *verbal, sensory, conceptual,* and
*emotional.***

As stated in Lesson 4, your mind's mental core is an intri-
cate network of raw information **plus** attitudes (emotions) about
that information. It is made up of what you "know" and how you
"feel" about what you know. The mental core also contains both
your self-image and your view of the environment. Each of your
attitudes concerning any piece of information stored in your
mental core is the result of conditioning or programming,
whether you did this deliberately or unknowingly. For most people it was done unknowingly. Almost all attitudes are conditioned. You start life with a blank slate, so to speak. Each attitude is then built piece by piece, brick by brick, through conscious thought and your responses to the world around you. Your
conscious mind is and always will be the programmer for your
subconscious mental core.

How is this complex subconscious mental core built? *In conscious thought humans use four modes that contribute to the
ongoing development of their mental core: **verbal, sensory, conceptual,** and **emotional.*** The one most widely recognized by
people is the verbal mode. You can think in terms of words. You
are reading this line verbalizing each word in your head. This
inner dialog is popularly known as "self-talk." It goes on all the
time while you are awake, when you read, listen to the radio,
talk to others, etc. This self-talk continues at about 300-400
words per minute for most people.

However, you didn't use this verbal mode of thought or self-
talk until you learned the meaning of words. You were taught
when you were a small child that words have *symbolic* meaning.
But what about before you learned of words? Before that time
your conscious thought processes used primarily two other
modes of thought to program the subconscious mental core, the
sensory and *emotional* modes.

Here are some examples to help illustrate the sensory thinking mode. Think of the word "house." Can you see a house? Think of the word "car." Can you see a car? This is what's known as your "mind's eye." Now use your "mind's ear." Can you hear a crying baby, a dog barking, a police siren? How about your "mind's nose"? Can you recall the fragrance of an irritated skunk, sewage, pizza, barbecued chicken, bacon, coffee? Now your "mind's tongue." Can you taste salt, coffee, spicy mustard, chocolate? Now your "mind's skin." Can you feel velvet, sandpaper, heat, snow, water? What you just did is called *sensory thinking.*

Chances are you can see visual images more clearly in your mind than you can imagine anything else with your other "mind senses." This is no coincidence. Your eyes have the largest area of the brain devoted to them of any sense organ. A few people can imagine sounds better than see visual images. They imagine more with their mind's ear than with any other mind sense. On rare occasions individuals will use another mind sense more. Note, however, that the human brain ranks the mind's eye first for imagination or *sensory thinking.* This is a critical point and is crucial to the later topic of **Imagineering**, which will be discussed in the High Achievement part of this book.

Your mind senses can conjure up sensory thoughts logged in from earlier experiences that you actually had **or** *imagined you had.* This is a key statement. It is truly amazing that your mind can call up prior experiences and allow you to "reexperience" them again very vividly. Once your mind has taken in information or experiences through any of your five senses, it can later "recreate" the actual experience or a *modified experience* for you through the power of imagination.

For example, notice what is happening in your mind as you read the next sentence. *There is a small brown poisonous spider crawling on the back of your neck.* First you read (verbalize) the words. Their meaning is instantaneously interpreted into visual images (sensory images). Then you search your mental core (evaluation) for what your past experiences with spiders are. You then think *emotionally.* What are the **feelings** that you "conditioned yourself" to have about spiders? Are you affectionate toward spiders, fearful of them, repulsed? Whatever your feelings are about spiders, can you acknowledge that you were not born with these feelings? You were born with a genetic ability to have feelings (emotions). But you *learned to associate* these emotions with people, places, events, objects, and ideas.

At birth you had the capacity to feel fear, security, frustration, joy, pain, pleasure, and a host of other genetically programmed emotions. As you live and experience life you associate specific emotions with everything in the world around you. This creates your attitudes about foods, sounds, smells, events, people, places, ideas, etc. At birth your thinking was only two dimensional: *sensory* and *emotional*. You didn't know any words (verbal thinking) and had no concepts to deal with. Nonetheless, these two early modes of thought served to build your mental core. Later you programmed the mental core with words (verbal thinking) so you could label your sensory experiences, emotions, and concepts.

The fourth mode of conscious thought is conceptual, dealing with abstractions such as the future, personal freedom, time, infinity, nothingness, subatomic. You don't experience these much with the sensory, verbal, or emotional modes.

As an adult you can now think with all four modes: **verbal, sensory, conceptual, and emotional.** The degree to which the human mind can think in terms of words is one of the prime factors that differentiates us from all other life on this planet. If you were born with an inability to communicate with language, your behavior would be more "animallike." Even among normal people who do think with language, there is a direct correlation between the size of a person's vocabulary and effective intelligent behavior.

The four modes of thought, verbal, sensory, conceptual, and emotional, are all free-flowing in your conscious mind. Any single mode can trigger a stream of thought; that thought usually causes the other three modes to quickly follow suit.

Self-talk has received the meaning in recent years of being purely verbal. So I will use the term "self-communication," which encompasses the other three modes of thought as well. It is crucial for you to understand all four modes, because this is how your subconscious mental core was built, is built, and can be **"rebuilt."** You will learn later how *autogenic conditioning* can be used as one of the fastest, most effective ways to reshape your mental core. It is extremely important to consider all four modes of thinking. Any thoughts you have are not just fleeting impressions that vaporize or disappear; your subconscious mind is always listening. It will store, record, and process each conscious thought you have and continuously reinforce, modify, and adjust the existing structure of information in your mental core. Every single thought you have in your conscious mind makes a contribution to the mental core. There are no exceptions!

Positive and Negative Attitude Formation

An "attitude" is defined as your inclination toward (favorable) or away from (unfavorable) something. The *degree* of inclination toward or away can be strong, weak, or anywhere in between. You can test yourself with the list below. For some of the items you may think you are completely neutral, but you probably aren't; you will usually have a *tendency* toward or away from anything you know about. Nothing is neutral. You have an associated attitude with every bit of information in your mental core. Put a P if you have a positive attitude and an N if you have a negative one next to each item on the list below. Try to really get in touch with your attitude about each one as you read them.

1. Eating dog food
2. Kittens
3. Puppies
4. Eating stewed tomatoes
5. Going to work on Monday mornings
6. Your car
7. Your boss
8. Your spouse
9. Your kids
10. Making public speeches to large audiences
11. People from foreign countries
12. Snakes
13. Spiders
14. Flying in airplanes
15. Money
16. Power

As you went through the list, could you sense your mental core at work, generating your attitudes toward or away from, positive or negative? Did you sense this emotional component, which was programmed into your mind? Could you feel how your attitude was instantly **associated** with each listed item? Keep in mind that all of your attitudes about anything are the result of earlier conditioning, and that adjustments and reinforcement of your attitudes are made through your four modes of conscious thought (self-communication).

You developed all of the attitudes inside your mind. No one else plugged them in. Your own past self-programming has resulted in the attitudes you harbor right now. You developed the attitudes in your own mental core for better or for worse, and you alone can change them!

As an aid in understanding attitude development, you can visualize your mind as the scales of justice or a simple pan balance, one pan representing the positive side, the other pan representing the negative side. Only one of the four modes of self-communication acts as a weight for information as it enters the positive or negative pan. It is the **emotional** component. As weight builds up on either the positive side or negative side of the balance, your attitude develops in regard to any given idea or object. It can also be about even, no weight (emotions) strongly for or against. The amount of weight is determined by your emotional intensity, also called **emotional charge**. A single fleeting thought has little weight unless the emotional charge is high. For example, the word "rape" has a high negative emotional charge for most people. The word "and" has little charge. The word "love" has a strong positive emotional charge for most people.

A constant flow of thoughts, each carrying a positive or negative emotional charge (weight) about any given idea or object, eventually builds up into a strong attitude and can have a great impact on the mental core, which in turn influences your behavior.

I'll use "speaking" as an example to illustrate how *emotional association* forms an attitude. Remember, before children begin learning how to speak they primarily use sensory and emotional thinking. Later on they learn the exciting world of speaking by first uttering sounds and then whole words. It is all new for them. As they learn whole words, their parents greatly encourage them to speak. They begin associating positive emotions with speaking. They sense approval from their parents; they get positively reinforced by them. It doesn't take long now before the genetic potential to speak gets fully expressed as the child starts speaking on a regular basis.

The child enjoys speaking. Speaking serves the child's needs quite well. Weights accumulate on the positive side of the mental attitude balance in regards to speaking. A positive attitude is forming in conjunction with speaking. But later a mixed message may come in. For example, little Annie happens to be speaking loudly in church. Mommy says, "Shhh, you must be quiet in church." and Sally is talking when Daddy is on the telephone with a potential new employer. "Shut up!" Sally's Dad barks out. "Go to your room right now!"

The prediction of what happens inside Annie's and Sally's minds is not certain, it's only a probability. However, Sally and Annie will now *internalize* what has been said to them. It is most likely some weights will now be put on the negative side of their mental attitude balances in regard to speaking. Annie probably won't be so enthusiastic about speaking in church, Sally probably won't be talking to her Daddy much when Daddy is on the telephone.

Let's project Sally and Annie a little further in time. If Annie is told by her parents to "shut up, be quiet" consistently and punished for speaking much of the time in public, she will probably have a lot of weight on the negative side of her mental attitude balance in regard to expressing herself. She becomes a quiet and reserved child.

Let's say Annie and Sally are now in school and the teacher asks the students to read aloud in class. How well do you suppose Annie is going to do? Does she have a lot of enthusiasm about doing this, when for years outside of school with her family she was supposed to be quiet? How about Sally? Let's say she got yelled at a few times by Daddy at home, but she also got a lot more encouragement for speaking than poor little Annie ever did. It's Sally's turn in class, she "feels" pretty good about this reading aloud business. In fact, she read a storybook to her mother the night before and Mom thought it was great! So Sally reads aloud in class and does well. The teacher enthusiastically says, "Fine job, Sally!" (more positive reinforcement for Sally from the teacher). Annie does her reading. She is very nervous but does OK. The teacher says, "That's nice, Annie," but there is no enthusiasm in her voice and she doesn't smile at Annie. I would bet after this is over Sally really likes reading aloud in class and Annie dreads it. Sally felt warm and good about herself; *proud positive* **emotions** are associated with speaking aloud in class for her. Annie may have felt uptight, embarrassed; maybe some of the kids laughed at her, ridiculed her; she may have been very upset. The emotional charge on the mental attitude scale was probably positive for Sally, negative for Annie.

Let's project into the future a little further now. Annie never quite got the hang of speaking in public, while Sally always did quite well. Now it's time to give some prepared speeches about summer vacation in front of the class. Well, Annie isn't hot on this idea at all; in fact, she starts **TELLING HERSELF**, "I can't do this. I'll screw up, the other kids will laugh at me. I feel stupid. I'm really nervous." (Her self-communication is very negative, generating strong negative emotions.) She gets up in front of the class, gives a *self-prophesied* terrible speech. Her **negative** attitude is then further reinforced. Sally does a great job; her **positive** attitude is further reinforced.

Move ahead in time ten years now. Sally and Annie hear about the Toastmasters public speaking organization. I bet Sally is pretty interested in it. I also bet Annie doesn't want anything to do with it. *Annie is behaving in a manner consistent with what was built into her mental core years before, and so is Sally!!!* Annie is probably not going to be very good at expressing herself to others in her relationships, to her family, or at her place of employment. Sally will probably do well.

Can you see in this simple scenario about Annie and Sally how future behavior can be shaped by past experiences and also how those experiences are internalized by the individual they are happening to? Positive and negative attitudes are built in this way. I realize this has been simplified, but I extrapolated this example to prove a point. The principle is sound. This does happen—*it happens all the time!*

Here is another example to illustrate this principle of attitude formation. Joey is seven years old and his friend Billy invites him over for dinner. Joey gets approval from his Mom, then calls Billy back, but Billy now says, "No, don't come over tonight, we're having tuna casserole." If we assume Joey never had tuna casserole before, how do you think he will internalize (self-communicate) tuna casserole? As a delicious food or a terrible one? This will be the beginning of an attitude about tuna casserole for Joey. A small weight goes on the negative side of the mental attitude balance for tuna casserole. Joey never had tuna casserole or heard the words before, but *by sensing* the tone in Billy's voice he *perceived* it to be distasteful. Joey **associates** negatively with tuna casserole from his *perception* that Billy doesn't like it. What Billy says and how he says it does not guarantee how Joey will start shaping his very first attitude toward tuna casserole; only Joey's own self-communication (programming) can shape his attitude. Joey may say to himself, "Gee, whatever tuna casserole is, it must be awful." Joey will internalize in his imagination a **visual** image, a **sensory** impression, and a negative **emotion** all revolving around the words (**verbal**) "tuna casserole," even though he has never seen or eaten it before. This one incident doesn't create a strong negative attitude for Joey against tuna casserole, however.

But a few days later Daddy asks Mommy what's for dinner. Mommy says, "Tuna casserole." Daddy says, "Oh no, I hate tuna casserole. I told you that years ago!" Joey overhears this conversation. Daddy has a pretty negative tone in his voice. Joey has heard that tone before. Joey **associates** this with what he already **"knows"** about tuna casserole, that it's "not good." He thinks, "Daddy hates tuna casserole, too. It must really be bad." Joey also smells (sensory) the tuna casserole cooking in the kitchen and now **associates** a smell with the negative attitude. Notice, that neither Mommy nor Daddy had any direct input into Joey's mind. They weren't even talking to him! But Joey was sure talking to himself a lot. Joey's own **verbal, sensory, emotional** thought processes put another heavy weight on the negative side of his mental attitude balance for tuna casserole.

Now Joey gets some new information. He sees a tuna commercial on TV, and those people seem to like tuna casserole. He probably puts a small positive weight on his mental attitude scale for tuna casserole. But at this point the negative weights still outweigh the positive ones.

Now Joey's older brother Tommy comes home. Mother says, "I thought you went to Heather's house for dinner." Tommy says, "Yeah, I was going to, but they're having that nasty tuna casserole stuff. I don't like it so I went out for a burger and fries." Joey hears this and says to himself, "Tommy doesn't like tuna casserole either." Another negative weight for tuna casserole. *Notice that Joey is now developing a strong negative attitude based on what he says to himself, not necessarily on what others are saying to him directly.*

Joey has now built a fairly strong negative attitude for tuna casserole in his mental core. His family members and friends whom he loves, admires, and respects, Daddy, big brother, and Billy, don't like it. *There is extra intensity and emotional charge attached to what his family and friends say. This is called social conditioning.*

A month later Joey's family is invited to a dinner party. Guess what they're having—**TUNA CASSEROLE!** Joey smells it as he enters the house; negative emotions are triggered in his brain by the smell. His apprehension builds. They all sit down for dinner. Joey may even be so worked up at this point he feels nauseous. He whispers to his mother, "I don't want any tuna casserole" (negative weight). Mother says, "Try it, dear, you'll like it." Joey says, "I don't like it" (negative weight). Mother says, "You've never had it before, sweetheart, just have a little." Joey says, "I don't care, I don't want any at all" (negative weight). Dad steps in and says, "He doesn't have to eat any, honey, if he doesn't want to." Joey says, "Thanks, Daddy" (another negative weight for the tuna casserole). Joey says, "I may have thrown up all over the table, Mommy, if I ate any. I hate tuna casserole" (negative weight).

Each time Joey **verbally affirmed** his negative attitude towards tuna casserole he was talking not only to others but to himself as well, continuing to reinforce his own negative attitude inside his own mental core. As the inner dialog described above went on, the emotional intensity of the whole situation increased until Daddy put the final kibosh on the tuna casserole. Joey was quick to pick up that weight and add it to his pile, reinforcing his already strong attitude **against** tuna casserole. Unintentionally Joey's Mom and Dad insisted that Joey develop a full-fledged hatred for tuna casserole. They were not programming his mind directly—Joey did that all on his own—but they created an environment that fostered the development of the negative attitude (social conditioning).

Joey's like or dislike for tuna casserole probably won't enhance or destroy his life. I used this example because it is an easy way to illustrate that most of your **attitudes are not genetic but are learned or socially conditioned.** Joey was not born liking or disliking tuna casserole. He learned to dislike it.

This principle of attitude development and reinforcement applies equally well to very significant areas of life. The attitudes housed in your mental core control the effectiveness of your behavior. When attitudes first develop they tend to progress in the same direction in which they started. Negative attitudes tend to become more negative, positive ones more positive. (Refer to Mental Core Diagram #1.)

The Emotional Gate

You saw from the attitude cycling diagram that the attitude held within your mental core influences your behavior to a large degree and that your behavior tends to reinforce that attitude. This means that what you expect to happen when you enter any situation will be enhanced or suppressed by how you **feel,** and what you **expect** is based on the attitude *already existing* in your mental core. Your attitude can be thought of as an "emotional gate." The setting of this emotional gate allows your potential to flow (opening the gate) or closes it off (shutting the gate). When Joey in our previous example takes his first mouthful ever of tuna casserole, he will influence his own *perception* of how it tastes. When you go through activities, whether making public

Mental Core Diagram #1

ATTITUDE CYCLING

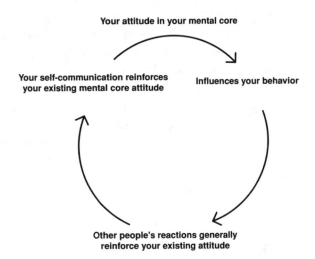

Your attitude in your mental core

Your self-communication reinforces
your existing mental core attitude

Influences your behavior

Other people's reactions generally
reinforce your existing attitude

Your behavior tends to be consistent with your existing attitude in your mental core. This then reinforces the same attitude, whether it is a positive or negative one. Once an attitude starts the cycle spinning, it tends to keep spinning in the same direction, feeding upon itself. You also tend to select things out of your environment that reinforce your initial attitude and to ignore things that go against it.

speeches, going on a job interview, preparing dinner, dealing on a car or a house, whatever the situation, is how you expect that event to proceed will have a great influence on the actual outcome. *YOUR EXPECTATION IS CONTROLLED BY YOUR ATTITUDE.*

"For, he that expects nothing shall not be disappointed, but he that expects much — if he lives and uses that in hand day-by-day — shall be full to running over."

Edgar Cayce
The sleeping prophet

Cayce's quotation above is a version of what is called the "self-fulfilling prophecy" phenomenon. You actually have much more control over events than you currently believe. There are two stages to this phenomenon. First, your **expectancy**, which is based on your attitude, positions your emotional gate, helping or hindering the flow of your natural potential. And second, your expectation is communicated to other people non-verbally through tone of voice, rate of speech, and body language and also energetically through superconscious thought waves. People will respond to these silent messages in such a way as to help create the outcome **you yourself expect!**

For example, many people dread getting up on Monday morning to go to work (usually because they aren't in a job that matches their natural talents). They say things like "Its going to be a terrible day, Mondays always are." The day probably will turn out terrible for them. Their negative attitude at the outset will limit their flow of potential throughout the day. Their general *mind-set* in the morning is negative, which closes their emotional gate. This will be immediately communicated to others they encounter through their tone of voice, facial expressions, posture, and other cues. Their decision early in the morning to project this image to others will affect all the events of their day, and their negativity will be reflected right back to them. They will focus on all the bad things that happen to them throughout the day, not the good. Other people will reinforce their negative expectation, perhaps saying, "Gee, you are a grouch today. What's your problem?" The difficult task that needs to be done in the office will seem impossible. Other people won't be very cheery or helpful towards them (I wonder why?). This all serves to reinforce their negative attitude about how lousy Monday mornings always are. (Refer back to the attitude cycling diagram.)

This self-fulfilling prophecy phenomenon works equally well in the positive direction. If you awaken on Monday morning and generate an optimistic attitude about the day, your emotional gate opens, allowing the full flow of your natural potential. You will be much more effective throughout the day, as people will respond to you more favorably. That difficult task at the office somehow won't seem so difficult after all. Your expectancy for success at the start of the day will be communicated to other people. This will have an extremely powerful impact on the outcome of the day's events for you. The internal attitude change in your own mind will affect your perception of events and have a direct influence on other people. This is no mere mental trick, it's a Universal Law!

Here is the mental programming process detailed out. As you sense people and events around you, you **associate** them with your preexisting attitude about such matters, in your mental core. Your perception of what you think is "supposed to happen" does, and you say, "That figures, that's just what I expected!" You now reinforce your **preexisting** attitude.

If there is a contradiction in what you perceive and your subconscious mental core attitude, you say to yourself, "This isn't normal. This is an exception to the rule." By doing this you **don't change** your preexisting attitude but reinforce it. You are **not internalizing** your perception of what is really happening. You are throwing away what's really going on by consciously editing it out! That's why it's so hard to change an attitude once the attitude is formed. Attitudes usually just tend to reinforce themselves. For example, you gave a presentation and you *"know"* your presentations are always terrible. But this one was different, it went quite well. You received many compliments. Instead of changing your mental attitude, you say to yourself,

"Boy, I sure was lucky. I'm really no good at presentations. This one was a fluke. I wore my lucky tie, that must be why I did well. I'll never give a good one like this again. This isn't me." None of the positive attitude is reinforced, all of the negative is. Your self-communication is serving to strengthen your negative attitude about how **poor** a presenter you are. Your preexisting attitude in your mental core reads like this: *"I'm really a poor presenter."* Instead of changing that internal attitude when you do a good job (which you had the natural potential to do all along), you have a tendency to reinforce the preexisting **negative** attitude. You say to yourself, *"I gave one good presentation, but I'm really still a poor presenter."* With this internal negative attitude in your mental core, becoming a consistently great presenter or expressing your true potential is impossible. I could tell you a hundred times that you can be a great presenter, but you would be quick to **affirm,** *"No, I can't, because you don't know me. You see, I'm really a poor presenter."* You will tend to cling to your preexisting negative **false belief** about yourself so strongly and defend it to others even though it may be making you unhappy, unhealthy, bitter, and full of despair.

Here is another example. Harvey knows he is no artist. As a general rule his paintings are quite consistent with his negative attitude about his ability to paint. In other words, much of what he paints is poor in his estimation and other people's. No one ever encouraged Harvey to paint, and when he did they put his work down. In high school art class, the teacher asked that each student paint a picture and bring it in the following week. Harvey didn't put much effort into the assignment. He "knew" he couldn't paint. His preexisting attitude about being a poor artist guided his behavior. He took his painting to class and the other students laughed at it. Harvey thought, "I knew it, I knew I couldn't paint, what a stupid picture." What if Harvey's painting had turned out well? What would Harvey have said to himself (self-programmed) then? Would he perceive the painting as beautiful, well made, colored to perfection because of his latent abilities, and quickly change his attitude about his artistic talent? Probably not!

This is a key point; it depends on how negative his artistic talent attitude really was. If he only thought he was a slightly poor artist, he might internalize a good painting as "Hey, maybe I can paint. This painting turned out great. I feel good about this painting and myself." He might have *accepted* and *internalized* his good painting to reinforce a more positive attitude concerning his artistic ability.

However, if Harvey firmly **believed** that he was a lousy artist he might say, "It was just dumb luck. Somehow this painting turned out okay" (negative programming). If he was given some compliments on his painting, he would immediately throw them away (consciously editing them out) and say to himself, "They are just saying that, they really don't think it is any good" (negative programming).

Harvey can also continue to reinforce his negative attitude about his painting even when he didn't paint the picture! For example, if Harvey goes to an art show with his friends, he may think to himself, "Golly, these paintings are great." He may even *verbalize* his attitude to the group in the form of a self-depreciating compliment to the artist, saying, "These artists are great. I wish I could paint like them but I know I can't" (negative programming for Harvey, reinforcing his own preexisting negative attitude).

Let's take one last example, a family situation. Sue, a sixteen-year-old, is waiting for her ride to go over to her girlfriend's house and has some time to kill. She notices her parents working hard on a large remodeling project and offers to help. "Can I help?" she says. "I've got some time to kill." Her parents have a host of responses they could use, positive or negative. But in this case they are shocked! They say, "We can't believe you are offering to help. Are you sick or something?" Sue probably won't internalize this in a positive way, thereby reinforcing a good attitude about her parents.

Why did her parents react so harshly anyway? Well, they have a preexisting attitude about Sue based on sixteen years of child rearing and "know" that Sue is a thoughtless, self-centered, arrogant, immature slob. They *"wish"* Sue would get better, but they don't seem to realize they need to help reinforce mature behavior in Sue when it happens. When Sue offers to help, they *perceive*, then *associate*, what they "know" about Sue. They evaluate it as "That's not normal for Sue to behave this way because *I know* Sue is a mostly irresponsible teenager." So the parents behave in a manner consistent with their attitude about Sue in their mental cores. They say "We can't believe . . ." They behave in a manner entirely consistent with their preexisting attitude about Sue!

What about Sue? How does she feel about this exchange? She was rejected and probably figures, "What's the use, I'm never going to offer any help to those bitter old people again." Had our well-meaning but ignorant parents understood the attitude amplification process and their own mental core, they would have gladly accepted Sue's help. They would say "Sure, we appreciate the help. We can sure use it." That's all, no big production on their part. Just a sincere show of appreciation. The parents would then be reinforcing the kind of behavior they want in Sue instead of reinforcing the behavior that they don't want.

If Sue understands the attitude cycling process, she will know that her parent's negative response need not be internalized in a negative way. She can respond calmly, by saying, "I just want to help out. Can I do some wallpapering?" It is in Sue's best interest to develop herself and her mind in spite of her parents!

Can you see how your attitudes, whether they are strongly positive or strongly negative, feed on themselves? Your perception of reality is influenced by your attitudes held within your mental core. Your perception feeds back on your attitude, amplifying it and influencing your behavior. This in turn feeds back into the cycle. The diagram below illustrates the process.

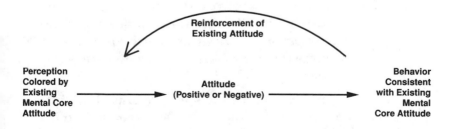

Even though the natural tendency is for an attitude to amplify itself, it does not have to be this way. If that were the case there would be no point in reading this section! It is normal for your conscious mind to **reaffirm** and reinforce your attitudes about yourself and your world. You adopted most of these attitudes years ago; however, you can consciously **decide** to take more deliberate control of what you are thinking. You can guide your thoughts more carefully to build the kind of attitudes into your mental core that will serve you much better than some of the ones you may currently have.

Your understanding of these concepts is important because as you use the principles of this book you may encounter reactions of surprise or shock from other people—family, friends, coworkers, etc. Others are going to notice changes in your behavior. Change is not bad, it's absolutely necessary for your personal success. The "that's not like you at all" response is to be taken as a compliment. Take the surprised responses from others as compliments, signs that you are changing, becoming more effective. This is rewarding evidence that what you are learning is working for you!

Take some time now to review and reflect on this material. Be sure you understand the attitude cycling, reinforcement principle, and self-fulfilling prophecy thoroughly. Go through the examples very carefully. Remember, attitudes tend to get stronger and stronger no matter what the outside events really are. *People color reality with the preexisting attitudes in their mental core.*

Childhood Conditioning and the Flow of Potential

Principle: **Destructive/restrictive attitudes elicit the emotion of anxiety when they are violated, shutting off the flow of potential. Constructive attitudes don't elicit the emotion of anxiety when they are violated.**

The first few years of a child's life are critical, in that a tremendous amount of learning takes place from birth to four years. Not only is information acquisition proceeding at a rapid rate, but the foundation attitudes, physical habits, and mental (thinking) habits are all being laid down at this time as well. A child has great emotional attachment to the parents during these "formative" years. Because of this the child has a great tendency to incorporate "messages" from his or her parents as true or real. These are internalized and begin to form the child's mental core.

Parents who repeatedly send negative messages, such as "no, no, don't, shut up, stop that," are stifling the child's genetically programmed curiosity and creative drive, effectively forming a mental prison in which the child must live. A child during this time will take communication messages to heart much more than would an adult in an exchange with another adult. (Still it should be noted the child's own conscious mind does the programming, not the parent.) These messages carry the emotional charges of pain, pleasure, fear, punishment, promise, reward, etc. These need not be physical in nature to be effective. Rejection of love by attention deprivation, popularly termed a "time out" session, can be considered emotional punishment or pain to a child. The emotional charges attached to messages can be on either end of the extremes, with pain and pleasure being the outliers.

EMOTIONAL RANGE

Extreme negative . . . . **Extreme Positive**

Pain	**Pleasure**
Isolation	**Partnership**
Fear	**Love**
Rejection	**Attention**
Scorn	**Praise**

The child will have a natural tendency to move toward or repeat behaviors that bring positive consequences and away from behaviors that elicit negative ones. This principle applies to all human behavior, but children are extremely susceptible. Why? As we learned earlier in this lesson, the emotional mode of learning is a very significant part of a child's conscious self-communication, more so than the verbal and conceptual modes.

A child's behavior is shaped in this way. Destructive behaviors tend to be inflexible and hard to change, while constructive ones are easily adjusted and shaped, allowing constructive behaviors to be honed to razor sharpness.

An example of how a physical constructive behavior develops is a child's learning to run. The child must first have the *desire* to learn. He knows he can move faster, get from place to place quicker by running. He sees other kids doing it, learning by *modeling*. The child then gains information on how it is done by his *sense* of sight, watching others. His parents teach him to walk, help train him, *praise* him (positive reinforcement). Trial and error also plays an important part; when he falls it isn't too painful, so he tries again and again, **correcting for errors each time** (this is a point to remember). As he moves faster and faster without falling, the coordinated effort and success skill is developing and being remembered. His skill and effectiveness are being developed. Repetition of the skill allows for the acquisition of more and more feedback information. A subconscious or automatic program for running develops in his subconscious memory banks. The conscious or deliberate actions during the learning phase are now becoming automatic or subconsciously controlled. The three steps involved in the development of constructive behaviors are:

1. Associating a positive emotion with a particular constructive behavior, object, situation, or idea

2. Gathering information from training (assistance or encouragement from others), personal experience (trial, error, and corrections), and modeling (learning from others)

3. Practicing or repeating the skill over and over to make the behavior **automatic or subconsciously controlled.**

Can you recall how these three steps played a role when you learned to drive a car, to print letters of the alphabet, to type, to sew, to golf, to bowl, to dribble a basketball, to catch a ball, to swim, to ski, to hit a baseball? It is easy to see how you acquired a good feeling about successfully accomplishing these tasks. You took lessons or watched others or read books, you used trial and error, made corrections, and you practiced, practiced, practiced (soon you will learn a powerful substitute for actual practice, called imagineering or mental rehearsal). The new skill became automatic, in other words, your potential flowed naturally and wasn't consciously forced. **You used no will power at all!**

You also may have learned other constructive behaviors, such as foreign languages, mathematical equations such as $2 + 2 = ?$, multiplication rules like $9 \times 3 = ?$ You don't have to think about these answers; they automatically flow into your consciousness.

A *destructive* behavior involves the three steps above as well. However, the associated emotions are negative, not positive. The emotional feeling associated may be hatred, anger, disgust, jealousy, envy, frustration, or the big F (Fear). A constant negative emotional association with any aspect of yourself or your environment builds a destructive behavior. You can recognize self-limiting destructive attitudes when you say things like "I can't," "I could never do that," or "I wish I could" about any activity. These are inhibitory phrases expressing a self-limiting belief.

Equally self-limiting are the "have-to" attitudes, such as "I hate doing this but, **I have to.**" This is very self-limiting, restricting the flow of your potential. You will never be as good as you can be at anything if you feel you have to do it. Do you have any destructive/restrictive attitudes about any of the following examples: painting a picture, speaking in front of five hundred people, crying in front of your spouse, making a million dollars per year, going back to school? How about have-to attitudes like eating all the food on your plate or answering a ringing telephone? Can you see how you have associated strong emotions with some of these behaviors? These attitudes have become part of your mental core and thus automatically control your behavior.

Here is an example of how a have-to attitude may develop. Karl sits down to dinner and doesn't like spinach. His mother asks, "Why aren't you eating your spinach, Karl?" He replies, "I don't like it." Mom says, "You should eat everything on your plate, Karl." He eats half of it. His mother is obviously angry. Karl feels bad about not pleasing his mother and internalizes his Mother's **rejection**. The next evening Karl eats everything on his plate; Mother is very pleased and notices, telling Karl he's a good boy. Karl internalizes this too. The next evening there is broccoli on Karl's plate. He doesn't really like broccoli, so he leaves it, but starts thinking, "Mom will be mad." He soon finds that mad she is. She goes into a long tirade and tells Karl he will get no dessert unless he eats the broccoli. He doesn't, and Mother sends him to his room early (rejection, scorn, and isolation punishment). Alone in his room Karl is likely to feel terrible about himself, all alone, rejected, feeling bad about his behavior at the dinner table.

The next evening Karl eats everything on his plate whether he likes it or not! Mother is pleased. The behavior is reinforced. It now becomes *automatic* for Karl to eat everything on his plate. Ten to twenty or more years later Karl will feel a strong urge to eat everything on his plate because he thinks something bad could happen. Karl in fact feels he has to eat everything on his plate even though Mom is long gone and he really doesn't have to do anything in order to avoid punishment from her. But in his mind he still feels **compelled** to eat everything on his plate and becomes uncomfortable if he does not. Even though he may not consciously realize why he will feel uncomfortable, he just knows he will, and indeed does!

When Karl doesn't eat everything on his plate later in life he will feel an emotion called **anxiety**, which is basically low-intensity fear. Anxiety is diffuse, it has no focal point. When Karl doesn't clean his plate he isn't really terrified and can't tell exactly why he is uncomfortable, yet he is experiencing anxiety (low-grade fear). The stress response in his body has induced hormonal balance changes in his body and his brain that cause him to be slightly "on edge."

When a person violates a destructive/restrictive attitude, anxiety occurs and can result in fretting, suffering, worrying, tension, etc. This anxiety is physically damaging to the body. *Destructive/restrictive attitudes elicit the emotion of anxiety when they are violated, shutting off the flow of potential.*

Constructive attitudes don't elicit the emotion of anxiety when they are violated.

Many attitudes that are the causes of destructive behavior such as racism, religious discrimination, low self-esteem, poverty, and lack of self-confidence are due to childhood conditioning. The transfer of an attitude from generation to generation is a secondary effect of the parent's own negative attitudes.

The amount of anxiety a person feels in violating a destructive/restrictive attitude depends on the amount of fear or other negative emotion associated during the conditioning period.

A destructive/restrictive attitude expressed by the "I can't" phrase has an important detrimental effect. It tends to limit your awareness of alternative possibilities. Whenever you "know you can't" do something it is very difficult for you to look at the situation any other way than "impossible." Your creative potential flow is stifled or blocked. A have-to attitude is even worse, because you are totally limited to one method of doing something. Awareness of available alternatives is cut off completely in both cases. The creation of narrow-minded thinking is the result.

Destructive/restrictive attitudes can form later in life, not just during childhood. They can develop any time. However, you developed most of your basic attitudes in your mental core early in life. Anytime later in life, by applying similar techniques to those by which your attitudes were formed, you can recondition or reshape them in your mental core to allow your natural potential to flow more freely. Changing your mind, your body, your environment, the people in your life and your world can be done. This is one of the foundation principles on which this book is based. The creation of a POWERMIND starts with a reengineered, stronger, more accurate mental core!

The Building of Mental Prisons

Principle: Your subconscious mind cannot protect you from your negative conscious thoughts or what negativity you expose yourself to.

Your mental core is directly shaped by what you think and expose yourself to. Continuous visualization and emotionalized repetition of thoughts tend to get the thoughts incorporated into your mental core. What you read in newspapers, watch on television, read in books, see in magazines, watch at the movie theaters, hear on the radio, listen to in the lyrics of songs, hear from parents, relatives, or friends bombards you constantly.

Some of these messages are helpful—encouraging you, motivating you, expanding your vision, improving your self-image—but all too often the messages are totally destructive, upsetting, and weakening. They ruin your self-confidence, self-esteem, and courage to act, turning you away from your goals and your purpose in life or, worse yet, encouraging you to never even set any goals. This makes your mind apathetic, helpless, hopeless, lifeless, and destructive towards others. Your natural potential is completely shut off.

"You are a product of your environment. So choose the environment that will best develop you toward your objective. Analyze your life in terms of your environment. Are the things around you helping you toward success — or are they holding you back?"

W. Clement Stone
Coauthor of *Success Through*
A Positive Mental Attitude

When you were born you were an information-gathering machine, mostly functioning on basic instinct from your genetic program. At that time and during most of your childhood (perhaps even now) you may have accepted outside influence from others, turning that into negative beliefs about yourself, your capabilities, and your world. You probably didn't know about conscious editing (censoring out negative inputs) and thus accepted some of these harmful negative messages and false beliefs, such as "You can't do that," "You'll never be anything," "Don't do that," "You have no chance," "You are wrong," "It won't work," "It isn't what you know that counts but who you know," "What's the use," "Who cares?" "Working hard doesn't pay," "Nobody wins," "Who do you think you are?" "Who died and left you in charge?" "Don't take risks, be safe," "You are a messy person," "You can't trust people," You are too old, too young, too fat, too thin, too ugly, too pretty, too smart, too stupid, on and on. **Can you think of any more?**

Your subconscious mind can't tell you that you must not say harmful things to yourself because they will damage you throughout life. When you say, "I can't do that," "I am too old," "I am too young," "I am a bad person," "I don't know the right people," "I'm uneducated," "I don't care," realize that by using these types of self-depreciating phrases, saying them out loud or even thinking them, you are imprinting your subconscious mental core with these negative thoughts. **You** are in fact blocking your own progress, bringing failure, limitation, fear, frustration, poverty, illness into your own life. **You** are setting up blockages, **you** are denying the wisdom and intelligence that is now and always has been at your side.

Those self-limiting phrases become your conscious commands to your subconscious mind. They say, "Don't help me, bring me failure." This leads inevitably to mental anguish, sometimes followed by serious depression.

Your subconscious mind cannot protect you from your negative conscious thoughts or what negativity you expose yourself to. Grab a newspaper, watch the evening news. Can you find any stories that instill fear, poverty, worry, anxiety, illness, unhappiness, violence, failure, impending doom for our country and the world? I'll bet you can find some without much searching. If you dwell on these negative ideas it can depress you to a point where you feel life isn't worth living. Many people start their day reading the horrors on the front page of a newspaper. What a way to start the day! No wonder they are depressed! When they get to work they ask their colleagues, "Did you read about that rape, murder, kidnapping, etc. today in the paper?" They then repeat the story if their colleague hasn't heard it, spreading the gloom and doom.

Many people become confused and frustrated by exposing themselves to the onslaught of negativity from their friends, family, newspaper, TV, etc. They learn to be helpless, to see no use in trying to improve their lot in life. The most potent will can be smashed to pieces by a continuous onslaught of negativity if it is not consciously edited out. Many people are confused and frustrated in large part by constant exposure to negative outside influence, which is causing all the trouble for them in the first place. Many of course have no worthy goals in life, adding to the frustration, bewilderment, terror, and despair that they must encounter as a result.

You must always be aware of the fact that what you consciously think about gets imprinted onto your subconscious mental core. You can choose to reject dwelling on or being personally influenced by such negativity (conscious editing). It isn't necessary for you to immerse yourself in destructive suggestions from others. **Be very alert to the negative suggestions people make to you.** You'll quickly see who is suppressing success in you because of their own feelings of helplessness. Be especially alert to what you say to yourself (self-communication). I guarantee you'll catch yourself in what I call self-condemning self-communications.

"Every experience in life, everything with which we have come in contact in life, is a chisel which has been cutting away at our life statue, molding, modifying, shaping it. We are part of all we have met. Everything we have seen, heard, felt or thought has had its hand in molding us, shaping us."

Orison Swett Marden
Author of *Pushing the Front*

As you look back into your past, can you remember your parents, relatives, friends, colleagues who engaged in such negative campaigns? Much of this "propaganda" was designed to **control** or **instill fear** into you. This propaganda is present in homes, schools, offices, factories, clubs, and other places even today. As you make a careful study of this, you'll discover the purpose is to make you think, feel, or act as others want, for **their advantage!**

Think for yourself and make your own decisions based on factual information. You can't be filled with fear, self-doubt, self-limitations, or a poor self-image when your mind is full of worthy goals and sound plans to achieve them. As long as you don't let negative thoughts, such as fear, limitation, and self-doubt, into the subconscious mind, it will continue to work on winning the goals you set. In other words, discipline yourself to be focused on your goals at all times. There is no need for you to live in a self-made prison!

The Self-Image

Principle: Your self-image sets the limits of both your thinking and your behavior.

Your self-image is your idea of what type of person you are. It is based on your current attitudes and beliefs and past experiences, which are stored in your subconscious mental core. When a baby is born, it has no self-image at all, but as it learns it begins to distinguish itself from its environment. Based on the way it perceives and internalizes the actions of others toward it, it starts to develop a self-image. The self-image has nothing to do with genetic endowment, inherited ability, or "real" ability. It is learned (conditioned in). Anything learned (conditioned in) incorrectly can be unlearned (conditioned out), allowing greater flow of natural potential. People often times put limits on their potential because of their self-image.

Your self-image sets the limits of your thinking and your behavior. A person can never outperform their own self-image. If you cannot imagine yourself as being a millionaire, you will never become one. You won't work toward becoming one because you don't believe it's possible for you to become one, even though you probably could if you tried! If you can't imagine yourself winning a sports event, you won't have the inner drive necessary to give you the "winner's edge" necessary for winning.

Olympic athletes are often of such great caliber it's only a slight edge, the millisecond, that separates the winner from the also-rans. The winner has the **mental advantage**—that's the winner's edge, not necessarily their physical condition. You can't take two swimmers and say, "Well, Jane's body is ten milliseconds faster than Tina's body, so Tina can never beat Jane." No! It's the difference in their mental attitudes.

People always act in accordance with their self-image. Will power can only temporarily override the subconscious self-image. Why? Because will power is the conscious mind overriding the subconscious. That causes the two minds to be operating in direct conflict, not harmony. Harmony between the two allows potential to flow, internal conflict, between the two stifles it. The powerbonding concept allows the conscious, subconscious, and superconscious minds to function in harmony, not discord, and that's real mind power!

A student who thinks of himself as poor in English will always do poorly in English; he sets about to verify his *false* belief by getting D's and F's on tests. Then he has proof that his self-image is correct, though it is proved with crooked thinking.

The poor person who claims she can never be rich and never does anything to try to get rich proclaims, "See, I'm poor and nothing can be done about it, so *why should I try?*" She never stopped to think, "I'm not doing anything to get rich, so why would I expect to be rich?" Lo and behold, she never ever gets rich; she sets no money goals, and that's the trap that snatches and catches practically everyone in the U.S. As I stated in the money goals lesson, this is the richest nation in the world, we have forty or more years in a working lifetime to learn the mental mechanics and secrets of financial independence, and only about 3% ever do! A poor self-image is at the root of personal poverty in all departments of life.

Mental Self-Defense

Principle: **Alcohol, sedative drugs, and lack of sleep inhibit the conscious mind's editing (reasoning) ability.**

Three main elements **weaken** the ability of your conscious mind to edit destructive influences that come from outside sources, such as TV, newspapers, radio, relatives, and associates: **alcohol, sedative drugs** (such as relaxants and depressants), and **lack of sleep.** If you think for a moment, it should become obvious. When your brain's ability to reason clearly is impaired it cannot consciously edit false information. The conscious editing function of the conscious mind is turned down or off by these three *weakening agents.*

As you learned earlier, one of the conscious mind's jobs is to edit or weigh incoming information on a set of mental scales. The mental scales determine the validity and importance of incoming information. If the mental scales are not working properly, incoming information is internalized into the subconscious mental core, bypassing the conscious editing wall. Then whether the information is actually true or false will not matter. Your subconscious mind will accept the information as true, incorporating it into the mental core. It is extremely important for you to avoid these three weakening agents so your subconscious mind is not allowed to incorporate damaging information *from outside sources.*

Realize that when you are under the influence of any of these agents, the people you are around or the information you are exposed to will be readily accepted to a high degree directly into your mental core. This information will then serve to guide and affect your future behavior and, more importantly, your future thinking. If the information is false and damaging, your future thinking will be wrong: your mental scales will be off, and your subsequent behavior will be self-destructive.

I'll explain how this works with an extremely powerful example. Religious cults usually use drugs such as marijuana, heroin, alcohol, or quaaludes to enhance the brainwashing impact that they have on their followers. Each day, the followers are continuously exposed to the false beliefs of the cult leader.

While the followers are under the influence of drugs, the false information is heavily emphasized with a strong **emotional** situation, such as a "religious" ceremony. Cult religious ceremonies often involve animal sacrifices, loud strange music, torture, sexual orgies, etc. Each of these has extreme emotional impact on the subconscious mind. If this sort of false direct subconscious programming is combined with the disarming of a person's conscious editing machinery, the mind control is highly effective because the mental core readily incorporates the damaging information.

Lack of sleep (sleep deprivation) is also extensively used by many cults to brainwash their followers. Sleep disruption techniques (waking people up every hour or so during the night) also disarm a person's conscious editing machinery. While a person is tired or disrupted during sleep, the cult preaches their beliefs or plays music with the cult beliefs injected into the lyrics. Lyrics of songs may also contain highly sophisticated subliminal messages.

Jim Jones, the cult leader responsible for the mass suicide of nine hundred people, and David Koresh, the 1993 Texas massacre leader, used sleep disruption/sleep deprivation extensively during the brainwashing sessions of their followers. Koresh would keep his followers up all evening and "preach" for hours on end, while the followers sat listening to the false beliefs. He incessantly programmed their weakened minds. **REMEMBER THIS!!! IT COULD ONE DAY SAVE YOUR LIFE OR YOUR CHILD'S LIFE.**

Classic Case: The Demonic Mind of Jim Jones

Infamous cult leader Jim Jones' philosophy included socialism, brotherly love, and racial equality. His first prey were the poor down-and-out people of California whom he could coerce into following him. He offered a sense of belonging and unity to these lonely, disrespected people. The individuals donated time, work, and anything they had to support their twisted religious leader and his People's Temple Church, as it was called.

Jones' cult was very appealing to people who were made outcasts by their family or society or who could not find spiritual well-being in a traditional church. Jones told his followers he was their father, and they called him "Dad." As his followers worshipped him over time, Jones' mind became increasingly warped and he thought of himself as Christ reincarnate. Later he even believed himself to be God. Jones would not allow people to leave his cult. Any "disloyal" followers were threatened with death or tortured severely. To speak against his authority was absolute heresy.

In 1977 Jones moved his religious cult to the socialist country in South America called Guyana. With the approval of Guyanese officials he set up a religious "Garden of Eden," as it was advertised to the people in the U.S. The truth of the matter was the **compound** was run Nazi-concentration-camp style.

Jones used a **sleep disruption** technique in which followers were awakened in the middle of the evening to listen to a few hours of preaching by Jones. Those who could not listen attentively were physically beaten. Jones, in an attempt to give longevity to his order, worked intensively on the mental programming of the cult's children. Those youngsters who did not smile when Jones' name was mentioned were electrically shocked on their arms. Adults who disobeyed "Jones' Law" were confined to the "hot box," a small wooden box that was set out in the sun for days. Jones cleverly made use of **sedative drugs**, the second most common method of eliminating a person's conscious editing capability. This kept his settlement followers in a zombielike state of total obedience and worship. In the later days of Jones' rule in Jonestown, he posted armed guards around the compound to intimidate anyone who tried to escape. Jones also taught and rehearsed mass suicide, involving everyone in the cult. He told his followers the U.S. was an evil place. The followers of Jim Jones were exhausted, tranquilized, and hopelessly brainwashed, with no choice but total dependency on the man.

Congressman Leo Ryan of California was horrified by reports from people in the U.S. who had relatives living in Jonestown, so he went there on a personal tour. Ryan, two newspapermen, and a temple member were shot in an ambush while trying to escape Jonestown. At the same time, back at Jonestown, Jim reported the deaths and ordered the mass suicide. He had a red drink prepared, laced with cyanide. Members who hesitated to drink it were threatened at gun point. However, almost all of the nine hundred followers took the cyanide drink *voluntarily*. When U.S. and Guyanese officials arrived at the cult site, over nine hundred dead bodies were found neatly lined up. Jones, 46, was dead of a bullet wound to the head, thought to be suicide.

This gruesome case of a classic cult leader is recounted for you in vivid detail to impress on you the need for careful conscious editing of all information that you are exposed to. Especially **TAKE CARE** and **BEWARE** of your surroundings if under the influence of any of the three mind-weakening elements, *alcohol, sedative drugs, and lack of sleep*, which all can shut down your conscious editing capability. This is a very serious matter, which most people are completely unaware of. *Protect your mind and your children's minds.* Don't wind up following a lethal false prophet like Jim Jones! **REMEMBER THIS!!! IT COULD ONE DAY SAVE YOUR LIFE OR YOUR CHILD'S LIFE!**

Taking Conscious Control of Your Subconscious Mind

Principle: The subconscious mind is controlled by conscious belief and enthusiastic faith.

At this point you should have the idea that your conscious mind has a *guardian* function. Part of its job is to guard the subconscious mental core against incorporating false information, false impressions, and false beliefs. Early in Mental Mechanics I said the conscious mind has the power to reason. The subconscious mind has no such reasoning capability. The subconscious mind is largely controlled by conscious beliefs. It can't protect itself. The subconscious simply *obeys* belief commands and has no preference for productive or destructive commands. It is neutral; it simply carries out orders.

If you give your subconscious mind "wrong" beliefs, they are accepted as true. The subconscious then brings your beliefs to pass in your life by influencing your thinking, decisions, attitudes, behavior, outward conditions, events, and experiences. Most of what has happened to you in your life is a result of what you've imprinted on your subconscious mental core by the power of belief. If you have incorrect beliefs about yourself and your world, you probably aren't very successful.

There are techniques, such as *autogenic conditioning*, that you can use to correct your thinking, allowing your natural potential to flow more freely, making you far more successful than you ever thought possible. Habitual thinking in your conscious mind serves to imprint the subconscious mental core. This is very beneficial if your thoughts are positive, not so beneficial if your thoughts are negative. Most people engage in negative thinking by focusing their thoughts on fear, worry, self-doubt, physical illness, etc. Don't worry if you are thinking like "most people." One of the main purposes of this book is to teach you the tools and background theory necessary to change your thinking in the right direction and in so doing revolutionize your whole life. Your mental core can be molded and reshaped just like a clay pot, making your thinking and behavior accurate and highly effective.

Remember this point: Your thoughts have no command power to the subconscious mind unless they are charged with strong emotion. Emotionalized firm belief, called faith, causes your subconscious and superconscious powers to flow in a focused direction. This **emotionalized belief** requirement is a primary reason why positive thinking and verbal self-affirmations don't work for so many people. Their affirmations have no emotional charge or faith attached to them. Words are powerless unless backed by emotionalized faith, then action! *The subconscious mind is controlled by conscious belief and enthusiastic faith.*

"Your belief that you can do the thing gives your thought forces their power."

Robert Collier
Early editor of Collier's
Weekly

An After-the-Lesson Visit with the Author

I hope you had a number of surprising realizations in this lesson. Many people need to be, and in fact are, shocked into conscious awareness after reading this vitally important lesson.

The four modes of thought section gave you a theoretical basis so you will be able to understand the techniques in the lessons on verbal self-affirmation and imagineering. Since you self-communicate with verbal, sensory, conceptual, and emotional modes, it should be possible to use specific techniques to modify the mental core by using them. Indeed, that's what you will learn shortly.

The concepts of attitude formation, cycling, and reinforcement have been covered here, as well as how they affect the flow of natural potential. I mentioned earlier that many people live in mental prisons of their own creation; you learned in this lesson exactly how that happens.

You were also notified of the three weakening agents, alcohol, sedative drugs, and lack of sleep, that inhibit/destroy the ability of the conscious mind to consciously edit false information. People who expose themselves carelessly to the extreme negativity inherent in our society could easily wind up with a poor self-image. In extreme cases they could conceivably end up in some type of a cult, eventually being totally brainwashed and dependent on a cult for survival. This is happening with surprising regularity in the U.S., as evidenced by the 1993 David Koresh Texas massacre.

People must always be alert to who is looking to control or influence their behavior in a negative way. I certainly don't want my child or yours to be ensnared in a cult, but education and awareness of mental mechanics is not widespread in the U.S.

YOUR OWN KNOWLEDGE IS YOUR BEST MENTAL SELF-DEFENSE! REMEMBER THIS!!! IT COULD ONE DAY SAVE YOUR LIFE OR YOUR CHILD'S LIFE!

By taking conscious control of your thinking, limiting your exposure to negative outside influences, driving yourself from within, and gaining the sophisticated precision techniques in the next part of this book, you'll fully unlock any mental prison doors!

This lesson has provided you with the required theoretical knowledge of the mental core necessary for you to understand why autogenic conditioning works. This lesson and the one before explained all you need to know in order to gain tremendous benefit from the verbal self-affirmation and the imagineering techniques coming up shortly. By learning the mental mechanics of how your mind operates, you'll be able to understand both how and why autogenic conditioning works.

"Blessed is the man who finds wisdom, the man who gains understanding, for she is more profitable than silver and yields better returns than gold. She is more precious than rubies; nothing you desire can compare with her."

Proverbs 3:13-15

◆6▶ The Changing Mind

Overview

This is a short lesson where a few of the more critical mental mechanics points mentioned in previous lessons are emphasized and more fully explained. This last mental mechanics lesson should wrap up a few loose ends for you. This will fully prepare you for complete understanding in Part IV of The POWER-MIND System.

The Changing Mind

Personal Change

Principle: The mind always changes first.

You are changing each and every day of your life. You can prove this to yourself by simply looking at photographs taken six months ago, one year ago, two years ago, five years ago. You have probably changed hairstyle, clothing, physical appearance, hobbies, interests, and more. Your body has certainly changed, but more importantly your mind has also changed. All changes in your mind are reflected in your body, behavior, and life circumstances. These mind changes effect your whole life. The mind always changes first.

"What's going on in the inside shows on the outside."

> **Earl Nightingale**
> **Self-development pioneer**
> **Author of *The Strangest Secret, Lead the Field*, and Cofounder of the Nightingale Conant Corp.**

You may not realize drastic changes in your mind on a day-to-day basis. But rest assured that each day your mind does change. You think differently today than you did yesterday, two days ago, two years ago, ten years ago. This is no shocking revelation, it's just a simple fact of life. As you live, learn, and experience life, you gain new information, and this changes you. The experiences you have each day are assimilated by your mind, affecting your reactions to opportunities and difficulties as they continuously present themselves.

You may not change dramatically from day to day, but the cumulative effects over time are always noticeable. Changes may be more pronounced in some areas of your life and less noticeable in others. For instance, it may take you six months to lose ten pounds but only one day to turn your life around if you attend the right seminar or **READ THE RIGHT BOOK!**

What are your feelings about change? Does it make you feel uneasy, not knowing what the future has in store for you, or do you view the future with eager anticipation because you have it so well designed? Most people are afraid of change, more so if they feel they have no control over it. If you would like to have more control over change you should recognize by now that you have come to the right place. The decisions, actions, and reactions you make now are what determine the direction of change for you. The only time you are in control is NOW. You are always directing your future every moment, whether you are consciously aware of this or not. What happens to you today affects your tomorrow, and so on.

When you finish this book you will be much more aware of this fact than you may be right now. The POWERMIND System is a lifesaving guide that teaches you how to manage your life using simple techniques that work and are universally applicable. It's like when you buy a new car. You read the owner's manual to see how everything works, all the knobs, switches, buttons, dials, etc. Inevitably there are certain gadgets that would be hard or impossible to figure out how to operate without a manual. However, once you read the manual and know how to turn everything on and off, it becomes a simple task for you. It becomes an **automatic** (subconscious) action. In a similar fashion you can, by understanding and training your mind, develop beneficial automatic actions and reactions—actions and reactions that will turn your dreams into reality, failures into successes.

You are not stuck with the past damage of poor childhood conditioning. You can change; you need not be dependent on others to determine your future for you. *They* are not at the helm of *your* ship. Here is a classic phrase said by a self-limiting person: "I can't change, that just the way I am." It's not true! You have the ability to decide for yourself and then deliberately guide the process of change in the direction you desire. You are learning scientifically how to do this with extreme precision by self-analysis, goal setting, learning how your mind works, and finally the high achievement techniques that follow this lesson.

The techniques in Part IV will greatly aid you in personal betterment. By obtaining more knowledge of how to take control of your own mind and how to condition it properly, you will look at yourself and your world in a profoundly different way. Many people are driving through life on a deserted dirt road with their headlights off. I'm turning your headlights on for you as you continue working through this book. You should be able to see the Light when you are through.

Your life experiences and knowledge are beginning to crystallize inside your mind, fitting together into a unified meaningful pattern. As you continue to learn, the carefully crafted self-improvement method in this book you will develop a deeper understanding of yourself, which can only lead you to positive change!

Creation of Self-Limiting Beliefs

Principle: After continued repetition of a self-limiting self-image phrase, you come to "believe" it as true, then "know" it to be true.

People have many beliefs about themselves formed by past experience, knowledge, and feelings. Over the years these have become truths for them, which they consider to be self-evident and never question. They know what some of their strengths and weaknesses are, their abilities and personality traits. This is their self-image, which is a major part of their mental core. Your self-image, which I introduced you to briefly in Lesson 5, is somewhat distorted because over time you have misinterpreted a wide variety of what was actually happening. The attitudes that you developed may have also been distorted. Can you remember any self-communication in the form of *verbal* phrases mixed with strong *emotions* that led to some distorted views you may have about yourself?

For example, have you used phrases such as these? "I'm not very creative." "I could never write a fiction novel." "I can't paint a barn door, let alone a wildlife scene." "I always drop things, I was born all thumbs." "I can never remember people's names." "I can't talk in front of groups, I'd forget my lines and screw up and they'd all laugh at me." "I just have no patience at all. I've always had a bad temper." "I'm just a worrywart." "I'm just not very attractive." "I'm always so tense. I try to relax but I just can't."

Do you see how some of these phrases elicit strong emotions? Can you recall the emotions clearly? Maybe you can even remember a situation very vividly, and say, "Yes, that certainly is true of me." These are examples of negative self-limiting phrases that may be beliefs that you may have built into your self-image over the years.

Think about and challenge some of these self-limiting self-image beliefs. *Are they really true?* Have you tried to change any of these recently, or did you paint a stick figure in the fourth grade, which Mrs. Smith didn't put up on the wall, causing you to decide you had no artistic talent from that day on? Maybe you would say to me, "But you don't understand, Michael, I really have no artistic ability." This is a nicer way of rationalizing to yourself the idea that you really **"believe"** you have no artistic ability, though you never really tried to develop yourself in art. *After continued repetition of a self-limiting self-image phrase, you come to "believe" it as true, then "know" it to be true.*

You may say, "You see, Michael, there is no point in me trying to become an artist because **I know I can't** do it." My response is this: If you **know** you can't, then you can't, but what you know to be true and what is actually true may be entirely different. Here is another self-limiting phrase I used to use myself years ago to build my own self-limiting self-image belief: "I can't change. That's just the way I am."

Obviously all of your self-communication isn't self-limiting or you wouldn't be reading this sentence. Did you notice how you are quite good at some things and very confident about your ability? For example, a person may say, "I'm no artist, but I can sure hit a baseball." I would bet this person isn't a very good artist but is probably a fairly good baseball batter. Can you recognize how the activities you tell yourself you are poor at or can't do are the same ones you aren't very good at? Funny how there is a direct correlation! In the words of Dr. Denis Waitley, author of *The Psychology of Winning,* "Winners never prequalify themselves in the negative." Winners never use negative self-limiting communication on themselves about their performance.

The point of this discussion is to demonstrate that you probably have natural potential far greater than you give yourself credit for, and you may be limiting yourself by your thinking.

"Whether you think you can or think you can't—you are right."

Henry Ford
Founder of the Ford Motor
Company

The Self-Image Range

Principle: People don't act according to their natural potential, they act according to their self-image belief about their natural potential.

People behave in accordance with their self-image stored in their subconscious mental core. You have that *emotional* gate I talked about in Lesson 5 that acts as a thermostat in your mind, a behavior regulator so to speak. This keeps your behavior consistent with your self-image, in much the same way a thermostat in a refrigerator keeps the chamber temperature within a certain range. In all areas of your behavior you have more potential than you are currently expressing.

Your maximum potential is constantly changing as you experience life. Few people in life ever express their maximum potential in any given area. For example, when an amateur tennis player takes lessons it doesn't mean he will immediately become a professional tennis player. It just means he now has more information and is developing more skill than he had before, and that increases his maximum potential.

How exactly does the emotional gate work? In a refrigerator an internal sensor detects when the chamber temperature rises above the manual setting, and an electrical signal triggers a sequence of events to engage the cooling mechanism to begin cooling the chamber. In a human being tension signals go off in the brain when boundaries of the self-image are reached. Whenever you behave outside your self-image boundaries you feel tension, negative stress, and discomfort. You say things like

"Things aren't going the way they are supposed to." A conflict is set up inside your mind because what is happening and what you expect to happen are different. This makes you tense mentally and, of course, physically. You will now strive to scurry back into your self-image range so this conflict is eliminated. You will change your behavior so that what happens coincides with what you expect to happen. You begin acting more like your internal picture of yourself (your self-image). (Refer to Mental Mechanics Diagram E).

This concept can be illustrated nicely with a bowling game example, but you can easily see the analogy in other activities as well. I'll use Bob the bowler for my illustration. Bob is a 150s average bowler and he **"knows"** it. He tells anyone who asks him (reaffirming it to himself in the process). In Bob's mind it is very natural for him to **"believe"** this. If you told him he could be a 220s pro bowler he would quickly tell you he couldn't, reaffirming the self-image he has of being a 150s average bowler. He would say, "I can't, you are mistaken. I'm a 150s bowler. I can't be a pro. I sure *wish* I could be though." When you watch Bob bowl he looks pretty smooth; he practices a lot, takes lessons, and wants to improve. Every now and then Bob strings a series of strikes together, looking real professional. As Bob looks at the strikes piling up on the scoreboard he senses he is on a roll and could end up with a 220 or better game. He starts to try real hard now, concentrating on not making any errors, so he can make the perfect shot. *It is at this point the natural flow of potential is gone; he is thinking too hard, trying too hard, not acting automatically anymore.* He begins operating outside his self-image range. He bowls a gutter ball, then open frames. He misses some easy spares, his score rapidly sinks back to the 150s. He's back in his self-image range. When asked about his game, Bob says, "Yea, I got *lucky* there for a while but I'm a 150s bowler. See I scored a 159. Pretty good for me! Huh?"

Mental Mechanics Diagram E

How Self-Image Effects Performance

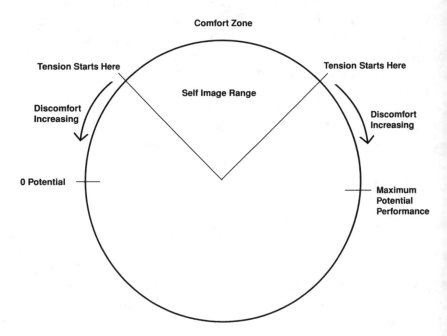

As a person behaves above or below their self-image range, tension begins. As they continue to operate outside their self-image range, discomfort sets in and performance tends to move them back into their comfort zone. Self-image ranges are set up inside the subconscious mental core.

Bob may also start out a game poorly then seem to make a *miraculous comeback* at the end to wind up in the 150s. He'll say when asked, "Yeah, I started out real bad, but I pulled it off in the end, right up to 151. Seems like I'm always in the 150s for some reason." If Bob does bowl below 150, he'll say, "That's not me, I was off tonight, I'm really a 150s bowler;" if he rolls 220 he'll say, *"Gee, I sure was lucky."* In both cases, he doesn't critically examine his scores. Any scores outside his self-image range are scoffed off!

Scores outside Bob's self-image range of 150-160, he always views as a fluke, an *unlucky* or *lucky* game. He is completely ignorant of his own mental self-image, which is controlling his scores. It all seems so logical to Bob that he may even get angry with you if you tell him he could be consistently much better than a 150s average bowler! You will be challenging his personal self-image belief about himself. Is Bob doomed to be a 150s average bowler forever? NO! But his natural tendency is to reinforce his existing attitudes and behave in a manner consistent with them. Changing his attitudes and hence his self-image requires a basic understanding first.

Here is another example. Frederica is a scientific supplies salesperson. She has a self-image in her mind about her earning potential. She's been working for ten years, her volume is $40,000 per month, and she gets 10% commission. This translates to a $4,000 dollar monthly earning. When you ask Frederica about her monthly earnings, she says it is about $4,000. Frederica really has the potential to sell a lot more. But despite circumstances, she always seems to somehow earn about $4,000 per month. One month, however, due to circumstances "seemingly" beyond Frederica's control she happens to sell $80,000 of product and doubles her monthly income. Does Frederica reevaluate the month to *determine the cause* for her success (in her personal journal) and set a new standard for herself (change her self-image setting)? Probably not!

Frederica is more likely to correct for the overselling "mistake." She says to herself "I worked so hard for the $80,000 volume, I must be exhausted. I need to rest up. I did two months of work in one month. I better relax, take it easy for a while. After all I don't need to work hard next month, I already made two months' salary in one month." She'll take it easy for a while, maybe even take a vacation for her "hard efforts." Perhaps she will rework her sales presentation (the really good one that sold $80,000 of products that month) and make it more like the old one, the $40,000 per month one. For the next month, Frederica's sales slack off. She gets right back into her old self-image range.

Will the doubled income month affect Frederica? Yes! But it is entirely dependent on how Frederica perceives what is happening. Her own self-communication, what she tells herself, how she thinks and feels about what she perceives—only that can change her self-image. Only Frederica can change Frederica. No one else and no outside occurrences can change her self-image. Frederica may view that month as a fluke, a lucky break or she may realize she has more potential than she originally thought. What interpretation she makes about the occurrence depends on the strength of her self-image belief and her knowledge of mental mechanics. If she believes she is only a $4,000 per month earning salesperson, she'll stay there. If she believes she can do better, she'll move up. If Frederica doesn't understand the self-image concept she might get very "logical" on us and find all the reasons why she doubled her income that have absolutely nothing at all to do with her or her abilities. She may "know" why it happened. She will be quick to tell you so and it will have nothing at all to do with her self-image, positive thinking, or any other mental mechanics mumbo jumbo. It will all be attributed to a lucky break. (How sad, how pitifully ignorant. To do well but be totally wrong as to the reasons why!) *People don't act according to their natural potential, they act according to their self-image belief about their natural potential.*

"Our self-image prescribes the limits for the accomplishment of any particular goals. It prescribes the 'area of the possible'."

Dr. Maxwell Maltz
Author of *Psycho-cybernetics*

The Ineffectiveness of Will Power

Principle: **All lasting change in human behavior starts with
an internal change, a change in a person's
subconscious self-image.**

Your self-image explains why straight will power is an ineffective method of changing your mind and long-term behavior.
Will power is a teeth-gritting forced behavioral change, which
can only *temporarily* override your subconscious self-image.
Will power is a **forced** effort to move outside your self-image.
You can do this temporarily and not act like yourself for a while,
but your potential will not flow naturally or automatically. *Your
conscious actions will be going against your subconscious self-
image.* Your conscious and subconscious won't be working in
harmony toward a common goal. This internal conflict will
result in negative tension, and you will feel very, very uncomfortable.

For example, if you hate dog food but you force yourself to
eat a bowl of it (will power), you probably still won't like it. It's
not normal for you to behave that way. If you were unaware that
it was dog food you might find it tasty. However, if you "knew"
it disgusted you, forcing yourself to try some probably wouldn't
change your mind. Using will power to make yourself behave
differently simply doesn't create lasting change.

Let's go back to the refrigerator example I used earlier. Is it
logical to set the refrigerator thermostat at room temperature,
then fill it with ice in the hopes of lowering the chamber temperature for the next six months? When the ice melts (will power
fades), the temperature will automatically rise to where the thermostat setting is (self-image). You aren't using the refrigerator's
built in mechanism at all. You aren't letting it operate the way it
was *designed* to. It is the same way with the human mind. If you
change the self-image and let the subconscious mind operate the
way it was designed to, it can allow your potential to flow, automatically. This is the most efficient and effective way. If you use
your mind the way it was designed to operate, it can work won-
ders for you!

Wouldn't it seem easier to just turn the thermostat down and let the refrigerator engage, allowing the cooling mechanism to work automatically the way it was designed to work? It is much easier to change your self-image and let the behavioral changes occur automatically, effortlessly, than to consciously try hard, using will power, to change. This key point is central to the POWERMIND system's effectiveness. *All lasting change in human behavior starts with an internal change, a change in the person's subconscious self-image.* How exactly do you change your subconscious mind efficiently? Read on—High Achievement is up next!

An After-the-Lesson Visit with the Author

In this lesson you were exposed to the idea that you are changing every minute of every day. This is a fact of life that no one can do anything about. You can, however, guide and direct this process of change with *specialized knowledge* so you change in the direction you want.

I also discussed how people tend to limit their own performance. They make self-limiting beliefs for themselves by continuous repetition of self-limiting thoughts and phrases such as "I can't." After time they come to believe this to be the case. They set up a self-image range for themselves inside their subconscious mind, within which they are comfortable operating. Whenever they move outside of the boundaries of their self-image range, they feel uncomfortable. These self-image boundaries, however, are not real, they are self-imposed or "self-programmed." They are imaginary, but their effects on a person's behavior are quite real!

Many times people try to use the brute force method of will power to move outside these self-image boundaries. This is ineffective because a person will always migrate back into their self-image range; the conscious mind can only override the subconscious self-image range for a short time, and it is mentally and physically exhausting for a person to do. Their natural potential doesn't flow automatically, it is forced. The way to get potential to flow is by changing the subconscious self-image so that the conscious and subconscious operate in harmony. This is done with relaxed *autogenic conditioning* techniques, which will be described in Lessons 7 and 8.

"Unless you have prepared yourself to profit by your chance, the opportunity will only make you ridiculous. A great occasion is valuable to you just in proportion as you have educated yourself to make use of it."

Orison Swett Marden
Author of *Pushing to the*
Front

HIGH ACHIEVEMENT

Part IV

Lesson Numbers
7,8,9,10,11,12

7 ▸ Autogenic Conditioning I. The Verbal Self-Affirmation Technique

Overview

The word "autogenic" simply means self-produced. "Autogenic conditioning" means conditioning your own mind rather than being conditioned by others.

This lesson is dedicated to explaining the verbal self-affirmation technique **in great detail**. It is a proven scientific method you can use to rapidly reshape your subconscious mental core, allowing more of your natural potential to flow freely. In this lesson you will learn how to direct your thought power to achieve your goals and gain all the riches you desire and deserve. Everyone has the ability to fully use their *mindpower,* but surprisingly few ever do.

The verbal self-affirmation technique is based on the principle that your habitual thinking affects your future more than anything else in life. You can now learn to consciously control your thoughts, thereby directly shaping your future. Through the self-affirmation technique described in this lesson, the door to controlling your destiny will be systematically unlocked for you.

This simple-to-do mental technique is a major tool for gaining true success in life. Mastery of the technique gives you the ability of scientific self-direction (SSD). You can in fact by applying verbal self-affirmations, mold, fashion, and create your destiny.

Your thoughts are like seeds, your subconscious mind is like soil. *"Whatsoever a man soweth, that shall he also reap" (Galatians 6:7).*

The POWERMIND System
Part IV. High Achievement

Autogenic Conditioning I. The Verbal Self-Affirmation Technique

Read on and absorb the wisdom of the ages, for it is now within your reach!

Introduction to the Verbal Self-Affirmation Technique

PULL OUT YOUR GOAL LIST!!! You have finally arrived. You are about to learn one of the most powerful high achievement techniques available. Throughout this book you have been carefully, *systematically* guided to this point. This lesson and the one that follows on Imagineering are the pivot points for the whole POWERMIND system. Everything you learned in the previous lessons will be utilized here.

Early in the POWERMIND system I started you off with a detailed self-assessment, where two of your tasks were to figure out what your life values and natural talents were. You then entered two elegant lessons on goal setting so you could determine absolutely what your burning desires are in several different life categories. You learned from the lessons on goal setting that you need to start with a clearly defined goal in mind. Then, starting in the future, you develop a plan by working backwards from the goal deadline to the point where you are right now. I then took you on an in-depth journey into the marvelous inner workings of the human mind, introducing you to the three basic parts, the conscious, subconscious, and superconscious. I also explained their separate functions as well as their interactions with each other. After that I elaborated on the basic mental structure housed within the subconscious mind, which dramatically effects your thinking and behavior. It is largely responsible for why you are where you are right now. This structure is called the mental core.

Now we come to one of the premier methods for reshaping the subconscious mental core. This technique allows you to actually "implant" your goals, new behaviors, and attitudes deep into the core of your subconscious mind, to develop focus, concentration, and single-minded purpose on a specific set of burningly desired goals. In the front of this book I said the POWERMIND system's method was "exactly what to do and how to do exactly that!" In this lesson you will learn not only exactly how to do the verbal self-affirmation technique but also exactly why it works.

You have already constructed many of the pieces necessary for the application of this powerful technique. You should have a list of well thought out goals that are all aligned with your personal life values. These goals should also benefit others in some way. It is time now to take those goals from paper and systematically bury them in your subconscious mind. Each one of your goals, whether it is a physical object, something you want to do, something you want to be, or a behavioral trait you want to develop, can be scientifically converted into verbal phrases or self-affirmations. These verbal self-affirmations can then be hammered deep into your subconscious mental core. Once buried there, they will begin to affect your thinking, your behavior, and all your actions *automatically, effortlessly,* without the use of "will power." By the process of superconscious thought induction, many of your goals will then begin moving toward you as well. Your reticular formation will also be properly set, causing you to be at a heightened state of mental alertness in regard to information and opportunities concerning your goals.

Autogenic conditioning in the form of the verbal self-affirmation technique must be done correctly for maximum achievement, so, as with all the techniques in The POWERMIND System, precise instructions will be given.

Two Historic Affirmation Pioneers

I will briefly introduce two pioneers of autogenic conditioning who utilized verbal self-affirmations to a high degree. These two historical examples capture the essence of the verbal self-affirmation technique you will learn in this lesson.

The Charles Baudoin Self-Affirmation Technique

Charles Baudoin was an early 1900s affirmation pioneer and a professor at the Rousseau Institute in France. Baudoin was considered to be one of the most brilliant psychotherapists of his day. He was a research director of the New Nancy School of Healing in 1910. There he taught people a basic subconscious imprinting technique.

He said that a person should enter a drowsy half-sleep state in which the body is completely relaxed and comfortable (called "alpha state" today). His formula for the technique, in his words, was as follows:

"A very simple way of securing this (impregnation of the subconscious mind) is to condense the idea which is to be the object of suggestion, to sum it up in a brief phrase which can be readily graven on the memory, and to repeat it over and over again as a lullaby."

This is very similar to standard self-affirmation techniques of today. When a person is in a drowsy state (remember, you learned in the mental self-defense section that drowsiness causes the conscious editing function of your mind to be neutralized. You want this to occur so that negative or contradictory thoughts from childhood conditioning, which would normally crop up from the mental core, are completely suppressed), whatever they affirm or repeat in this state is then immediately "graven on the memory" or accepted into the subconscious mental core as a new operating instruction.

Just before nodding off to sleep and immediately upon waking in the morning are the best times to repeat verbal self-affirmations. Later, with practice you can consciously induce the relaxed, drowsy, alpha state with the deep relaxation method I'll outline for you shortly.

Frederick Andrews and Self-Affirmations

In the March 1917 issue of *Nautilus Magazine* there was an article about a boy who had tuberculosis of the spine, called Pott's disease. The boy was Frederick Elias Andrews of Indianapolis. He later became minister of the Unity School of Christianity in Kansas City, Missouri.

The doctors, after examining him, told Andrews his case was "hopeless." Andrews decided to start an autogenic conditioning program to "pray," using intensive verbal self-affirmations. He was at the start of his program a twisted cripple, moving about on his hands and knees. He made up his own self-affirmation and repeated it daily many times. His affirmation was as follows: *"I am whole, perfect, strong, powerful, loving, harmonious, and happy."* He said this affirmation just before falling asleep and as soon as he awoke in the morning, as well as multiple times during the day.

Frederick Andrews' *attitude of mind* also extended out to other people. Even though at the time he himself was a "hopeless" cripple, he envied no one; he wished these same qualities used in his affirmation on others. He also used a *thought substitution technique;* when he found his mind wandering to fear, anger, jealousy, envy, he would immediately start saying his affirmation quickly *out loud* over and over again. He would not allow his mind to focus on negative destructive thoughts.

Andrews' self-affirmation technique worked! After doing his affirmation over time, he did indeed become straight, well-formed, and able to walk normally.

Outlining the Verbal Self-Affirmation Technique

There are four basic steps in using this technique to reshape your mental core or implant your goals. These are identification, definition, phrasing, and conditioning. I will explain each one briefly for you here, then go into more detail afterwards.

1. **Identification** is in two forms for our purposes. The first form you have already done. You should have identified your goals or the things you want to be, have, and do in life.

   The second form is to identify specific behaviors or personality traits that you feel can be more fully expressed if a negative self-limiting self-image attitude is eliminated. In other words, identify the behavioral traits you would have in order to become your "ideal self."

2. **Definition.** In this step you are to get a clear idea of your new self, with the new behavioral traits and specific goals already *achieved*. Then you decide on what positive emotions you would like to have *associated* with each of them.

3. **Phrasing.** This means creating a short phrase or set of phrases describing your "new" self with your goals or behavioral traits already in your possession. When you write these descriptive affirmation phrases, you should incorporate words that trigger the positive emotions you defined in step 2.

This step is a key step. Improper phrasing has resulted in many people being completely ineffective and frustrated with all verbal affirmation-style techniques.

4. **Conditioning.** The affirmations are then self-communicated both *verbally* and *emotionally* by reading them intensely at least three times a day as emphatically, faithfully, and convincingly as you can. The critical times are early morning, noon right after lunch, and right before you go to sleep at night. You should experience the positive emotions as much as possible while you read and think about each affirmation. You mentally acknowledge the fact that your newly affirmed self-image and goals that have been charged with strong positive emotion will *automatically* guide your thinking and behavior.

I will assume from earlier lessons that you have steps 1 and 2 pretty much covered. That is to say, you have identified a specific set of life goals and behavioral traits and have a clear idea of what they are (that was the purpose of all the lessons in Part I. Self-Assessment and Part II. Goalsetting). However, Step 3 *Phrasing* and Step 4 *Conditioning* need to be covered in much more detail for you to properly utilize the verbal self-affirmation technique.

Step 3. Phrasing: The 11 Affirmation Design Rules

1. Use positive phrases

Include only what you want, NOT what you DON'T want. For example, this affirmation is incorrect: "I don't get nervous talking in front of people." This affirmation is correct: **"I am cool, calm, and confident talking in front of people."** Cool, calm, and confident are all positive. Here are other examples. Incorrect affirmation, "I am not an impatient person." Correct, **"I am a patient, loving individual."** Incorrect affirmation, "I would feel awful if I didn't earn at least $200,000 per year." Correct, **"I love earning $200,000 per year."** Incorrect affirmation, "I hate spending the winter here." Correct, **"I like spending my winters in the sunny warm Caribbean, it's terrific!"**

The correct affirmations all focus your mind properly. You can't engage the subconscious mind on the negative of a command. Why is this so? The subconscious mind tends to delete negatives and focus on the overall meaning of the phrase. You can prove this to yourself in the following test: *Don't* think of a red Corvette. *Don't* think of a pink elephant. Try not to think of a rainbow. *Don't* think of a jet airplane. *Don't* think of your car keys. In reading these statements did you find yourself *automatically* thinking briefly about each one of them? Perhaps you even pictured (visualized) each one of these items in your *mind's eye.* Remember whatever you think about or visualize is what gets imprinted onto the subconscious mental core!

I was once in a class with two hundred people and the instructor gave us a quiz like that, having everyone close their eyes and try **NOT** to visualize ten different objects that she said "NOT" to see. Everyone in the room saw at least eight of the ten vividly; the two they didn't actually see, they thought about, which is what they **WEREN'T** supposed to do! It was automatic for us, just like it's automatic for you! "I don't," "I won't," "I can't," "I shouldn't" are all ineffective for use in verbal self-affirmations.

2. Use "I" language

Make sure "you" are included in each verbal affirmation. A first-person pronoun like **I, me,** or **my** must be used. Blank statements and platitudes such as "patience is golden," "enthusiasm makes happiness," "honesty is the best policy" are all useless in modifying your mental core.

You may become uneasy using I language in a statement that is not true of you at the present time. *However, you must recognize that affirmations are "tools," not true/false statements.* The point of a verbal affirmation is to create a long-term mental change inside your subconscious mind. Your subconscious mind will only respond to commands pertaining to you.

It is the essence of the verbal self-affirmation technique to set up a constructive conflict between you and your environment or you and your current personality. (Remember, in Mental Mechanics I told you that the subconscious mind has a *conflict resolution* function.) If you affirm the way things currently are, no change will take place. The conscious command to the subconscious is NOT to change the way things are. This is obviously ineffective. Subconscious activity is induced by constructive conflict. The subconscious mind will work to bring whatever conscious commands are given it into reality, using all its available resources, including its memory banks and the superconscious mind. This is exactly what you want to happen.

3. Make it individualized

Comparisons between you and *other people* can have serious detrimental effects on other people. For example, don't say, "I am much better at selling product than Tim and Sue are." Instead say, *"I am an extremely productive salesperson, in the top 1% of my company, and I love it."* Unconsciously you may find yourself undermining or sabotaging other people's work automatically if you improperly phrase your affirmation. Comparisons to others will divert your thought energy from your own self-improvement and could actually hurt others. "I have $500,000 more than Mr. Jones" is also an example of a faulty comparison self-affirmation. A better way to phase it would be, *"I have X dollars."* Don't say <u>more than</u> so and so.

4. Use present tense

Referencing **past** or **future** events, behaviors, or attitudes also destroys the effectiveness of a verbal self-affirmation. For example, "I am doing better now than I used to" or "I used to be a smoker. Now I'm not." This stimulates the past memory, behavior, or attitude you are trying to eliminate instead of the new one you are trying to develop.

Affirmations regarding the future are also ineffective. For example: "<u>Someday</u> I'll be a millionaire," "<u>Someday</u> I'll be patient," "<u>One of these days</u> I will be a nice pleasant person." The "someday" or "one of these days" statements are ineffective as well.

"Someday" statements reinforce your current behavior, not a new one. Remember the subconscious mind engages on conflict resolution. No conflict is set up if you say "someday I'll" or "one of these days" or "I used to be." Say instead *I am, I own, I have*. The affirmation must conflict with your current situation and focus on a new improved one. After all, you want to change your current situation *now*, not someday!

5. Write the affirmation as if the goal were already achieved

An affirmation should be worded "as if" you already possess the desired behavior, attitude, or goal. For example, **"I am an excellent time manager"** has a greater effect than "I could be a little better at managing my time." The point here is to design the affirmation so it allows you to vividly imagine the ideal. An example of a self-esteem, self-image builder affirmation would be **"I like myself,"** not "If I liked myself, I would feel great" or "I should like myself more in order to feel better." It is extremely difficult to imagine or visualize a changing ongoing process. However, it is easy to imagine the *end result, the perfect you, or the already achieved goal.*

For goals with future deadlines, instead of saying you have it right now, attach the date by which you expect to have it. For example, **"I have a million dollars in XYZ Bank by January 1 (such and such a year)"** is correct.

6. Be realistic (Remember the 50/50 rule of goal setting!)

You must have at least a 50% belief that you can achieve what you affirm at the time the affirmation is created. If you believe you only have a 5% chance to achieve, then don't affirm it. You need to start with at least a 50% belief. Don't affirm that which you can't possibly conceive yourself of having, either. This only leads to frustration. Perfection and ludicrous affirmations are also worthless. For example, someone making $200,000 per year may affirm **"I am earning $250,000 annually,"** but affirming "I am earning $10 billion by the end of next week" is silly. Or a 300-pound person affirming "I am weighing 200 pounds by next month" is ludicrous! Affirmations like that aren't effective.

7. Use caution with the words "always" and "all"
Using "always" and "all" generally leads to a harmful affirmation. There are times when you don't want to behave like you affirmed. If you affirm "I am <u>always</u> excited and enthusiastic," you don't want to be that way at someone's funeral, do you? Clarify, quantify, and qualify your affirmations. Attach positive emotion to *specific* behavior traits or goals. For example: **"I am enthusiastic when I concentrate on my goals"** or **"I am excited and happy as I labor in my chosen field"** are better than "I am enthusiastic *all* the time."

8. Design affirmations for your use only
It is tempting to see if your affirmations will effect someone else's behavior. An affirmation you use about someone else will have no effect on you. For example, the affirmation "My coworkers respect me" is not going to affect them. However, another properly designed affirmation will affect *your behavior*, which may in turn cause them to respect you. Here is a better way to phrase it to achieve the same result: **"I enjoy being the kind of employee who is honest, caring, and considerate towards my coworkers."** Or "My wife loves me" should be rephrased to **"I love myself and my wife."**

9. Use accuracy for goal-oriented affirmations
If a specific measurable objective is desired, then include this in the affirmation. Plug the goal you desire in accurately, with measurable results and/or deadlines. For example, if it's a weight loss goal, put the number of pounds you desire to weigh by the date you desire to weigh it into the affirmation. For a desired bowling average, put the number of your desired average in and when you want to be at that average. Be clear about exactly what you want to achieve. If it's an annual income, put the dollar amount into the affirmation, don't say "plenty of money." NOTE: Deadlines are not necessary with behavioral trait affirmations.

10. Use action words

Wording such as "I am able to" or "I have the ability to " diminishes affirmation potency and makes it difficult to experience in your mind. Better wording is **"I remember,"** not "I am able to remember," or **"I relax when. . . ."** not "I have the ability to relax when. . . ." or **"Effortlessly I. . . . "** not "I am able to with little effort. . . ." Use present-tense action words!

11. Use positive emotional charging (THIS IS THE PASSKEY RULE)

Put emotionally charged elements into each affirmation. For example, "I am weighing (xx lbs.) and *I feel great!*" or "I am smoke-free and *love it*" or "I manage my time well and *it feels terrific*" or "I am earning $100,000 per year and *it's wonderful!*" are all excellent. All affirmations are greatly enhanced and much more effective with positive emotional charging. Why? As a positive emotional response is generated inside your body, it helps you develop firm belief in the affirmation.

Emotional charging is a key element in this technique. It also explains why self-talk tapes work for some people and not for others. If the words on the self-talk tapes stimulate positive emotions in you they will be effective; if they don't, they won't. If the wording doesn't stimulate healthy constructive thinking in your mind, the tapes will be rendered ineffective. You need to use your own "emotionally charged language."

Perhaps you can remember very vividly from your childhood kind words said to you at a particular birthday or Christmas. The positive emotions of that event were so strong you easily recall the whole experience. Use those types of words in your affirmation. The subconscious memory record function is turned on, with strong positive emotion enhancing the affirmation's effect on the mental core. This is especially true if you use words carrying a positive emotional charge from a childhood experience!

Categorical Examples of Properly Phrased Self-Affirmations

Listed below is a series of properly phrased verbal self-affirmation examples. Remember, these are only examples to serve as basic guidelines. You must use your own wording. However, these examples are consistent with the eleven design rules and will aid you in designing yours. In the examples the goal is abbreviated; however, your written goals should be much more detailed. These examples are to demonstrate properly phrased affirmations, not written goals. I assume you will have a clearly defined written goal in mind before you design an affirmation for it.

Material goal affirmations: Things you want to have.

Goal: A new car
Affirmation: I enjoy owning my silver gray Mercedes. I feel my hands running over the cool slick paint. Today is December 25, 1998.

Goal: A new house
Affirmation: I own a beautiful 4,000-square-foot log mansion in Bangor, Maine. I feel wonderful, warm, and cozy sitting by the fireplace. It is January 3, 1999.

Goal: Earning $100,000 per year
Affirmation: I happily earn $100,000 per year. This money comes to me in various sums as I render my best possible service at (whatever you do for a living) in exchange for it.

Goal: A Rolex watch
Affirmation: I am wearing a stunning Rolex President's watch on January 5, 1997, and it looks awesome on my wrist. I have a strong feeling of personal pride as I now check the time.

Goal: A new boat
Affirmation: It's July 4, 1997. I'm cruising up and down Lake Seneca in my new 40-foot 200-horsepower blue and white Bayliner. The wind in my face is exhilarating.

Goal: Earning $500,000 per year
Affirmation: I earn $500,000 per year. This money is attract-
                   ed to me at various times throughout the year. I
                   offer (<u>whatever you do for a living</u>) to the best
                   of my ability to earn this money. I deal fairly
                   and squarely in all my business negotiations, for
                   I know the only way for me to enjoy money is
                   to honestly earn it. My family and I relish the
                   fruits of my labor. I am a financial success!

Activity goal affirmations: Things you want to do.

Goal: A trip to Europe
Affirmation: I am happily touring Europe June 10-June 24,
                   1998. It is a grand, memorable experience for
                   me visiting France, Holland, Germany, England,
                   and Spain.
Goal: Mountain climbing in the Rockies
Affirmation: My rock climbing trip September 10-20, 1998,
                   in Colorado is exhilarating. The sun is shining,
                   the sky is ice blue. I feel the clean crisp air rush-
                   ing into my lungs as I scale the mountains.
Goal: White-water rafting
Affirmation: My husband and I are enjoying white-water raft-
                   ing down the Snake River canyon May 10-20,
                   1997. Experiencing the splash and roar of the
                   rapids is thrilling.
Goal: Writing a book
Affirmation: I am engrossed in writing my romance novel.
                   The manuscript is complete on February 10,
                   1998. I feel the great sense of joy and personal
                   achievement that accompanies being an author.
Goal: Attending the Superbowl
Affirmation: I am having a blast at the 1999 Superbowl game
                   and am loving every minute of it.
Goal: Quit smoking
Affirmation: I am increasingly energized and healthy every
                   day of my smoke-free life. I breathe easily.

Goal: Achieve ideal body weight

Affirmation: I weigh 115 pounds, look stunning in a red bathing suit, and love showing off my shapely tight figure to others. It is July 4, the year 2000.

Career goal affirmations: Things you want to be.

Goal: A graphics design artist

Affirmation: I am a senior graphics design artist at Acme Graphics Company in the year 2000. What a fun job this is for me.

Goal: A world-renowned professional speaker

Affirmation: I am touring the globe in 1996, teaching and entertaining millions of people. My heart pours out to touch the masses. I am fulfilled.

Goal: An Olympic athlete

Affirmation: I feel fantastic as I train my body and mind every day. I am competing in the 1998 Olympic games, representing the U.S. in speed skating.

Goal: A multimillionaire

Affirmation: I have a personal net worth of over $5 million. This is in the form of stocks, bonds, and real estate. The titles of ownership are all in my portfolio by January 1, 1998. I offer (whatever you do for a living) in exchange for this money. I am proud of my financial accomplishment.

Goal: A super salesperson

Affirmation: I sell well to prospects that are in need of (your product). I confidently and quickly set about to assess their need for (your product). I recognize this quickly and proceed with showing them how (your product) will benefit them. I sell (your product), which benefits my customers. If (your product) does not suit my prospect's needs, I direct them to someone else's product that will. I am a super salesperson. I live an exceedingly good life at the top.

Goal: An M.D.

Affirmation: I am a general practitioner in Texas. The date on my medical degree is June 1998. I am enthusiastic, confident, and happy each day as I work toward my medical degree. I am satisfied and fulfilled.

Goal: Building a small business

Affirmation: My product helps humanity. I attract men and women who are talented and loyal by expressing these traits myself. I am an irresistible magnet, whose force and power grows daily. Fabulous wealth and prosperity comes to me from the manufacture and sale of (your product). I radiate goodwill to all my employees and customers, treating each one with complete honesty and fairness. I am the architect of my business. I am thankful and accept my good fortune now.

Goal: Save 15% of annual income

Affirmation: I take great pleasure in saving 15% of my annual income for retirement. I find that I live quite well on 85% of my income. The joy of building my personal fortune is unbeatable.

Behavioral trait affirmations: How you want to act.

Behavioral Trait: Patience with family

Affirmation: I feel at ease with myself as I deal patiently and lovingly with my wife and children. I control my temper well.

Behavioral Trait: Honesty

Affirmation: I am scrupulously honest in all my dealings with other people. This gives me the feeling of inner peace of mind and satisfaction.

Behavioral Trait: Creativity and memory

Affirmation: Novel ideas and stored information come to my conscious mind effortlessly, wonderfully, magnificently.

Behavioral Trait: Goal orientation (Option 1)

Affirmation: My actions and thoughts are consistent with and focused on achieving my goals. I enjoy focusing my power.

Behavioral Trait: Goal orientation (Option 2)

Affirmation: My mind is constantly on the lookout for ideas to propel me toward my goals. Finding these ideas is a thrilling, wonderful experience for me.

Behavioral Trait: Personal effectiveness

Affirmation: I reinforce successes in my life and correct for errors, using my experiences to become increasingly effective. I am confident, logical, and happy as I do this.

Behavioral Trait: High self-esteem

Affirmation: I recognize the high value of my work, respect my ideas, myself, and my purpose in life. I like myself! **I like myself! I LIKE MYSELF!**

Behavioral Trait: Physical attractiveness

Affirmation: I appear well groomed, neat, well dressed, handsome, and I project this image instantly to myself and others. My personality is charming, charismatic, and magnetic.

Behavioral Trait: Personal power

Affirmation: Physical, mental, and spiritual power flows in me. God is my partner. I am unstoppable!

Behavioral Trait: Self-confidence

Affirmation: I achieve the goals I set for myself. I have a clear mental picture of my life goals. I have all the necessary components to bring these goals into reality. I press myself onward, daily building my self-confidence as I see my goals materializing before my eyes. I am power!

Behavioral Trait: Personal responsibility

Affirmation: I gladly pull my own weight in life. I make no excuses for my circumstances. I am fully responsible for what happens to me. This gives me full control over my life, which I cherish dearly.

Behavioral Trait: Problem-solving skill

Affirmation: There is no problem that I cannot solve. Problems are only opportunities in disguise. I like challenges and successfully conquer them. My own strong abilities and knowledge are what I rely on to successfully solve problems. I am confident in my creative problem-solving capability.

SPECIAL AFFIRMATION FOR THE ILL

Goal: Good health

Affirmation: God's revitalizing energy is flowing through my veins now, healing me, making my body whole, strong, beautiful. I center my mind on the healing powers of God. I sense a oneness with the Divine. I feel myself growing physically and mentally stronger each day. I believe in and mentally accept my good health. I open my mind only to thoughts of good health. God heals all, and heals my body now. I am at peace.

SPECIAL UNIVERSAL AFFIRMATION TO FIND A PRACTICAL PLAN OF ACTION TO ACHIEVE ANY GOAL, USING YOUR OWN CREATIVE ABILITY!

As stated earlier, a practical plan for the attainment of a particular goal can itself become a goal. You simply start affirming *the finding* of a practical plan as your goal.

Goal: Obtain a practical plan to achieve my goal of (insert your goal here)

Universal Affirmation: I am patiently awaiting a plan for me to accomplish (insert your goal here). This fantastic practical plan is revealed to me now!

These two special affirmations are to be repeated more than three times per day. They should be repeated six to ten times a day until the desired result is achieved.

For the second affirmation, many people find that the whole plan or pieces of a plan come to them at unexpected times, such as while taking a shower, while driving to work, first thing in the morning, or in a dream. You might also be suddenly struck with the whole plan at once. It may be triggered by something someone says to you casually in passing. A seemingly insignificant chance event may trigger the plan that you need. Keep a small notepad and pencil handy at all times, and one by your bed or on the nightstand to write your ideas down. Be prepared for ideas beforehand, because they will come. Write them down immediately so you don't forget them, then be prepared to act on them.

◆ ◆ ◆

In converting your goals into a set of personal self-affirmations, be sure to take the necessary time to think each one out carefully. The more clarity and specificity you build into your affirmations, the better off you will be. Don't look up words in a dictionary, don't worry about making complete sentences. Use your own words, words you know and understand. Affirmations are personal mental tools, designed by you for your use, not for someone else. Limit your definition to just a few short sentences or phrases. The point is for the affirmation to trigger exactly what you truly desire in *your own mind*. As long as you follow the eleven design rules and conditioning procedure your affirmations **will be effective!**

You should at this time convert all your goals and desired behavioral traits into short multiple-phrase or single-phrase affirmations. Armed with your own personal set of custom-designed life goal affirmations, you will be ready to proceed with step 4, **conditioning.**

Step 4. Conditioning: Implanting Affirmations into the Subconscious Mind

"... *any goal set up by a human mind can be achieved by that mind's possessor.*"

> Napoleon Hill
> Success Philosopher
> Author of *Think and Grow Rich, Law of Success, Science of Personal Achievement,* and *Mental Dynamite*

Listed below are the nine steps used in the autogenic conditioning procedure.

1. Get comfortable. Use a sitting or lying down position. Place your body in an open position so no part of your body is touching, that is, no crossed arms or fingers, legs and feet apart, arms out from the body. If sitting in a high-back chair, rest your head against it. If you are not using a chair and are sitting on the floor, balance your head right between your shoulders, don't lean it on your hand. (Remember, no body part touches any other part.)

2. Close your eyes and tilt your head up slightly (this aids in air intake), breathe in deeply, hold it for five seconds, then exhale. Do this once, then breathe deeply five times. Now breathe regularly as you would at any other time. As you breathe, be alert to any tension in your body. This short breathing exercise charges your blood and brain with oxygen, aiding concentration.

3. Go from your toes to your head, relaxing each part sequentially. Start with your toes, then move to your feet, legs, torso, chest, hands, arms, shoulders, head, and forehead. As you relax each body part, breathe once, allowing any tension to go out of your body with your exhaled breaths. *Repeat out loud,* "The tension in my toes is gone now, the tension in my feet is gone now," and so on until you arrive at your forehead.

4. Imagine a relaxing situation you've been in from your past or would like to be in the future. A situation or setting where you feel totally at ease and peaceful is the aim. A serene fantasy or past situation is good. You may imagine yourself as a feather floating gently in the air, or perhaps you are a floating cloud. As you get into your imagined experience notice how good you feel, so peaceful, so relaxed. Let any remaining tensions be released by increasing the vividness of the peaceful imagined experience. Try to stimulate all five of your senses.

5. Slowly move out of the relaxing scene by counting down from 25 to 1. You could slowly ride down an escalator or elevator from the twenty-fifth floor to the first. As you count down each digit from 25 to 1, try to relax even more deeply. Think about how good it feels to be so thoroughly relaxed. If there are background noises around you, recognize them but don't let them bother you. Stay focused on your relaxed **feelings.**

6. When you hit the number 1 say, "I am now totally relaxed" out loud. Here is where your conscious mind is dramatically reduced in its ability to reason and edit out incoming or imagined information. Its ability to logically evaluate is almost gone. This is called "alpha state." The subconscious mental core is highly impressionable to affirmations at this time.

Now say your affirmations enthusiastically out loud to yourself or play a tape recording of yourself saying them. The verbal self-affirmations will go directly into your subconscious mental core as a **strong command.** The effects of any commands programmed into your subconscious mind when you are in this alpha state will be lasting. Goals, behavioral traits, and attitudinal changes are accepted as new operating instructions and are automatically processed by the subconscious mind.

NOTE: Now is also the ideal time to try to solve a problem, to resolve a conflict in your life, or to use the special universal affirmation I gave you earlier to find a practical plan for achieving any goal. Don't be alarmed if a number of possibilities or just one solution immediately flashes into your mind. Have a pen and paper handy just in case you latch onto one. Write it down, or better yet have a tape recorder handy, press record, and talk. Say whatever you are thinking.

The reason this problem-solving method works is again because your conscious mind's editing power is reduced. Your subconscious and superconscious can now flash answers more readily to your conscious mind, and your conscious mind won't suppress them. Any conscious preconceptions that serve to block your natural creative abilities are bypassed in the alpha state.

7. When you are done going through your entire affirmation list once, add these last affirmations. "Every time I review my self-affirmations, total relaxation is easier and easier for me." "I relax easily whenever I want to, and this is a pleasant experience for me." These last affirmations will help you to gain mastery of the deep relaxation technique quickly.

8. Count up 1 to 25 or ride up in the elevator or escalator from the first to the twenty-fifth floor, telling yourself, "I am now becoming more energized with each number increase." This brings you out of the alpha state and charges your body up for normal activity, putting you in a wide-awake state.

9. When you hit the number 25 stand up, take three deep breaths, stretch, and walk around. Notice how good you feel. You will feel much more energetic than when you started the procedure.

This conditioning technique practiced three times a day allows you to rapidly reprogram your subconscious mental core. The best times are upon first waking in the morning, noon after lunch, and just before going to sleep.

This is a valuable skill for *high achievement*, perhaps the most potent skill in the entire POWERMIND system. Everyone should have it in their repertoire of self-mastery techniques.

As you become more adept at this technique, you will be able to do the conditioning procedure almost any place. In just a few minutes you can be less tense, more energized, more focused on your goals than when you started.

When you use this conditioning technique to reprogram your mind, the effects are very rapid. In one day you'll notice changes in your thinking. In thirty days you'll be a firm believer in your own capability. Any change in your life can be had with this technique!

When you are comfortable that the behavioral trait changes have become habit or a goal has been achieved, substitute new affirmations to replace them. Never stop using this autogenic conditioning technique to unlock your potential. Use it every day all your life!

Reasons Why Some People Get the Opposite of Their Affirmations

Principle: **The subconscious mind accepts and acts on the thoughts carrying the highest degree of emotional charge.**

Emile Coue, the famous French psychologist and early affirmation pioneer, defined a law of reversed effort as follows: "When your *desires* and *imagination* are in conflict your imagination invariably gains the day."

As you affirm a phrase such as "I earn $100,000 dollars per year and love it" but in your mind you are thinking "I can't possibly do it. I'll just say these stupid affirmations a couple more times but they won't work," you undermine the affirmation. You are putting your dominant underlying thoughts in direct opposition to the affirmation. In the long run you always lose out, and you get the opposite result of what you "thought" you had affirmed.

Continuous repetition of thoughts in the relaxed *alpha state* I described earlier will **reshape the underlying belief inside your metal core so this doesn't happen.** That is, you make your desire **congruent with, not opposed to,** your dominant underlying thoughts (mental core beliefs). It is when conscious desire and subconscious imagination are perfectly aligned that you generate real power.

If you attempt mental coercion, that is, using an affirmation then quickly replacing it (thought substitution) with a negative affirmation such as "My life is awful," "I could never do that," "I won't amount to anything," "My life is meaningless," "I feel sick," "There is no solution," "It's hopeless," "I'm all stressed out," these emotionally charged negative thoughts counteract your positive verbal affirmation. You tend to get nowhere, or even worse, if you firmly believe the negative thoughts more than the affirmation, you'll bring negative circumstances into your life. Whichever has the strongest *emotional impact* is what gets imprinted onto your subconscious mental core as a command.

The subconscious mind can be analogized to a small child taking orders. If you order a small child to walk toward you, then say, "No, go the other way," then say, "No come here," he will most likely do one of two things. He may become confused and just stand there doing nothing, or he may go in the direction he thinks you *really want him* to go. The direction he decides to go in is based on the *emotional* cues he gets from you. If you yell at the child and shout with force, energy, determination, directness, "Come here right now!" he'll probably quietly walk straight toward you with his head down. Once you arrive at a clear, definite, **emotionalized instruction**, the child silently obeys.

The subconscious mind takes orders in a similar way. Command it with clear-cut, concise affirmations charged with strong positive emotion, and it will move you in that direction automatically. *The subconscious mind accepts and acts on the thoughts carrying the highest degree of emotional charge.*

Wishy-washy affirmations are ineffective as well. If you say, "I kind of want to be rich someday" or "I want things to be okay" or "I might be healthy in the future" or "I sort of like myself" or "I wish I was smart" or "I might achieve my goals" or "I think I might be able to someday" or "I sure hope things will work out," these will all be ineffective. They aren't designed right and are depleted of a strong positive emotional charge. In two words, they *"lack power."*

Affirmations and Truth: The Confusion Explained

Affirmation effectiveness depends on following the eleven design rules and the nine conditioning steps and on your understanding of how the human mind operates. You just received most of this vital background knowledge here and in Mental Mechanics, but you also need to understand what truth is.

When you were in grade school, you learned 5 + 5 = 10. If you said 5 + 5 was any number other than 10, you would have been told that was the "wrong" answer. Had you said 11, you would learn the correct answer is 10 because the teacher, a respected authority figure, told you so. The teacher and your other classmates would now "know" that 10 is the correct answer. But what if the teacher was wrong and she said the answer was 11? You, your classmates, and the teacher would all "know" 5 + 5 = 11, but that's wrong!

It is true that you *learned* 5 + 5 = 10 from somebody, you were not born with this knowledge. It is also true that human beings are meant to be productive and happy, have riches, help others, and set, seek, and achieve worthy goals. If you were taught this isn't "true," your teacher was wrong!

When you affirm in your mind sickness, sadness, failure, harm to others, poverty, despair, hopelessness, helplessness, you are going against Universal Truth. You would do this basically for one of two reasons: either you are ignorant of Universal Truth or your teacher(s) was wrong! It is easy to think you "know" the truth in our society, because so many people are programmed by others who have no idea that they are indeed wrong. Our society is very negative, and the majority of children were and are in fact lied to for much of their lives about their true potential. It only takes a cursory glance at our society to see the *truth* in these statements.

Armed with the knowledge that your conscious thoughts effect your behavior and these are reflected in events, occurrences, and circumstances in your life, why would anyone think that they had no power to change their own future? It is totally unreasonable to think that way; however, people do it all the time. They say, "I feel like I'm lying when I affirm what I do not now possess." Remember, affirmations are tools to effect positive changes. As you start autogenically conditioning your affirmations, in a remarkably short time (less than one week) they will begin to manifest themselves as visible changes in your life. You are causing yourself to come into harmony with a more natural state of living. If you really want to be scientific in your understanding, you'll realize true and false don't apply to verbal self-affirmations at all. Affirmations are simply instructions given over to the subconscious mind to effect mental and physical changes. You should realize by now that whatever is impressed on the subconscious mind is brought into reality.

Affirmations set up an inner homing devise or default program that guides your thinking, your perception of the environment, and your outward actions. As affirmations are repeated over and over, they continue to keep your inner orientation properly set. Just as a compass needle always points north, you will always be pointed in the direction of your affirmations, moving toward them. All your thoughts, decisions, and actions will move you toward your self-set goals AUTOMATICALLY, without the use of teeth-gritting will power! If you choose not to focus your thought power, it will be dissipated, your thoughts will become random and disorganized, you will become inconsistent, your actions will become haphazard and your life meaningless. You will function with no inner guidance system and thus be rendered powerless to control your future!

As stated earlier, affirmations are verbal tools charged with strong positive emotion that are used to guide your thoughts and actions in a specific self-chosen direction. Affirmations should be evaluated on the basis of how well they are crafted. Do they meet each of the eleven design rules I listed? Do they make you feel a certain way? Can they trigger the proper mental response? "Design," "construction," and "emotional impact," not "true" or "false," are terms applicable to verbal affirmations!

If an affirmation was an accurate "true" statement of you right now, you wouldn't need it! The affirmation's purpose is to automatically stimulate change; therefore they *must* conflict with your present situation. The "lying to yourself" trap catches so many would-be users who could benefit tremendously from affirmations, it boggles the mind!

Skeptics often play on this particular aspect, trying to shoot down affirmations as silly nonsense only used by fanatics. Their ignorance of an affirmation's purpose and their lack of understanding of mental mechanics keeps them forever criticizing others.

If you think for a moment, you've really been using affirmations all your life, probably to bring ill health, unhappiness, poverty, failure, and misery into your life by the process of worrying and putting yourself down. Remember, if you use your subconscious mind in a negative manner you'll get negative results.

It's just like when you put a car into reverse gear; the engine runs fine, and when you depress the accelerator pedal the whole car, you, and anyone else in it move *backwards*. The car and engine have not changed one bit, but you changed gears. Just a small part of the whole machine was changed, *but the transmission is a critical controlling part of a car.* Your conscious mind is like the transmission of a car: put it in forward gear, you move forward; reverse gear, you move backward. But humans don't have a gearshift lever on the side of their head to do this. Instead we have our thoughts. Positive, healthy, goal-directed thoughts put our whole subconscious mind machine in forward gear; negative thoughts put our subconscious mind machine in reverse gear.

If you are sick, poor, apathetic, or unhappy, your conscious mind is in reverse gear. To shift into forward gear, you must change your conscious thinking first, then drive this new thought into the subconscious mind. The verbal self-affirmation technique is exactly how you do it!

One final point on truth and affirmations. Is the car transmission "true" or "false" if it is set in forward gear? Do you see how the question does not apply? It also doesn't apply to setting your subconscious mind in forward gear with your conscious thoughts (verbal self-affirmations). Affirmations are just like the transmission of a car. They can take you forward through life or backward. The words "true" or "false" or "lies" don't apply to automobile transmissions any more than they do to verbal self-affirmations. If you shift your mind into forward gear, your whole life goes forward. If you shift your mind into reverse, your whole life will go backwards—and that's the TRUTH!!!

"Whatever we plant in our subconscious mind and nourish with repetition and emotion will one day become reality."

Earl Nightingale
Self-development pioneer
Author of *The Strangest*
***Secret, Lead the Field* and**
Cofounder of the Nightingale
Conant Corp.

Common Mistakes in Using Affirmations for Wealth Creation

Many people say they have used wealth creation affirmations for months and they "didn't work." Here are some of their *incorrect* affirmations: "I have money," "I want plenty of money," "I am wealthy," "I will have plenty of money," "I'm rich," "I wish I had a million dollars." I might also add these people don't usually pursue any ideas they have or *take any action.* **AFFIRMATIONS ARE MENTAL TOOLS; YOU STILL NEED TO WORK AT ACHIEVING WHATEVER YOU AFFIRM.**

I'll be the first to say wealth creation affirmations not backed by action aren't effective at all; you still need to act. The incorrect affirmations above also have multiple design flaws. If you check them against the eleven affirmation design rules, you'll see why.

Some people also tend to repeat their affirmations with the *emotionalized* feeling that it is not true or that they don't deserve to be wealthy. They think it's impossible for them to ever get wealthy. These are their underlying dominant beliefs.

They are trying to violate the Universal Laws of **belief** and **expectation**. They don't *believe* and they don't *expect* to be wealthy. When this occurs, their subconscious mind will direct their actions, making financial circumstances much worse for them because they are really affirming **poverty**. Their belief, expectation, and emotions are all in opposition to their weak verbal command (self-affirmation). The subconscious acts on belief, emotion, expectation, and imagery, not idle words. Since messages of poverty are actually what is conveyed to the sub-conscious mind, they actually attract poverty to themselves. *Here are two techniques to avoid this common mistake.* First make your affirmation more practical and believable. Say, "I am learning every day in my chosen field, this knowledge helps me earn 25% more annually, and it feels great!" Or "My actions and thoughts are consistent with and focused on obtaining a million dollars over the next five years. I am energized!" Remember, affirmations and goals need to be at least 50% believable at the start. The 50/50 rule of goal setting also applies to affirmations, obviously!

Second, you may try affirming your capability to get rich. It might be easier for you to believe the idea that learning, growing, and becoming more *capable* will aid you in earning more money. With this approach you merely affirm your potential, but you also tie the way you say the affirmation in with wealth creation. That is, you tie learning directly to earning. This style of affirmation becomes more believable and builds you in more ways than just an ability to get rich. It makes you more receptive to wealth-creating ideas, and your "money consciousness" is stimulated.

For example, affirm "Each day I gain information to aid me in earning more money. My mind is highly receptive to wealth creation ideas as I continue to think about an annual earning increase of 25%. I feel happy, confident, and powerful as I take daily action to achieve this goal."

An Advanced Technique: The Signed Contract Method of Affirmation

This is an EXTREME variation of the verbal self-affirmation technique. Many of the steps are identical to the ones used in the verbal self-affirmation technique; however, in this method you draw up a contract with yourself and God, describing what you will do in return for what you want to receive. You also include the date for the exchange to be completed. Then comes the all-important factor of signing your name in full and dating the contract. Once this is complete, you are to read your signed contract each morning upon awaking and each evening right before going to sleep.

What you are actually doing in this technique is making a commitment to yourself and God, and of course conditioning your subconscious mind. Many of the more "serious" individuals will enjoy using this advanced technique because it also serves to build an *"iron will"* and a high degree of *personal honor.* Whenever you sign your name to a document and date it, your personal honor is *on the line.*

When you were born you were given a name. That name represents you and all that you stand for. This contract is drawn up by you and you alone. Take care to be sure it is accurate in every detail *before you sign it!* Then put your commitment in ink, review it twice a day, and do what you contracted to do. If shivers run up your spine before you sign your name, it is a well-written contract. This is a very serious method. You'll see why in the two examples that follow.

Signed Contract Example for Wealth Creation

I (your name) hereby swear to become a millionaire in the next five years. I will render (your product or service) to the best of my abilities throughout this time period in exchange for the money. Each day I will commit at least one hour to improving myself so that I become more effective in rendering (product or service). I now commit myself to excellence in (your field). I will become a world authority, an expert, a specialist.

In all my dealings with people in my business I will be scrupulously honest, and never infringe on the personal rights or freedom of others. I now set all my actions and thoughts toward achieving this money goal. I concentrate easily on this goal. I feel confident, powerful, and happy when I work on its achievement.

I will induce others to help me in attaining one million dollars over the next five years by my willingness to help others. My main mission in life over the next five years is to become a millionaire. My conscious, subconscious, and superconscious minds are all unified and focused on this objective of obtaining one million dollars.

I am now successful and will continue increasing my success. I am unstoppable in my purpose! I demand financial success of myself! In return for this great financial success I will render my best at (your product or service). I will never quit. I will never stop trying. I will never give up until my goal of one million dollars is won! Each evening I will silently, solemnly pray for God's help in achieving this money goal. By God's grace it will be done!

Signed _____

Date _____

Signed Contract Example for the Creation of Good Health

I (your name) have a body in good condition. It is strong and healthy and serves my purposes well. I will take care of it as my most cherished possession on earth.

The foods I eat, the exercises I do are all geared toward maintaining it in top condition. I am proud of its appearance and gladly, honorably accept compliments concerning it. I will clean and adorn it with the best garments and enhancements that I can afford.

My body is my holy temple on earth and I will treat it as such. Each evening I will focus my thoughts on a future vision of my body as perfect, healthy, and strong. This image will become real by (whatever date you chose) as I continue my efforts each day to achieve that end.

I will silently, earnestly pray each evening for God's help in doing this. The power of God flows into my body now, healing me, charging me, rebuilding me, making my perfect image a reality.

I will never stop trying. I will never give up, until my good health goal is won!

Signed _____

Date _____

As you can see from my two examples, this method is not for the timid. It is highly effective as a more advanced technique. It is to be used usually for one or two main life goals. For instance, you probably wouldn't use the signed contract method to buy a new house next year.

You'll notice that my examples use the invocation of God as a "power partner." This adds the most powerful aid you could possibly have, so be sure your goal is a worthy one. Many beginning success students will obviously shy away from this particular method; however, for completeness I included one advanced technique in The POWERMIND System. You would be amazed at the miraculous results people get with this method!

An After-the-Lesson Visit with the Author

In lesson 5 you learned that there are four modes of thought or self-communication: verbal, sensory, conceptual, and emotional. The verbal self-affirmation technique in this lesson utilized mainly the **verbal** and **emotional** modes of thought.

It is a method of autogenic conditioning that can be used as an aid in either achieving goals or developing specific behavioral traits. This allows you to more effectively utilize your **true** potential.

With self-affirmations your thoughts and behaviors become automatically aligned, falling under subconscious control to a greater degree. It is one of the most important high achievement techniques you could possibly learn. I will review it briefly.

The verbal self-affirmation technique begins with the construction of a sentence or a series of short phrases called affirmations. A separate affirmation or set of affirmations is designed for each behavioral trait you want to develop or each personal goal you want to achieve.

The design of verbal self-affirmations is absolutely crucial for their effectiveness. There are eleven design rules that you must follow to build your verbal affirmations correctly. Read, reread, and study the eleven design rules and the categorical examples I gave in this lesson. Affirmations must be properly engineered to get the right response. One rule missed can render the affirmation completely ineffective.

I then discussed the nine-step procedure for conditioning or implanting goals into the subconscious mind. If you are doing the conditioning procedure one day a month, it will only lead you to frustration and disappointment. The nine-step procedure is scientifically based on the physiology and operation of the human brain. It must be done AT LEAST TWO TIMES PER DAY.

Many people have tried various affirmation-style techniques but were not thoroughly schooled. They didn't learn all the various facets necessary to be successful at it. After an unsatisfying trial effort, they became discouraged and started thinking affirmations are for weirdos, fanatics, and fortune tellers. If you are in this category, I strongly urge you to carefully reread this lesson to discover what you were doing wrong!

The main purpose of this technique is to instruct the subconscious mind as to how it should direct its power. Various verbal self-affirmation techniques have been around for thousands of years, and people throughout history have obtained mixed results. Sometimes they worked, sometimes they didn't, they worked for some people, not for others. I often wondered why this was the case until my extensive research in this particular area uncovered the reasons for the inconsistencies. I was then able to ferret out the exact causes for failure in using verbal self-affirmations.

The cause for failure was that they did not precisely follow the complete step-by-step procedure outlined in this lesson. They did not know exactly what to do or how to do exactly that!

"It is psychological law that whatever we desire to accomplish we must impress upon the subjective or subconscious mind."

Orison Swett Marden
Author of *Pushing to the*
Front

Lesson

8 ◆

Autogenic Conditioning II. Imagineering

Overview

This lesson is split into two separate modules. In Module I, you will learn a second autogenic conditioning technique, called imagineering. This technique basically utilizes all five of your senses to condition your mind for goal achievement. It is a simple technique you can use to rapidly reprogram your subconscious mental core.

In Module II of this lesson, I will wrap up all of autogenic conditioning by explaining the science behind both the verbal self-affirmation technique and the imagineering technique. This will give you complete understanding of exactly how autogenic conditioning techniques work and why they are so effective.

In uncovering exactly how autogenic conditioning works, I spent extensive time and effort going through very technical research on the human brain and memory development. A partial listing of research literature has been included for those of you who are interested in how autogenic conditioning works. You will find Module II quite fascinating!

Autogenic Conditioning II: Module I. Introduction to Imagineering

Autogenic Conditioning II: Module I. Imagineering
Introduction to Imagineering

"The whole idea . . . is to enable you to see mentally the pictures at all hours of the day."

> Claude M. Bristol
> Author of *The Magic of Believing* and *TNT: The Power Within You*

This autogenic conditioning technique involves all four modes of thought. The verbal and conceptual are used to a lesser degree, but the *sensory* and *emotional* modes are used to a very high degree. Imagineering is yet another tool to add to your success chest. As you work through this lesson I will fully explain imagineering. Here is an example of a brief imagineering sequence, which will provide you with a basic introduction of how the technique works.

Let's assume you love chocolate ice cream cones. Early in the afternoon on a hot summer's day you **decide** that you want one. However, you are at work and can't leave until 5 P.M. Well, from the moment you catch hold of this idea that you want a chocolate ice cream cone, it starts to *play on your mind.*

You start to think about the ice cream shop just down the street . . . *You can see the red and white shop sign vividly in your mind's eye. You imagine pulling up to the drive-through window in your car. Jill is working today. You can see her pretty smile as she says, "What would you like, Mrs. Jones?" You say, "A large chocolate cone, please." You watch her as she fills the cone with the smooth chocolate soft-serve, your mouth waters, you can already taste that icy sweet cream on your tongue. She brings the perfectly made chocolate cone to the window. Your hand reaches out and grasps the white-napkin-wrapped cone, it's soft on your fingers, a firm heavy cone made just the way you like. As you raise it to your mouth you can smell the frosty chocolaty aroma. You open wide to take your first bite, it chills and fills your mouth with flavor! It tastes, oh, so sweet!*

After you've "imagineered" this sequence a few times while you are at work, by five o'clock nothing in the world is going to stop you from heading straight to the ice cream shop to get that super duper double-size chocolate cone. Your desire will intensify each time you "imagineer" this pleasurable experience.

In my example, were you vividly imagining the ice cream cone sequence? Could you see, hear, taste, touch, and smell the whole experience? Do you want a chocolate cone now?

It may take you some time to get the hang of creating this type of synthetic experience in your mind, but this is a high achievement skill that anyone can develop. This synthetic experience style of mental programming is what imagineering is all about—imagining an activity or achieving a goal in your mind *beforehand*. Usually a paragraph, sentence, phrase, or word triggers an entire imagined experience sequence, and strong, positive emotions flow together with it to make an "imagineered" experience.

A key point in this technique is that you are to be the participant in the imagineered experience, not a spectator. You don't see yourself happily engaged in the behavior like watching yourself on TV, but you are actually doing it in your mind. In our ice cream cone example you were watching the cone being made and then holding, biting, smelling, tasting the cone, not watching yourself eat a cone.

What you will learn in this lesson is how to imagineer goals so that they supersede and dominate your thoughts and actions both consciously and subconsciously. Vividness of the imagineered experience, using all five senses (if possible) plus strong positive emotion, is what makes the technique highly effective. Positive emotional charging is again very important, just as it was with the verbal self-affirmation technique. You must feel the enthusiasm, joy, pleasure, happiness, and sense of accomplishment, letting your positive emotions run wild as you live out the imagineering sequence in your mind. Strong emotions make a lasting impression on your memory, locking the imagineered experience into the subconscious mental core.

The human mind is capable of imagining anything for which it has pieces of past experience or knowledge. For example, if you have seen an eagle at the zoo or a picture of an eagle you can imagine a "giant" one, a "tiny" one, a "blue" one, a "red" one. If you have ever felt happiness, enthusiasm, pleasure, you can recall and reexperience these positive emotions. These emotions can then be associated with newly created synthetic experiences in your mind. If you associate positive emotions in your mind repeatedly on a daily basis with an imagined experience, this association will become automatic, creating intense desire for whatever is "imagineered." Belief in your ability to actually live out the imagineered sequence also dramatically increases. This belief and desire will influence your subconscious mind, guiding your thoughts and actions, automatically moving you toward accomplishing the imagineered goal.

As in using any tool, the way to become skilled is to practice using it. You have already used imagineering all your life, probably unconsciously. I'm just providing you with a highly effective way to consciously control this process to guide your thoughts and actions, which will subsequently effect your destiny. Instead of using your imagination in a haphazard, unfocused, slipshod fashion, why not take precise deliberate control and use it with maximum efficiency for *maximum achievement?*

5 Foundation Principles

You can combine imagineered experiences (synthetic experiences) with virtually any positive emotion. These newly imagineered experiences will then allow you to use more of your true potential. This is not really a new concept since you have set limits on your potential with imagineered experiences ever since you were born. All your imagineered as well as real experiences make a contribution in shaping your desires, beliefs, and attitudes about yourself and your abilities, either to allow more of your true potential to flow or to completely cut it off.

Imagineering is mental engineering that is used to design your future in the magnificent workshop of the mind. It allows you to consciously guide your thought processes more deliberately. This results in changes to your subconscious mental core in regard to any goal. These core changes affect your thinking and behavior in a natural, automatic, free-flowing manner, requiring no use of energy-draining will power.

Imagineering is scientific and practical. It works for anyone, anywhere, anytime, has universal application, and requires no special schooling. It has been proven to work time and time again; in fact, it even explains why other "snake oil" methods don't work.

Imagineering is based on five foundation principles of human behavior, some of which were touched on in earlier lessons but are worth special review for this lesson. Each of the five principles can easily be tested and observed. It is absolutely necessary for you to fully understand these five principles. If you doubt the validity of any of them, experiment for yourself. Read other self-development books until the truth of each of these principles is finally revealed to you.

Principle 1:   Every human behaves in a manner that is consistent with the beliefs held within their subconscious mental core.

Everyone's actions and decisions make perfect sense to them because they are based on what they believe to be true about themselves and the world around them. Everyone behaves normally or in a manner consistent with their own subconscious mental core beliefs. For example, believers in voodoo may believe so strongly in the power of a "death curse" that they could actually die if they knew one had been placed on them.

When people believed the earth was flat there wasn't any point in trying to prepare for a journey to sail across the ocean. Christopher Columbus was an insane man to hundreds of people.

Trying to put a man on the moon was also utter nonsense to many thousands of people. You see, they believed deep in their mind it was not possible. So there was really no point in thinking about it or trying to build a silly rocket ship for space travel. In their minds it couldn't be done! They behaved in a manner consistent with their beliefs, which are held in their subconscious mental core.

Principle 2:   YOU influence your own subconscious
mental core with the thoughts, feelings, and
experiences YOU hold within YOUR
conscious mind on a continuing basis.

All your life experiences and how you felt about them made
a contribution to your subconscious mental core. Once you
experience something it is immediately stored in your subconscious memory banks and makes its mark on the core. Once in
the core it can never be erased.

You may not be able to consciously recall every experience
you ever had, but rest assured they are in there, and they affected
your attitude, which has been in turn reflected in your thinking
and behavior from that second onward. Reading this book right
now is changing your life, *unfolding your consciousness.* You
are learning and thinking thoughts you never had before. This
will most certainly affect you!

Changes in your mental core result from what you think
about often, what you are highly emotional about, and the ideas
you believe in. By the process of thinking certain emotionalized
thoughts often, you alter your mental core.

Principle 3:   YOUR subconscious mental core is the result
of how YOU interpreted all YOUR life
experiences, how YOU perceive yourself and
YOUR external environment.

Your parents or whoever raised you did not give you life
experiences. No one handed you a life experience diskette when
you were a small child and said, "Stick this in your ear, it's your
life experience memory bank." No religious leader, political
leader, teacher, or friend gave you your life experiences. You
built your own experiences both real and imagined into your
own mental core and continue to build it layer by layer every
day. Some people are building an ornate place for a mental core;
others are building an ugly maximum security prison. Some
build shacks, others cities; some build torture chambers, others
gardens of Eden. All of your behavior is a result of how you
yourself built your mental core, what you yourself programmed
in by yourself!

Principle 4: **One of the main components you can easily control to alter your mental core quickly is your IMAGINATION and your FEELINGS about what you imagine.**

I wondered for a long time why "positive thinking" didn't work for everyone. Many thousands of people attribute their life success to positive thinking. Why then do other intelligent people see it as a joke, a foolish delusion?

Positive thinking is the oldest form of psychological folk medicine. It has been written about in Egyptian, Oriental, and European cultures. Dr. Norman Vincent Peale's classic book, *The Power of Positive Thinking*, has been an invaluable aid to millions of people. Why then doesn't it work for everyone? The answer is quite simple. The difference in opinions has to do with how the information was *interpreted* by the reader. Like everything else in life it's how you interpret and internalize the information that counts.

If you view positive thinking as simply a "fun" exercise, nothing will happen, nothing will change for you. But if your positive thinking is backed by serious thought, concentration, burning desire, unshakable faith, vividly imagined experiences charged with especially strong positive emotion, changes in your behavior will inevitably result. Strong feelings combined with imagined experiences will quickly alter your mental core.

Principle 5: **To the degree that you vividly imagine an experience, person, place, or event, it is registered as REAL in your subconscious mind. This is the hallmark principle of imagineering. The subconscious mind cannot distinguish between a REAL and a VIVIDLY IMAGINED experience.**

Principle number 5 means that experiences can be synthetically created in the design studio of the mind. Since real or vividly imagined experiences affect the mental core the same way, it becomes a hallmark foundation principle on which to build a mental technique for high achievement. Any goal, as well as most behavioral traits, such as courage, self-confidence, charisma, all can be autogenically conditioned or cultivated with imagineering. *Positive emotions can be combined with synthetic experiences to PREPROGRAM future behavior, which will enhance current performance.* This recombination of positive emotions with vividly imagined (synthetic) experiences enable you to totally reshape your mental core. By using your imagination to autogenically condition in future experiences, you can make your true potential unfold.

This lesson is designed to teach you exactly how to perform the imagineering technique. Once you have the knowledge of this technique, you can then practice it daily to develop skill. Practical application of knowledge and skill combine to form personal power.

Imagineering is simply the fusing of imagined experiences with strong positive emotion. This causes changes to occur in your mental core. You can learn how to consciously control these changes; and as you do, your whole life will rapidly change for the better.

The Imagineering Technique

1. Establish what personal goals you would like to achieve or behavioral traits you would like to possess. (You should have already done this in Part II, Goal Setting. If not, review that part at this time.)

2. Write out a few paragraphs to serve as the "imagineering sequence." Some people prefer to write out the entire imagineering sequence, using descriptive language, when they first start. They then read the whole sequence to help train their mind. This helps them stimulate positive emotions and graphic detail of the desired goal better.

3. Select a word to serve as a memory "trigger." The only purpose of the trigger is to remind you of the imagineering sequence.

4. Relax, close your eyes, and live out the imagineered experience in your mind.

5. Allow strong positive emotions to fill your body and mind during the entire imagineering sequence.

6. Repeat this procedure at least two times per day, preferably early morning right after waking and late evening before sleeping. NOTE: Anytime when you have a few free minutes can be used to imagineer your goals. When you're stuck in traffic or waiting in lines are also excellent times. Whenever you can and as often as you wish, you can imagineer your goals. Remember you can imagineer anything you want to be, have, or do as well as behavioral traits. Your only limits are the limits of your own mind!

"For imagination sets the goal 'picture' which our automatic mechanism works on. We act, or fail to act, not because of 'will,' as is so commonly believed, but because of imagination."

Dr. Maxwell Maltz
Author of *Psycho-cybernetics*

Categorical Examples of Goal Imagineering

Imagineering enables you to program your goals into your subconscious mind as well as increase desire and belief in your ability to achieve these goals. Here are some categorical examples of imagineering sequences for you to study carefully. Examples of something you may want to be, have, and do are given as goals. Imagineering is a more advanced technique than the verbal self-affirmation method. However, both techniques are highly effective used individually or in combination. You may find it easier to imagineer some of your goals and easier to use verbal self-affirmations for others, or you can use both techniques together on the same goal for a synergistic effect.

Goal: Being president of your own company
                   (An example of a goal of something you want
                   to be)

Trigger: President

Imagineering
Sequence: *You are driving to your office in your brand new blue Mercedes. You feel the soft gray leather on your back, bottom, and legs as the seat completely envelops your body. It has that classic "new leather" smell. You notice a few passersby on the street taking second glances at you, admiring the car. As you pull up to your factory, the workers are putting the finishing touches on the red neon sign bearing your name, which is written across the side of the building. "J. Smith and Sons Inc." You get out of your car, open the glass and brass door of the building. The receptionist ever so politely says, "Good morning, Mr. Smith," with a big smile. You greet her kindly but hurry to the elevator and push the third-floor button. You glide on up. As the doors open, you see at the end of the hallway the shimmering gold nameplate on your door. You walk down the richly carpeted hallway with an air of success. The striking black letters on the nameplate stand out, "John Smith, President," written in scroll. Your hand clasps the cool smooth brass knob of the solid black walnut door. You are thrilled as it opens, because your new cherrywood desk and red leather chair have arrived and await your presence. The whole office smells of leather and new carpet. You lay your briefcase on the desk, you hear the familiar "snap, snap" as it opens. Just then your telephone rings. It's your secretary. She says "Jane Johnson, the President of XYZ Company, has arrived. Shall I send her in?" You know it is to negotiate the sale of widgets. You say with confidence, "Send her in, please." The door opens. Jane walks in with a bright eager-to-buy smile.*

Goal: Owning a summer home in Maine
                 (An example of a goal of something you want
                 to have)

Trigger: A-Frame

**Imagineering
Sequence:**   *You are driving your 4x4 up the winding moun-
                 tain road. The buds are just greening up on the
                 trees from a long hard winter. Just as you crest
                 the top of the hill, the beautiful cedar A-frame
                 comes into view. You notice the huge front trian-
                 gular window reflecting the rich blue sky and
                 puffy white clouds. You step out of your car and
                 smell the fresh pine air while walking up the
                 redwood sidewalk to the door. You see that the
                 realtor is inside with the others, getting all the
                 paperwork in order. You walk in and slip your
                 coat off. The thick gray carpet feels cool on
                 your feet. You stride into the living room, being
                 careful not to trip as you enter the expansive
                 sunken room. A fire is crackling away in the
                 green Italian marble fireplace. The strong
                 aroma of hickory smoke fills the air. You shake
                 hands with everyone, sit down, and sip a cup of
                 cinnamon cider. After the introductory remarks
                 have been made, you begin signing the papers
                 of ownership with your 14K gold Cross pen you
                 purchased especially for this momentous occa-
                 sion. When the final signature is made the real-
                 tor clasps your hand warmly and says,
                 "Congratulations on your purchase of this won-
                 derful cedar A-frame. I know you'll enjoy many
                 wonderful summers here!" You say, "Thank
                 you, it feels great to be here . . ."*

Goal: Winning a national speed skating title
                 (An example of a goal of something you want
                 to do)

Trigger: Champion

**Imagineering
Sequence:**   *It's your turn on the ice at the start/finish line.
All the other skaters have done unusually well.
You are paired with a strong competitor. You
know you need to beat her. You look down at the
steel blue ice while digging your blades in. You
hear "ready." Your muscles are tense, ready to
fire you down the track like a Patriot missile. All
the practice, all the mental rehearsals have
been for this moment. You know you can win.
"Bang!" the gun fires. Instantly you are on
automatic pilot. You are thirty feet down the
track and moving into your rhythmic stride, left
hand on your back now. You are maintaining
perfect focus, your body is exploding with each
stride pushing you on. You know it's going to be
a personal best time. The wind rushes your face.
It's exhilarating; the blades work the ice in perfect harmony under your feet. You feel like you
are flying. On the home stretch you can hear
nothing, all goes completely silent. Your body
and mind are one speed machine, it's just you,
ice, and a championship title. You see the finish
line, your peripheral vision narrows to see only
that line. You cross it, stand up straight, and
wait for the time. Ten seconds later you see your
time on the board, it's your best time ever.
You've beaten everyone else. Your arms raise
high in victory, the roar of the crowd rings in
your ears. The dream is now reality!*

Goal: Getting an A+ in chemistry class
                       (An example of a goal of something you want
                       to do)

Trigger: A+

**Imagineering
Sequence:**   *The shiny purple and gold chemistry book is on
                       the desk in front of you. You pick it up and feel
                       its smooth glasslike cover. You have an inner
                       sense of curiosity and desire to understand the
                       chemical principles contained within it. As you
                       read each chapter you underline points and
                       concepts that stand out in your mind. Anything
                       you don't understand you put a star by so you
                       won't forget to ask the teacher about it later.
                       Each homework question is an interesting chal-
                       lenge for you to conquer. During class you
                       detect no other sounds but the teacher's voice
                       and questions asked by other students.
                       Somehow you are acutely in tune with chemical
                       principles for each class. It seems to excite you
                       as you learn more and more from lectures, read-
                       ing, and your homework. A week before each
                       test you review your class notes, homework, and
                       book chapters, especially concepts you at first
                       didn't understand. As each test time approaches
                       you feel increasingly relaxed because you know
                       the material and absorbed the information.
                       Each test is fun! You think carefully before
                       answering the questions. When the semester is
                       finished there it is, your A+. You have a strong
                       sense of accomplishment, not so much for the
                       A+ itself but for the knowledge you gained. A
                       warmth rushes over your body; you feel happy.*

◆ ◆ ◆

In the examples given, notice how there were elements included to stimulate most of your five senses, sight, sound, touch, taste, and smell. In imagineering goals you simply create in your own imagination the experience of the goal.

If your goal were to become a millionaire you might create an imagineering sequence that would answer many of these questions: What will you look like? What will you wear? Where will you live? What will you own? What people will be in your life? What will you eat? Where will you go? How will you get there? How will people react to you? How will you talk? How will you feel? On and on and on.

The imagineering technique is basically to experience in your mind as vividly and completely as you can, with full sensory stimulation and strong positive emotion, the "end result" of your goal. Remember, without strong positive emotional charging there is no impact on the mental core. Imagineering uses the power of synthetic experience charged with strong positive emotion. Imagineered experiences are quickly internalized into the subconscious mind and become part of the mental core, where they will guide and direct your thoughts and actions automatically.

This may all sound quite simple to some. DON'T BE FOOLED!!! The most complex problems often yield themselves to simple solutions. The plain truth is that imagineering works for anyone!

"Begin to imagine what the desirable outcome would be like. Go over these mental pictures and delineate details and refinements. Play them over and over to yourself."

Dr. Maxwell Maltz
Author of *Psycho-cybernetics*

6 Helpful Tips for Imagineering

1. Trigger cards. Keep a list of imagineering triggers on a 3x5 card(s) by your nightstand and in your wallet or purse so they are conveniently available. Read the trigger, then imagineer the experience with full-blown positive emotion. This should only take a minute or less for each goal with practice.

2. Imagineer daily. Just like you brush your teeth, do the imagineering technique at least two times per day. Imagineering done in the early morning will be the most important part of your day in terms of happiness, health, and future high achievement. It will put you in a good mood, setting the tone and color for your entire day. Each time you imagineer you will be pushing yourself closer to your goals. Know in your heart that when you imagineer an experience you are taking control of your future.

3. "Live" the experience. Actively engage in the imagineering sequence as if you were actually doing it, **NOT** as if you were watching yourself perform. If you see yourself in your mind like you are watching yourself in a movie, the subconscious programming won't have as strong an effect. Why? The proper neural-muscular circuits in your body will not be stimulated if you imagineer as a spectator. You must vividly experience, feel, and sense the act being performed *by you as if you were actually doing it.* For example, when I imagineer a speaking engagement, I don't see myself on stage speaking. I'm on stage speaking. I see the audience and their reactions to me.

4. Act on your hunches. Imagineering has its main effects in your subconscious mind. Imagineering will cause you to get certain feelings or flashes of inspiration to do things that will move you toward your goals; these are called hunches. Be very alert to all of your hunches as soon as you start imagineering a goal. Start acting on these, because most of the time what "feels" right for you to do to move you toward your goal is something you should in fact do!

Unique creative ideas will also pop into your head at various times in regard to goal achievement. Be alert to them and consider them carefully!

5. Imagineer before sleep. Imagineering is highly effective right before you fall asleep, even if it's just a short nap. Here's a short review of the reason.

As you relax prior to sleep, the conscious mind gradually loses its editing ability, causing the subconscious to be more susceptible to conscious commands. You then become less inclined to consciously argue the logic of an imagineered experience, thereby giving the subconscious a more straightforward command. The subconscious mind is always hungry for new commands, new experiences, and new goals. It will readily accept and take action, processing the imagineered commands while you sleep. Once you fall asleep, the conscious mind is shut off completely, and subconscious activity will be turned way up.

6. Aim for full sensory stimulation. Try to stimulate as many of your five senses as you can when imagineering a goal. You will probably stress sight and sound, but try to incorporate taste, touch, and smell cues as well. This makes the imagineered experience more realistic and trains all your senses to be on the lookout for anything that can move you toward your imagineered goals.

Imagineering and Subconscious Activity

Imagineering goals in your mind's eye is an excellent way to imprint your subconscious mind. As you experience your goals vividly in your imagination, you have actually created and realized them to a certain degree. This is the start of high achievement. Once goals are planted in the subconscious mind, they begin to grow and become more and more real to you. As you continue imagineering, your subconscious mind's activity increases. You now begin to get novel ideas and hunches from the subconscious about how you might actually achieve your imagineered goals.

An architect first builds a model of a new building in her head; then a small scale model is built; then finally the real thing is made. Construction workers and contractors build the actual building according to the architect's design, which was first conceived in the architect's mind. YOU are the architect! YOU are charged with the job of designing, building, and achieving your own self-set life goals!

You have been using imagineering all your life, probably unconsciously, but you can now use it consciously, more scientifically, to guide your tremendous mind power. For example, you may have the idea to go to college. At first you aren't even sure if you can afford it. Your idea is born but it's still young and helpless. As you talk about your idea with others and imagineer going to school for your degree, your idea grows into a mature picture of what you really want. The idea continues growing. You now focus in on which college you want to attend, what you will study, what moving to a new town will be like, etc. Then you start to figure out a way to get exactly what you have imagineered. If you have enough money you just go out and enroll, but if you don't have the money you'll still get to go if your desire is strong enough, because you will now start to think of ways to raise the needed money. Your desire, creativity, thoughts, and actions will drive you straight to realizing your going-to-college goal.

Your subconscious will be fully activated and serve to aid you in finding practical methods of acquiring the funds to go to college. It works the same way for any goal you care to imagineer. The imagineering technique induces subconscious activity no matter what the goal is.

The Importance of Full Sensory Stimulation in Imagineering

Why is it important to imagineer your goals specifically and precisely and try to stimulate all five of your senses? Because the subconscious mind now will have a more complete set of conditioned or PREPROGRAMMED information to serve as instructions. The subconscious mind stores all the sensory information from all five senses from before you were born to today in its primary memory banks. It will work twenty-four hours a day, seven days a week to scan these ever-increasing memory banks and your environment for leads, opportunities, and ideas for attaining your autogenically conditioned (imagineered) goals. It has the ability to create a workable plan for you or assist you in your current plans, but it is absolutely crucial for you to preprogram in a complete sensory experience as specifically and emotionally as you can.

A general instruction or vague imagineered experience will lead to vague and erratic results. If you visualize a goal in detail and get into the full sensory experience as I have described them, whenever your subconscious mind "senses" anything related to that goal's attainment, based on associated information in its memory banks, it will immediately point it out to the conscious mind. Since your conscious mind is also focused on the same goal it will be receptive to the information, recognize it, and evaluate its usefulness using its power of logic and reason.

Each time you repeat an imagineered goal sequence, you notify the subconscious mind that this is still important to you and that it should keep searching for ways to attain it. The more precise you can be about your goals, the better.

Your aim in imagineering is to actually see, hear, taste, smell, touch, and emotionally feel what you want in your mind. A complete detailed imagineered experience, with full-blown sensory stimulation and full-blown emotion, serves as excellent instructions for the subconscious mind. If you give the subconscious mind an exact complete sensory/emotional instruction in the form of an imagineered goal experience, it will help you to get exactly that!

Autogenic Conditioning II: Module II. How Autogenic Conditioning Works

Training the Mind's Eye

"Concentrate all your thoughts upon the work at hand. The sun's rays do not burn until brought to a focus."

> **Dr. Alexander Graham Bell**
> **Vibrational theory scientist**
> **Inventor of the telephone**

Verbal self-affirmations and imagineering are two autogenic conditioning techniques that help you train the mind's eye. The results of verbal self-affirmations and imagineering are that your goals will be "locked" or "preprogrammed" into your subconscious mental core.

Three important activities occur in the mind as a result of either of these two autogenic conditioning techniques. First, the mental filter or *reticular formation* (discussed in earlier lessons) is set so that your subconscious mind makes you instantly aware of ways and means existing in your environment to help you achieve your conditioned goals. The subconscious mind will use its massive memory bank to instantly associate all incoming sensory information as it relates to goal achievement, enabling you to perceive what you could not perceive before. You in effect fine tune your mind with affirmations and imagineering.

Second, you will start to get all sorts of creative ideas, hunches, and inspiration bubbling up to your consciousness, all aiding you in goal achievement once you autogenically condition your goals. Most of your actions will also become automatically aligned, speeding you toward your goals.

Third, the subconscious mind will activate the superconscious mind if necessary. When this happens, favorable circumstances outside your direct physical control seem to "miraculously" occur. "Gifts from the heavens," as they say, are bestowed on you, meaning your goals start moving toward you!

Your conscious, subconscious, and superconscious minds all begin working in perfect harmony to achieve your clearly defined goals. This is exactly the mental state you want to be in. *If you do this, everything in your life will change, moving you in the direction of your goals.*

Here is a simple illustration of how autogenic conditioning instructs the subconscious mind. I take a six-year-old child and *show* him a Spanish gold piece so he can see it and say, "Do you see this?" He says, "Yes." I say, "Hold it in your hand, *feel* it, *look* it over carefully." He now has a fairly good idea of what a Spanish gold piece is. I then tell him, "They are very precious. If you bring me more of these I will richly reward you" (create desire). Finally I say, "Go out into my backyard, find as many of these as you can, and bring them to me for a reward" (clear direct command). (Beforehand I secretly hid a number of Spanish gold pieces in the yard.)

This boy is now well on his way to finding Spanish gold pieces because he knows *exactly what he is searching for in the environment.* He has clear instructions and strong desire. He is well equipped to recognize the gold pieces when he finds them. He knows his goal well, he knows what it looks like, feels like, his senses are tuned. He is properly programmed for his mission!

Now, imagine I take a second boy who is really better educated and far more intelligent than the first boy and tell him, "There are *some very valuable things* in my backyard. I will reward you greatly for them if you find them and bring them to me." Then I turn him loose.

In a contest, I would bet the first boy would bring me back many of the Spanish gold pieces, while the second boy *wandered aimlessly* with *no idea* of what I really wanted. The second boy's programming (instructions) was poor. He is a much smarter boy than the first and his senses are equally good, but he is *not tuned in on the goal.* He has strong desire for the reward but he has no clearly defined instructions, no vision, no picture in his mind's eye of what he is to search for.

This is a good analogy for many thousands of people in the world today. "Riches" in life are everywhere to be found, but those people with no clear-cut goals preprogrammed into their mind wander around aimlessly. Some are highly motivated and very intelligent but have not autogenically conditioned their minds to pursue self-chosen goals. They are at a severe disadvantage to those people who use autogenic conditioning to train the mind's eye on self-chosen goals. If you aren't working on any goals of your own, you are probably working on someone else's!

Preprogramming the subconscious mind with autogenic conditioning is similar to the clear instructions I gave to the first boy. After I gave him clear instructions, he knew exactly what to look for and could use his five senses and memory banks effectively. I hope you see the value of autogenically conditioning your goals now!

Here is one more example just for *clarity*. An experienced game hunter sees deer, pheasants, ducks, and rabbits while on a Sunday drive in the country with a city dweller. The city dweller on the other hand never even notices them, and it is hard for her to see them *at first* even when the experienced hunter points them out. After the hunter points them out a few times, however, the city dweller starts to "tune in" and learns to "spot" game for herself.

Opportunities in life are the same way. Even though opportunities for goal achievement may be presented to them on a regular basis, it is difficult for people to "spot" them if they have not autogenically conditioned their goals into their mind. We all stand in our own acres of diamonds! But you need to train the mind's eye so you can spot their sparkle. Autogenic conditioning techniques help you to see the blue-flash brilliance of a diamond in the rough.

All the raw materials necessary for you to achieve your goals are all around you right now. But if you aren't mentally conditioned you aren't receptive, and they will all go unnoticed! As you focus on your goals using autogenic conditioning techniques, you become aware of and start to notice the people, opportunities, events, and ideas necessary for you to achieve them. The subconscious mind can be consciously programmed for this because it is goal seeking by nature. Autogenic conditioning is actually quite simple. It is not magic, it's just a method of sensitizing and training your mind.

When you verbally, sensorily, emotionally, conceptually program your subconscious mind it performs its job well, making what it is ordered to do into reality. As you sensitize your mind it begins to select the necessary raw materials from the world around you, to build your dream. It's not that these things weren't in the world before, it's just that YOU WEREN'T TRAINED TO NOTICE THEM BEFORE. With autogenic conditioning you can "see" what you couldn't see before. Your mind's eye becomes keen, sharp, and accurate.

Physiological Changes in the Human Brain Caused by Autogenic Conditioning: The Dendrite Cabeling Process

"Autogenic conditioning" is defined as the process of impressing a goal or behavioral trait on one's own subconscious mind by verbal, sensory, emotional, and/or conceptual self-communication.

The two autogenic conditioning techniques described in this book cause physiological changes in the human brain. In order for you to understand these physiological changes, you need to have some basic knowledge of brain physiology. This discussion will be brief; however a reference list is provided at the end of this section for those interested in delving into this particular subject further.

◆ ◆ ◆

The human body is composed of individual living units called cells. These cells are microscopic and cannot be seen with the naked eye. They are like the millions of individual sand grains that compose a sand castle. The sand castle appears as a solid structure from a distance; however, upon closer inspection it is seen to be composed of a collection of millions of individual sand grains. The human body is like the sand castle. All the millions of cells in the human body can be classified into types of cells with different names. The type of cells we are concerned with for this discussion are brain cells called "neurons."

The human brain contains an estimated 100 billion individual neurons. These neurons in your brain communicate with each other when you think by way of both electrical impulses and chemicals called "neurotransmitters." The communication from neuron to neuron is thus said to be "electrochemical" in nature.

When you think a certain thought, specific neurons and sets of neurons are activated to send *electrochemical* impulses to other neurons, and they in turn are stimulated to send the message on to other neurons in a type of chain reaction. The brain is like a magnificently complex computer circuit board, but instead of being made of metals it is made of living cells. ***This feature endows it with the ability to change and grow***. Unlike a fixed, unchanging circuit board made by humans, the biological circuits in the human brain can change. Each neuron can be thought of as having thousands of wires extending from its center, sort of like a spider with thousands of legs. These "wires" are called dendrites. Dendrites can connect a single neuron (brain cell) to thousands of other neurons (brain cells). These neuron branches (dendrites) can respond rapidly to changing patterns of neuron activity (Stryker, 1993). These changing patterns of neuronal activity can be ***self-induced*** by thinking the same thoughts over and over on a continuing basis.

Individual neurons can grow ***more dendrites*** and communication nobs, called "synapses," thereby increasing their communications network. Neurons can also reinforce their existing connections to one another. So we see that the biological machinery of the human brain is both *electrochemical* in nature and capable of *rapid physical restructuring* (Lynch, 1986).

Why is this important? Thoughts are caused by a specific sequence of neurons sending electrochemical impulses or communicating with each other. Any particular thoughts that are repeated generally use the same set of neurons. A verbal self-affirmation or imagineered experience repeated daily over and over stimulates a particular set of neurons. This causes a structural change, called "dendrite cabeling," to take place for the neurons involved. Repeated performance of sensory tasks can cause structural changes in specific areas (intracortical and subcortical networks) of the brain (Pons, 1991). Neural circuitry, especially in sensory areas (cerebral cortex) of the brain, is capable of radical structural changes (Newsome, 1994).

I have mentioned time and time again that a critical time for autogenic conditioning is just before sleep. Not only is it possible for neural connection patterns to change, but entire cortical networks may reorganize during sleep (Sejnouski, 1993). Dendrites from neuron to neuron will cable or fuse themselves, locking into position, becoming "hardwired." This *dendrite cabeling process* enables neurons to actually cable themselves to each other so that a specific thought can become physically fixed (hardwired) in the biological machinery of the human brain. Being trained formally for eight college years in cell and molecular biology and working in the field of genetic engineering for fifteen years, I still find the reality of this simply staggering!

As dendrite cabeling proceeds "belief" in the thought also develops, getting stronger and stronger. Old dendrites used in previous thoughts (beliefs) atrophy, causing the old beliefs to be superseded by the new ones. The tremendous importance of developing this type of strong belief is discussed in the next section.

Autogenic conditioning techniques are powerful mental techniques that physically change the structure of your brain. Human brain structure can change and is shaped by learning as well as genetics (Posner, 1993). By the process of living and learning your brain's physiology changes. Structural changes in the brain, more specifically connections between neurons, can be modified by experience (Pennisi, 1994). Just as muscles grow from proper use, becoming stronger, so does your brain power! Neural networks increase in complexity; others become more efficient through repeated use. This serves to improve your thinking efficiency and increase creativity. As your brain grows and changes, so does your thinking ability.

Scientific References Cited in the Text for the Dendrite Cabeling Process Section

1. "Rapid Remodeling of Axonal Arbors in the Visual Cortex," Antonella Antonini and Michael P. Stryker, *Science* 260 (1993).

2. "Neuroanatomical Plasticity, Its Role in Organizing the Central Nervous System," Christine Gall, Gwen Ivy and Gary Lynch, *Human Growth* 2 (1986).

3. "Repeated Performance of Sensory Tasks can Cause Structural Changes in Intracortical and Subcortical Networks in the Brain," T. P. Pons, et al., *Science* 252 (1991).

4. "Neuronal Plasticity that Underlies Improvement in Perceptual Performance," Ehud Zohary, Simona Celebrini, Kenneth H. Britten, William T. Newsome, *Science* 263 (1994).

5. "Thalamocortical Oscillations in the Sleeping and Aroused Brain," Mircea Steriade, David A. Mcormick, Terrence J. Sejnouski, *Science* 262 (1993).

6. "Seeing the Mind," Michael I. Posner, *Science* 262 (1993).

7. "Seeing Synapses: New Ways to Study Nerves," E. Pennisi, *Science News* 145 (1994).

Additional Scientific References Not Cited in the Text

1. "A Theory of Pavlovian Conditioning: Variations in the Effectiveness of Reinforcement and Nonreinforcement," R. Rescorla, A. R. Wagner, in *Classical Conditioning* 2 (1972).

2. "Enduring Brain Effects of Differential Experience and Training," W. T. Greenough, in *Neural Mechanics of Learning and Memory* (1976).

3. "Postlesion Axonal Growth Produces Permanent Functional Connections," G. Lynch, S. Deadwyler and C.W. Cotmas, *Science* 180 (1973).

4. "Theta Pattern Stimulation and the Induction of LTP: The Sequence in which Synapses are Stimulated Determines the

Degree to which they Potentiate," J. Larson, G. Lynch, *Brain Research* 489 (1989).

5. "Electron Microscopic Studies of Brain Slices: The Effects of High Frequency Stimulation on Dendritic Ultrastructure," K. Lee, M. Oliver, F. Schottlar, G. Lynch, in *Electrical Activity in Isolated Mammalian Central Nervous System Preparations* (1981).

6. *The Synaptic Organization of the Brain*, G. M. Shepherd (1979).

7. "Synapses as Associative Memory Elements in the Hippocampal Formation," W. D. Levy, O. Steward, *Brain Research* 175 (1980).

8. "Growth and Reshaping of Axons in the Establishment of Visual Callosal Connections," G. M. Innocenti, *Science* 212 (1981).

9. "Hippocampal Neuronal Firing, Context and Learning," J. L. Kubie, J. B. Ranch, Jr. in *Neuropsychology of Memory* (1984).

10. *"Mechanisms of Memory,"* L. S. Squire, Science 232 (1986).

11. *Synapses, Circuits and the Beginnings of Memory*, G. Lynch (1986).

12. "Structure-Function Relationships in the Organization of Memory," G. Lynch, M. Baudry, in *Perspectives in Memory Research* (1988).

13. "Long Lasting Morphological Changes in Dendritic Spines of Dentate Granule Cells Following Stimulation of the Entorhinal Area," E. Fifkova, A. Van Harreveld, *Journal of Neurocytology* 6 (1975).

14. "Cortical Encoding of Memory: Hypothesis Derived from Analysis and Simulation of Physiological Learning Rules in Anatomical Structures," G. Lynch, R. Granger, J. Larson, M. Baudry, in *Neural Connections, Mental Computation* (1989).

15. "Watching the Brain Remake Itself," Marcia Barinaga, *Science* 266 (1994).

The Power of Belief

As you continue autogenically conditioning your goals, you increase **belief** in your ability to accomplish them. Whatever goal you want to achieve, affirmation and imagineering techniques help you tap into your true potential. This will surely help, especially if you use your mind and your natural talents in a harmonic, free-flowing manner. This puts you on the royal road to high achievement in life. Single-minded concentration on a goal or set of goals over time followed by direct action produces firm belief in their ultimate attainment. Concentrating on your goals every day with words (affirmations) and synthetic experiences (imagineering) as if you already achieved them is the key to creating strong belief.

"Picture yourself in your mind's eye as having already achieved this goal. See yourself doing the things you'll be doing when you've reached your goal."

Earl Nightingale
Self-development pioneer
Author of *The Strangest Secret* **and** *Lead the Field* **and Cofounder of the Nightingale Conant Corp.**

Some may ask, why think of the goals "as if I already achieved them." Because you become much more enthusiastic and **emotional** if you are in possession of the goal rather than hoping someday to attain it. This enthusiastic feeling is highly motivational, thereby energizing your desire, readying your body and mind for **action**, charging up the electrical activity of your brain, improving its ability to process information, enhancing the strength and vitality of your entire being!

How you think you feel has a great effect on how you actually feel. Your thoughts immediately change the balance of brain and body chemicals. Your nervous system responds to your self-generated thoughts. If your mind is happy your body is energized, if your mind is sad your body is weak. The state of your mind determines the state of your body to a great extent. The famous cliché of being "psyched up" to perform or "psyched out" is very real. By having strong belief in your ability to achieve your goals, you supply your mind with a constant energy flow, empowering you to accomplish.

"The mind tends to transmute all beliefs into their physical equivalent."

> **Napoleon Hill**
> **Success philosopher**
> **Author of *Think and Grow***
> ***Rich, Law of Success, Science***
> ***of Personal Achievement, and***
> ***Mental Dynamite***

An After-the-Lesson Visit with the Author

"The great successful men of the world have used their imagination . . . they think ahead and create their mental picture, and then go to work materializing that picture in all its details, filling in here, adding a little there, altering this a bit and that a bit, but steadily building—steadily building."

> **Robert Collier**
> **Early editor of <u>Collier's</u>**
> **<u>Weekly</u>**

The pivotal point of The POWERMIND System has now been revealed to you in full detail. Autogenic conditioning techniques are star methods for turning you into a high achiever. Autogenic conditioning is so very important to your success. I'll illustrate it with two final simple analogies, then we'll move on.

If you set a plane on autopilot and then try to override it by taking hold of the controls forcefully (consciously), you will be working against the automatic (subconscious) mechanism of the plane. When you stop your conscious forceful efforts, the plane will automatically (subconsciously) resume flying to its prepro-grammed destination. Consciously you were working against the plane's built-in automatic pilot.

Another way to change the course of the plane is to repro-gram the autopilot (subconscious) with a new destination (goal). Now the plane flies in the direction of the new destination **auto-matically.** This illustrates will power (conscious energy-draining control) versus autogenic conditioning (subconscious energy-supplying automatic control).

If you consciously try to change with force (will power) without autogenically conditioning yourself, your automatic mechanism (subconscious) will try to correct for these "errors" based on what it was programmed to do in the past. The subconscious mind is the automatic mechanism just like an autopilot on a plane. It is much easier, more efficient, and healthier for you to reprogram your subconscious mind.

"When the imagination and will power are in conflict; are antagonistic, it is always the imagination which wins, without any exception."

Emile Coue
Noted French psychologist
and early affirmation pioneer

Here is another analogy. If you have a magnifying glass and move it about constantly on a sunny day it will not burn paper. But by holding it steady you can harness the rays of the sun, burning a hole in the paper. A single magnifying glass has the potential to start a forest fire if held steady on some readily available tinder. So it is with your mind. You can harness the energy of your whole mind by using autogenic conditioning to bring about a firestorm of positive change in your life. By hold-ing goals steady in your conscious mind, using autogenic condi-tioning daily, you can bring about the necessary positive changes in thinking and behavior, allowing goal achievement to proceed rapidly!

Up to this point in this book you have been exposed to the principles and techniques that allow you to operate as a well-organized, successful individual. You have seen that emotional, spiritual, mental, and physical unification is key. The ability to unify and focus yourself will allow you to bring tremendous power to bear on achieving any goal.

Many, in fact most, people don't know how to condition their mind. Their energy is sapped by inner strife because they have no clearly defined life values, they don't know what their natural talents are, they have no real goals in life, no tools for high achievement, no knowledge of mental mechanics, and of course they live in emotional chaos! This is not an effective existence—the rewards are sparse! A mind, body, and spirit working harmoniously will continuously become stronger in every way. Age and circumstance need not deprive you of health, wealth, power, success, consciousness, a sovereign soul, and a happy fulfilled life (The Seven Highways of Life's Riches). You now have enough *specialized knowledge* to start taking charge and controlling your future. Two powerful methods of high achievement have been placed in your hands, many more patiently await you in the next lesson!

◆ Three Methods of Superlearning

Overview

The POWERMIND System will now take an interesting turn with this lesson and lesson 10. These two lessons are devoted to teaching you very practical methods you can implement immediately to help you actively progress toward your goals. None of the methods require large amounts of money or influential friends.

I have stated in the autogenic conditioning lessons that you must take action in addition to autogenically conditioning your mind. This lesson and the one that follows will provide you with specific actions you can take. These actions are in the form of *superlearning* techniques and *creative problem-solving* methods.

In this lesson you will be exposed to three practical methods of superlearning you can immediately use. These three methods are **modeling, systematic book reading,** and **journaling.**

Modeling involves the specific study of an individual or a preselected group of individuals. These people can be living, deceased, or a combination of both. The purpose of modeling is to have at least one successful person whom you can strive to be like. By making a careful study of a role model you can begin incorporating the features he or she possesses into yourself as well as learning *how* that person gained the great success you desire.

Systematic book reading is the process of reading a book using a scientific method. This method, called the OS Triple R Method, will allow you to extract and retain far more information from the books you read than you ever thought possible. It is based on the information processing mechanisms of the human mind. It also turns book reading into an exciting active process instead of a passive boring chore.

Journaling is the third method and is one of the best kept secrets of superlearners. It is simply the process of keeping a daily diary. However, most people were never taught how to do this properly. Journaling is a vital success tool. Personal journals allow you to learn from your own unique set of life experiences.

Three Methods of Superlearning

Modeling: Learning by Studying Role Models

"He that walketh with wise men shall be wise. . . ."

Proverbs 13:20

Modeling is a method of superlearning in which you study a person(s) who can serve as an example for you to follow. You then systematically incorporate or copy his or her personality characteristics, behaviors, and methods he or she used to become successful. There are two distinct ways in which you can study role models: (1) direct observation and (2) indirect observation.

I will illustrate how the direct observation method works in children, because it's easy to understand, and the same principle applies in adult direct observation learning. When children are little they *watch* their parents perform a certain behavior, then they imitate it. For example, if a parent performs an action such as using a stool to grab a cereal box that is out of reach, the child will directly observe this. Later the surprised parent finds the child standing on a stool to get the cookie jar that was placed out of reach!

Another more complex example is that children will learn about male/female relationships by directly observing how their mother and father interact. If there is little show of affection or love between their parents, the children will grow up having difficulty showing affection and love in their adult relationships. They learned this relationship behavior through direct observation of how their role models (their parents) interact.

Direct observation of a role model can be done by making a vigilant study of that person. This person would be someone you aspire to be like, someone who has qualities you admire. You would then set about to directly observe the person and then imitate his or her actions as best you can, trying to incorporate the admirable qualities into yourself.

Direct observation is a very potent method of superlearning because you can actually observe the role model(s) in person (or on video). This allows you to avoid your own personal trial and error experiences; you can observe what works for the person and simply do what he or she does.

Indirect observation modeling is a little more difficult, but is the method most people must initially use because they can't get around a superstar for one-on-one direct observation. It is also the method that you must use if your role model is deceased. In this case modeling can still be used, but indirect observation is required. How can you indirectly observe them? By reading about the person in an autobiography or biography or studying books written by or about the person. You might be able to obtain cassettes to further assist you in *indirectly observing* the role model(s) you choose to mold yourself after.

You can model virtually anyone who lived, who left a legacy behind, and adopt their "success habits." The average public library has more than what most people would ever need. It contains a gold mine of information for anyone **willing to search.** You can study people who did or are doing what you want to do. The great, shrewd, and keen-thinking people throughout all of human history are at your fingertips in a local library. They are definitely within your reach, and it's all free! It just takes a little effort on your part to go and **seek them out.**

Modeling allows you to benefit from **other people's experience.** You can easily adopt the success habits of others and use many of their ideas, saving yourself tremendous amounts of time, money, and energy.

Modeling works because you inevitably pick up habits from the people you "hang around." You don't just pick up habits of action but also habits of thinking. Picking up an action habit can be illustrated with speaking accents. When a Southerner moves north, the accent is softened by being surrounded by Northerners, and vice versa. When I moved from New York to Texas, I had never heard of "ya'll," but I picked it up in about a week because everyone *I was around* said it.

You might adopt a bad financial thinking habit if you are surrounded by people who spend all they make, never saving anything for their future. If the people you model yourself after think that way, you will probably think that way too, and end up broke and embarrassed just like them!

Don't ever underestimate the power of the individuals you are around and those whom you choose to be your role models. Be sure your role models are people you want to be like.

The real key in modeling is that it isn't necessary to learn from role models directly (although that would be nice). You can observe them **indirectly**. That releases you from the shackles of your current environment, allowing you to study virtually any great successful person or persons you want to be like in this generation or past generations. You could actually live in the worst environment and still surround yourself with great successful role models. You can feed your mind with ideas and inspiration from the greatest, most successful people throughout all of human history by reading their books!

Now, ask yourself these six key questions:
1. Do I have any role models now?
2. Who are they?
3. Do I really want to be like them?
4. Would it be **easy** for me to make a careful study of them?
5. Are there books, tapes, or videos I could obtain to further my studies of them?
6. Is there any way I could directly observe them?

Systematic Book Reading: The OS Triple R Method

I cannot stress enough the importance of reading books pertaining to your goals. Only about 3% of the population in the U.S. owns a library card. So why not cash in on some of those tax dollars people complain about so much? There is more wealth readily available to you in your average public library than you'll pay in taxes in one hundred years.

Yet most people aren't *interested* in any of this life-saving knowledge. They are too busy watching cartoons, horror movies, violence, sporting events, soap operas, or a host of other mind-numbing shows. They may be in bars drowning their sorrows in alcohol every weekend, trying to forget their awful lot in life rather than actively changing it. *They curse the results of their behavior while nursing the cause!*

These are the people who can't quite seem to figure out why they aren't happy. They live in poverty and are suffering needlessly in quiet desperation. If they would only set specific life goals, and start reading books that would help them achieve those goals, it would expand their consciousness and open doors for them they never dreamed possible.

Reading stimulates the mind, it stirs the soul. Reading dramatically improves vocabulary, which in turn greatly improves your ability to think and process ideas. It is not enough to casually read a book, however. *The goal in reading books is to spark creativity in your mind and retain the information that you read so it can serve you well in the future.*

Wouldn't it be great if you could remember more of what you read in books? Did you ever have the problem of falling asleep when you read? There is a simple method, which I will now introduce you to, that allows you to more actively read, spark latent creativity, and retain more of what you read.

The system is called the **OS Triple R Method**. It is one of the most powerful superlearning techniques available.

Briefly the **O** stands for **Overview**, the **S** stands for **Survey**, the first **R** stands for **Read**, the second **R** for **Review**, the third **R** for **Remember**. Each one will now be detailed out for you.

OVERVIEW

To overview a book you simply familiarize yourself with the book. There are two parts to overviewing. **First** you read the front cover, back cover, inside jackets, table of contents, glossary, preface, dedications, etc.—everything *except* the actual text. This whets your appetite, stimulating your desire to discover the information contained on the pages of the text.

The **second** part of overviewing a book is to rapidly skim through the whole book page by page as fast as you can, using a pen or your index finger as a point guide. You make large, sweeping motions in the shape of the letter Z, covering the whole page, starting at the top of the page, working the pen or your finger down quickly. You do this fast, keeping your eyes focused just above the pen point or your fingernail. *Don't* try to read the text, just skim it fast! (Refer to Long Z Stroke Diagram.) It should only take you about fifteen to twenty minutes to overview a four- to five-hundred-page book. You should be going almost as fast as you can turn the pages.

LONG Z STROKE

Eyes focus here

Pen point or fingertip travels along the "Z"

In the long Z stroke, your pen point or fingertip should be moving along the Z from the top of the page to the bottom. Your eyes should be focused about one-eighth of an inch above the pen point or fingertip, following it along the Z.

This may all seem pointless to you; however, you will *subconsciously* pick up a surprising amount of information by overviewing. You will learn the general format or layout of the book, such as position of charts, tables, photographs, and diagrams as well as a good idea of the book's scope from this.

Before actually buying a book it's a good idea to overview it in the bookstore. You will be able to quickly determine if it contains what you need simply by overviewing it.

SURVEY

The **S** in **OSRRR** stands for **survey**, which comes next. If you did a good job overviewing you are well practiced for surveying. Surveying is a more in-depth, slower form of overviewing. Like overviewing, surveying has two basic steps also.

First select a chapter or specified section you wish to read *in one sitting*. Again use a point guide, but use a pen, *not* your finger, this time. Read the chapter title, chapter introduction, then skip over to the end of the chapter and read the chapter summaries. If there are any charts, tables, photographs, or diagrams in the text study these for a few moments as well.

The **second** step in surveying is to **slowly** scan using *many* shorter Z strokes as you move down the page. At this stage you are encouraged to make special note of chapter subtitles, quotes, captions, and print in boldface type or italics. If there are any words or phrases that happen to catch your eye, circle them at this time with your pen. (Refer to Short Z Stroke Diagram.)

READ

You are now ready for the reading step. This means actually reading the text at your normal speed. Do you see how familiar you are already with the information you are about to read? You've basically seen all the words twice, you are going over them for the third time here. Again use a pen or pencil as a point guide for your eyes. Run your pen just under the line you are reading, then, like the return key on a typewriter, move it to the beginning of the next line down, read that line, and so on. (Refer to Mini Z Stroke Diagram.)

SHORT Z STROKE

Eyes focus about one eighth of an inch above pen point

Pen point travels along here

In the short Z stroke, your eyes should be focused just above the pen point. The pen point should follow the short Z's down the page.

MINI Z STROKE

Eyes focus on text

Pen point travels just under text on Z's

In the mini Z stroke, your pen point travels along just under each line
of the text. Your eyes should focus on the actual text as you read it.

The reason for using a pen as a point guide is twofold. First, your pen is serving to guide your eyes so they stay focused only on the line you are reading. As you end reading one line, your eyes will automatically follow the pen, moving down to the next one without getting "lost." This point guide reading technique alone will nearly double the reading speed of anyone who is not currently use a point guide for their eyes.

Second when you come to key words, phrases, or ideas, you can immediately circle or underline them "on the fly" as you read. If a paragraph is important to you, circle it or put an X outside in the margin.

The **second** part of reading involves a subtechnique called **Idea Capture**. If as you read you think of a new idea that "flashes" into your mind, write it in the margin of the book immediately, or keep a notepad handy where you can write it down.

Idea Capture is an extremely valuable technique because it is a method that unlocks your own natural creative powers. Almost everyone has experienced this while reading. They read a sentence or paragraph, which in turn "sparks" an idea to come to mind. Have you ever experienced that? If you did, do you also remember that you forgot what that "great idea" was? Did you lose it? The idea capture technique is your written insurance policy against idea loss!

REVIEW

After you have finished with an intensive reading of the chapter, you are prepared for the fourth step. In this step you simply go back to the beginning of the chapter or section and reread *only* the words, phrases, paragraphs, or ideas you noted with your pen.

REMEMBER

The final, remember, step should be done once the entire book is finished. After you've finished the whole book you should go through it all from beginning to end, rereading *only* your specially noted words and sections and ideas you captured. At this time you may also want to transfer any especially unique ideas to your personal journal.

"Everything you need for your better future and success has already been written. And guess what? Its all available. All you have to do is go to the library. But would you believe that only three percent of the people in America have a library card? Wow, they must be expensive! No, they're free. And there's probably a library in every neighborhood. Only three percent!"

Jim Rohn
America's foremost business philosopher; author of *The Five Major Pieces to the Life Puzzle, Seven Strategies for Wealth and Happiness,* and *The Seasons of Life*

Why is the OS Triple R Method So Effective?

When you overview a book exclusive of looking at the actual text, you are "prepriming" your mind, getting it into a receptive state for learning. You are in effect telling it, "information about X topic is on the way, get ready to receive input."

As you fast-scan the actual text in the survey step, your subconscious mind picks up bits and pieces of information, building a "memory file." In the second part of the survey step you preprime it once again to be receptive to specific information concerning a central topic or theme, creating another, more detailed, memory file.

By reading chapter summaries, your mind is given the basic points of the chapter beforehand; these are just like filing tabs in a filing system. This helps your memory because the information now goes into the subconscious memory banks of your mind in an organized fashion instead of helter-skelter. All the information gets filed neatly, systematically, in place for easier retrieval later.

When you read a section making special notation of words, phrases, or ideas, these serve as *memory enhancers* since you made an active conscious effort to star, underline, or circle them.

The *idea capture* technique allows you to tap effortlessly into your own natural creative powers. Ideas arising from this technique often turn out to be extremely valuable to people. In the review step you once again drive the important points deeper into your memory.

Then in the final remember step you lock the whole book in your mind, making sure all the information is neatly organized in your memory banks.

By using the OS Triple R method you saw every word of the *text* at least three times, and the important information that was also reviewed and remembered five times. They say *"repetition is the mother skill of all learning."* It should be quite obvious to you now that you will extract and retain much more information from any given book using this systematic superlearning method.

Another side benefit of the method, which enhances retention of information, is that you can concentrate better because you are *actively* reading. You'll notice you don't fall asleep reading if you use this method. Most people assume reading is a passive, somewhat boring, chore. Many adults and children hate reading because no one taught them how to read actively using a scientific method. I wish someone had taught me this when I was in grade school. It would have enhanced my knowledge tremendously.

If you are reading this section and have children in school, I encourage you to take the time to teach them this simple super-learning technique. You will be giving them a gift that will serve them well for the rest of their lives. They'll get more out of what they read and score higher grades because they will be actually *learning*, not just mouthing words.

Most people "read" a book and two weeks later couldn't even give you a brief synopsis of what the book was about. What a colossal waste of time. Don't get caught in this trap or let your children get ensnared in it either!

Perhaps the most important benefit of the OS Triple R Method is that you will retain more information from the books you read so you can invest it in your own future!

"I suppose that every old scholar has had the experience of reading something in a book which has significance to him, but which he could never find again. Sure he is that he read it there, but no one else ever read it, nor can he find it again, though he buys the book and ransacks every page."

> **Ralph Waldo Emerson**
> **American success philosopher**
> **Author of numerous essays,**
> **including the famed**
> **"Compensation"**

(With the OS Triple R Method, the old "scholar" problem won't be yours!)

Michael Monroe Kiefer's Power for Success Library

1. *Success—Cybernetics* and *The Secret of Secrets*, U.S. Andersen
2. *Magic of Thinking Success*, Dr. David J. Schwartz
3. *Think Like a Winner*, Dr. Walter Doyle Staples
4. *Sell! Sell! Sell!*, Robert Conklin
5. *The Five Major Pieces to the Life Puzzle*, Jim Rohn
6. *Power for Success* and *Business Power*, Dr. Frank Channing Haddock
7. *The Greatest Salesman in the World* and *The Greatest Miracle in the World*, Og Mandino
8. *Think and Grow Rich*, Napoleon Hill
9. *The Richest Man in Babylon*, George S. Clason
10. *Thrift*, Samuel Smiles
11. *Pushing to the Front*, Orison Swett Marden
12. *Your Infinite Power to be Rich*, Dr. Joseph Murphy
13. *How to Get Rich in Mail Order* and *How to Self Publish Your Book and Make it a Best Seller*, Melvin Powers
14. *Charisma—How to Get "That Special Magic,"* Marcia Grad

Journaling: The Power of the Written Word

I've stressed writing your thoughts on paper throughout this entire book in the lessons on self-assessment, goal setting, affirmations, imagineering, etc. There are four very important reasons for this.

First, almost all highly successful people are very good at *"thinking on paper."* Second, writing focuses your mind, forcing you to concentrate. Third, you tend to express your thoughts more clearly if you have to write them out. Fourth, the very act of writing your thoughts causes you to focus your mindpower on a specific point. These four reasons help you develop what is known as "thought power control."

Personal journals (daily diaries) provide you with a chronologically organized written record to show how your thinking has evolved over time. This inevitably leads to self-awareness. They also allow you to objectively determine if you are moving forward toward your goals, are working at cross-purposes with yourself (your values), or are stagnating in life. Journals have the uncanny power to uncover weaknesses and reveal your hidden strengths. A personal journal is a book written by your own hand in which you summarize and highlight daily life experiences.

Keep in mind journals are for your personal use. They are self-discovery tools for *serious people.* You might be keeping a journal mainly to chart progress toward your goals, while someone else's main interest with their journal is to benchmark their current lot in life. Another person may be detailing their life experiences to leave for their children to learn from. It's all up to you. As you work with a personal journal, you may discover many more uses.

The guidelines for keeping a personal journal are general. The following is an easy to understand question and answer section detailing the fundamentals of keeping a personal journal.

1. **What should I consider writing or putting in my personal journal?**

   A. *Significant events in your life and your feelings about them. For example, the achievement of a long sought after goal, the death of a loved one, a recurring dream*

   B. *Personal problems you are trying to solve*

   C. *An occurrence in your life that made you very happy, sad, or angry*

   D. *Your goals*

   E. *Mistakes you've made and ideas on how to correct them in the future*

   F. *Unique ideas, yours or **someone else's** (remember the idea capture technique in the OS Triple R section!)*

   G. *Peculiar observations you've made about your own behavior or other people's behavior*

   H. *Progress you are making toward your goals*

   I. *Interesting quotes you come across*

   J. *Personal photos, for example, of birthdays, graduation, award ceremonies, vacations, etc.*

   K. *Drawings, artwork*

   L. *Interesting newspaper or magazine articles or photos from literature you read*

2. **Should I always summarize the major events of the day?**

   Yes. Even though your specific purpose for keeping a journal may be more focused in one area, such as solving problems or dream analysis, you should still capture and summarize the major events of your day.

3. **How often should I write in my journal?**

   Every day! Every day! It's also a must to date each page with month, day, and year. Oftentimes it's useful to record the time of day and where you are when you make an entry. You could also purchase a journal with the dates already marked.

4. **Should I take my journal with me on vacations or business trips?**

   *Yes. How else can you write in it **every day?***

5. **How much information should I put in my journal?**

   That is up to you. You might buy one journal each year, writing one page per day, or you might get twelve journals per year, filling one per month. It's all up to you.

6. **How often should I review my journals?**

   *This is an important question that gets asked regularly. Some people are very disciplined, meticulously recording information in their journal, but they never review it. What a major mistake! The point of a personal journal is to **learn from your own unique experiences in life, not to develop penmanship!***

   Here is an excellent formula that I use. Every day review the previous day's entry. At the end of every week, review the previous week's entries. At the end of every month, review that month's entries. At the end of the year, take a weekend and review the past year's entries.

7. **What type of journal should I buy?**

   Styles and sizes vary, but you should get a high-quality journal that appeals to you. Office supply stores, bookstores, and gift shops have them. If you like it and it feels good in your hands, you'll enjoy writing in it. Some people prefer lined pages, some unlined, it's all up to you here. However, I would never recommend one that's cheap, with pages that could easily tear out and get lost.

9 Special Pointers for Journaling

There are a few pointers for personal journals that I think you'll find very helpful in getting started.

1. It is useful to put photographs of yourself in your journals so you can see graphically how you have changed over time. If you go on a diet it's always nice to see before and after shots. If you neglect your diet that will show up in your photos, too! If you change hairstyles often, you can see what best suits you. You can see if you are transfiguring yourself in a positive direction or deteriorating. Special events that you attend or award ceremonies should be photographed and put into your journal as well. Pictures are worth a thousand words, so be sure to put them in.

2. Another use of a journal is to solve difficult life problems. You ask, how can I solve problems with a personal journal? Just like this. If you have a particularly pressing life problem, write it at the top of the page in your journal entry for that day in the morning. Then in the evening before you write your entry of the events of the day, read it over. Think about it for a few minutes, writing down any ideas on how to solve it that come to mind. If none come, write your day's entry, review the previous day's entry, then read the problem over again. Finally, close the journal and go to bed so you can sleep on it. The next morning write the problem at the top of the next page for that day's entry, read it, write out any ideas that come to mind. If none come, repeat the whole process every day until the answer finally does come.

Writing problems on paper objectifies them so they don't seem quite so personal. This allows you to think more logically, because you aren't so emotionally wrapped up in the problem. Seeing it on paper emotionally detaches you from the problem. When you write it down, it also forces you to clarify and be a more accurate thinker.

If an obstacle is preventing your progress toward a goal, attack it on paper with the power of objective reasoning. The removal of personal emotion is one key to unlocking your mind's creativity. It is extremely hard to think logically when you are upset, angry, or frustrated. Writing obstacles out on paper clears your head. (Remember, in Mental Mechanics you learned the conscious mind's reasoning ability is inhibited by negative emotional stress!)

Major problems or obstacles often surrender to simple solutions, such as simply writing them in a personal journal and thinking about how to solve them for a few minutes each day. Don't forget to write down any solutions you come up with, no matter how silly or impossible they may seem at the time. This basic creative problem-solving technique has universal application.

3. Along these same lines you may want to write your goals, verbal self-affirmations, and imagineering triggers at the front of your personal journal. By reviewing them every day, you will press them into your mind. This allows you to be constantly on the alert for information in your environment to speed you toward your goals. Each time you review your goals and think about them, you focus your thought power on achieving them. This gives you your guiding light, motivating you on your purpose, while everyone else stumbles and fumbles through the day. You can be confident you are not among them because you are on a *scientifically self-directed* mission!

4. I encourage you to get a high-quality journal. There is nothing worse than a cheap personal journal. Your life experiences are valuable, they are important! Take a special pride in your personal journal work. Your life has meaning; record it carefully in the confines of a high-quality book, worthy of you.

5. It is also especially important to capture unique ideas in your journal. If an idea hits you during the day, be sure to get it down in your journal. Good ideas are all around us and inside of us, but how many of them can you recall from the past week, month, year? I have them *all*, and if you had a personal journal you would too! They would all be there awaiting your use at any time if you so *desired*.

6. If you make mistakes, write them in your journal too. Why? So you will remember to not repeat them.

7. I also like to write peculiar things that I can't explain in my journal. Later I usually find an explanation, and that's a very satisfying experience for me.

8. A personal journal can be used to explore new courses of action to take in overcoming problems or achieving goals. These can all be worked out and analyzed on paper first. You can project yourself into the future on paper, make plans and refine plans on paper, so they are as perfect as possible before you act!

9. I find it best to write in my journal during the evening at the end of the day before I retire. I reflect on the day. If I have notes from the day I transfer them to my journal at this time. They serve as an aid in reliving the experiences while they are still fresh. Writing engraves the experiences into the subconscious gold of the mind.

◆ ◆ ◆

In the future you may be able to reach back into your past for the solution to a problem or a unique idea. Your personal journals may hold the key. Reviewing your own life experiences and good ideas may cut short your search for answers. Over the years your journals of ideas and life experiences are like creative weaponry you can use to do battle in life. Life is a struggle, but a well-armed soldier is better equipped on the combat field than an unarmed one. A journal is your paper guardian speaking to you from your past, aiding you in your self-discovery mission.

On reviewing your journal at the end of the year, you may find that many seemingly unrelated events "magically" come together. Mental changes over time will become obvious when you review your old journals. Your journals will reflect your own mental evolution, its unfoldment or its decline, perhaps allowing you to catch yourself before it's too late! Wouldn't it be wise for you to at least learn from yourself, your own personal life experiences?

An After-the-Lesson Visit with the Author

"If you employed study, thinking, and planning time daily, you could develop and use the power that can change the course of your destiny."

W. Clement Stone
Coauthor of *Success Through a Positive Mental Attitude*

The three methods of superlearning covered in this lesson are all near and dear to my heart. Much of my own personal struggle for success has been greatly reduced by the diligent unwavering practice of these three methods. The people that I have personally coached in these three superlearning techniques have also reported similar beneficial results.

I myself have used a multitude of *role models*, many of whom you have probably ascertained by now. In the front of this book many of my role models are listed, each one making a significant contribution to my thinking and behavior. These people kept me burning the midnight oil night after night. Many a Friday and Saturday evening were given up as I pursued my goal. The call of friends and family had to be temporarily sacrificed for future gains. It was during these late hours of loneliness when my thoughts would often turn to these great people for inspiration as I toiled relentlessly, crafting words, ideas, and ideals into a practical method of life management. I will be forever grateful to self-development superstars like Brian Tracy, Jim Rohn, Dr. Denis Waitley, Dr. Alan Zimmerman, Earl Nightingale, Napoleon Hill, and a host of others for providing me with guiding light when I needed it most.

Systematic book reading allowed me to gain knowledge about a topic without going through trial and error experiences of my own. This accelerated my learning tremendously. The key here was to know exactly which books to systematically read, because no one has time to systematically read them all. This is why proper goal setting technique is crucial. My goals served as guideposts in my book-screening process, enabling me to quickly determine which books to systematically read.

I had to decide on my goals beforehand, otherwise my reading time would be wasted. I wouldn't know exactly what to read, what to study, or what to practice. I would drift aimlessly.

By reading the right books and learning from other people's experiences, I was able to "beat the clock." A person's major life knowledge, which may have taken them thirty, forty, fifty years or more to acquire, was plugged into my memory banks in a week or less. I was able to communicate and learn from the greatest minds that ever lived on this planet by reading their books. I learned across generations, *across time*; the knowledge and wisdom of the ages and sages was captured by reading their books.

Can you imagine how powerful your mind can become if you do this? You also have a brain with an infinite capacity to store information and the wisdom of the ages available to you in a local library. It's all yours for free! Perfect health, great wealth, power, success is virtually yours for the taking! When I learned from other people's experiences I noticed a multiplication effect because their knowledge was invested into my mind and instantaneously assimilated with my own knowledge, amplifying my powers of mind.

As the information age is upon us we have more access to information now than ever before in the history of mankind. Personal and financial betterment becomes such an easy task for the serious person. With continuous literary research your rewards will be unbelievable!

But reading is a tedious, boring chore for most people. They hate reading because they were forced to read material in school that was *not interesting* to them. They thus developed a negative *conditioned response* to reading.

I was guilty of this myself. When I graduated from college I foolishly vowed "never to read another book for the rest of my life." My days of reading were over (I thought). I had my degrees, it was now time to sit back and enjoy the good life, reap the rewards of my labor. In a relatively short period of time I became very dissatisfied with my lot in life.

I was lulled by the siren song of sinister video rental stores. I can remember going out on a Friday night with my wife and renting six to eight videos so I would have "something to do" for the weekend. What a tremendous waste of time!

After a very fortunate unique series of events occurred I was able to turn my life around, to *transfigure* it. In the process I made an interesting observation. I had started voraciously reading again like I did when I was in college. I observed that the successful people I was modeling were also voracious readers. I designed the OS Triple R Method to help me maximize my reading effort, stimulating both my mind and soul.

What a tragedy it would be if you were unable to learn from your own life experiences. Yet most people learn little from themselves, repeating the same errors over and over again, wondering why their life isn't working out well. Journaling enables you to avoid this pitfall, unearthing causes of life problems. Journals are also an invaluable aid for keeping track of progress toward goals, which is one of the main reasons I started keeping personal journals. I discovered a core of thirteen specific uses listed below, most of which I mentioned in the lesson, they but are worth listing again.

1. Improve the accuracy of your thinking
2. Allow you to chart progress toward goals or show lack of progress
3. Show you how your thinking has evolved over time
4. Show you how you've evolved over time
5. Uncover weaknesses and show strengths
6. Uncover elusive positive or negative patterns of behavior
7. Impress goals into the subconscious mind by reviewing them daily
8. Objectively solve problems by writing them out and pondering solutions
9. Capture creative ideas (yours or other people's) on paper
10. Teach your children who you are and what you did with your life
11. Help you learn from your own mistakes
12. Motivate you on your goals
13. Improve the accuracy of your memory

There are no doubt many other benefits of journaling yet to be discovered by you!

I now ask you to take these three superlearning methods and use them to **THINK AND GROW RICH!**

"If you share a good idea long enough, it will eventually fall on good people."

Jim Rohn
America's foremost business philosopher; author of *The Five Major Pieces to the Life Puzzle, Seven Strategies for Wealth and Happiness*, and *The Seasons of Life*

◆10▶ Unleashing Natural Creativity

Overview

In this lesson you will learn both theory and practical application of natural creativity. This will aid you in developing your hidden powers of creativity. This lesson is geared toward directly applying creativity for goal achievement and problem solving, which are two sides of the same coin. All major goals will require you to solve problems along the pathway to their final achievement.

The lesson is divided into three separate modules. The first is creative thought, which covers creativity theory and two separate problem-solving techniques. One technique is an individual method and the other is a group method.

The second module teaches sensory enhancement techniques, which will enable you to become a more creative thinker by developing keener senses of sight and hearing.

The third module details the attitude required to solve major problems. A series of Divine Guidance techniques are discussed to help you attain "right thinking" with regard to creative problem solving.

Henry Ford was once asked what he would do if he somehow lost all of his money and his business. He said, *"I would think of some other fundamental, basic need of all people, and I would supply that need more cheaply and more efficiently than anyone else. In five years I would again be a multimillionaire."*

It is interesting that Henry Ford was one of the wealthiest men on earth in his day and never graduated from high school!

Unleashing Natural Creativity: Module I. Creative Thought

Unleashing Natural Creativity: Module II. Sensory Enhancement

Unleashing Natural Creativity: Module III. Problem Solving

Unleashing Natural Creativity: Module I.   Creative Thought

Introduction to Creative Thought

The human mind has the tendency to arrange information so it fits the owner's perception of the way the world is supposed to be. The human mind seeks order. For example: Some people keep a meticulously arranged desk, others keep a sloppy desk. A neat desk would make the sloppy desk keeper uneasy or irritated. They would quickly set about "messing it up." If the neat desk keeper were to have their desk messed up, they would quickly set about to "tidy it up." Both people would be working toward their internal mental idea of the way their desk "should look." This is what I call the "not right" thinking pattern.

If there is something about you or your environment that's "not right," a **conflict** is set up between your internal mental idea of the ways things "should be" and what you are perceiving. When this happens the subconscious mind's conflict resolution mechanism is activated.

The first step the mind goes through is to search its memory files for past experiences to find a quick solution to the conflict in order to "set things right." If an easy solution cannot be found immediately, a second step occurs. The subconscious mind will now exert effort to find a more *creative* solution. For example, when you first realize that you are hungry, your subconscious mind has alerted you to the fact that there is a problem within your body. Something is "not right." This causes you to do a quick memory file search to see how you resolved this type of conflict in the past. You then *evaluate* the memory files for the best solution in this particular instance. Do you need a hot dog, pizza, ice cream, steak, potato chips, candy, an apple? You then make a conscious *decision* and take appropriate *action*.

This "thought followed by action" sequence based on stored information (memory) is efficient and practical. You simply do something you have done in the past. However, it is **NOT** creative.

If during the **evaluation** process you have no personal experience options to draw on, an alternate thought sequence is set into motion. You will start to rescan memory files for shreds of information from experiences, observations, or knowledge you have gained of *other people* who had a similar problem. Your mind will now start to *synthetically* manipulate the information or become creative. This mental manipulation (creativity) may be a logical systematic analysis of related information or a "nonsensical juggling" of bits and pieces of stored information resulting in a totally novel solution. For example, with our hunger problem, perhaps you aren't hungry for anything you've ever eaten in the past, so you decide to try something you've never had before—a totally new gourmet dish or a new **combination** of food you've had before, perhaps a peanut butter, shrimp, and pickle sandwich! Some of the best recipes have actually come from the "nonsensical juggling" type of creative thought.

It should be apparent now that the main difference between simple mechanical thinking and creative thinking is that the creative thinking act involves either a new twist on an old idea or something totally "out of the blue".

The foundation on which the fast achievement of large long-term goals rests is in creative thought. Once you drive a goal into the subconscious mind with autogenic conditioning, you have set up a constructive conflict in your mind between your perceived self or world and your *desired* self or world. In essence you have artificially made something "not right" with you and your environment.

One reason for concentrating, verbally affirming, and imagineering is to enhance stimulation of this *subconscious conflict resolution process*. The faster and stronger the conflict is driven into the subconscious mental core, the sooner a creative answer or plan of action will come to you. This is why I stated earlier that **"you don't need a plan for achieving a goal when you first set the goal."** As long as you keep the final goal in mind and go through the autogenic conditioning techniques, your own latent creative powers will present you with practical plans for its accomplishment. All problems along the way will eventually be overcome.

The entire goal setting process is like giving your mind a difficult puzzle to solve. You have some raw information to start with, which constitutes some of the pieces of the puzzle, and a mental picture of what you want to end up with (the final goal). The subconscious mind then goes to work on sorting, organizing, and assembling the pieces of information you already have to come up with a practical plan of action to make the mentally pictured goal a reality.

This is the exact point where many people fail, because when the subconscious mind provides them with a plan or pieces of a plan in the form of a hunch or a seemingly nonsensical idea they are too timid, fearful, or shy to take action (risk). They listen to well meaning but ignorant friends or relatives who tell them they are "stupid" or their plan "won't work" or that they "can't do it." Thus, they ensure their own failure by never taking any action at all! Success is never guaranteed, but failure is easily guaranteed by not taking any action.

Once you start autogenically conditioning your goal or a specific problem into the subconscious mind, be very alert to your hunches from that moment onward. Many people throw all their hunches into the trash can by not acting on any of them. Others throw their valuable creative ideas away by thinking they are stupid, because of their own low self-esteem or negative feedback from friends and relatives.

This is a tragedy, because everyone is a creative genius. We all have a wondrous human brain. It's just that some people know how to use it better than others. This lesson will teach you precisely how to develop your latent powers of creative thought.

"And after you get a good idea, your boss and business associates will marshall a thousand reasons why it won't work."

Earl Nightingale
Self-development pioneer
Author of *The Strangest*
***Secret* and *Lead the Field* and**
Cofounder of the Nightingale
Conant Corp.

4 Barriers to Creativity and How to Eliminate Them

Let's take a closer look at what is happening subconsciously to solve problems and/or resolve conflicts. It is often the case that too much conscious (logical) effort may retard the **flow** of an exciting creative breakthrough. Earlier you learned that when environmental perception and subconscious self-image are in conflict, creative subconscious activity is induced. I will illustrate this point further.

Most people have had the experience of working diligently to solve a difficult business or personal problem. They think about it often, carefully running various alternatives or options through their head over and over, weighing the pros and cons of each. But none seems to be "quite right." They then give up and go on to an entirely different activity with the conscious intent of thinking about the problem later. Then an amazing thing happens. When they least expect it, an ideal solution pops into their head. The time may be in the middle of the night, or when they first awake in the morning, or at any time during the day when they least expect it. It often happens when they are working hard on an *unrelated activity*.

The key here is that the subconscious mind did NOT set aside the problem. In fact all that conscious concentrated effort served to drive the conflict deep into the subconscious mind, telling it to quickly find a solution. What happened was their subconscious mind developed a solution for them, then shuttled it to the conscious mind later. When you are deeply relaxed or distracted with an unrelated activity, that's when the subconscious can communicate readily with your conscious mind. A subconscious solution may have actually been made immediately, or it may have taken some time to "process" the conflict. The subconscious mind often does this *during sleep*. The subconscious may also need more information to solve the problem. In this case it will start sending you signals in the form of hunches to search for additional data in certain specific areas. Then when it has all the necessary information and all the pieces have been fitted together in the form of a practical solution, your subconscious mind awaits the proper time to send its answer up to the conscious mind. But it can't send the conscious mind answers efficiently unless mental barriers are removed first.

Four major mental barriers inhibit creative thought flow from the subconscious to the conscious mind. These are all in the area of negative attitudes. (Note: Each attitude can easily be changed with the two autogenic conditioning techniques described in this book.) Reversing or neutralizing any one of these will allow more of the creative genius inside you to be unleashed.

1. *Fearing change (Rigid Thinking Barrier)*
2. *Thinking you are not creative (Self-Image Barrier)*
3. *Telling yourself the problem is "impossible to solve," "too difficult for you," or "too hard for you" (False Belief Barrier)*
4. *Feeling there is only one way of doing something (Linear Thought Barrier)*

1. Fearing change is a very basic human reaction. It is a triple combination of self-doubt, fear of the unknown, and the human nature to form habits. "Habit" meaning to think or do things the same way because that's the way you've always done them.) Here are some negative phrases diagnostic of people harboring this fear: "If things change will I be okay?" "Do I have the ability to do well if my circumstances change?" "Will I be safe if my surroundings change?"

Fear of change centers around self-doubt. Self-doubt causes people to restrict creativity flow within their mental circuitry. It is also doubly dangerous in that it causes them to have a strong negative reaction to new ideas and new ways of doing things. One reason people don't use self-help techniques is that they are afraid of change. It's ironic, because they are desperately in need of exactly what they fear! I liken these people to the ostrich that buries its head in the sand so as to become "invisible," thereby stopping any change from occurring in the world around it. This is a tragic exercise in self-delusion, which millions of people are currently engaged in.

Change is occurring in the world at a rate faster than it ever has since the history of humankind.

How do you feel about that statement? Does it make you uneasy? Do you feel threatened? Is your attitude positive or negative? A negative attitude sets up constant low-level anxiety in your body. This low-level stress inhibits the free flow of creativity in your mind.

It's a fact that our world is changing rapidly. Look back and see what is different now from the way things were ten, twenty, fifty, one hundred years ago. One hundred years ago there were no computers, no TVs, and no radios. What will change one hundred years from now?

The more positive your attitude toward change, the more creative you will be. Change is good; it enables you to improve yourself and your world. Without change you would be stuck with your current self forever, never growing, never learning, never advancing. The way to overcome the fear of change is simply to focus on your own self-chosen goals. In doing this you eliminate the fear of change and look forward to change with the positive attitude of eager anticipation.

2. Thinking you are not creative is a self-image barrier. If you think this way it's because at sometime in your life you convinced yourself you weren't very creative. You may have said, "The world has two kinds of people: creative and not creative. I'm in the second category." Or you may want to blame your apparent lack of creativity on your genetics, saying, "I wasn't born with any creativity genes." Or maybe you blame your negative relatives, saying, "My parents told me I wasn't creative." There are hundreds of other examples. (I find the genetics one particularly amusing—"creativity genes"?)

Remember our old friend, the self-fulfilling prophecy? If you "know" (believe) you are not creative, sure enough, you won't be. When you tell yourself this, it means you've given up before you started.

Can you believe the real truth about yourself? The fact is that you aren't using all of your creative potential. If you can freely admit you have more creative potential than you are currently using, I suggest you turn your attention once again to autogenic conditioning to overcome whatever negative attitude is keeping you from fulfilling your true potential.

A verbal self-affirmation to increase your creativity may go something like this: "I am an extremely creative person by nature. Creative ideas crackle in my conscious mind effortlessly. I enjoy the abundance of new ideas I now possess." Get in touch with the positive emotions you had when you solved a difficult problem in the past, then link those emotions to the above verbal self-affirmation to alter your negative attitude.

3. Telling yourself the conflict or problem is "impossible to solve." Many people when presented with an obstacle along their goal path label it as "impossible" or "unsolvable." These word labels immediately send a verbal command to their sub-conscious mind, saying, "Forget this one, it's too hard! Please don't find an answer." They are in fact programming their minds with the failure attitude, damming up the creative river of ideas. They made the problem into a larger one than need be by their negative **impossibility thinking**.

Words are not empty, they all contain meaning and emotion (positive or negative). All words in your vocabulary have meaning in your memory banks based on your past experiences. They all have attached feelings as well.

In order to eliminate this "impossible to solve" attitude, substitute less ominous words like "this is an interesting situation." These words imply a solution is possible and it will be fun trying to find it. At the root of "problems" are opportunities. Problems should be treated as valuable learning experiences. If you alter your attitude by expecting solutions to *situations* you are encouraging creative ideas to flow into your mind.

When you find yourself clogged up or your mind coming up blank, take the objective approach. Determine how you are looking at the problem. Did you label it as "impossible," implying a miracle would be needed to resolve it? Shift your attitude to one of *positive expectancy*: think of how wonderful you will feel when an ideal solution is received. This positive expectant attitude will then enable your river of creativity to flow once again.

4. Feeling there is only one way of doing something is called *restrictive conditioning* and serves as a linear thought barrier. This severely limits the flow of creativity. If you think certain activities **must** be done a certain way and there is no other way, your subconscious ideas will never surface. The conscious command to the subconscious is "I know how to do this, I don't want any new ideas on how to do this differently." The subconscious responds to this command exquisitely. Your orders are followed to the letter, and your mind becomes dull and devoid of creative power. This restrictive conditioning very effectively eliminates your awareness of alternatives. Even if a new idea does come your way, you'll quickly eliminate it with ridicule, ignorance, and fear, without ever seriously considering it! This is called the "narrow-minded thinker syndrome."

A simple way to overcome this and stimulate creativity is based on the reverse exclusion principle. Exclude the current way you are doing something. Say, "If I can't do this the way I have always done this, how might I accomplish the same end result?" This forces you to broaden your scope which is just what a narrow-minded thinker needs!

The Written Problem-Solving Technique

Outlined below is a simple technique you can use by yourself to generate creative ideas on how to solve any problem you might have. This technique allows you to tap into your own vast subconscious storehouse for a solution by inducing the creative "flow" state.

1. *Sit down and write out your problem in as much detail as possible on a sheet of paper. Really try to be precise as to exactly what the problem is.*

2. *Condense what you have written to one paragraph.*

3. *Read that paragraph carefully three times, closing your eyes for a few seconds after each reading.*

4. *Once you've read it for the third time, focus as much attention as you possibly can on the problem for five solid minutes by shutting out all other thoughts, noises, and sights. Keep your eyes closed and concentrate!*

5. *When you are done, get up and go do something totally unrelated for 30-60 minutes. Try NOT to think of your problem. Now is the time to shut the problem out. Getting physically active at something is a very good way to get your mind off the problem.*

6. *At the end of this time sit back down! Reread your problem paragraph, relax, and see if any ideas begin to "flow" into your mind.*

7. *As they do, write them down! Spend about 30 minutes or more writing ideas from your mind to paper. Intensive concentration activates the subconscious mind and induces the ideal "flow" state.*

8. *If no ideas come immediately when you sit down to write, just sit relaxed with your eyes shut, opening them only to reread the problem paragraph about every five minutes. If at any time ideas start to "flow," start writing until you can't come up with any more.*

Special note: Don't worry about ideas seeming crazy or "nonsensical," just write them down. You should never fully evaluate the ideas you generate with this method the day they are generated. Wait until the next day to evaluate. Also be alert to ideas that may "flash" into your mind when you are doing the alternative activity in step 5. If an idea comes to you at this time, start writing without waiting for the full 30-60 minutes to be up.

If at the end of the whole process you can't come up with any ideas, don't tense up or worry, try again the next day. But again be especially alert to ideas that may flash into your mind at any time in between. When any ideas come, write them down!

Repeat this technique once each day for up to seven days or until you generate the solution. If no ideas come at the end of seven days, try turning the solution to the problem into a daily verbal self-affirmation or imagineering trigger and add it to your list of these.

Here is a short explanation of what is happening during each step of this technique.

Step 1. This focuses your thinking and clarifies the problem in your own mind.

Step 2. This further focuses your thinking, cutting straight to the root of the problem.

Step 3. This step programs the problem into the subconscious mind.

Step 4. The purpose of this step is to drive the problem so deeply into the subconscious mind that it induces subconscious activity.

Step 5. In this step you are giving the subconscious mind time to process the problem (conflict), unfettered by conscious interference.

Step 6. This step refocuses your conscious mind back on the problem in a "relaxed" state. This condition allows the subconscious to easily transmit ideas up to the conscious mind.

". . . it is often on such occasions, while one is alert but not heavily concentrating, that the subconscious feeds back answers to questions and problems which may have lain within it for a long time."

Napoleon Hill
Success philosopher
Author of *Think and Grow Rich, Law of Success, Science of Personal Success,* and *Mental Dynamite*

Step 7. This is the "flow" state, in which ideas move rapidly, effortlessly, freely from the subconscious to the conscious mind. Idea generation is most prolific at this time.

Step 8. This step continues to prime the subconscious mind in order to jump-start you into the flow state.

This technique enables you to utilize your mind more fully in a very efficient manner to solve problems. It has universal application, so it can be adapted to virtually any problem, obstacle, difficulty, or challenge you might be facing in life. Remember, there are usually multiple solutions to any given problem but *you only need one!*

"Men give me some credit for genius. All the genius I have lies in this: When I have a subject at hand I study it profoundly. Day and night it is before me. I explore it in all its bearings. My mind becomes pervaded with it. Then the effort which I have made is what people are pleased to call the fruit of genius. It is instead the fruit of labor and thought."

> **Alexander Hamilton**
> **American revolutionary**
> **Leader of the Federalists**

Generation of New Ideas: The POWERMIND Session

This is a *group method* that can be used to generate unique ideas or solve problems. A POWERMIND session consists of a collection of people gathered together in one place to generate ideas on how to achieve a goal or solve a problem. It begins with the formation of a POWERMIND group.

The size of the group can be anywhere from two to twelve. (If more than twelve are present, the group becomes too unwieldy to manage properly.) Individuals in the group should be gathered together only for a limited time in order to generate ideas on solving one specific problem or the achievement of a single goal. POWERMIND sessions are highly effective because whenever two or more minds meld in the spirit of perfect harmony, a third or group mind is created. Each person's ideas help to induce creative thinking or "flow" states in the others.

Each person's background and life experiences cause them to operate on a different mental database. Their ideas, twists, and slants will expand the scope of thought for everyone in the group. This leads to creative ideas. Many of these ideas would normally be hidden from view if any individual was alone and tried to think creatively.

The individuals in the group should not all be at the same formal educational level or age, and definitely should not be trained in the same area of expertise. For example: They shouldn't all be Ph.D. physicists, all trial lawyers, all MBA accountants, etc. Cross-functional varied age and education-level groups of people work best for POWERMIND sessions.

The 6-Step Procedure For Holding a POWERMIND Session

Step 1. Notify the people who are to be involved in a POWER-MIND session one to two weeks ahead of time. In a memo or letter, let them know what the goal or problem to be worked on is. Spell it out as clearly as you can in fifty words or less. If it gets too wordy, people will be confused as to exactly what the objective is, so be very concise. If you can't distill it down to fifty words of less, you yourself don't have a clear idea of the objective. You better think some more, until you can whittle it down to fifty words or less, before you hold the session.

The reason for doing this is that advance notification plants the session objective in the other members' subconscious minds so they can stew on it before the actual meeting is held. This will start their creative juices flowing.

Step 2. At the start of the meeting post the objective on the wall in big letters so everyone can see it. This will maintain everyone's mental focus throughout the session. The meeting room should also be well stocked with large tablets or whiteboards, so every single idea generated can be immediately placed on the walls in clear view of everyone at the meeting.

Step 3. One or two people should be designated "scribes," who have the additional job of writing all the ideas generated during the meeting on the charts or walls. They should write neatly and large enough so everyone in the room can read them. There is a very important reason for doing this.

If all the ideas aren't clearly visible, the last idea generated will stick in people's minds, replacing all previous ones, which will serve to *limit* everyone's thinking to that idea alone. When you limit attention to one idea, the inspiration of the others is completely lost. *Sequential linear attention from one idea to the next makes for a boring, unproductive session.*

Putting all the ideas on the walls leads to a frenzy of fast-paced excitement, which is exactly what you want. Each idea continuously serves as fuel throughout the session, inspiring a host of other ideas. As the walls fill with ideas, you'll be astonished!

Step 4. Run the meeting quickly at high intensity for one solid hour, then quit. If there are still many more ideas to list, go no longer than another 15 minutes, then stop. If ideas peter out quickly (within thirty minutes) during your first session, stop it and have another session the very next day if you feel you don't have enough ideas already.

If you hold a second session, be sure the objective as well as all the previous session ideas are posted on the walls.

Step 5. Record and keep all ideas for an evaluation meeting. Never throw any of the ideas away!

Step 6. Hold an evaluation meeting.

4 Ground Rules for a POWERMIND Session

1. Have the objective (problem or goal to be worked on) clearly written out large enough for all to see and posted on the wall. This maintains the groups focus.

2. *Never criticize* an idea, no matter how silly it may seem to you! Criticism instantaneously suppresses creativity in the individual that had the "silly" idea, and to a lesser degree stifles the whole group. If someone breaks this rule, have them stand up and read out loud, "I encourage all the ideas generated in this meeting. All ideas have the potential for greatness." Then have them sit down and move on with the meeting.

3. Compliment or praise *all* ideas. This doesn't have to be a long involved compliment, just a quick "good idea" or "that's interesting, how about another." This puts everyone in a relaxed positive mood.

4. No evaluation of ideas is ever to be conducted *during* the POWERMIND session. A separate evaluation meeting is held later for that purpose.

The Evaluation Meeting

After a POWERMIND session has been held, an evaluation meeting should be conducted in order to evaluate the ideas that were generated.

A new group of individuals should be selected for this job. Some members could be the same as in the POWERMIND session, but these should *represent less than half of the total group.*

The evaluation group must first define the requirements for an idea to "make the grade." Each requirement should be listed on a chart. Each idea is then compared to each requirement on the chart systematically, going down the list checking off if an idea meets the requirement. As soon as an idea fails to meet a requirement on the list, it is kicked out. If an idea meets all the requirements, it is placed on a separate "first cut" list.

Depending on how many ideas you have left after the first cut you can increase the stringency of your selection criteria with a new set of requirements. You then simply repeat what you did for your first cut. You systematically check all ideas against your second cut requirements, kicking out ideas that don't make the grade. Keep doing this until you have the very best idea or a very small manageable set of ideas.

The next step is to assign an individual or team to research each idea further or implement the single idea that is left. This is a very systematic scientific group approach to determine the very best idea(s) among many.

A consultant friend of mine told me of a company that held a POWERMIND session to save 100 million dollars in two years for a company. They had one session from 9 A.M. to 10 A.M. and generated sixty-five ideas. They held an evaluation meeting to make a first cut from 10:30 to 12, then broke for lunch. They made a second cut list from 1 to 2 in the afternoon, a third cut list from 2 to 3 o'clock. They then had five ideas left on the third cut list. They assigned teams from 3:30 to 5 to research and carry out the five ideas. At the end of just one year they had saved 125 million dollars as a direct result of a one-day POWERMIND session.

POWERMIND sessions and evaluation meetings apply not only to business settings; clubs and *families* can form POWERMIND groups to achieve goals or solve virtually any problem. For example, a family could have a POWERMIND session to figure out how to save money for a new car, house, family vacation, etc. An individual could organize one with friends to determine how to get a better job, improve a relationship, get a promotion, start a business, or achieve any other goal. POWERMIND sessions are excellent powerful ways to generate unique creative ideas that work!

"Industry is at the feet of creative thinkers begging for ideas."

William H. Danforth
Chairman of the board,
Ralston Purina Co., 1940
Author of more than twelve
books, including *I Dare You!*,
Power,* and *Four Golden Keys

10 Tips for Creative Problem Solving

1. Know and believe all problems have solutions.

2. Stay cool, don't let a problem overwhelm you. Relax your mind so your creativity can flow.

3. Systematically break a big problem into smaller more manageable ones.

4. Objectively analyze problems by clearly writing them out on paper.

5. Make sure your facts are facts, not assumptions. This will greatly clarify your thinking, and any lack of facts will become obvious.

6. Concentrate single-mindedly on solving the problem for ten minutes each morning.

7. Know God is helping you in your mission to solve the problem.

8. Listen to your subconscious mind (intuition), *follow your hunches!*

9. Think about the problem often during the day; review your problem before you go to bed so your subconscious mind will work on it while you sleep.

10. When an idea pops into your head on how to solve the problem, write it down!   Carry a small notepad or your personal journal with you at all times for this purpose.

Unleashing Natural Creativity: Module II. Sensory Enhancement

Introduction to Sensory Enhancement Techniques

In earlier lessons you learned about the "acres of diamonds" principle, which states that all the raw materials for you to acquire riches are all around you. Affirmations and imagineering are two types of autogenic conditioning techniques that enable you to focus your mind power on specific goals, solutions to problems, or desired behavioral changes.

If you could somehow enhance your physical senses to increase the amount and accuracy of information coming into your mind, you would gain a heightened level of awareness in regard to your surroundings. This would result in your being better able to "spot" clues in your environment related to achieving your goals or solving your problems. These clues would ordinarily escape you without sensory enhancement training.

In this module, I will describe a series of visual and auditory sensory enhancement techniques. These are short, simple exercises anyone can perform in order to physically improve their sense of sight and hearing. These exercises will also improve the accuracy with which you **perceive** your environment. They are advanced techniques that will help you hone your natural physical sensing capabilities. I will deal only with the senses of sight and hearing since most people rely on these two senses more than the others in daily living.

You can think of the benefits of these exercises in this way. Imagine someone put a pair of very dark sunglasses and a pair of blinders (like the ones for horses) on you. Then they stuffed cotton balls in your ears. If your senses were restricted in this way, don't you think you would miss out on quite a bit of what might actually be happening around you every day? Do you think some information would be misinterpreted or missed altogether? Don't you think some of what you miss out on might help you achieve your goals or solve your problems? These exercises are designed to take the dark sunglasses and blinders off and take the cotton out.

With improved sensing capabilities you increase your chances of finding clues leading to goal achievement and problem solving. With enhanced senses of sight and hearing you are better equipped to mine your own *acres of diamonds*. Always remember you are now standing in your own *acres of diamonds*, if only you could see their brilliance and hear their call!

The Standard Regime

Each sensory enhancement exercise in this section should be performed once each day for five days, then skipped for two days, then repeated for five more days. This enables you to complete an enhancement exercise in a two-week time frame. This is known as a standard regime. Standard regimes for each exercise should be done about every six months to keep your senses fine tuned.

Visual Enhancement Exercise for Visual Acuity

Sight is clearly the most used sense. Scientists estimate over 80% of all the information a person takes in comes from their sense of sight. It is therefore in your own best interest to try to increase the accuracy, amount, and acuity of information from this most important sense.

This series of visual and auditory enhancement exercises heavily stimulates your brain's cerebral cortex circuitry, increasing your capacity to perceive, think, remember, utilize stored information, and of course become more creative.

Visual Acuity Exercise Steps:

1. Sit in a comfortable position indoors or out, take six deep breaths, relax, and observe your surroundings.

2. Notice how certain objects tend to catch your attention.

3. Select one of these objects and gaze attentively at it without straining your eyes. Study it carefully.

4. When you feel you have studied it well, look away and don't look at it again.

5. Write out or talk into a tape recorder the answers to the following questions.

   A. What was the exact size of the object? (Estimate measurements or use comparisons to commonly known objects.)
   B. What was the distance of the object from you?
   C. What was its exact shape?
   D. Did it stand out from its background? Why or why not?
   E. Exactly what color or colors did it have?
   F. What materials do you think it is made of?
   G. What purpose does it serve?
   H. How did it come into existence?
   I. Could it be improved upon in some way or made more efficient?
   J. Does it have a unique texture or temperature?
   K. If you were to touch it, how would it feel?
   L. Does it make any sounds; if so, what kind?
   M. Why did you select this object?

6. When you are finished, turn and look at the object. Check to see if your answers are accurate.

7. Correct any inaccuracies by saying the correct answers out loud *while you look at the object.*

8. Repeat steps 1-7 with two other objects.

This exercise may seem almost ludicrous to some people, but it is a serious visual enhancement exercise, which will help in many additional ways I haven't even mentioned.

Exercises like this one improve accuracy of thought and brain circuit efficiency, honing your mind to razor sharpness. As sight *perception* becomes more accurately linked to memory recall, you refine your ability to interpret your surroundings as they really are, not as you think they may be. If the link between what you see, what's really there, and what you remember is all fuzzy, you can imagine the problems that can cause in your thinking. If your mind is full of inaccurate fuzzy perceptions of what's real and what you think is real, you are in serious trouble!

Visual Enhancement Exercise for Calibrating the Mind's Eye

Calibrating the Mind's Eye Exercise Steps:

1. Sit comfortably inside or outside. Take six deep breaths to relax.

2. Scan your surroundings and gaze at the first object that catches your attention for exactly 30 seconds. (Use a timer.)

3. Shut your eyes and try to see it as vividly as possible, in full color, in full detail.

4. When you have a clear mental picture, open your eyes and check to see if your mental image is accurate.

5. Close your eyes and repeat until what you see with your eyes open is exactly what you see with your eyes closed.

6. Select two more objects and repeat steps 1-5.

At first most people will either have a hard time seeing the object at all or the object will seem dim, fuzzy, less detailed. With practice your mind's eye will be able to lock onto exactly what you saw quickly and you'll be able to recall the image perfectly, weeks later.

The special benefit of this exercise is that it allows you to capture exactly what you see, enabling you to form an exact mental picture that corresponds precisely to reality, not a dim shadow of reality. It also allows you to sharpen your memory because clear vivid pictures are more easily remembered than shadowy images.

Your mind will quickly become trained to remember accurately whatever you briefly focus your attention on. It can then log accurate images into your subconscious memory banks. The more accurate the mental pictures in your memory banks, the more precise your thinking will be. This is a method of calibrating your mind's eye to make it more accurate.

Visual Enhancement Exercise for Peripheral Vision

This exercise is specifically designed to increase "field of view." Your sensitivity to that which is out of your direct line of sight will dramatically improve after this exercise. As field of view increases you'll start to catch bits of information in your environment that might have otherwise escaped you. This expansion of sensory perception will then be reflected in your thinking, allowing you to open new windows of opportunity that the untrained person would miss.

Information and valuable ideas often come from the "periphery"; your alertness and attention to these outer fringes of information will be of great value. Be alert to information coming to you from this "outer margin." A glimpse of something that suddenly catches your attention from the corner of your eye is often quite valuable.

This exercise enhances your sensitivity to small bits of visual input that at first may seem unimportant or lie at the fringes of your conscious awareness.

Peripheral Vision Exercise Steps:

1. Sit in a comfortable position inside or outside. Take six deep breaths to relax.

2. Look straight ahead, but don't strain your eyes.

3. Focus on an imaginary point directly ahead of you. Without moving your eyes, make a mental note of everything to the far right, to the far left, higher up, and lower down.

4. Do this for 30 seconds. Set a timer.

5. Look away, and without looking back describe everything you saw in writing or on a tape recorder.

6. When you have finished writing or recording, look back to the point you were watching, then visually scan around it.

7. Correct for items you missed by describing them out loud.

8. Repeat steps 1-7 in two different locations.

Make special note of colors, textures, distances, shapes, sizes. This is also a descriptive exercise that aids in developing memory recall.

Most people report dramatic noticeable improvement from this particular exercise even before the first five days of the *standard regime* are up!

Auditory Enhancement Exercise for Visualization of Sound

This short exercise develops your ability to link sound with visual images for enhanced memory development. Sounds are more easily remembered if they are associated with a visual image.

Visualization of Sound Exercise Steps:

1. Sit in a comfortable position inside or outside. Take six deep breaths to relax.

2. Close your eyes, and listen intently.

3. Notice all the sounds you can hear for one minute. Set a timer.

4. Write out or record on a tape recorder all the sounds that you heard.

5. For each individual sound you listed close your eyes and try to imagine a picture of what was making that sound.

6. Move to two different locations and repeat steps 1-5.

Auditory Enhancement Exercise for Auditory Acuity

This exercise develops auditory acuity. You will focus your attention by using conscious control of your auditory sense. This exercise first sensitizes you to all sounds in your surroundings to increase your auditory awareness. Then it asks you to consciously focus your attention on a single delicate sound, shutting all others out.

The main objective is for you to train yourself in becoming more sensitive to the softest sounds in your environment. This develops your power of auditory control so you can consciously shut out all other sounds in your environment. It also develops your ability to hear what is on the fringes of your hearing *perception*.

Auditory Acuity Exercise Steps:

1. Sit in a comfortable position inside or outside. Take six deep breaths to relax.

2. Close your eyes and notice all the sounds you can hear.

3. Focus your attention on the quietest, least obvious sound you can hear.

4. Try to shut out all the other sounds for about one minute by drawing all your attention to that single sound.

5. Open your eyes and answer the following questions in writing or out loud on a tape recorder.

   A. What direction did the sound come from?
   B. What made the sound?
   C. How else could a sound like that be made?
   D. Does the sound have any unique features?
   E. Where else have you heard that sound or one similar to it?

6. Move to two different locations and repeat steps 1-5.

Unleashing Natural Creativity: Module III. Problem Solving

Mind-Set of the Major Problem Solver

Principle: You have within you the power to overcome all difficulties, rise above defeat, and solve all major problems.

Most problems appear large or small depending on your attitude toward them. When you change your attitude toward the problem in either direction, positive or negative, that affects how the problem appears to you. Did you ever hear the phrase,

"You're making a big problem out of nothing?" Well, you can also do the reverse, that is, you can literally make a big problem into much smaller ones and then systematically attack each little one. In fact most big problems are just that, a collection of many little ones.

Almost all problems, no matter how large or difficult, even the seemingly impossible ones, may be overcome. The most important single factor is your attitude toward them. A "big" problem can overwhelm you mentally, causing you to block it out of your mind rather than thinking creatively about how to solve it. However, if you are provided with a battery of proven techniques to help you solve big problems, that overwhelming feeling instantly fades, being replaced by creative thought. This puts you suddenly on the road to solving it.

A confident, optimistic, faith-filled attitude can overcome many "insurmountable" problems. If you feel you have no control and unseen forces are against you, you can build this attitude up in your subconscious mind, turning it into a formidable opponent indeed. This negative attitude prevents you from expressing your true creativity. If you rid yourself of this negative, self-defeating attitude you will solve your problems and be lifted from certain defeat to assured victory.

Oftentimes very difficult personal problems lend themselves to proactive solution methods. You first need to specifically identify the problem, then devise a plan of action to solve it. The key is to keep working a plan of action. The very fact of knowing you are working on a plan brings energy and enthusiasm to bear, which will result in the ultimate demise of the problem. Working on a specified plan of action brings you closer to the solution and the solution closer to you. This is not magical but a fact of human nature. Attitudes become more positive as we become actively involved in a plan of action that we believe has the potential to eventually solve the problem.

If you have no set plan, then start following your hunches; they are instructions from the subconscious mind and are almost always correct for you. The ability to solve all your problems is inherently within your reach.

In emergency situations (life-and-death situations), the human brain is capable of remarkable creative thought power. This creative power is always present but only tapped by most people in an emergency situation. People who fall apart at the least little problem in their lives have never learned to draw upon their own innate creative strength. *You have within you the power to overcome all difficulties, rise above defeat, and solve all major problems.*

The day you realize this will be one of the greatest in your life! The sleeper will have awakened. Believe in your own creative intelligence to find answers. Don't fret or worry. Relax, use the following scientific techniques, and behold, the perfect answer will be yours!

Strength through Scientific Prayer

"When every physical and mental resource is focused, one's power to solve a problem multiplies tremendously."

Dr. Norman Vincent Peale
Author of *The Power of*
Positive Thinking

"Scientific prayer" means to boldly, intensively, purposefully ask God in solemn prayer to provide you with practical means to achieve your goals or aid you in solving a problem. Scientific prayer can open up the floodgates of creativity, which is available to all of us. It can give you such confidence you'll walk nine feet off the ground. Asking God to help solve problems, get you through difficult times, and help you win your goals is a major key to high achievement in life. Faith in God can unlock the mental prison door. God has the key, so let yourself free!

Physical health scientists recognize prayer can be a potent asset in helping people to heal their bodies. Prayer can also be used to restore mental harmony. These are not the preachings and teachings of religious fanatics. Most people experience tremendous tension release during and after intensive scientific prayer.

By allowing your mind to concentrate on Divine Guidance, you feel relief, which allows your mind to generate creative thoughts. It's like a mini physical and spiritual rebirth each time you scientifically pray. So how exactly do you pray scientifically? Simply ask God to help you physically, mentally, and spiritually. God is with you always. It is always your *choice* to be close to God and have this miracle-working power at your side.

"Draw nigh to God and he will draw nigh to you."

James 4:8

I encourage you to scientifically pray so that magnificent power can flow into you, strengthening your mind, body and soul. This universal energy is unused by many people because they never learned how to "scientifically pray."

As you may well suspect by now this is a practical method of putting the supreme power of God to use in a very practical way in your life everyday to help you lead a stronger, happier, healthier, more fulfilling life.

"What things soever ye desire, when ye pray, believe that ye receive them, and ye shall have them."

Mark 11:24

The Presence of God Technique

The presence of God technique can help you solve all major problems.

1. Imagine God is with you, assisting you, standing by your side, helping you solve the problem.

2. Verbally affirm daily, regularly, religiously, "God is with me. God will see me through. God is all knowing, kind and caring, revealing to me the perfect answer to my problem now. I ask for Divine help in complete faith and love." Say this verbal affirmation, believe in it, and you will see solutions appear before your eyes that will astonish you!

3. When you receive a "sign," take action immediately.

4. Have faith in yourself and in God. This will condition your mind and body, parting the red sea of hopelessness and despair, enabling you to walk through to the promised land of opportunity for the rest of your life.

"According to your faith be it done unto you."

Matthew 9:29

6 Tips for Divine Guidance

1. Ask God to provide you with inspiration and strength in carrying out your actions, then your actions will be "God guided." Ask for strength at any time in any place. Remember God is omnipresent and all powerful.

"Finally my brethren be strong in the Lord and in the power of his might."

Ephesians 6:10

2. Practice scientific prayer, which means, asking God to specifically give you the means for achieving goals and solutions to your problems. Go off to a quiet place and do this by yourself. Be confident that what you pray for can be made so.

"But when you pray, go into your room and shut the door and pray to your Father who is in secret; and your Father who sees in secret will reward you."

Matthew 6:6

3. Be thankful for all the good things you have had and now have in your life.

"I thank thee father that Thou hast heard me and I know that Thou hearest me always."

John 17:24

4. Never pray for ill will or bad things to happen to someone.
   These thoughts tend to come back magnified sevenfold on
   you, and will most certainly hurt you.

*"When an evil spirit (thought) comes out of a man, it goes
through arid places seeking rest and does not find it. Then it
says, 'I will return to the house I left'. When it arrives it finds
the house unoccupied, swept clean and put in order. Then it
goes and takes with it seven other spirits more wicked than
itself, and they go in and live there. And the final condition of
that man is worse than the first."*

Matthew 12:43-45

5. Spend time reading the Bible and thinking about God working in your life.

*"Acquaint now thyself with him, and be at peace: thereby good
shall come unto thee."*

Job 22:21

6. Always remember the supreme law of the universe:
   Whatever you do will have future consequences that will
   come back magnified at a later date and affect you. It is the
   law of action and reaction, sowing and reaping. If your
   actions are good, the future reactions will be both good and
   magnified. If they are evil, this too will be brought back to
   you magnified. There is no escape from this law; it is not a
   law made by humans, but a Universal one. The law of sowing and reaping is inviolate!

*"Do not be deceived; God is not mocked (fooled), for whatsoev-
er a man soweth, that shall he also reap."*

**Galatians 6:7
(Supreme Law of the
Universe)**

An After-the-Lesson Visit with the Author

All major goals will present you with a series of problems that must be solved along the way to their final achievement. In my discussions with people who have difficulty solving problems, I find that most of them simply have the wrong attitude. They don't feel that they are very good problem solvers. This is called creativity lockdown, and it stops many would-be high achievers as soon as a problem is encountered. By changing their frame of mind from negative to positive they can quickly transform their whole outlook. The very act of having a confident positive attitude can unleash natural creativity.

It is difficult, however, to solve problems and be positive about it without any proven techniques to help you. Thus we come to the second major obstacle people run into: They don't know any scientifically proven step-by-step techniques for problem solving.

In Module I of this lesson, I instructed you in two techniques for major problem solving. The first one was a technique you could use by yourself, called the written problem-solving technique. The second one required you to gather one or more individuals who would be interested in helping you. This was the POWERMIND session method. The principle operating behind a POWERMIND session was written about by Napoleon Hill in his great book *Law of Success*. This principle also dates back to ancient times, and it is stated in the Bible.

In Module II, I introduced you to a series of sensory enhancement techniques. I have found these particularly intriguing in that a specialized physical training regime of the two major senses organs can actually sharpen thinking processes. Natural creativity is unleashed as you heighten your sensory perception of the world around you and improve your memory of life experiences.

Sensory enhancement exercises develop the machinelike sensing capabilities of a human being. Most people gain noticeable benefit from the exercises even before the first two-week standard regime is complete. Realistically speaking, it's as if someone turned the lights on in a dark room so they could see and hear clues leading straight to their goals. ***Don't ever underestimate the power of the sensory enhancement techniques!***

Module III is a highly personal one because I believe God can work miracles in people's lives if only they would ask and believe in this Divine power. Millions of people in the world will testify to the miraculous power of God in speeding them toward their goals and helping them to solve serious problems in their lives. You will notice most principles in this book are in fact supported by the Bible.

I encourage you to read the Bible more, not just when you have a problem but often. Some Friday night when the masses are out drinking their lives away in a bar or being hypnotized into helplessness by the television programmers, grab yourself a Bible, get in a comfortable chair in a quiet place, and let the **Word** affect you.

This lesson on unleashing natural creativity has provided you with more than enough information to tackle most major problems. Move with confidence as you attack all obstacles along your goal path with these weapons of wisdom!

"If God is for us who can be against us?"

Romans 8:31

Lesson

11

The Four Essential Personality Traits for High Achievement

Overview

In this lesson you'll be exposed to four personality traits required for high achievement in life. These are also essential traits for personal power. They are **personal responsibility, personal honor, self-discipline**, and **persistence**. All historical as well as contemporary success masters would agree on these four. A deficiency in any one of these will inevitably lead to disaster! I'll explain and illustrate each trait with one or more poignant vignettes.

The 4 Essential Personality Traits for High Achievement: Module III. Self-Discipline

The 4 Essential Personality Traits for High Achievement: Module IV. Persistence

Module I. Personal Responsibility

The Universal Law of Sowing and Reaping

"Personal responsibility" is defined as *the act of holding oneself 100% accountable for the circumstances of one's own life*. The idea that you are the primary cause of the circumstances of your life through both your thoughts and actions is personal responsibility. In order to be a true high achiever, a person must accept the fact that they are 100% accountable for their thoughts and actions *and the consequences of both.*

It may seem like your lot in life is caused by external factors or forces. Whether you are doing well or doing poorly in life, it is caused by your own thoughts and actions; no one else is at fault. You alone build the mental structure (mental core) that governs your behavior. You must live with the consequences of what you build in your mind.

The idea that you are personally responsible for your current station in life may indeed be hard for an irresponsible person to swallow. They would much rather give up responsibility and say they are "victims of circumstances outside their control." This is called crooked thinking.

In earlier lessons I've touched on two Universal Laws that you must understand. The first one is the **Universal Law of Accountability**, which says, "You alone are personally responsible for how your life works out." The second one is the **Universal Law of Sowing and Reaping**, also called the law of action and reaction, or cause and effect. It is the supreme law that governs the universe. It's been stated in the Bible and also by all the great philosophers since the beginning of man's recorded history. It says, *"Whatsoever a man soweth, that shall he also reap"* (Galations 6:7). It is an immutable law. It cannot be broken. This law is at the very heart of personal responsibility. It has been stated throughout this book consistently in various forms.

Another part of the law of sowing and reaping that is often missed is that effects are produced *in kind* and *magnified* in relation to the causes. The meaning of this, is that if you do kindness to others, kindness will be returned to you magnified.

If you are mean to others, others will be mean to you magnified. If you sow good, you reap greater good; if you sow evil, you reap greater evil. It's a simple law, *yet a severely unforgiving one!* **THIS LAW CRUSHES MILLIONS OF PEOPLE'S LIVE'S INTO DUST WHO DO NOT ABIDE BY IT!** It also glorifies, energizes, and rewards those who rightly understand and obey it.

This is so important for you to understand I'll further illustrate it. If you plant one kernel of corn in the soil you expect to get a corn plant, not a tomato, pepper, or bean plant. You also expect to get an abundance more of corn kernels back from that single plant. You don't expect to just get one or two kernels back. And so it is with your thoughts and actions. A good thought planted in the fertile soil of the subconscious mind, well cared for (followed up by action), produces an abundance more after its kind. An evil thought planted in the soil of the subconscious mind also produces an abundance more after its kind. A good deed you perform for others produces an abundance more good after its kind *from others to you.* An evil deed also produces an abundance more evil after its kind *from others to you.*

You can ignore, disagree, or argue this law to your heart's content but it operates in a very merciless, unforgiving way regardless of you. This law is not made by humans, it's a *Universal* one.

The law of gravity can be used to help explain what a Universal law is. The law of gravity is not made by humans. It is universal. If you jump off a cliff you will fall down, not up, sideways, in circles, but down. You may not be *aware* of the law of gravity, but you fall just the same. You might think the law of gravity is stupid, false, unfair, and even argue the point; however, you still fall!

The Universal law of sowing and reaping applies very directly to human beings. You don't need to believe in it, it always operates regardless of how you feel about it. However, you can easily put this law to work in your favor by understanding it and using it to your benefit.

Skydivers and hangliders *work with* the law of gravity for their enjoyment. You can also work with the Universal law of sowing and reaping to live a phenomenally successful life simply by helping others whenever you can.

"Whatsoever a man soweth, that shall he also reap."

Galatians, 6:7

This Biblical quotation is also worth your committing to memory.

"For with the measure you use, it will be measured to you."

Luke 6:38

The Personal Responsibility Continuum: Where are you?

0% Responsible	50% Responsible	100% Responsible
Believe that magical forces, luck, other people, or circumstances control their destiny. Believe their thoughts and actions don't matter.	Realize their thoughts and actions matter *in some cases.*	Realize their thoughts and actions completely control their destiny.

If you are on the 100% responsible end of the scale, the low end probably seems ridiculous; this is good. If you are on the 100% responsible end, you are in an excellent position to correct for your errors and reinforce your successes. The *awareness* that you are in total control of your destiny is the starting point for high achievement in life. Responsible people recognize that things going well or poorly can be and is directly controlled by them. If something goes poorly they analyze it, find out where they made the mistake, learn from it, and make the correction for *next time.*

Irresponsible people who believe "magical forces" have predetermined their destiny for them simply accept whatever fate befalls them. They shuffle through life shiftlessly with the rest of the crowd, whining and complaining about their circumstances. They take no action to improve themselves because they are too busy complaining about external circumstances instead of looking at their own lack of personal responsibility. If only they would wake up, they would see how much power for success they could easily garner in a relatively short period of time!

"If it's to be, it's up to me."

> Brian Tracy
> Human achievement expert
> Author of *Maximum Achievement, The Psychology of Achievement,* and *The Universal Laws of Success and Achievement*

Skill Development

Responsible people take charge of their life. They consistently take action, trying to improve themselves, knowing that by doing so they'll change the circumstances of their lives for the better. Many times these people are extremely unskilled at the start, but by practicing, getting feedback, coaching, making corrections, and *researching* they eventually develop skill.

Here's a simple example to illustrate this point. Let's say you are throwing darts at a dart board. Your first try might not even hit the board. Your second and third tries will probably be better, and so on. After a little practice you can hit the board with every try. Now you start to hone your skill by focusing on hitting not just the board but the bull's-eye. You get better and better to a point, then peak out.

What would you do next? You could practice all the time, developing your own technique over months and months of hard work, OR you could take a shortcut by gaining *specialized knowledge*. You could get books on darts and research the game. You could watch pros and get coaching, combining other people's specialized knowledge with your own experience to trim time off becoming a pro yourself. Let me ask you this question: If you followed that procedure, would your dart throwing improve? Would you attribute it to luck, chance, "magical forces," or would you accept personal responsibility for the consequences of your thoughts and actions? Would you be willing to accept a prize after months of study and practice if you won a tournament, or would you say, "It was nothing, I just got lucky?" You see, *a responsible person takes action to develop their skill* no matter where they start. An irresponsible person takes no such action.

Here is another important point. Let's say as you practice at darts, you happen to be "on" one evening, doing really well. If you are a responsible person you will try to *figure out why* you did so well. If you are an irresponsible person you will consider your performance just "dumb luck." You will simply scoff it off, attributing the performance to just a "lucky break." This is an extremely important point! This particular situation could have great value to the person with the personal responsibility mind-set, because they will figure out exactly why they were "on" that evening and later be able to *repeat it at will!* The irresponsible mind-set person would gain nothing from the situation because they would never *search for a cause* as to WHY they performed so well that evening.

Just like in the darts example. If you are searching, you will find the causes for success in life; if you aren't searching, you not only won't find the causes but you *can't find* them!

The irresponsible mind-set person usually has lots of "bad luck" and is very superstitious. They think if things go well for them it's because of "good luck," and if things go bad for them its because of "bad luck." They don't reinforce effective behavior or correct for errors because they don't view themselves as personally responsible for what happens to them. They aren't in a position to develop success skills because their mind-set is all fouled up. The personal responsibility mind-set is the first step in success skill development.

The Power of Decisions

The power of decisions and their relationship to personal responsibility is nicely illustrated with a parenting example. If you are in a restaurant and you ask your child what he would like to order, he may say, "A hot dog and fries." He may later see his younger sister eating the hamburger and chips that she ordered. He then *decides* he no longer wants what he ordered.

At this point many parents would allow the child to change his order. "What's the big deal?" they say. The "big deal" is this: They are teaching the child to be irresponsible for his *decisions*, that his decisions don't really matter. If you tell the child he must "stick to his decision," the next time you are in the restaurant the child will consider the options much more carefully. You could even remind him of what happened last time. You could help him in the decision-making process, but make him personally responsible for his decision. In this way the child learns the direct connection between personal responsibility, decisions, and the consequences of those decisions.

Many parents won't allow the child to suffer any inconvenience caused by the consequences of their decisions at all. In doing this they are breeding an irresponsible child who will have serious difficulties in life. They are enforcing irresponsibility, not responsibility.

It is cruel to teach irresponsibility to a child, because later on in life they learn Mommy and Daddy will not always be there to bail them out when they make a bad decision. In a sense parents program the child for failure because the child never develops the awareness that they are personally responsible for the consequences of their decisions.

What about you? Do you feel fully responsible for the consequences of your decisions? This parenting example usually hits home because many people were in fact raised in that sort of a childhood environment themselves. They then see from this example how they developed irresponsibility and may be repeating the same teachings to their children.

The point that should now become obvious is that your decisions all have direct consequences and that you should take due care in making all important decisions. You are personally responsible for the results in your life because of your decisions. If you make bad decisions, you must suffer the consequences. If you make good ones, you must also be entitled to *reap the rewards!*

The 10-Point Decision-Screening System

Because of the Universal law of sowing and reaping, you will most certainly be held accountable for all your decisions. Since this is so, I'll provide you with a ten-point decision-screening system to help you make excellent decisions throughout your life.

This ten-point decision-screening system is to be used whenever you make any major decision, such as a career change, financial investment, or life direction decision. It will help you immensely and become an ever-present guide for you to use at any time. Most people use no systematic screen at all when making crucial life decisions. They use haphazard thinking regimes, which inevitably lead to poor decisions, failure, loss, procrastination, and future regret.

An interesting experiment you can do to test the validity of this system is to put three of your most recent important decisions on trial. If the decision was a good one, see if the system is valid. If a decision was a bad one, see if this system would have caught the error for you so that your decision would not have been poorly made. Write your decisions at the top of a sheet of paper and check them against the following.

Check Point 1. Was I in a calm state of mind when I made the decision? All important decisions should be made when you are calm, thinking logically and clearly. Decisions made in a very emotionalized state, such as high stress, anger, sexual passion, or severe depression or under the influence of drugs are poor because all these inhibit your conscious mind's ability to reason.

Check Point 2. Did I consider whether the decision was moving me toward or away from my major goal(s) in life?

Check Point 3. Did I know what was really motivating *me* when I made the decision? Many people make externally motivated decisions, never considering whether it's the right choice for them personally. They listen to others and let others decide for them.

Check Point 4. Was the decision in conflict with any of my personal life values? Any decision that conflicts with your personal values will always be regretted!

Check Point 5. Was the decision morally correct? Morally incorrect decisions will also be regretted.

Check Point 6. Did I have any strong inner negative or positive feelings (hunches) about the decision? For example, it felt wrong and I knew I shouldn't have, but I went ahead and did any way. Or it felt right and I knew it. Always listen to that still small voice within!

Check Point 7. Did the decision infringe on the personal rights of anyone? Remember the Universal law of sowing and reaping!

Check Point 8. Did I consider the long-term future consequences of the decision? Most people think in the short term, which is usually devastating to them in the long term!

Check Point 9. Did I seek the counsel or advice of other people more knowledgeable than myself in the area or topic under consideration before I made the decision? Special note: Relatives or friends may not qualify for decision consultation because of total ignorance *in the topic area*. For example, if your friends are all heavily in debt, don't ask them how to invest your money!

Check Point 10. Did I write down on paper the pros and cons of the decision, weighing them on my mental scales before I made the decision? Putting all the reasons for and against on paper objectifies them and enables you to be a much more logical decision maker.

Remember, you can check all your future major and even minor decisions using this ten-point screening system. Simply change the tense of the questions from past to present and ask them. For example, Question 1 would read, Am I now in a calm state of mind, feeling capable of thinking logically about the decision I must now make? Question 2 would read, Is this decision going to move me toward or away from my major goal(s) in life?

Do you think using this decision-screening system would help you make better decisions in the future? **THINK ABOUT IT!** This system only takes about thirty minutes to use, and it's definitely time well spent!

It's Your Fault: A Personal Responsibility Self-Awareness Poem

This is a personal responsibility poem designed to create SELF-AWARENESS.

*If you hate your job and you **decide** to stay there, it's your fault.*

*If someone offers you a better job, but it requires you to move to another city and you **decide** not to take it, it's your fault.*

*If you **decide** to save no money during your working lifetime, winding up broke and embarrassed at age 65, dependent on charities for survival, it's your fault.*

*If you **decide** not to study or read in your chosen field and find yourself never rising above mere mediocrity, it's your fault.*

*If you **decide** to spend more money than you make, running yourself into debt by satisfying one capricious whim after another, it's your fault.*

*If you **decide** to waste all your time on meaningless activities, neglecting all the important things you could do with your life, it's your fault.*

*If you **decide** never to read a self-help book and then suffer dramatically because you are ignorant of success principles, it's your fault.*

*If you **decide** to smoke three packs of cigarettes a day, then get lung cancer, it's your fault.*

*If you **decide** to spend no time building a loving relationship with your spouse and your spouse divorces you, it's your fault.*

*If your life isn't working out well and you **decide** to do nothing about it, it's your fault.*

*If you **decide** never to help anyone else in life and wind up lonely, it's your fault.*

*If you **decide** on goals that are completely self-serving and you have a hard time getting others to support you, it's your fault.*

*If you **decide** never to pray and find that God works no miracles in your life, it's your fault.*

This little poem is not meant to depress you, but simply to make you *aware* of the fact that you are personally responsible for the way your life works out. *The decisions are all up to you!*

"You always do what you want to do. This is true with every act. You may say that you had to do something, or that you were forced to, but actually, whatever you do, you do by choice. Only you have the power to choose for yourself."

> **W. Clement Stone**
> **Coauthor of *Success Through a Positive Mental Attitude***

Module II. Personal Honor

30 Pieces of Silver

"To every man there openeth
A way, and ways, and a way.
And the high soul climbs the high way,
And the low soul gropes the low!
And in between, on the misty flats,
The rest drift to and fro.
But to every man there openeth
A high way and a low.
And every man decideth
The way his soul shall go."

> **John Oxenham**
> **AKA William Dunkerley**
> **Author of *God's Candle,***
> ***Christ and the Third Wise***
> ***Man*, and *Anno Domini***

Personal honor is the pivotal personality trait that is used as a *winnowing stick*. People with true personal power always have personal honor. This trait is defined as *adherence to high standards of justice or ethical conduct*. It sounds simple enough, yet millions lack it. People with personal honor will never allow someone lacking it to enter into their *inner circle*. They cannot do so, because doing so would compromise their own personal honor. They would be **contaminated by association** with the dishonorable person.

The highly skilled *manipulator* who devotes all their time to learning "tricks" to gain power over people falls quite nicely into the *valueless* category of people lacking personal honor. The person who lacks personal honor can easily be illustrated in business management circles. I'll explain. The one they call "Mr. Yes Man," who faithfully obeys the commands of unethical superiors, is lacking in personal honor. He is like a chameleon, always taking the view of those whom he believes to be in power. He licks the boots of bosses and will sell out anyone around him or under him if he sees the opportunity for personal gains.

It is interesting to track how these pitiful people can sneak their way into organizations and then even move up to a certain level by aligning themselves with equally pitiful, egotistical, unethical superiors. Mr. Yes Man feeds the egos of his insecure superiors like a dog hoping one day to be thrown a bone for his meager efforts. The sad part is that Mr. Yes Man is trying to break the *Universal law of sowing and reaping*, which is a relentless unforgiving law for those who do not abide by it.

Then one day a man possessing personal honor comes on the scene and all recognize this man as a true leader. He commands **respect from** everyone because of his **respect for** everyone. When he ferrets out the cancerous "Mr. Yes Man," he makes one swift slice with his sacred scalpel, and Mr. Yes Man is cut from the organization, looking for work, pink slip hot in hand. Mr. Yes Man's family suffers from the terminal cut, wondering what happened! The people in the organization rejoice because they realize a true leader has arrived!

People who lack personal honor never seem to attain any real leadership status. (Leadership status meaning being **respected** by subordinates, peers, and higher leaders.) They are often perplexed by events that happen to them in their lives. They don't realize that their own self-serving goals impress no one, not even others who also lack personal honor.

A person with personal honor does not lie or knowingly withhold helpful information from others. They keep their word. When they say they will do something they do it! No one is left wondering whether they can count on them or not. Written legal contracts are often unnecessary with this type of person. They stand by their word like a marble pillar. In this way they build reputations of rock-solid reliability. Often they put in extra time and energy, performing their work at a much higher standard of excellence than the rest. They work by their own personal code of excellence, not an externally imposed one.

"Your character and mental attitude will make or break you."

> **Dr. Joseph Murphy**
> **Author of** *The Power of Your Subconscious Mind, Your Infinite Power to be Rich,* **and** *The Amazing Laws of Cosmic Mind Power*

I can't provide you with any technique to help you develop personal honor; it is a *decision* you have to make by yourself. You can *decide* to be a person who sells out everyone around you for personal gain, giving up your pride in your work, but OH! the tremendous cost of that single decision. There is no gray area or in-between region as far as personal honor is concerned. You can live your life honorably or dishonorably. You have the God-given free will in this matter, the choice of good or evil.

I'll direct your attention to perhaps the most famous story ever written about personal honor and the tremendous *cost* of selling out to the dark side. It's in the Bible. You may have heard it before, but it's worth repeating. It's the story of **Judas Iscariot**.

Many will recall that Judas sold out to the dark side by betraying **Jesus Christ** for thirty pieces of silver. Thirty pieces of silver was a substantial fortune in those days, so it would seem that after being paid, Judas would have been delighted with his deed. A fortune now his, to be, have, and do whatever he wanted. But there was a catch. Judas wasn't happy with his great fortune. After he got the money he tried to give it all back, to regain his personal honor. But the money givers laughed and threw him out. Judas, in a last-ditch effort to regain his personal honor, threw all the money away.

Finally, when he realized he could not violate the Universal law of sowing and reaping and that he had paid the heavy price of all his personal honor for a mere material fortune, he hung himself!

"I'm sure if Judas could speak back to us from some dark corner of the universe he would say 'beware! BEWARE! BEWARE!' of what you give up in pursuit of what you want."

> **Jim Rohn**
> **America's foremost business philosopher; author of *The Five Major Pieces to the Life Puzzle, Seven Strategies for Wealth and Happiness,* and *The Seasons of Life***

Indeed, the decision is all yours, but remember the story of Judas Iscariot and **BEWARE!** *The Universal law of sowing and reaping is immutable!*

Module III. Self-Discipline

Little by Little, Day by Day

"Self-discipline" is defined as *systematic, willing, and purposeful action taken each day, leading to the completion of a self-assigned goal(s).* (A goal that must be achieved by delaying gratification.)

You probably at this moment possess sufficient knowledge to **begin** moving toward any one of your goals. Many people know what they "should do," what they "could do," but they don't. Why? Lack of self-discipline.

It is true most people think they employ self-discipline if they act for a short period of time, which is relatively easy, but self-discipline is maintenance of this action until the goal is finally attained. The latter part is where the majority fail to make the self-discipline grade. They fail to consistently apply effort over an extended period of time until the goal is ultimately won. This is the key to self-discipline.

Once the initial enthusiasm for the goal has faded, self-discipline must be employed to keep you moving toward the goal's ultimate attainment. If you always quit when the going gets tough, you'll never achieve anything worthwhile. Self-discipline is simply working toward your goal(s) regularly on a continuing basis until it is finally realized.

The voice inside your mind that says, "Give up, quit, it's no use, you won't succeed," attacks all of us, even the most successful, powerful individual. It is the weed that consistently tries to grow in the garden of the mind. It must be torn out every time it sprouts! How do you tear it out? By taking action. Do an activity that pertains to the specific goal that the weed of procrastination or self-doubt is choking. Self-discipline is the iron fist that grips the insidious weed, and action rips it out!

It also takes self-discipline to deal with the jealous ridiculers and the rest of the herd of small mean voices who tell you your efforts are in vain. These are mean *little people*, with mean *little salaries*, mean *little goals*, and mean *little souls*. These voices could even be those of respected individuals such as parents, relatives, teachers, or friends. If your goal(s) is morally correct, and will help others, hurting none, rest assured it is worthy of your effort, warranting the self-discipline you will need to achieve it.

Self-discipline is an essential personality trait in the science of personal power as well as high achievement. Sporadic impulses will show you how quickly your lifetime is eaten away, leaving you with dust to show for your intermittent efforts.

"No great work has ever been done 'at a heat.' It is the result of repeated efforts, and often of many failures."

Samuel Smiles
Author of the classic self-help
series *Thrift, Character,* and
Self Help

It is not as important how long you engage in working toward your goal(s) each day, but it is important that you do at least one thing every day to move you toward it. Every day counts, not twenty hours on a Saturday once every few months. Labor, *little by little, day by day,* is what counts, and that takes self-discipline!

Godspeed on Your Journey

Be relentless in the pursuit of your goal(s). High achievers must always remember, for the short term it is always easier NOT to employ self-discipline. The really big payoffs in life, however, come from dedication and the consistent application of self-discipline.

Of course it's easy to work as little as possible. Its easy not to work on your goals, not to set goals, not to manage your time well, not to read, not to take self-improvement courses, not to be honest with yourself. It's easy to overeat, to watch endless hours of TV, to use illegal drugs. All of these are "easy outs," or escapism-type behaviors The short-term gain appears appealing to many, but the long-term pain is the agony of self-defeat. Imagine that, an entire life wasted on TV or a life cut short from drug abuse!

What is "easy" also has the least payoff. It's easy to work at a fast-food restaurant; the pay is low. It's harder to become a brain surgeon; the pay is high. If the effort required to become either one were equal, which funny hat would you rather wear? It's easy to get drunk on a Friday night, it's much harder to study. The drunk's payoff is nonexistent, the serious success student's payoff is high. So you see, the difference here again is in self-discipline. There is no shortage of low wage workers. The hoards line up at the gate from just one small newspaper ad. But I have yet to see a throng of brain surgeons walking the streets in search of a job.

Personal honor is also a form of self-discipline, which so many people lack. When you say you will do something for someone else, it takes self-discipline to carry out the promise. Lack of self-discipline in this case shows up as a loss of credibility, leaving behind a trail of broken promises, half-finished projects, and severed relationships that mark failure's devastating path.

Long term, the price of self-discipline is low (short-term pain for long-term gain), and the price of procrastination is high (short-term gain for long-term pain). Everyone must pay a price; there is no escape! You, however are *personally responsible for deciding* which price you wish to pay.

Do you hope for a rewarding life or an empty, wasted one? Delaying the final payoff while you labor for the goal is always worth the wait. When you employ self-discipline your ultimate rewards will far outweigh your effort; this is **Universal Law!**

If you have the self-discipline to plant and protect one apple tree, does it yield apples the first few years? No, not a single one. Should you then kill the tree or keep fertilizing, watering, protecting, and nurturing it until it yields for you an abundance? It will yield bushels and bushels of apples for many, many years if you have the self-discipline to plant and care for it with unwavering action.

Disciplined efforts always pay high dividends, not only in terms of money, but in terms of a rewarding life. Your life is not a practice session for something else. As you discipline yourself in all areas of your life, watch that effort closely as it multiplies into cherished experiences for you.

Your life will add up to being either a warning or an example for others. I encourage you to have your life serve as an example for others, not a warning. Work now, coast later, pay now, not later, pay the full price for success in advance! Don't look back on your life when it's too late, as millions must, and say, "I should have, I could have, but I didn't!"

I'm glad you are reading this. If it shocks you into reconsidering your present lifestyle, good! Better you get on the high road of human achievement while you still can. If you're already on that road, I salute you and wish you *Godspeed on your journey!*

Module IV. Persistence

The Iron Will

Persistence is the last essential personality trait I will cover. "Persistence" is defined as *perseverance in the pursuit of a goal(s)*. Ridicule, fear, self-doubt, worry, depression may all come calling, but *he who perseveres to the end will ultimately win out.*

How do you deal with these vicious intruders of the mind? Answer: We've already covered it. Imagineer your goal with strong positive emotion, hold it in your conscious mind often, think of the infinite power of your subconscious and superconscious minds. Keep on keeping on through difficulty until the red sea parts and you stride triumphantly to your promised land.

As with the other essential personality traits, no high achievement is possible without persistence. This personality trait separates the great one from the mass of also-rans. The person that keeps trying and trying, who never gives up, is persistent.

In Mental Mechanics, I described the complete unification of the triune mind (conscious, subconscious, and superconscious) called powerbonding. When a person becomes bent on a goal in this way, they develop an "iron will."

Having an *iron will* means their very soul (superconscious mind) is bent on the achievement of the goal. That's why it's so important that you become powerbonded on a goal that you burningly desire and that this goal be morally correct. An iron will by definition is capable of bringing universal forces to its aid to accomplish its mission.

Any great goal will inevitably have you crashing into barriers along the way. An iron will enables you to smash right through them. A goal wouldn't give you any feeling of fulfillment if it was simple to reach.

Barriers and problems along the goal path make you stretch, forcing you to dig deep into your own divine mind within for answers. They make you tap into your soul for power. Eventually the whole universe must yield to an *iron will!*

"There has been altogether too much talk about the secret of success. Success has no secret, her voice is forever ringing through the marketplace and crying in the wilderness and the burden of her cry is one word, WILL."

Dr. Russell H. Conwell
Author of *Acres of Diamonds*

The Spirit-to-do

Did you ever solve a very difficult problem or achieve a difficult goal in your past? How did it make you feel? Didn't you feel great? Looking back now, was the struggle worth it?

The persistent person has a philosophy in regard to "challenges." It goes like this: "Problems, obstacles, and mistakes are my teachers in life. Sometimes they are brutally harsh and unforgiving, but their lessons are always thorough." The person that takes the seemingly easy road or quits early at the least little sign of difficulty never accomplishes much because they lack persistence.

If you watch ants, you will see that an ant has more persistence than most humans. If you put a brick in an ant's path, it will immediately *begin searching* for a way over, under, around, or through the brick. The ant does not stop, roll over on its back, and die. It doesn't quit! Many people, however, do quit. They quit far too early. If your goal is a worthy one, you must persist.

"Nothing in the world can take the place of persistence. Talent will not; nothing is more common than unsuccessful men of talent. Genius will not. . . . the world is full of educated derelicts. Persistence and determination alone are omnipotent. The slogan 'press on' has solved and always will solve the problems of the human race."

Calvin Coolidge
Thirtieth President of the
United States

Persistence is a matter of never-ceasing application of mental concentration followed by action. You must continuously work at your goal(s) both mentally and physically. You can afford little rest; the spirit-to-do needs to be fanned until its flare becomes a brilliant white light on the high road of human achievement. You need to constantly stoke it with the fuel of plans, modifications to plans, creative ideas, focused attention, and action! ACTION! **ACTION!** When the spirit-to-do is gone, physical death soon follows. A person with no dream, no vision, wastes away mentally and physically. The brilliance of the spirit-to-do fades to black.

"What this power is I cannot say; all I know is that it exists and it becomes available only when a man is in the state of mind in which he knows exactly what he wants and is fully determined not to quit until he finds it."

Dr. Alexander Graham Bell
Vibrational theory scientist
Inventor of the telephone

Batter Up!

"And if you feel that everyone has rejected you and your ideas let me tell you this, you are most assuredly in good company."

Dr. James K. Van Fleet
Subconscious mind power
expert; author of eighteen
books, including *Power with
People* and *Hidden Power*

In a match between two individuals, all things being equal except one is persistent and the other is not, the persistent person will win every time. Perhaps the best way for me to illustrate the power of persistence is with a few historical examples.

The greatest scientific inventor in American history was Thomas A. Edison, but in trying to make the incandescent light bulb he tried over ten thousand times before he was able to produce it. One time when he was being interviewed by a haughty young reporter before he had accomplished the great task, the reporter said, "Mr. Edison, you have tried thousands of times to make the incandescent light bulb and failed." Edison said, "Young man, I haven't failed at all, I have succeeded in finding thousands of ways that absolutely will not work!"

The first book author Irving Stone wrote was about the world famous artist Vincent Van Gogh. It was taken to an elite publishing company. The company never opened the envelope containing the manuscript to look at it. The rejected manuscript arrived at Stone's home unopened before he himself arrived from his delivery trip to the publishing company. The manuscript was later read and rejected fifteen more times by publishers before Stone's manuscript *Lust for Life* was finally published in 1934. It has now sold **over 25 million copies!**

Gone With the Wind racked up thirty-eight rejections before Macmillan publishers latched onto it and Margaret Mitchell's work became immortalized as a classic.

Joe Brooks won a Grammy award for the song (words and music) "You Light Up My Life." At the awards ceremony, Brooks said, "As I look out there tonight I can't help but think that just about every company in this audience turned this song down. As a matter of fact, about ten of you turned it down twice. So I must admit that this award tastes oh, so sweet!"

Best-selling author and world-renowned human achievement expert Brian Tracy recounts an insightful little story. *"Life is like a baseball game in that you are both the batter and your own umpire. When you get three strikes in a real baseball game you are out. But in life, since you are also the umpire, **you decide** when you are out. You can stand at the plate and swing as long as you like. You probably won't hit a home run on your very first swing, but if you persist in swinging long enough and hard enough eventually you will!"*

The Final Message of Persistence

My final message of persistence to you is this:

If you are pursuing a worthy goal and it is aligned with the forces of good, never, never give up. Just when you think it's all over, press on one more time.

I am not much of a believer in superstition, but I will tell you this, based on many years of personal life experiences and the life experiences of hundreds of other intelligent, successful, powerful, sophisticated people. The human mind has a completely spiritual component, which I call the superconscious mind. This component has the ability to draw on a higher power (God, Infinite Intelligence) to bring "unseen forces" to its aid. This is not coincidence, chance, or luck, it's a scientific fact!

I have experienced and experimented with the "superconscious effect," as I call it, enough times in my own life (and have worked closely with others who have) to be sufficiently convinced that it is real, workable, and controllable. This is something many of you who read this message will need to experiment with for yourself.

If you persist long enough and hard enough in your studies and are a conscious observer of your own life and the world around you, you will come to see the undeniable truth in what you've just read!

"What we do not see, what most of us never suspect of existing, is the silent but irresistible power which comes to the rescue of those who fight on in the face of discouragement."

Napoleon Hill
Success philosopher
Author of *Think and Grow*
Rich, Law of Success, Science
of Personal Achievement, **and**
Mental Dynamite

An After-the-Lesson Visit with the Author

My mission in this lesson was to impress on you the dire need to incorporate the four personality traits required for high achievement in life. There are perhaps a total of twelve personality traits necessary; however, I view **personal responsibility, personal honor, self-discipline,** and **persistence** as the top four.

Lack of personal responsibility was a very subtle trap that ensnared me for a good portion of my life. Since I myself was caught, I know what it feels like. I had carefully assembled a blame list that I could use with anyone who would challenge me as to why I wasn't doing well in life. No one I had ever met in the early portion of my life could defeat me in an argument on this point. I was securely *irresponsible.*

I had absolved myself of personal responsibility, therefore my own name did not appear anywhere on my blame list. With my blame list to cling to, there was no need to engage in any study after college. I thought you just worked at a job, collected your pay, and did the best you could on what you earned for the rest of your life.

I found out later from various *success masters* that this was crooked thinking. Many of them at one time in their lives were ensnared in the same trap I was in, but they had each escaped. What you read in this lesson on personal responsibility enabled me to escape. The mind-set of the serious success student as well as the success master is one of 100% personal responsibility.

I fared much better on personal honor. In my life I gave up many apparent gains in order to stand by my own code of honor. Many offerings were made to me for exchanging just a little bit of personal honor. All were denied. I have also suffered short-term ridicule from many small, mean people lacking personal honor. *This is to be expected!*

One of the most tempting offerings to give up some personal honor came to me in graduate school, but it was declined. Had I given up some of my personal honor at that time for a short-term gain, my life would have followed an entirely different track. You would not be reading this book right now if I had decided to give up some of my personal honor at that time. Looking back with hindsight, it was the best decision I ever made, but at the time it seemed like the worst!

My advice to you is this, never give up any of your personal honor no matter what is offered in exchange for it. Your personal honor should be priceless—never for sale no matter how much silver is offered!

Self-discipline is one of the more interesting personality traits. Most people are very disciplined in some areas of their lives but completely undisciplined in others. The trick is to maintain self-discipline in areas where you are strong and to work on areas where you are weak.

A lack of self-discipline, if severe enough, can render self-discipline in all other areas of life worthless. Oddly enough, my battle with self-discipline is in eating sweets such as candy, cookies, donuts, ice cream, cake, and the like. I can maintain high degrees of self-discipline in every area of my life, but my fight for self-discipline is waged on a *candy-coated battlefield.* In order for me to be self-disciplined I must focus my attention there, with emerald eyes on the cupcakes. You must determine for yourself where your lack of self-discipline is and battle it out. I'll be in your corner rooting you on, warrior to warrior, soldier to soldier.

Finally, we come to persistence, whose death bell tolls loud and clear for more than most. Just a select few persist tenaciously enough at a big life goal until it is finally achieved. If you persist when all others fall back into the ranks of quitters and it seems like you are all alone, you will have the supreme joy of experiencing the "superconscious effect"!

I've touched on this topic more than once throughout this book, and most readers won't understand it because they've never observed life carefully enough to recognize it. The fascinating part about it is that it can be *indirectly* consciously controlled. I was a doubting Thomas myself, needing experiment after experiment to become sufficiently convinced. My *personal journals* now contain more than enough firsthand evidence for me.

Perhaps the best way for you to experience it is to persist in a morally correct goal when it seems like you've reached an immovable obstacle. At this time I suggest you let a wry smile creep across your face, bow your head, and solemnly scientifically pray. If a "miracle" soon follows, you can wave to me on the *High Roads of Human Achievement, Success Master to Success Master!*

"It takes a little courage
and a little self-control
and some grim determination,
If you want to reach the goal.

It takes a deal of striving,
and a firm and stern-set chin,
No matter what the battle,
If you really want to win.

There's no easy path to glory,
There's no rosy road to fame.
Life, however we may view it,
Is no simple parlor game;

But its prizes call for fighting,
For endurance and for grit;
For a ragged disposition
And a don't-know-when-to-quit!"

Anonymous

12 The Illuminated Mind

Overview

We round the corner now as you embark on the last leg of your journey. There are no more step-by-step techniques for you to learn here. This lesson reveals the full force and power behind all previous lessons. The entire POWERMIND system philosophy can be summarized in this lesson. Since you have been a serious student in coming this far, it's only fitting that the science of true success in life be engraved indelibly onto your mind with this last *lesson of life*.

In the last section of this lesson I will awaken you to the tremendous *personal responsibility* you now carry since you will be a new keeper of the ancient *specialized knowledge* that can turn *dreams into reality, thoughts into things!*

The Illuminated Mind

"Man, alone, has the power to transform his thoughts into physical reality; man, alone, can dream and make his dreams come true."

Napoleon Hill
American success philosopher
Author of *Think and Grow
Rich, Law of Success, Science
of Personal Achievement,* and
Mental Dynamite

Peace and Despair

The key to fulfillment in life is not to compete against others but rather to compete against yourself. You should strive to do better today and in the future than you did yesterday and in the past. This means experiencing joy for coming in tenth in a race when you came in fifteenth last time.

When you make a mistake in life don't punish yourself for it, but learn from it so you can make the correction for next time. Always work on self-improvement. Learn from the daily experiences life offers you. If you live each day to the fullest, your future will be one of hope and your past one of happiness.

You can set a positive example for others by working on your mind, your skills, your natural talents, and your goals. Life asks that each of us *unfold,* making the most of what we have in order to better serve others. This is our solemn duty.

If you follow this philosophy, when you look back over your entire life at some time in the distant future as we all necessarily must, you will be able to safely say, "I have no regrets, I am at peace because I did the very best I could with what I had."

There are only two types of people in the world when death is near: those filled with *peace* and those filled with *despair!*

Self-Mastery

You should realize by now that your attitude of mind tends to attract circumstances to you. You are like a living magnet because your subconscious and superconscious minds tend to bring about what you think about. The subconscious and super-conscious minds are servant machines. They do as ordered for your benefit or for your destruction. Your thoughts and feelings have tremendous power because your entire life is largely deter-mined by what you think and feel.

Here are three quotes for you to **think about** in regard to this. The great Roman philosopher Marcus Aurelius said, *"A man's life is what his thoughts make of it"*; Ralph Waldo Emerson, the great American philosopher, said, *"A man is what he thinks about all day long"*; and American self-development pioneer Earl Nightingale said, *"We become what we think about."*

Your habitual thinking tends to materialize into real life cir-cumstances. Since this is the case, you must take great care to *discipline your thinking.* Consciously edit out all unkind, depressing, hurtful, sad, evil thoughts and focus your mind on your goals, success, high achievement, and of course happiness. When your mind wanders from your goals, the first thing it will begin to see is defeat.

Autogenically condition your mind; use words and imagina-tion to create your future, feel how wonderful it will be, then get busy working on making that future your reality.

When a person truly understands the concept that they have the power to create the conditions, circumstances, and events in their own life by their thoughts and feelings held in their con-scious mind on a continuing basis, they will have reached a higher plane of human existence. When they become aware of the fact that their external environment is not the cause but only the effect of their own thinking, they will have gained a true understanding of *self-mastery.*

"Self-suggestion makes you master of yourself."

W. Clement Stone
Coauthor of *Success Through*
a Positive Mental Attitude

The Iron Law of Belief

"What the mind of man can conceive and believe, the mind of man can achieve."

> **Napoleon Hill**
> **American success philosopher**
> **Author of** *Think and Grow Rich, Law of Success, Science of Personal Achievement,* **and** *Mental Dynamite*

The iron law of belief is now stated for your consideration: *Whatever you imprint on your subconscious mind becomes belief and will be expressed externally as conditions, experiences, and events.* This law is the reason why various lessons in this book stressed combining strong positive emotion with verbal affirmations, imagineered experiences, and scientific prayer. The emotional component is what facilitates the development of strong belief, which is necessary to enforce the iron law of belief.

See now illustrated before your very eyes, in biblical quotations from **Mark**, the iron law of belief.

"Whosoever shall say unto this mountain, be thou removed, and be thou cast into the sea, and shall not doubt in his heart, but shall BELIEVE that these things which he saith shall come to pass, he shall have whatsoever he saith."

Mark 11:23

"What things soever ye desire, when ye pray, BELIEVE that ye receive them and ye shall have them."

Mark 11:24

"If thou canst BELIEVE all things are possible to him who believeth."

Mark 9:23

Thoughts held firmly in the conscious mind become dominant and get imprinted into the subconscious mind, creating firm belief. These thoughts must then be realized and materialized because the actions you take will *automatically coincide with your belief.* Your subconscious and superconscious minds will also actively engage, affecting external circumstances over which you had no direct physical influence; they will assist in the materialization of your belief. The superconscious mind has the capability of drawing energy from an infinite power source for this purpose.

You now have been exposed to the full force operating behind the iron law of belief. If you discipline your conscious mind to contain only thoughts of harmony, health, wealth, power, success, wisdom, and worthy goals, these must be brought into your life. This is Universal law!

"Power in its highest expression is the science of organizing the individual mind in the service of the Universal."

Benjamin Kidd
Author of *The Science of Power*

Social Reform

Definitions

Social*: — of, relating to, or concerned with the welfare of human beings as members of society. "The desire for removing human error, clearing human confusion and diminishing human misery. . . . motives eminently such as are called social." Matthew Arnold.

Reform*: — to put an end to (an evil) by enforcing or introducing a better method or course of action or behavior.

*Definition Source: *Websters Third New International Dictionary* (unabridged).

If you study the teachings of success philosophers through-out history, you will find that all of them stress self-develop-ment. This starts with the movement of the mind upward, pon-dering the idea of improving its current station by the achieve-ment of worthy goals. This is then accomplished by an aggres-sive search for *specialized knowledge.*

Every individual can help him- or herself by self-education. People are not pieces of driftwood thrown into the sea of life whose only purpose is to mark the changing currents. Each per-son has the God-given power to rise above circumstances in life, charting a new, definite, self-determined course.

We can all elevate ourselves by educating ourselves. We can read books written by the wisest *teachers through time.* We can attend seminars by the master teachers of our day. We can devel-op our spiritual awareness by making a careful study of our reli-gion. We can fill our minds with good, pure, helpful ideas, lead-ing to the performance of right actions. We can live frugally and provide well for ourselves and our families. We can place our-selves under the divinest influences on earth. We can live for high purposes during the short time we have here.

The people that study and improve themselves improve the world. They add one more intelligent unit to the population. The natural result of this individual improvement is improvement of the whole population.

Social reform is merely the cumulative result of individual self-improvement. Society reflects the mental condition of all the individuals within it. There is no surprise in what you are now reading, but seeing it on paper sometimes sharpens the point.

A person self-improved in this way is better able to improve those who come into contact with her. She has more power, knowledge, and experience and wider vision. She sees more clearly the **causes** of suffering in others, which might easily be remedied. She is in a position to lend a more active hand in help-ing others in need.

The self-improved person has fulfilled his duty to himself. In so doing he commands more respect when he urges others to see the necessity of doing like duty for themselves. Is it possible for a person to be a social elevator when he himself walks in the mire of ignorance, selfishness, weakness, poverty, and self-pity? How can he teach if he does not know? How can she give if she is selfish? How can she strengthen if she is weak? How can he make others rich, if he is poor? How can he be compassionate if he is self-centered?

The point of this message is this: In all *social reform* we must begin with self-improvement, **the root of which is self-education.** To help others we must begin by helping ourselves. To elevate others we must first elevate ourselves. To be a *master teacher* we must first be a *serious student*. We must lead by example.

Each person can study and learn. It is a decision one must make between study and play. The uncertainty of life should serve as strong inducement to study. Those who play all the time and study little will find themselves outclassed, outmatched, and outwitted in any endeavor.

Dedicate yourself to lifelong learning; become a leader in your chosen field. Become a self-respecting, self-improved, self-educated, self-directed individual, who is committed to benefiting others with both your *natural talents* and *developed skills*. In this way you contribute to the betterment of society as a whole and effect *social reform.*

"Social advancement is the result of individual advancement."

> **Samual Smiles**
> **Author of the classic self-help**
> **series, *Character, Self Help,***
> **and *Thrift***

The Author's Call to Action: Can One Person Change the World?

"In the country of the blind, the one-eyed man is King."

> **Michael Apostolius**

It is the people within organizations that determine how well they function. This is true for families, companies, clubs, churches, towns, states, or entire nations. When groups of people function well together, it makes it easier for individuals within the group to achieve their personal goals. When you think about this concept, think about how it would be to your advantage to improve yourself.

By practicing the life management method laid down in this book, you can help your family, your employer, your country, or any other group to which you belong. When you master the teachings in this book you will emerge as a true leader, a life guide, and an inspiration for others.

The crux of leadership is the idea that your behavior dramatically affects not only you but the people around you. Many people are looking at what you are doing even without your realizing it. If you have children, no matter how bad your relationship with them, they still look to you for leadership.

Scientific studies have shown that even physically abused, battered children still look to their own parents for leadership and guidance. As terrible as this sounds, it's true. I mention this extreme to emphasize a point. Children are highly impressionable because their conscious editing machinery is not yet fully developed. I urge all parents to set the best possible example for their children; they are indeed watching in ways *you* or *they* may not even be aware of. Your behavior will have a profound effect on them and on their children's lives as well.

I saw a powerful antidrug commercial one time that illustrates this fact quite nicely. A counselor was talking to a father and son about where the son had learned to snort cocaine and why the boy thought it was okay to do so. The counselor and father kept pressing the boy for an answer until finally the boy broke down in tears and said, "I learned it from you, Dad. I thought it was okay because you did it and I wanted to be just like you!" The burden of teaching a child right actions lies with the parent.

Consider the various organizations of which you are a part—your family, your company, sports teams, social clubs, and so on. Each one has a "group personality" all its own. The attitude and behavior of each person has an effect on this group personality. Each person contributes to the effectiveness of the whole.

I will illustrate this with another family example. At the dinner table the mood of any one person can set the entire tone for everyone else. One person's attitude, positive or negative, is contagious. If a father has a good day at work, is very happy and noticeably thrilled, this will immediately be transmitted to his wife and children. Everyone will quickly become "happy," escalating the positive group mood. *One individual can easily trigger the mind-set of the whole group.*

This can also be illustrated graphically with a sports team. One person can pump the team up or send them into emotional peril. If a coach tells the team at half time. "We are behind but we haven't lost," and then pumps them up, do you think the players will do better for the second half? You have probably seen this dozens of times, when a team makes a "miraculous" comeback in the second half to win. *All groups of which you are a part are influenced by you. Everyone has influence; that includes you!*

This concept can be extrapolated to the human race in general. Does humankind have untapped potential? You better believe it! As an individual how can you contribute to the betterment of humankind? By fulfilling yourself, becoming the best person you can possibly be. If you develop your natural talents, set goals, achieve them, and help others win their goals in the process, this behavior benefits not only you but others around you as well. In this way you contribute to the betterment of humanity. There are millions of people in this world looking for the rare *brilliant light* of true leadership.

As you trace back through human history, you can find countless examples of people who started at what seemed to be an insignificant position early in life with seemingly insurmountable odds against them, yet rose to greatness. One person's mind can produce an idea that illuminates millions, stunning them into action, thereby altering the history of humankind.

There is no question that you or anyone else can affect the world. The question is, do you want to? The only person you have *direct* control over is yourself. The only parts of you that you can directly control are what you are thinking in your conscious mind, moment to moment, and what your daily actions are.

If your life changes for the better, you'll serve as a catalyst for positive change, affecting others around you in a positive way. If they change, they'll affect others around them, and so on and so forth. Each person who reads this book will set off a chain reaction of events affecting all the people around them. These people in turn become agents for positive change. In one clean sweep, the POWERMIND system's life management method can *make the world* a better place by *teaching* individuals how to grow and develop themselves.

If you found any information in this book to be of service to you in your life, it is your duty to pass it along to others. The information contained in The POWERMIND System is revolutionary to say the least, enabling readers to gain not only supreme earthly success for themselves but the ability to **teach others** around them how to do so as well. It is one of the great riches of life to have the privilege of contributing to the success of others. Because you have read this book, it is your *personal responsibility* to do what you can to lead the fight against ignorance, poverty, weakness, confusion, and failure so common among the masses today.

I know that there will be readers of this book who wield tremendous power, money, and influence, who are searching for a worthy cause to put these behind. These people especially are urged to make their contributions by teaching others what they learned here or by providing books for others who so desperately need to read this message for humanity!

In taking on the personal responsibility of being the principal investigator for the POWERMIND system research project, writing this life management textbook, and presenting educational life management seminars worldwide, I'm doing the best I can with the *natural talents* I possess. With all the **needless suffering** in the world today, who else will step forward among the masses and help?

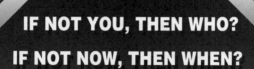

IF NOT YOU, THEN WHO?
IF NOT NOW, THEN WHEN?

*"Godspeed on Your
Journey"*

Michael Monroe Kiefer

Get an Edge on Tomorrow with. . . .

PRIVATE NEWSLETTER

"I want to hear from you! Through my private newsletter, we can help others help themselves."

Stay in touch and in tune with the mind of the world's foremost success scientist. This newsletter is designed to keep you informed and intrigued with interesting insights on the psychology of success and entrepreneurialism. All subscribers will be offered the opportunity to contribute personal articles for publication. This is your chance to be heard!

Exclusive advance notice and special discounts on future POWER-MIND system products will also be available for all subscribers. This newsletter is a nice blend of fascinating information for inquiring minds like yours!

AUDIO BOOK

Hear the dynamic, motivating voice of Mr. Kiefer as he reviews a carefully selected series of inspirational highlights from The POWER-MIND System. Keep your mind on the *high roads of human achievement,* day in the day out. Don't sell yourself short, listen to a caring, knowledgeable, supportive *voice of value!*

Don't Delay, Order TODAY!!!

Newsletter - 10 issues annually	$60.00 postpaid
Audio Book - (approx.) 2 hours of power	$22.00 postpaid
Save $4.00 <u>Both for only</u>	$78.00 postpaid
Extra copies of The POWERMIND System for your friends with handsigned bookmark	$20.00 postpaid
Official POWERMIND system bookmark handsigned by Mr. Kiefer	$ 4.00 postpaid

List items *desired* and send check or moneyorder to:

> Kiefer Enterprizes International Press
> Box 3N
> 22320 Albatross Circle
> Farmington, Minnesota 55024

Coming Soon!

The Secret Power of Personal Journals

(Step-by-Step Instruction on Journaling)

Audio ◆ Book

Available November 1995

In Preparation!!!

POWERMIND II
?
❖

Your opinion counts at Kiefer Enterprizes International Press!

Our mission is to publish life changing, awareness creating, inspirational self-help material. You can assist us in accomplishing this goal by sending us your answers to the following questions.

1. Why did you buy this book?
2. Did you enjoy reading it?
3. What lesson(s) impressed you most?
4. What techniques did you find most useful?
5. Are there any subjects contained in this book you would like to learn more about?
6. What pieces of information from this book have really made a difference in your life?

We would be delighted to read your answers and *any other comments* you care to make. Please mail correspondence to:

Kiefer Enterprizes International Press
POWERMIND Opinion Survey
22320 Albatross Circle
Farmington, MN 55024

Michael Monroe Kiefer

American Success Scientist
Principal Investigator for
The POWERMIND System Project